TOMBS OF THE GREAT LEADERS

TOMBS OF THE
GREAT LEADERS
A CONTEMPORARY GUIDE

GWENDOLYN LEICK

REAKTION BOOKS

Published by Reaktion Books Ltd
33 Great Sutton Street
London EC1V 0DX
www.reaktionbooks.co.uk

First published 2013

Copyright © Gwendolyn Leick 2013

All rights reserved

No part of this publication may be reproduced, stored in a retrieval system, or transmitted, in any form or by any means, electronic, mechanical, photocopying, recording or otherwise, without the prior permission of the publishers

Printed and bound in China by 1010 Printing International Ltd

A catalogue record for this book is available from the British Library

ISBN 978 1 78023 200 3

Contents

Preface 7

1 Enduring Signification: Mounds, Monuments and Mausolea 11
Stone Age Burials – Bronze Age Elite Tombs – Hellenistic Eclecticism and the Invention of the Mausoleum – Roman Imperial Tombs – Royal Burials of Christian Monarchs in the Middle Ages – The Impact of the French Revolution – Napoleon's Tomb – Lincoln's Tomb in Springfield, Illinois

2 Safeguarding the Immortality of Revolutionary Leaders: Mausolea in Communist Countries 31
Lenin's Tomb – The Mausoleum of Ho Chi Minh – Mao Zedong Memorial Hall – Kumsusan Memorial Hall, 'The Sacred Temple of *Juche*' – Destroyed Communist Mausolea

3 Fantasy and Reality: The Burial Places of Fascist Leaders 98
Mussolini's Crypt in Predappio – Franco and the Righteous Fallen in Santa Cruz del Valle de los Caídos

4 New Nations, New Monuments: Mausolea for Fathers of the Nation 119
Sun Yat-sen's Mausoleum (*Lingmu*) on Purple Mountain – Anıtkabir: The Memorial Tomb of Mustafa Kemal Atatürk – Mazar-e-Quaid-e-Azam, 'The Mausoleum of the Great Leader', Muhammad Ali Jinnah, in Karachi – The Mausoleum of Shaheed President Ziaur Rahman in Dhaka

5 Not the Final Resting Place: Temporary Mausolea 188
Chiang Kai-shek at Chihu, Taiwan – Yasser Arafat at Ramallah

6 Appropriated Traditions 213
Sukarno and Suharto in Java – The Mausoleum of Ayatollah Khomeini in Tehran

7 Political Mausolea in Africa 240
North African Mausolea – Sub-Saharan Mausolea – Dr Kwame Nkrumah Memorial Park in Accra – The Mausoleum of *M'zee* Laurent-Désiré Kabila in Kinshasa – The Mausoleum of Hastings Kamuzu Banda in Lilongwe, Malawi – The Tomb of Dr John Garang de Mabior, Juba, South Sudan – Reinventing the Political Tomb in Africa

References 283
Chronological List of Tombs and Mausolea 301
Bibliographies 303
Acknowledgements 309
Illustration Acknowledgements 311
Index 313

Preface

There are architectural works that stir desires and memories in all our lives, quite apart from the primary shelter of the home, so eloquently explored by Gaston Bachelard. When I was a child growing up in a village in Styria, Austria, my grandmother would take me to a delicately carved Gothic church that I loved all the more for it being called 'Maria Buch', a name that evoked Mary, mother of Jesus, with the idea of a book (*Buch*).[1] The reward for having undertaken the long walk to this sanctuary was to be given a dark-red fizzy soda in a distinctive bottle, with a marble-like glass stopper. Inside the sanctuary, I could not tear myself away from staring at the yellowed faces of the embalmed old priests, who had been placed in glass coffins along the aisles. Later, when we had moved to Graz, one of my favourite buildings there was simply know as the 'Mausoleum' – a High Baroque oval-domed church, squeezed between the bulk of the thirteenth-century cathedral and multi-storeyed townhouses from the same medieval period. One always looked up to it from the narrow streets to its position at the end of a steep flight of steps. The richly articulated facade included two paintings, free-standing sculptures, swags of garlands, Corinthian giant order columns and a finely balanced superposition of triangular pediments and shallow arches. This mausoleum had been built in the seventeen century for the Habsburg Emperor Ferdinand II (1578–1637), who was born in Graz. In the context of the then still raging Thirty Years War, he nearly succeeded in eradicating Protestantism in Austria. This mausoleum happens to be the only purpose-built mausoleum for a European emperor. Although it was part of the familiar urban 'furniture', the mausoleum retained its mystery largely because it was always closed when I was still living in the city. The word 'mausoleum' thereafter evoked this particular building for me, which, despite its tyrannically inclined and intolerant incumbent, was delightful and gracious in its urbane, Italianate architectural composition.

Many years later, in quite a different context, the mausoleum of Atatürk in Ankara, Turkey, exerted a similar fascination for me. I began to think of what sort of messages such self-consciously constructed *architecture parlante* (architecture that 'speaks' to the viewer and makes its purpose clear) was trying to convey and how, with the passing of time, subsequent generations react to such a defined programme.

All monuments are produced within the coordinates of historical and cultural circumstances of the time they are envisaged and created (Ferdinand II's commitment to the Counter-Reformation, for instance). With works of art and architecture, form and content respond not only to aesthetic notions current at the time but also to an iconographical, even ideological programme, which passing time can render vague and obscure. Monuments and tombs built for national leaders are even more intensely determined by political ideas and expediency. They often form the setting of a posthumous personality cult and serve to legitimize a government keen to take credit for maintaining the public worship of a significant or revolutionary leader. Such places can also become attractive and meaningful to the public in ways not envisaged by the authorities, and become sites of protest or mere recreation. The present catches up with the past in unexpected ways, and what was deemed a significant and potent symbol of national unity can also become an embarrassment; an uncomfortable reminder of a historical period that citizens would rather forget.

I was also interested in the role of the architects who had to respond to political content and the often vaguely defined notion of 'cultural identity', while trying to do justice to the 'longevity' of architecture and their desire to create a building and a place that would continue to inspire and 'delight' generations to come.

I have tried to discover why a particular ruler would be entombed in a mausoleum, where and how his political heirs and successors chose to bury him and what sort of ritual they instituted at the site. I also sought to ascertain the concepts that the architects, artists and landscape designers developed and how their designs were executed, changed or thwarted by circumstances. Most rewarding, however, was the experience on site itself. I have visited eighteen of the 24 tombs discussed at some length in this book. If possible, I tried to make several visits to see what people did, how they used the place, what the general atmosphere was like and what visitors were willing to say about their experience (in this case I had to rely on sometimes self-appointed guides or local friends to interpret). Of course, in most cases, especially at faraway sites, lack of time meant that this research gathering provided little more than a snapshot; a necessarily superficial encounter but one that could nevertheless stand for a particular time. Political and ideological changes naturally affect such buildings that were meant to encapsulate ideas and circumstances prevailing at the time of construction. I was sometimes surprised at the almost jovial and joyful atmosphere at a mausoleum that I had expected to be largely irrelevant now and deserted. I found that people who frequented such sites did so with a sense of purpose and were willing to share their experience. For those sites I could not reach in person, especially the more recent ones in Africa, I had to rely on first-hand accounts, such as online articles and blogs.

The book is divided into seven main sections in order to contextualize the different tombs and establish certain common denominators. I begin with the prehistory of burial monuments generally, the 'development' of tombs chiefly in the ancient Near East and the classical world, and go on to examine medieval practices, the funerary structures of the post-Enlightenment period, up to the graves of Napoleon and Lincoln. Chapter Two is devoted to the mausolea of revolutionary leaders in communist states, most of which took Lenin's Moscow tomb as a precedent. A shorter section on Fascist dictators follows in Chapter Three, including Franco's Valley of the Fallen. Chapter Four brings together tombs that have been built for the Fathers of the Nation in China, Pakistan, Turkey and Bangladesh, and then come two temporary mausolea whose incumbents (Chiang Kai-shek in Taiwan and Yasser Arafat in Ramallah, on the West Bank in Palestine) are officially there only temporarily. I discuss the monuments in Indonesia and Iran in a separate chapter because they do not fit other categories of mausolea and can be best understood within the specific cultural and religious practices of their region. The final chapter is dedicated to African examples, which are arguably architecturally the most diverse and interesting cases.

All of the rulers who ended up in a state-built mausoleum during the last 100 years were not ordinary politicians. They achieved political power in exceptional circumstances, as revolutionaries, anti-colonialists or military leaders. They were almost always charismatic and all, at least on some occasions, resorted to violence and repression to achieve their aims. It was this readiness to overcome obstacles by any means that brought them to prominence, and also, in some cases, to a violent end. Particularly brutal dictators, especially those whose grip on power depended on both ruthless suppression at home and substantial support from abroad, as was the case with such figures as Mobuto, Bokassa, Idi Amin, Pol Pot or 'Papa Doc' Duvalier, were not placed in a mausoleum because their period of rule left only bitter memories which no subsequent government wished to commemorate. There have also been instances where a hated ruler was buried in a mausoleum, only for the building to be attacked and violently destroyed, once the regime was overthrown. This happened in Haiti to Duvalier and to some communist rulers. The majority of the 'tyrants' discussed here have been reconfigured as benign ancestral figures, and said to have initiated a new era, as well as also engendering a 'nation'. They have become the famous and revered 'founding fathers' of new states; vital figureheads of new 'imagined communities'.[2] The problematic moral aspects of these leaders form an important part of the dense layers of meaning that these sites encode. The mausoleum makes death and the dead an intrinsic component of architecture, which in turn operates under the aegis of eternity. However, when the compromising details of an individual life have been forgotten and, if the architect had done his job right, only delight remains, made more palpable by the frisson of mortality.

CHAPTER ONE
Enduring Signification
Mounds, Monuments and Mausolea

Bones and corpses, coffins and cremation urns, are material objects. Most of the time, they are indisputably there, as our senses of sight, touch, and smell can confirm. As such, a body's materiality can be critical to its symbolic efficacy: unlike notions such as 'patriotism' or 'civil society', for instance, a corpse can be moved around, displayed, and strategically located in specific places. Bodies have the advantage of concreteness that none the less transcends time, making past immediately present.[1]

The death of a human being constitutes a rupture of social ties. Mourning rites were invented to safeguard the continuity of the collective and to mend the broken fabric of relations, of kin and clan, of generations. All known societies acknowledge death with some form of ritual but the corpse or the ashes of the deceased might not merit any special treatment beyond disposal. However, even in early history, the remains of *some* people were cared for in a special way. In the *Sima de los Huesos* (Sierra de Atapuerca, Spain) (dated to 300,000 years ago) the skeletons of 28 individuals were found that seem to have been thrown into the very deep rock fissure. The presence of a remarkably beautifully stone axe suggests that this may constitute the earliest known site for the conscious disposal of these bodies for whom a particularly remote and inaccessible site was selected.[2]

Anthropologists living with contemporary hunters and gatherers have commented on the fluid nature of personhood in such societies and on their dread of the dead. This fear seems to be based on the notion that the living cannot be truly living unless the dead are completely dead. For example, a dirge sung at a funeral by an Amazonian tribe tries to banish the harmful influence of the recently deceased:

> Do not call me son (or sister, or father...) any more! You are lost! Now you have gone for good! Do not look at me! Do not take my soul away! Above all, do not take my soul away![3]

Where dead humans are perceived as dangerous 'no longer humans', their former belongings must not circulate amid the living; in such societies the dead must never be mentioned again. It appears that as long as human beings lived exclusively from hunting and gathering, there were no permanent reminders of the former presence of the dead in the form of graves.

Stone Age Burials

The change of attitudes towards the dead, from perceiving them as harmful to potentially helpful, seems to be connected to changes in the modes of survival and the beginnings of sedentariness and agriculture during the Neolithic period. With the end of the Ice Age and the beginning of the Holocene period, some 11,000 years ago, the large mammals of the glacial period disappeared but new forms of subsistence became viable. The warm earth sprouted grasses bearing hard grains that could be ground and cooked. It became possible to stay in the same place and to 'multiply', that is, to expand the size of families, since larger groups had an advantage in clearing the ground, tilling the soil, sowing and reaping and turning produce into food. The agricultural revolutions in all of the different parts of world that they occurred in introduced not only new ways of surviving but also new ways of thinking about the world and new ways of living together. In a permanently settled community the house became the most important place, where life had its beginning and end. Speaking about Neolithic sites in Syria, excavators noted:

> Many burials were distributed within the settlement, at places where the dead had lived and worked. No separate, formal graveyards outside the areas of occupation have yet been found.[4]

The importance of the dead to the Neolithic communities can be gauged in the elaborate treatment of their remains, such as the plastered skulls found at Jericho (dating from around 7000–6000 BC). At Çatalhoyük in Turkey, a densely populated settlement inhabited from *circa* 6500 to 5000 BC, the living resided above the dead, who were sealed into clay platforms and thus remained tied to the homestead, as part of an elaborate symbolic ensemble that fused cultural artefacts such as pottery, sculpture, wild animal remains (the horns of giant wild cattle) and human bones.[5] In these settlements the dead became ancestors whose continuing presence anchored successive generations to the home. The practice of keeping the dead within the family home persisted in the ancient Near East for millennia, and well into the historical period.

The development of agriculture occurred rather later in Europe than in the Middle East, not least because dense forest cover and swamps made land clearance much harder than in the Fertile Crescent. A remarkable feature of British and other northwestern European areas are the conical or rectangular mounds, usually called 'barrows' to distinguish them from natural mounds, of which often only the inner structural components, huge slabs of stone, remain. The long-held assumption that all of these were prehistorical burial sites has recently been reconsidered:

> Linear mounds may simply have been designed to seed the ground with representative elements of the local human community. Such material (be it bone, pottery flint or organics) could indicate a desire to establish a communal or territorial statement, or it may have been intended to tame or claim an area of wild land. If this is the case, then the evidence for the disposition of articulated, disassembled or cremated human bone within linear mounds may have little to do with burial in the conventional sense.[6]

As containers for the remains of people who must have been considered as important representatives of a group, as well as examples of material culture, such barrows were fashioned in such a way as to became a permanent feature of the landscape. Yet, at the same time, their difference from the natural surroundings was stressed through their geometric configurations. Although covered with soil, they were originally kept free from vegetation and would, in places where the soil was mainly chalk, have been far more conspicuous than they are today. Huge upright stones often formed an impressive entrance and signalled from afar that these barrows and mounds contained an inner space; one arranged in such

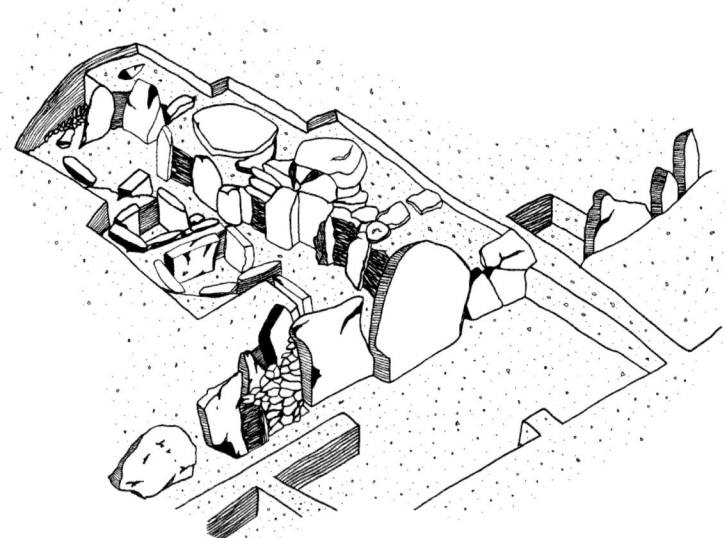

Isometric view of West Kennet long barrow.

a way as to create a highly affective interior. Although many European Neolithic sites contained intramural burials, the soil-covered stone mounds and barrows that dominated the landscape can be said to constitute the first monumental architecture, signalling the desire to impose a new order on the land. Miles Russell evokes the impact of these structures when they were first seen:

> The linear mound, the enclosure and the shaft may look harmonious, mysterious, idyllic and tranquil to us, but to our ancestors these structures were as intrusive and as psychologically shocking as the motorways, airport and nuclear power plant are today. The new buildings created massive scars upon the land; new ideas caused profound shifts in ideology and human organization.[7]

The transition from nomadic hunting to settled communities where it did occur (which, in some isolated places, continues to be resisted to this day) was not a sudden change but a long process. The social transformation from equal to ranked societies was equally slow. The Neolithic house burials, as well as the mounds that stored the physical remains of the representative of the whole community, appear to have served to retain the ethos of social equality.

Bronze Age Elite Tombs

In some places and societies this egalitarian ethos was superseded by a more unequal access to resources. The power to make decisions could shift from a council of adults or elders to highly ranked elite groups. Examples of such social differentiation can be found in the ancient Near East from the end of the fifth millennium BC. A few houses within a settlement would be significantly larger than all the others and the burial sites of the privileged personages who had inhabited them contained exquisitely painted pottery, as well as personal ornaments and weapons made of high-quality materials. Lavish funeral ceremonies and burials in monumental tombs demonstrated the deceased's superior rank and gave rise to demonstrations of loyalty by his descendants. The preparations necessary for such a funeral are described in a cuneiform letter written at the beginning of the second millennium BC. The sender was trying to impress with his share in the goods destined for the deceased Amorite chief Abda-El.

> Say to Bilalama: 'I am your brother of your flesh and blood [...] hear my words! Make me look important in the eyes of the Amorites. The objects destined for Abda-El so far retained: one gold vase, three silver vases, a first quality *lamahussum*-garment, bronze vases, one copper kettle. You know all this, let them be sent. In addition, messengers from all over the country will come to Abda-El's funeral and all the Amorites will gather together. Whatever you intend to bring for the tomb of your father-in-law Abda-El, have it brought separately.'[8]

The most common form of a Bronze Age chief's burial, known as a tumulus, consisted of an inner chamber solidly constructed from timber or stones and finished with an earthen mound above. Although such a tumulus now looks the same as many of the Stone Age mounds described above, they served primarily for single burials and were not to be disturbed or entered thereafter. Their interior chambers did not serve as a space for holding commemorative ceremonies once the burial was completed.

The greater the power of ruling elites to make decisions on behalf of the whole society the greater their need to substantiate their claims to this power through ideology. The supreme rulers of some Bronze

Age societies were said to mediate with the gods on behalf of their peoples and to enjoy such intimacy with supernatural beings to assume a measure of divinity themselves. Such a quasi-divine ruler would not simply die as other mortals would, but was thought to continue to influence the fate of his erstwhile subjects. Some dead Sumerian kings in the early third millennium were laid to rest surrounded not only by luxury objects of gold and lapis lazuli but together with members of their court, who rather than joining their master on his demise more probably joined his posthumous retinue after their own death.[9] In ancient Egypt even greater investments into funeral cults were needed in order for the elite to achieve a mode of immortality. It is not surprising that the most labour intensive and longest lasting examples of the monumental Bronze Age tombs are the Egyptian pyramids. They are perfect geometrical manifestations which conjure up the 'melancholy image of arid mountains and immutability', as the Enlightenment architect Étienne-Louis Boullée put it. Just as in the more earthen tumuli, their interior spaces were sealed. Once the coffin had been placed in its chamber, the passageways were blocked; the temporary entrance obliterated and concealed. The pyramids proclaimed the disappearance or transformation of the pharaoh's mortal remains but the rituals of commemoration and veneration took place in other edifices and at other places. When all these measures failed to deter grave robbers searching for the treasures buried with the dead kings, the sites of royal tombs disappeared into the barren rocks at the edge of desert, while huge mortuary temples

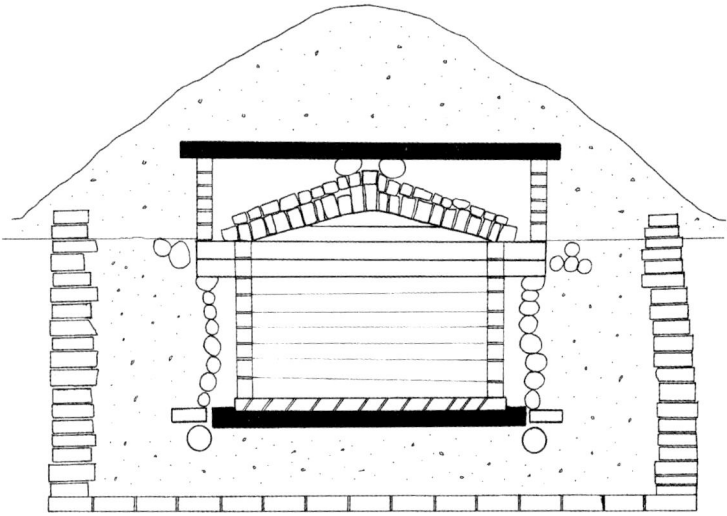

Section through the Great Tumulus at Gordion.

serviced the cult. The geometric configuration of older pyramids however, retained its symbolic connotation with death and the desire for immortality. Indeed, often reduced to an ornamental feature, it kept its original signification for millennia.

Hellenistic Eclecticism and the Invention of the Mausoleum

Alexander's conquest of the Persian Empire in 331 BC resulted in the wide dissemination of Greek culture far beyond the original *oikumene* (the civilized region) of Hellenism. The outward trappings of 'modern' Greek civilization, such as modes of dress and public buildings in Greek style, were widely adopted by locally signalled elites during the following centuries, when Alexander's successors divided up his conquered territories amongst themselves. Local traditions were subject to many different influences because goods and people circulated much more widely and faster than ever before across the Hellenistic world. Literacy in Greek increased, which in turn was influenced by Mesopotamian, Egyptian and other non-Hellenic ideas, histories, and religions. It was an age where religious syncretism, a more or less free mixture of different religions, thrived and where traditional identities were overlaid with imported new ones. Minor local kings and potentates, who managed to maintain not only a certain measure of independence but also to amass considerable wealth by obtaining trade monopolies, began to portray themselves as either heroic figures or semi-divine beings, favoured by the gods and striving for immortality. At the same time, their hold on power was precarious; subject as it was to complex and unpredictable political events. Given their 'spending power' and the insecurity of their position, an investment in lavish tombs made sense. Indeed, it seemed a safe manner to achieve lasting fame and status.[10]

The local potentates of the small oligarchies and petty kingdoms in Western Asia could choose from several different methods of funerary monuments: mounds, rock tombs or free-standing, purely architectural structures imitating single-room pitched roof houses, as well as so-called *heroa* that celebrate the memory of particularly heroic

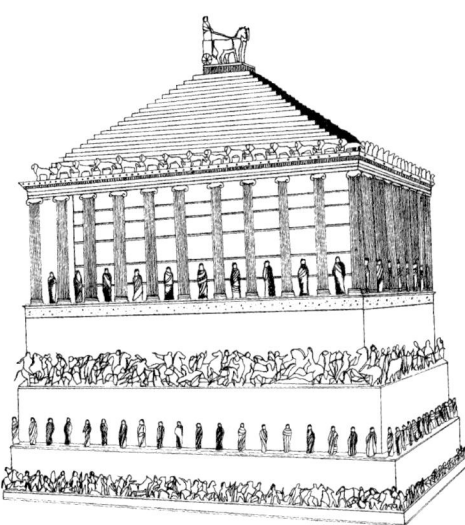

Reconstruction of the tomb of Mausolus at Halikarnassos.

personages. The Nabatæans and Lycians preferred to place their dead kings in rock tombs with huge and elaborate Grecian facades and simple, hollowed-out chambers behind to host funerary cults.

The best craftsmen and artists, mainly Greeks, were asked to embellish these monuments. The most famous was the latterly eponymous *Maussolleion* of Mausolus at Halicarnassus (fouth century BC), stupendous enough to qualify as one of the Seven Wonders of the World. Pliny the Elder reports on the monument and especially the sculptures in his *Natural History*:

> the Mausoleum; such being the name of the tomb that was erected by his wife Artemisia in honour of Mausolus, a petty king of Caria, who died in the second year of the hundred and seventh Olympiad. It was through the exertions of these artists more particularly, that this work came to be reckoned one of the Seven Wonders of the World. The circumference of this building is, in all, four hundred and forty feet, and the breadth from north to south sixty-three, the two fronts being not so wide in extent. It is twenty-five cubits in height, and is surrounded with six-and-thirty columns, the outer circumference being known as the 'Pteron'. The east side was sculptured by Scopas, the north by Bryaxis, the south by Timotheus, and the west by Leochares; but, before their task was completed, Queen Artemisia died. They did not leave their work, however, until it was finished, considering that it was at once a memorial of their own fame and of the sculptor's art: and, to this day even, it is undecided which of them has excelled. A fifth artist also took part in the work; for above the Pteron there is a pyramid erected, equal in height to the building below, and formed of four and twenty steps, which gradually taper upwards towards the summit; a platform, crowned with a representation of a four-horse chariot by Pythis. This addition makes the total height of the work one hundred and forty feet.[11]

Mausolus was the ruler of Caria, a very wealthy city-state at the time, who had invested heavily in beautifying the coastal town of Halicarnassus. Very little survives of his efforts (he also built a sumptuous palace) as the area was substantially rebuilt in the sixteenth century. Excavations, conducted first in 1856, have not yielded a great number of significant artefacts that would allow a definite reconstruction of what the whole edifice would have looked like.[12] The whole monument was certainly hugely impressive on account of its size, the high-quality sculptures and the gleaming white marble that rendered it visible from afar. The building was sited to dominate the town and the shore; it stood within a vast and beautifully landscaped precinct. Stylistically, it was a combination of many ideas about funerary architecture current at the time. The *Maussoleion* was mainly admired more for the quality of its sculptures than as a funerary monument. It was the ultimate memorial to an exceedingly rich potentate in Asia Minor whose aspirations were out of step with his importance. The mixed messages of his tomb and the contradictory references to widely different customs and beliefs lacked inner coherence. It tried to communicate too much and ended up as empty rhetoric. Nevertheless, the *Maussoleion* gave rise to the term 'mausoleum' that is still in current use. Ironically perhaps, it was the first monumental example of the temptation to overload a public tomb with symbolic significance from which few subsequent examples were entirely free.

Roman Imperial Tombs

When Octavianus became 'Augustus', Rome's first emperor in 27 BC, he commissioned a new symbolic landscape around the Campus Martius ('Field of Mars') – a prime site for elite burials from the Republican period. He ordered the construction of the monumental 'Altar of Peace' (*ara pacis*), put up an obelisk taken from Egypt and transformed the whole Field of Mars into a site dedicated to the cult of Augustus and his dynasty. It presented the newly created autocratic form of government as the culmination of a long line of Roman history. Augustus therefore decided to build his own monumental tomb as the focal point of the newly created ceremonial site. It resembled the so-called *tholoi* burial mounds (large earthen heaps on circular stone socles) that had been built for the Etruscan elite but also the *heroon* in Lavinium, the reputed tomb of Aeneas, the mythical Trojan founder of Rome. The choice of such an archaic form was a conscious decision. Augustus rejected the fashionably exotic forms of contemporary Roman elite burials as much as those of the overly ostentatious *Maussolleion* at

Plan of the mausoleum of Augustus.

Halicarnassus. There is no scholarly consensus on exactly how the building looked 2000 years ago, and whether it was surmounted by a *quadriga*-chariot (drawn by four horses), like Mausollos', in addition to a grove of trees. It is clear, though, that it meant to evoke ancient tumuli and at the same time appear suitablly impressive and express Roman appreciation of Greek architecture. The building was very large – 89 metres (291.11 feet) in diameter – and it contained a series of interior spaces large and sumptuous enough to serve as the setting for complex ritual observances. According to Jane Clarke Reeder, these rituals would enforce the idea of the new emperor's divine status on various levels:

> The Mausoleum of Augustus [...] was not merely a funerary monument but a cultic one as well. It served as an Augusteum or temple for the living ruler and later for a daily sacrifice to the *divus Augustus*. Thus sacrificial libations were probably poured both to the chthonic powers in the Greco-Roman custom and to the dead emperor as a deified hero in a *heroön*, and in particular in the manner of those to Alexander in the Sema at Alexandria. It is even possible that sacrifices or libations took place at the Mausoleum while Augustus was still alive.[13]

It was a considerable technical challenge to build an accessible interior and support the superstructure; the ring-shaped corridors and internal buttresses took up much of the space. It was finished before the death of Augustus. After the cremation of his body, so Suetonius relates,

> his remains were gathered up by the leading men of the equestrian order, bare-footed and in ungirt tunics, and placed in the Mausoleum. This structure he had built in his sixth consulship between the Via Flaminia and the bank of the Tiber, and at the same time opened to the public the groves and walks by which it was surrounded.[14]

Subsequent emperors were also entombed in the Augustan mausoleum, even some, like Vespasian (9–79), who was not of the Julio-Claudian line. Trajan (*c.* 53-117) departed radically from this tradition by ordering his ashes to be interred beneath his monumental column near the Basilica Ulpia (built in AD 113). Trajan's successor, Hadrian, built the last of the great Roman imperial tombs. Now known as the

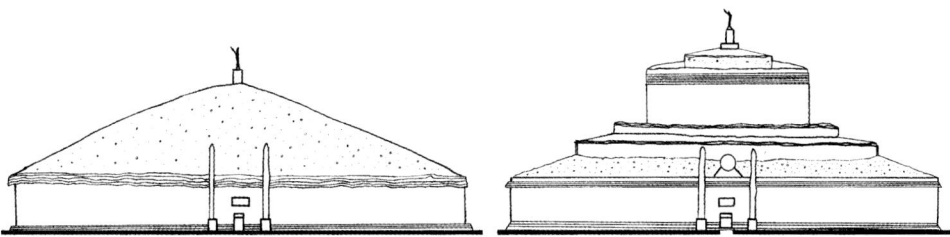

Different reconstructions of the elevation of the Augustus mausoleum.

'Castello degli Angeli' and substantially altered exteriorly, its form recalls the mausoleum of Augustus, which it matched in diameter, though it was probably higher. The main difference was in the interior, which was much loftier and comprised several burial chambers that were circular in plan and roofed with domes. By this time, the technique of using an early form of concrete (*opus caementicium*) was applied to monumental and not just utilitarian structures, and this allowed much wider spaces to be spanned, as for instance, in the still-functioning Pantheon in Rome. The architectural and symbolic importance of the dome, which came to signify the well-ordered cosmos, as well as eternity, was the main feature of the late Roman mausolea.

Royal Burials of Christian Monarchs in the Middle Ages

Roman mausolea were sacred spaces that served the cult of divine emperors. Once Christianity was officially adopted as the Roman state religion, emperors were no longer deified but instead were said to have a particularly close relationship to Christ. The mausoleum of Constantine, known as an '*apostoleion*', was a church dedicated to the apostles and intended to house the relics of the apostles. It also indicated that Constantine could be seen as the thirteenth apostle or an 'omitator of Christ'. The mausoleum was completed before the emperor's death in 337 and stood until 1462, when the Turks razed it to make room for the Fatih Mosque. Little is known of its appearance. It was possibly still a domed rotunda, not unlike the Church of the Holy Sepulchre, which Constantine had ordered to be built in Jerusalem. In Rome, he erected a grand basilica to mark the burial site of St Peter, which would become the spiritual centre of Western Christianity. After his death, Constantine's own tomb became a centre of pilgrimage and the sarcophagi of the emperor and his mother were believed to have miraculous powers.

The last imperial Roman mausoleum was built by Honorius in the early fifth century. Soon afterwards, Italy was invaded by Germanic tribes:

Mausoleum of Theoderic in Ravenna.

in 455 the Vandals sacked Rome and in 481, Theodoric (c. 454–526) King of the Ostrogoths, who had spent his youth as a hostage in Constantinople, made himself the ruler of Italy. Keen to shown himself as the protector of Rome, he ordered the restoration of destroyed monuments. He also had a new mausoleum built for his own use in Ravenna (northeast Italy), his capital. It was a free-standing, double cylinder surmounted by a flat dome. This was to be the last mausoleum in the Christian world until the eighteenth century and such was the fame of this king and his architectural projects in the Middle Ages that he was long believed to have built the much earlier mausoleum of Hadrian in Rome.[15]

In both realms of the Christian world, kings and emperors were henceforth buried in funerary churches (discussed below). Medieval kings would also fund monasteries and abbeys and it is not surprising that these would serve as their last resting places. The Church of St Geneviève in Paris, for instance, founded by the Merovingian King Clovis in the early sixth century, was to house his tomb, whilst the convent of Las Huelga at Burgos, set up by Alfonso VIII in 1199, became the royal necropolis of the House of Castile. While the royal burials enhanced the prestige of these monastic foundations, they were not intended to attract pilgrims or serve as sites of anniversary celebrations.

Quite different in purpose were the funerary churches that formed part of a palace complex, which was a practice initiated by Charlemagne (742–814), king of the Franks and later Holy Roman Emperor. His Palace Chapel at Aachen in western Germany (built between 786 and 789) was the first large edifice to be erected in transalpine Europe since the fall of Rome.[16] The emperor wished to demonstrate that the prestige of his court rivalled that of the Byzantine rulers, after having admired the architectural splendours of Ravenna. Instead of the circular plan of Theodoric's tomb, the chapel at Aachen was formed of an octagon in the centre and surrounded by a sixteen-sided groin-vaulted ambulatory. The interior was sumptuously decorated with marble slabs shipped from Rome and Ravenna and embellished by craftsmen from all over the empire. It was *the* imperial palace chapel; the cosmic centre of the Carolingian and Ottonian empires, the seat of coronations and the site of imperial burials. Housing the venerable remains of pious Christian rulers, it attracted countless pilgrims throughout the Middle Ages. Charlemagne's politico-religious complex at Aachen remained the original model and the ultimate source of inspiration for any ruler aspiring to universal power.[17]

During the High Middle Ages the possession of royal corpses was politically valuable and a means to confer legitimacy to a new or hitherto minor lineage. In 1264, for example, the bodies of eight Carolingian and eight Capetian kings and queens were moved to the abbey church of St Denis outside Paris at the request of Abbot Suger, who had 'identified the well-being of the royal house with its own interests' and who hoped to induce future kings to choose St Denis not only as a place of burial but for coronations.[18] This was a successful strategy. The subsequent sanctification of Louis IX (St Louis), who had died in Tunisia during the Second Crusade, and whose boiled bones were exhibited in a precious reliquary at St Denis, ensured the enduring importance of the church as the royal necropolis for the French monarchy.

The fusion of royalty and religion was not restricted to the Middle Ages but continued to flourish, especially in Catholic countries, and with renewed vigour after the Counter-Reformation. The complex political and dynastic configuration of the Habsburg empire led to several sites being constructed as dynastic '*loci sancti*', that is, churches that housed dead kings and queens (including those Prague, Wiener Neustadt, Graz and Vienna).[19] Philip II, an obsessive collector of relics, and keen to secure the legitimacy of Habsburg rule in Spain, created the sixteenth-century equivalent to the Charlemagne's palace complex at El Escorial. He did not try to assemble every relic of St Lawrence but instead desired to erect a mausoleum, where his body and those of the other Spanish Habsburgs could rest for all eternity. Having sacred relics of saints in physical proximity in a holy place would secure legitimacy for the new ruling dynasty:

> By treating the bodies of his father and family as holy relics to be transferred to the pantheon of the Escorial and placed directly under the basilica's main altar – a space usually reserved for saints – Philip II wished to appropriate the entire spiritual legacy of the Habsburgs as a cornerstone for his still somewhat precarious authority.[20]

The Impact of the French Revolution

While the revival of classical scholarship, the growth of scientific rationality and the beginning of capitalist economies in Western Europe all contributed to the intellectual climate of 'Enlightenment', it was the French Revolution, with its radical demotion of the Church, that profoundly affected attitudes to death and burial through a process of enforced secularization. In Revolutionary France the closure of church graveyards meant that bodies were interred in mass tombs. Garden-like, pantheistically inspired Fields of Rest (*champs de repos*) were to replace the older forms of burials. Instead of dead kings, the Republic wished to honour great, dead citizens. Hence, while the royal graves were attacked at St Denis, the bodies of intellectuals and revolutionary leaders were disinterred and moved to a new site, the secularized church of St Geneviève in Paris, which was transformed into the Pantheon in 1791. St Geneviève was also meant to be surrounded by a woodland grove. The example of this first national pantheon, which assembled the remains of those deemed to have made significant contributions to the fatherland, was taken up during the nineteenth century in many countries, and most assiduously in post-colonial Latin America.

Funerary architecture and the design of mausolea and cenotaphs became a popular subject for architects. Best known are the efforts of Claude-Nicolas Ledoux and Louis-Étienne Boullée, who despite not building extensively, made copious drawings of imagined buildings. Boullée favoured especially huge monuments in the shape of pure geometric forms such as pyramids and spheres which he placed in 'landscapes of eternity'. The dread of death as final separation was suggested through sunken and dimly lit interior spaces and densely packed masonry, an 'architecture of shadows', which emphasized the sense of loss and absence:

> they define a place set off from the world of the living either by making a temple-like enclosure, by opening a cavity in the ground, or by gathering a dense mass of stone around a constricted area. They often employ a descent into earth or an ascent toward the sky; they sometimes use a special light, luminous and crystalline or somber and ghostly.[21]

In Britain too, such funerary architecture became fashionable. Aristocratic landowners commissioned private mausolea to be added to the architectural incidents and 'follies' within their artfully landscaped estates. They were generally built in a classical idiom, modelled on the examples of Roman funerary monuments such as those that lined the Via Appia. In the early Victorian public cemeteries, such as Kensal Green, such neo-Classical family mausolea enjoyed great popularity, together with those that recalled Gothic chapels.

Napoleon's Tomb

Napoleon I (1769–1821) did nothing to restore the remains of the French royals who had been committed to mass graves during the Terror (between mid-1793 and July 1794). The restoration of the Bourbon monarchy entailed a search for the corpses of Bourbon royalty which were ceremoniously reinstalled in St Denis. When Napoleon died on St Helena Island (in the South Atlantic) in 1821, the government of Louis Philippe I decided on the repatriation of his remains, owing to the enduring popularity of France's national hero. The question of where and how to bury them then followed. Louis-Napoleon (1808–1873) had hoped to bury his uncle at St Denis, thus placing him in the hallowed context of French kings – a notion firmly rejected by the Orléans family which was not keen 'to excite followers of [the] Napoleonic cult'.[22] An alternative site, the Hôtel National des Invalides, which had been one of Louis XIV's grand architectural projects and had served as a retirement home for ex-soldiers, was finally agreed upon. In selecting this reseting place, Napoleon's status as a military commander of genius was emphasized. At the same time, the choice distanced him from the long line of French royalty at St Denis, as much as from the dead freethinkers and revolutionaries assembled at the Panthéon. Interior Minister de Rémusat offered the commission to the French architect Félix Duban and the Italian sculptor Marochetti, but following public protests over this autocratic proceeding, an open competition was held and the commission was given to Louis Visconti. Louis Philippe and his son and heir, the Duke of Orléans, rejected their design and Visconti's tomb was only completed 30 years later, by which time Louis-Napoleon had become Emperor Napoleon III in 1848. The dome and crypt were opened to the public on 14 August 1853 but the emperor's dislike of the tomb and his desire to bury at least his uncle's heart at St Denis delayed the final inauguration until 1861.

The architect's task was to insert the tomb within the body of the Baroque church and to create a secondary space for the sarcophagus and a sculptural memorial. Visconti's solution was to place this in a sunken crypt situated below Mansart's dome and make it visible through a large round opening surrounded by a balustrade. The coffin was made of red porphyry, like those of later Roman emperors, with scrolled ends but without an effigy. Twelve colossal female figures by Pradier, allegories of Napoleon's main victorious battles, surround the crypt. The tomb set

Napoleon's tomb.

the memory of Napoleon within the heroic tradition of the victorious soldier and, at the same time, as a unique moment in French history. In response to the architectural setting, Curl mentions the possible influence of early prison designs:

> to be sure Visconti would have intended no reference to incarceration in his design, but the unseen ruler in a sealed sarcophagus in the center of a circular space, at the periphery of which lesser members of society stand in attitudes of reverence, is an arrangement that the panopticon prison and the tomb of Napoleon have in common.[23]

Whether the attitude of those who visited this public place was one of reverence or censure for Napoleon's hubris, the gaping hole within the monument of the *ancien régime* allowed a perspective view from above to the stone sarcophagus below, and therefore a certain distance to reflect and evaluate the incumbent's legacy. The Beaux-Arts neo-Classicism of the design and the cold blankness of the sculptures dispelled a more emotional or romantic engagement with the entombed emperor. The monument in its final form, as well as the history of its construction, can be read as embodying the conflicting tensions of nineteenth-century France, caught between a revolutionary legacy, attempts to restore the Bourbon monarchy, and the triumph of the bourgeoisie under a Bonaparte autocrat.

Lincoln's Tomb in Springfield, Illinois

Another eighteenth-century revolution led to the birth of the United States of America. One of the most outstanding early presidents was Abraham Lincoln and his violent death in office at the hand of an assassin in 1865 shocked the nation and occasioned the development of a great popular interest in his person. Lincoln's tomb was built on the initiative of an association of former friends from his native Springfield in Illinois. Although this was to be a private memorial, set within the Oak Ridge Cemetery that had only been opened in 1860, the aspirations for national significance were spelt out in the sermon spoken at the funeral service at the White House:

> The friends of Liberty and of the Union will repair to it in years and ages to come, to pronounce the memory of its

occupant blessed, and, gathering from his very ashes, and from the rehearsal of his deeds and virtues, fresh incentives to patriotism, they will there renew their vows of fidelity to their country and their God.[24]

As with Napoleon's tomb, a competition was announced and a thousand dollars offered for the winning entry. Out of the 37 submissions, the design of Larkin G. Mead was chosen, which featured an 25.9-metre-high (85-feet-high) obelisk set on a terraced platform and surrounded by statuary. In the initial version of the tomb, this obelisk was more than a symbol of immortality – it was a vantage point to allow visitors a panoramic view of Springfield. From the very beginning, while laying claims to its status as a sacred site of the nation, the tomb was also made to function as a place of entertainment and instruction. In addition to the burial chamber that contained crypts for Lincoln and members of his family, a memorial room exhibited personal articles of the dead president. The dedication ceremony for the Lincoln Tomb was held on 15 October 1874 and it opened to the public the following day. When in 1876 a plan to steal Lincoln's body to exact a ransom nearly succeeded and the poorly constructed foundations caused some of the supporting vaults to collapse, substantial alterations became necessary. The burial chamber was replaced and Lincoln was reburied in a steel-caged coffin set within an underground crypt, while a 'symbolic' marble sarcophagus on the publicly accessible level indicated the placement. The management of the monument passed from a private association to the Illinois Department of Public Works in 1917, and it continued to be a popular attraction. Indeed, visitors could still climb the obelisk and inspect the growing collection of memorabilia. Uneasy with the notion that the private tomb of a former president – who after all was not a king and held office only temporarily –- be a sole memorial to the much revered Lincoln, the Administration under Woodrow Wilson commissioned an alternative site of veneration: the Lincoln Memorial in Washington, DC, where a Grecian temple holds the colossal seated statue of the president. By 1930 officials had grown increasingly concerned by the lack of dignity and the physical deterioration of the Springfield tomb and suggested a further rebuilding to 'transform the monument into a hallowed shrine'.[25] New rules were to curtail the entertainment aspects, the observation tower was closed, the erection of picnic tables forbidden and the tomb was meant to be transformed from a tourist attraction into a national site sacred to the memory of

Lincoln's Mausoleum at Springfield, Illinois.

the Defender of the Union, and one of the founders of the nation. President Hoover inaugurated this final version of the tomb in 1931. Following attacks by vandals in the late 1980s and 1990s, the site was placed under 24-hour surveillance managed by a private security company. The controversies surrounding Lincoln's tomb prefigured and paralleled those of other politicians buried in much more controlled circumstances in a national museum. Its architectural form, much in the spirit of nineteenth-century eclecticism, drew on a whole range of funerary monuments: it provided a crypt sunk into the earth, where the bones of the great man were held; a cylindrical chamber to exhibit objects he had handled and used. In addition, the stepped terraces, the dramatic statues and the gleaming white stone recall the mausoleum of Halicarnassus, while the tall obelisk, the main feature of the tomb, points to the funerary temples of ancient Egyptians. The statuary and shields on the platform and inside the burial chambers were to symbolize the heroic deeds and acts associated with the incumbent in the manner of medieval monuments. The striking absence of any Christian symbolism underlines the secular nature of American democracy (as expressed in the First Amendment to the Constitution in 1791) and is in keeping with the pantheistic imagery of the Enlightenment.

We have seen that the custom of preserving the mortal remains of individuals in conspicuous monuments has ancient roots. The bones of ancestors embedded in the earth suggested a link between past and future generations within a particular landscape and was all the more powerful when the site became a landmark. Indeed, in urban, stratified societies, supreme rulers could eternalize their prerogatives through solidly built tombs. The usefulness of bones and ashes of prominent dead leaders as a tool of legitimating claims to power could lead to their being disinterred and moved to different locations. Rites and cults tied to these sites of memory would keep their meaning alive for as long as that had any relevance. To some extent, the loss of a specific historical context allowed the material remains a greater resonance, and evoked a wide range of associations. The repertoire of forms and symbols in funerary architecture relies on simple generic models, that is, essentially the mound in the landscape and the hole sunk into the ground, in combination and varied composition that is rich in meaning and can be elaborated to evoke complex ideas and messages.

CHAPTER TWO

Safeguarding the Immortality of Revolutionary Leaders
Mausolea in Communist Countries

> The Mummy is the greatest communist. The stem of the Party.
> The Mausoleum is the Center-accumulator mastering the collectivized people's libido.
> The Mummy-stem in the Mausoleum-laboratory – this is the grand installation of modern political art and science.[1]

Mass graves marked the French Revolution of the late eighteenth century. In 1871 the executed *Communards* (supporters of the Paris *Commune*) were also given such anonymous and collective burial. In the October Revolution of 1917, mass graves again held revolutionaries as well as their enemies. The abolition of social distinctions and inequality, two of the primary aims of all these revolutions, were to extend beyond death.

In November of that year 240 pro-Bolshevik victims were buried alongside the Kremlin wall in Moscow. This was the beginning of a revolutionary necropolis and the Soviet equivalent of the national pantheons, which in other countries held the assembled mortal remains of worthy individuals in named and often sumptuous tombs. Such posthumous distinction, and the possibility that one's corpse or ashes might become objects of veneration, like the relics of saints, were abhorrent notions to revolutionary heroes. However, just as the corpses and skeletons of saints and monarchs could be appropriated by subsequent generations for political ends, dead revolutionary leaders were also too 'useful' to be granted private burials, as they might have wished. They could instead be elevated to the status of secular sainthood and thus serve to provide an emotional outlet, especially at times when the observance of traditional forms of religion was repressed. Unlike in the United States, where the Lincoln tomb as a private initiative could be exploited for commercial gain, in communist countries the state and the party kept a tight control over all aspects of these posthumous cults.

All the tombs I have discussed so far served to safeguard the remains of their incumbents, such as the ashes of Roman emperors or the bones of Christian monarchs. Even when certain of these corpses were embalmed after death, their bodies were not put on show. This was unlike the practice of exhibiting the bodies of some Christian saints whose saintliness was proven by the incorruptibility of their dead flesh. It is one of the great ironies of history that the acknowledged leader of the October Revolution (1917), which swept away so much of the old Russia and its medieval superstitions, should end up preserved and contained in a glass casket, just like the old priests I saw as a child, or a long dead saint. Lenin, however, had to be made 'incorruptible' by science, and the survival of his body was presented as one of Soviet science's great achievements. At the same time, the Politburo could be seen to react to the unexpectedly passionate manifestations of public grief and to be able to find means of giving the bereaved populace a near miraculous example of the system's power in overcoming even death. Although, as we shall see, the procedures applied to Lenin's corpse were at best improvised, the dead revolutionary was kept in a state of freshness, giving the impression of being merely asleep.

Having acquired the necessary expertise, the scientists at the Moscow mausoleum were keen to practise their skills and whenever a communist head of state happened to die while in the Soviet Union, he would be given this treatment. It became an honour and a sign of allegiance for countries with political ties to the Soviet Republic to have their own prominent leader embalmed and subsequently exposed in a grand mausoleum, which in turn was often built by Soviet engineers or at least with their expert guidance.

These mausolea were great national shrines, characterized by Vladimir Todorov in the quotation at the beginning of this chapter, as 'the grand installation of modern political art and science'. They were places where the people could silently commune with the dead leader, where choreographed public rituals were performed, and from where government leaders addressed the masses at solemn occasions. They were potent symbols of state Communism in the capitals of Eastern bloc countries and as such, could become the target of popular resentment after the break-up of the Soviet Union.

In the following sections, I will examine the still functioning tombs of Lenin, Ho Chi Minh, Mao Zedong and Kim Il Sung, which I have all visited in the last few years. Those of Mao and Lenin have endured, despite the fact that they are no longer deemed ideologically useful to the government. What began as a substitute focus of mass devotion in the aftermath of the Russian Revolution, that is, the shrine containing the embalmed leader, reaches its most exaggerated manifestation in the context of North Korea, where the grand mausoleum at Kumsusan now houses two defunct members of the ruling Kim dynasty. I will also review what happened to the tombs of the other embalmed communist leaders once they were removed from public sight.

Lenin's Tomb

The dead man who lies in the crystal sarcophagus in the mausoleum that bears the laconic inscription 'Ленин' was born Vladimir Ilich Ulyanov, on 22 April 1870 in Simbirsk, a town on the Volga.

By his own account, he had a happy and affluent childhood. His father held the office of a state councillor, and was raised to the nobility for his services as an inspector for schools. He died in 1886 when Lenin was sixteen. The execution of his elder brother Alexander in the following year – he had been part of a revolutionary group trying to assassinate Tsar Alexander III – has often been cited by Soviet biographers as the crucial event that triggered Lenin's radicalization. He was expelled for engaging in 'revolutionary activities' by the University of Kazan, where he had been studying law, and moved to St Petersburg University, completing his degree in 1891. Returning to the east, where he practised as a barrister at Samara, he gained first-hand experience of the hardships endured by the Russian peasantry. Rather than continue to serve the legal system, the young lawyer joined revolutionaries in St Petersburg and became involved in the international labour movement. This entailed giving lectures for workers, distributing leaflets, organizing strikes and protests, setting up committees, as well as travelling abroad to establish a broader base of support. Lenin made his first trip to Europe in 1895. Back in St Petersburg, he founded the 'League of Struggle for the Emancipation of the Working Class' (together with Martov) and met his future wife, Nadezhda Krupskaya, a comrade from St Petersburg University. As a result of his ceaseless activities, he was arrested and exiled to Siberia, along with Krupskaya, where they married in 1898. She remained his lifelong companion and collaborator.

After the Siberian exile, Lenin went back to Europe, with his wife joining him soon after, to continue the organization of the Labour movement and to set up the revolutionary paper entitled *Iskra* (*The Spark*). He argued for the necessity of an organized, collective party leadership to direct the revolutionary struggle, a stance that led to an ideological split within the Russian labour movement, which was henceforth divided between Lenin's Bolsheviks (literally, 'majority') and Martov's Mensheviks ('minority') factions.

Like many other revolutionaries, he used pseudonyms, one of which was 'Lenin' (or the full 'Nikolai Lenin' in 1902), possibly derived from the Siberian Lena River. In 1905 Lenin joined the first Russian Revolution and was elected to the Presidium of the Russian Social Democratic Labour Party. However, when the tsarist forces suppressed the revolution, Lenin and his wife resumed their exile in Europe, developing and clarifying his political and ideological position. He argued that workers should bond in international solidarity and engage in a class war rather than take part in the 'imperialist war' that had begun in 1914.

When the tsar was forced to abdicate in 1917, and a provisional government had been put in place, revolutionary councils (*soviets*) sprang up which opposed it. The Germans, who hoped that Lenin's presence would weaken Russian military resistance, allowed him to travel to Russia in a sealed train. On this journey he composed the *April Theses*, which set out the programme for the Bolshevik Party and its aim for a full socialist revolution that would hand over the leadership of the party from the bourgeoisie to labourers and peasants. Accused of being a German spy, Lenin went into hiding again but emerged after three and a half months to take part at the Second Congress of the Soviets on 25 October 1917. During the night of 27 October he proposed a draft decree about signing a peace treaty with Germany. This was accepted, and the Bolshevik majority, supported by the left wing of the Socialist Revolutionaries, declared that supreme power was now to be vested in the Soviets and appointed Lenin to head the Soviet of People's Commissaries and, as such, the government. In this capacity he signed the peace treaty of Brest-Litovsk with Germany on 3 March 1918. Lenin directed the deposition of the Provisional Government in early November 1917 in the famous storming of the Winter Palace. On 26 October he issued the following decree:

> All private ownership of land is abolished immediately without compensation. All landowners' estates and all lands belonging to the Crown, to monasteries, church lands with all their live stock and inventoried property, buildings and appurtenances,

are transferred to the disposition of the township Land Committees and the district Soviets of Peasants' Deputies until the Constituent Assembly meets.[2]

The country was by no means united in the acceptance of the new regime's policies. The proposed peace with Germany, achieved at the cost of considerable territorial losses, was much resented in particular and seen as too high a price to pay for Lenin's internationalism. Civil war broke out in 1917, pitching Bolsheviks and their supporters, relying first on the Red Guard, then the conscripted Red Army, against Allied forces, groups loyal to the former Russian governments, as well as various nationalist groups united by the so-called White movement and the White Army. Intense fighting lasted from 1918 to 1920 and major military operations only ended in 1922, while skirmishes continued until 1923. Lenin, as head of the Soviet Bolshevik government, directed military operations, as well as organizing the economic recovery from the devastations of past and ongoing warfare in a backward country. His ambitious programmes for electrification, free universal health care, free education and civil rights for women could only be partially implemented. Lenin also created a Secret Police (*Cheka*) to repress criticism of the Bolshevik regime and control the press.

In 1918 Lenin was the target of two assassination attempts. The second attempt was nearly fatal, when he received two bullets in the neck shot by a Social-Revolutionary named Kaplan. While the effects of this wound were to contribute to Lenin's declining health, the fact that he had survived these attacks gave fuel to the rising personality cult. In the end, the damage wrought by the attack, together with the effects of overwork, led to a series of strokes. In 1922 Lenin was forced to retire to the country, where he continued to work, defying his doctors' advice. Realizing the severity of his affliction, he dictated a series of letters to Krupskaya, in which he expressed his view of the main personalities in the Politburo. He was particularly critical of Josef Stalin, who had become the Party General Secretary in 1922. This document, known as 'Lenin's Testament', was not made public until much later. In December 1923 Lenin's condition worsened, he became paralyzed in the right arm and leg and lost the ability to speak. He died on 21 January 1924, at 6.30 p.m., at Gorky, near Moscow, with the cause of death being cited as 'arteriosclerosis of the brain'. He was in his 54th year.

Lenin had effectively wielded power for a mere five years. Yet he was the figurehead of the new Soviet Republic and was presented as the very spirit of the Revolution by the Russian mass media. None of the other members of the Politburo matched his charisma and popular appeal. His image, often portrayed as passionately exhorting the people, was widely reproduced and disseminated, even more so in his final two years from 1922 to 1924, during his retirement to Gorki. The news of Lenin's death caused a terrific shock and a sense of collective bereavement and bewilderment. Arthur Ransome described the scene at the Congress in the Guardian edition of 23 Wednesday January 1924:

> When Congress met at eleven this morning, Kalinin, who was hardly able to speak, announced Lenin's death in a few broken sentences. Almost everybody in the great theatre burst into tears, and from all parts came the hysterical wailing of women. Tears were running down the faces of the members of the Praesidium. The funeral march of the Revolutionaries was played by a weeping orchestra. Lashevitch announced that January 21 will be a day of mourning in the Russian calendar.[3]

Common reactions to Lenin's sudden demise were the refusal to accept the finality of his passing and to express a passionate wish for his continuing vitality and relevance, as expressed in Vladimir Mayakovsky's poem 'On the Death of Lenin', written a few days later. Mayakovsky praises 'the man, the champion, the avenger, the fighter', the one who, 'alive as ever', urges the workers for 'the last assault' and concludes with the rousing statement that

> There's no one
> > more alive
> > > than Lenin in the world,
> our strength,
> > our wisdom,
> > > surest of weapons.[4]

In a country that had been through the violent transition from medieval serfdom to a union of Soviet republics and that had experienced a devastating civil war and the radical *Umwertung aller Werte* ('revaluation of all values'), Lenin was seen to have embodied the revolutionary vitality of the Russian people and their hopes for a better future. It was therefore vital that the members of the Politburo should show themselves to be enthusiastic disciples of the great leader and his legitimate and worthy successors. They were far from united in this endeavour and Zinoviev, Stalin and Trotsky engaged in fierce rivalry about who should assume Lenin's mantle.[5]

Stalin was to prevail in this struggle. He had set the tone in his famous speech to the Congress of Soviets with the incantatory intensity he had learnt at the Seminary as a youth:

> In leaving us, Comrade Lenin ordained us to hold high and keep pure the great title of member of the party. We vow to thee, Comrade Lenin, that we shall honourably fulfill this thy commandment. For twenty-five years, Lenin trained our party and made of it the strongest and best-tempered workers' party in the world [. . .] In leaving us, Comrade Lenin ordained us to guard the unity of our party like the apple of our eye. We vow to thee, Comrade Lenin, that we shall fulfill this thy commandment, too.[6]

However, solemn promises were not enough. Lenin's immortality was not to be simply metaphorical. Immediately after Lenin's death, a funeral committee was formed under the direction of Felix Dzerzhinsky who declared publicly that 'if science permits, Lenin's body must be preserved'.[7] Two committee members were particularly engaged in the discussions. Anatoly Lunarchsky, as 'Commissar of Enlightenment' and the main exponent of the so-called god-building movement, wished to turn Lenin into a deity, to become an object of devotion for the new era.[8] Leonid Krasin believed that science would one day be able to bring about immortality and argued that the body of the dead leader should be prepared for this eventuality. Josef Stalin argued that Lenin be embalmed and placed in a publicly accessible mausoleum, an idea that was angrily rejected by Trotsky and Bukharin, who argued that making Lenin's body into a relic was an insult to his memory. Lenin's widow, Krupskaya, would not hear of it either. She wrote an open letter that was published in *Pravda*, where she took issue with the very idea of sanctifying Lenin in this manner:

> I have a great request to you: do not allow your mourning for Ilyich to take the form of external reverence for his person. Do not raise memorials to him, palaces named after him, solemn festivals in commemoration of him, etc. To all this he attached

so little importance in his life, all this was so burdensome to him. Remember how much poverty and neglect there still is in our country. If you wish to honour the name of Vladimir Ilyich, build crèches, kindergartens, houses, schools, libraries, medical centres, hospitals, homes for the disabled, etc., and, most of all, let us put his precepts into practice.[9]

Her plea was ignored. Stalin had his way. Lenin's embalmed corpse was to become the main focus for a new cult and to be displayed in a mausoleum on Red Square. The official reasoning was that millions of workers and peasants had demanded the preservation of their deceased leader.

While some members of the Funeral Committee subscribed to the belief that Lenin could actually be revivified at some future stage, the reality confronting the team of physicians dealing with his corpse was that decay had already set in. Vladimir Vorobiev, professor of anatomy at Kharkov University, removed the first signs of putrefaction with acetic acid and hydrogen peroxide.[10] He recalled that there was an ancient Russian tradition of preserving corpses in honey and argued that instead of drying out the body as in mummification, the tissues should be kept moist by injecting the veins and soaking the whole body in a solution of glycerin and drops of acetate. This would allow the body to keep its natural appearance and give the impression of being peacefully asleep. Vorobiev was confident that given regular maintenance and submersions in the right liquid, Lenin's body could be kept in good condition for an indefinite number of years. Of course, this treatment was not preparing the body for potential revitalization on any scientific basis. Moreover, the most important point was to present the dead revolutionary leader as lying in a state of suspended animation, and still being in some mysterious way 'with us forever'. The Center of Biomedical Technologies at the All-Russian Institute of Medicinal and Aromatic Plants (VILAR), as the centre where the team of experts entrusted with looking after Lenin's remains was called, eventually moved into purpose-built rooms situated directly beneath the mausoleum complex. All the necessary mechanisms and paraphernalia, from the large glass tub used for submersions to wax models and substitute corpses of Lenin lookalikes, were kept within this hidden substructure, completely out of sight from visitors.

Immediately after Lenin's death, while the embalmers were busy with his body, the Funeral Commission entrusted V. D. Bonch-Bruevich with the task of supervising the construction of Lenin's tomb. In order to engage the general public, a competition was announced and people sent in hundreds of proposals. The artist Vladimir Tatlin, for instance, proposed to house Lenin in a building comprising a huge auditorium and an information bureau equipped with hundreds of telephones.[11] There was very little time and the commission promptly accepted the design by the architect Alexey Shchusev. At a meeting at the Funeral Commission on 23 January he said:

> Vladimir Ilich is eternal [. . .] How shall we honour his memory? In architecture the cube is eternal [. . .] let the mausoleum, which we will erect as a monument to Vladimir Ilich, derive from a cube.[12]

He spontaneously sketched a cube and the Commission accepted the proposal. A hastily constructed makeshift timber structure was to serve as a temporary mausoleum until a more permanent version could be built. Controlled explosions were necessary to excavate solidly frozen ground on Red Square and workers, as well as volunteers, laboured day and night. The temporary mausoleum was made of a timber frame covered with grey painted boards. It had the form of a central cube, measuring six metres (nineteen feet) on each side, topped by a shallow three-sided pyramid.[13] 'The Hall of Mourning', containing Lenin's sarcophagus, was sunk below ground and could be reached through a shaft-like entrance on either side. Within the first six weeks after the funeral on 27 January, some 100,000 people braved temperatures of minus 30 degrees centigrade (86 degrees Fahrenheit) to pay their last respects to 'Comrade Lenin'.

This first makeshift structure was only in use for a few months, before being replaced by a more solid and monumental version that was officially inaugurated on the occasion of the 13th Party Congress on 23 May 1924. Shchusev, again entrusted with the commission, maintained the concept of the immortalizing cube, although this was now hidden behind a rectangular facade. The central placement of the coffin room was emphasized on the outside by a platform consisting of three tiers, supporting a step-pyramid topped by a temple-like feature. An important addition was the external rostrum that was reached by steps on either side, in order to allow the Politburo members to address the assembled populace. This new mausoleum was twice as big as the temporary one. Despite being similarly constructed from timber, it had

TOMBS OF THE GREAT LEADERS

much more elaborate panelling. It was a curiously Babylonian-looking building, recalling a ziggurat in its stepped outline and the recesses and niches of mud-brick temples. Following the Grand Opening on 1 August 1924, the people were given open access and were able to see Lenin's body dressed in a khaki tunic, ornamented by the Order of the Red Banner, lying in an elaborate, diamond-shaped, crystal sarcophagus designed by Victor Melnikov that was the only truly constructivist feature in the rather conventional timber mausoleum.

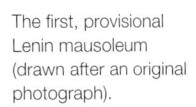

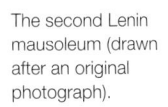

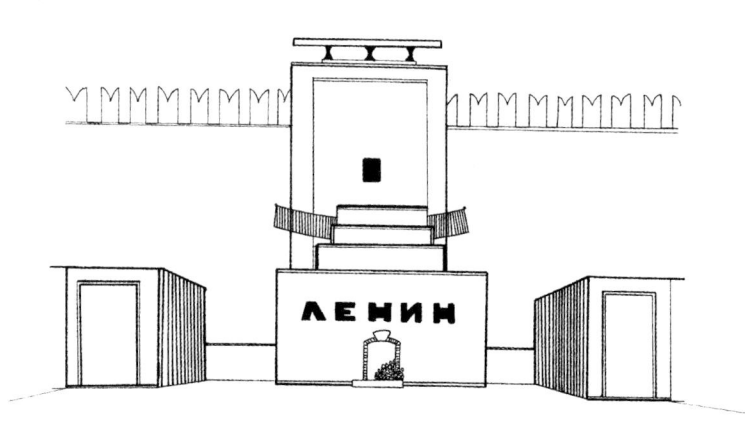

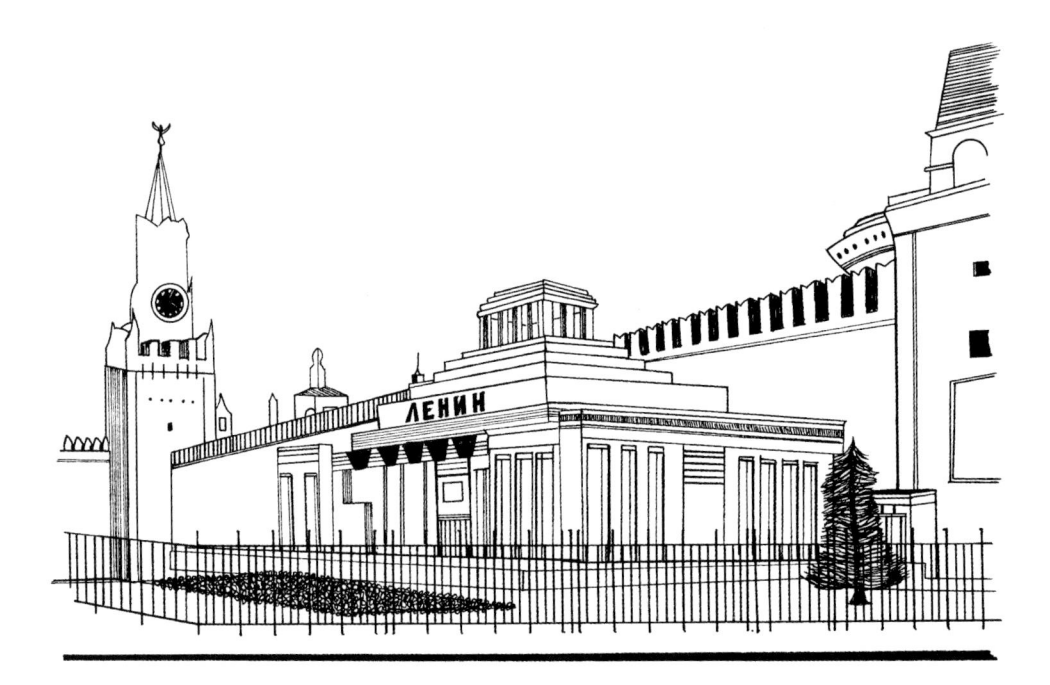

The first, provisional Lenin mausoleum (drawn after an original photograph).

The second Lenin mausoleum (drawn after an original photograph).

40

Given the continuing symbolic and political importance of Lenin's tomb and the by now perfected technology of keeping his body for an indefinite period, Stalin decided in 1929 on a further transformation of mausoleum, which was to make it truly monumental and commensurate with the aspirations to eternity. The timber structure was to be replaced by one of stone to resemble the great tombs of ancient times. Shchusev, again the architect in charge, was sent to source suitable materials from around the Soviet Union, and selected marble (for the interior), porphyry, red granite and black labradorite for the external wall cladding. The interior too was clad in stone, with the artist Ignaty Nivinsky being responsible for the striking black-and-red wall design of the tomb chamber. The design for this third mausoleum was based on the second version, but made more coherent and compact. The rostrum was made bigger, although this function was concealed by integrating the access to it within the lateral corners of the facade and by placing it above the entrance bearing Lenin's name. The recesses and niches were replaced by smooth stone cladding, and the little 'temple' at the top now had a flat roof, consisting of a single massive slab supported by 36 pillars. On either side of the mausoleum, alongside the Kremlin walls, seating for 10,000 party members, who assembled there on ceremonial occasions, was provided on grey granite benches.

Elevation and plan of Lenin mausoleum.

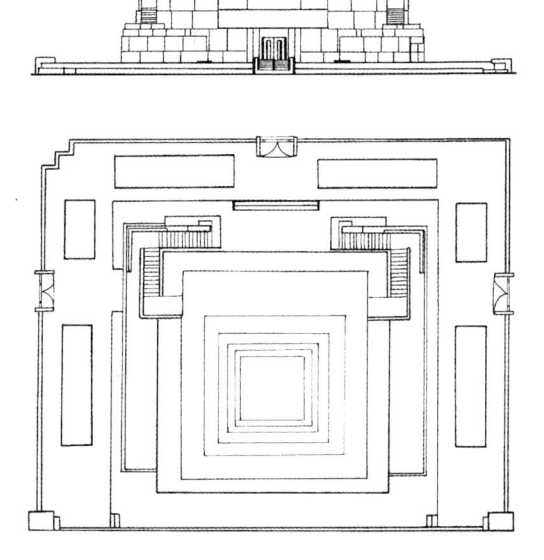

It was at this stage that the laboratories for the maintenance of Lenin's corpse were accommodated underneath the mausoleum and seating areas. The whole of Red Square underwent refurbishment and repaving to be turned into the largest ceremonial space in the capital. Tramlines were removed, and the statues of Minin and Pozharsky shifted from a previously central position to a peripheral one close to the cathedral. All of these works were carried out in great haste and were completed by October 1930. The mausoleum has not undergone any significant change since then.

We have seen that Stalin presented himself as Lenin's most faithful comrade and follower after Lenin's death. Since Trotsky had spoken against the sacralization of

Lenin's body and was prevented from attending Lenin's funeral, Stalin not only officiated as chief mourner but presented himself as the only one who understood the feelings of the populace and their need to have Lenin with them forever. At first, the ensuing cult of Lenin was marked by the sense of loss and mourning. From 1926 onwards, once Stalin had consolidated his grip on the party, Lenin's cult underwent a process of standardization, with less emphasis on mourning. Stalin's 50th birthday celebrations on 21 December 1929 mark the beginning of his own personality cult that grew in proportion to his assumption of complete power, relegating Lenin to the position of a forerunner. By 1933 Stalin had taken over the sacred sphere of the Lenin cult, replacing 'Lenin the Redeemer' with his name and 'personality', as slogans such as 'Stalin is the Lenin of Today' or 'Stalin is the Living Lenin' demonstrate. The famous film *Three Songs About Lenin* by Dziga Vertov, made in 1934 as a montage of striking images, summarized the popular devotion to Lenin and frames Stalin as a faithful follower. The inter-titles to the second film read:

> In Moscow, in a big stone city,
> Where those chosen by the people gather
> There is a nomad's tent on a square
> And in it Lenin lies.
> If you have a great sadness,
> And nothing comforts you,
> Go up to this tent,
> And look upon Lenin,
> And your woe will disperse like water
> And your sadness float away like leaves in a stream
> Lenin can dissolve your grief
> Lenin can give you courage.
> Stalin, great pupil of Lenin, carries on the fight.[14]

When the body of Lenin, having been taken for safekeeping to Siberia during the war, returned to Moscow in April 1945 is was placed into the reopened mausoleum. Henceforth, the mausoleum, equipped with the additional tribune, became Stalin's favourite spot to appear on Revolutionary holidays, thereby expressing the idea that he had safeguarded the founder of Bolshevism. In addition, it suggested, as Nina Tumarkin has remarked, that the dead Lenin was but a stepping stone for the living Stalin.[15]

Stalin also stood there for his final apotheosis, on the occasion of the victory parade over Hitler's Germany on 26 June 1945, which culminated in hundreds of captured Nazi flags and standards being thrown before the mausoleum and, as it were, at Stalin's feet.

When he died on 5 May 1953, there was no question that he would not be accorded the same treatment as Lenin. He was duly embalmed and laid to rest in a second sarcophagus next to Lenin's and the name 'Сталин' was added below Lenin's. He was not to remain there for long. The general unease at having Stalin, who, while winning the war, had inflicted great suffering on many thousands of his compatriots, was expressed at the 22nd Party Congress in 1961. One delegate, Dora Lazurkina, announced that Lenin had appeared to her whilst she visited the mausoleum, saying that it was 'unpleasant for me to lie next to Stalin'.[16] Soon afterwards, as part of Krushchev's de-Stalinization process, Stalin's body was unceremoniously removed one night and re-buried just outside the mausoleum within the Kremlin wall necropolis.

After the dissolution of the Soviet Union in 1991, the leadership increasingly jettisoned communism. Since Lenin's body was the single most sacred artefact for Russian Communists, his mausoleum on Red Square began to represent the archetypal 'contested' memorial.

After Boris Yeltsin came to power in 1990, he made several announcements declaring his intention to bury Lenin's remains. Like the Bourbon kings in nineteenth-century France, he wished to connect to the glory days of the Russian monarchy. He made it clear that he considered the removal of Lenin from the Red Square mausoleum and the ceremonial re-burial of Tsar Nicolas II, who had been executed by the Bolsheviks, as the 'two key goals for his final term in office'.[17] The intended symbolism of such an act was clear. However, such pronouncements met with resistance both from within the Russian political elite and the masses. Long queues formed outside the mausoleum, and some supporters held up placards reading 'Hands Off Lenin!'

Since then, Russia's leaders have kept their distance from the former sacred spot and no speeches have been made from the rostrum. Leningrad became St Petersburg again and countless statues of Lenin were removed from offices and public squares. Although the closure of the mausoleum and the removal of Lenin's body is occasionally requested, no Russian government has yet been bold enough to take this step.

My own visits to the mausoleum took place in July 2010, at the time when Dmitry Medvedev was president and Vladimir Putin prime minister. It was no longer possible to access the mausoleum from Red

Lenin mausoleum and the Kremlin.

Square. Instead, people had to queue on Revolution Square and enter through the northeastern corner of the necropolis alongside the Kremlin Wall, where the Memorial to the Unknown Soldier attracted much attention with its theatrical 'living flame' and goose-stepping, Mikhail Baryshnikov (the ballet dancer) lookalike guards in skintight black trousers. The majority of people waiting to pass the security checks, in order to be admitted to the mausoleum, were foreign tourists and predominantly European and Chinese, though there were Russian families too. I overheard a middle-aged man from the United States urging his compatriots to go and see Lenin in his mausoleum, 'if they really wanted to understand Russia'. As the queue moved slowly, different perspectives of the mausoleum unfolded one by one, producing a montage-like effect of juxtaposed images, reminiscent of Vertov's film. Shuffling up the slight slope towards Red Square, the squat ziggurat outline of the mausoleum appeared as a sharply delineated scissor-cut silhouette against the sky, while a few paces away the onion-domed and extravagantly swelling contours of St Basil's Cathedral nearly obliterated the modernist temple-form of Lenin's tomb. At the checkpoint, police ordered that all large bags and cameras be left and that everyone pass through a security scanner before entering the necropolis precinct, which is closed off from Red Square. Some of the tombs were marked by wall plaques or by flat stone tablets set into the lawn, and There were also some busts on plinths. Single red carnations deposited here and there meanwhile suggested that old loyalties prevailed.

Arriving at the east side of Lenin's monument, the variegated gorgeousness of the smooth, polished brown-red stone of its walls was revealed. The single word 'Ленин' indicated that the man buried there had superseded the boundaries of ordinary time, even historical contingency.[18]

Having entered the mausoleum in bright summer light, I was momentarily blinded by the sudden darkness inside and chilled by the icy air. Stern-looking guards motioned impassively to keep moving, when I had stopped to get my bearings after becoming disoriented by the mirroring sheen of black marble. Two flights of broad marble steps led to Lenin's tomb chamber where the glass-walled sarcophagus is set into a hollow depression in the centre. A soft-pink glow illuminated the bearded 'sleeping beauty' Dressed in a dark suit, a white shirt and his favourite polka-dot tie, he looked peaceful enough. The glass casket has a pyramid top that echoes the shape of the mausoleum, while the lower part made of metal, is profusely ornamented with emblems, flags and wreaths. This bombastic sarcophagus dates to the mid-1950s, when Krushchev ordered it to replace Melnikov's constructivist original.

The most extraordinary design element in the dark tomb chamber is the decoration of the black walls, with their violently zigzagging, crimson red marble inserts. The artist responsible for the interiors, Ignaty Ignatevich Nivinsky, had wished to evoke the billowing red banner of the Revolution. However, they reminded me of the ring of fire protecting Brunhild in a performance of the *Valkyre*.

No stopping is allowed inside the mausoleum and the guards urged visitors to move at a brisk pace. Indeed, the whole visit was timed to take no longer than two minutes. After another turn down a dark-panelled corridor, we were once again in the sunlight to complete the walk that leads past the busts of buried Soviet grandees, past the plinth

Corner detail of Lenin mausoleum.

Embalmed Lenin.

with Stalin's oversized sculpted head, past Andropov, Brezhnev and other former presidents and past the burial sites of cosmonauts, athletes and soldiers.

Seen from the vastness of Red Square, Lenin's mausoleum looks small and is initially hard to make out against the reddish-brown background of the Kremlin wall. The ranks of grey stone terraces extend on either side. Now empty, they were once filled with Soviet dignitaries during official celebrations. To the south, is the precinct of St Basil, spared from plans to rationalize Moscow's public spaces by Stalin's intervention. The sixteenth-century turrets and towers are a link to the distant past of feudal Russia, while the pompous eclecticism of the History Museum on the northern end represents the nineteenth-century *fin de siècle* worldview. In such a context, the straight-edged geometry of the mausoleum speaks of a new, unsentimental modernity, despite its evocation of archaic prototypes of the ziggurat and temple. On closer inspection, the building shows considerable volumetric complexity that is the result of the architect's hiding the access to the tribune from view. The solidity of the successive tiers and the tightly packed mass of smooth stone surfaces, suggest a hermetically sealed solid body, evocative of the 'architecture of shadows' characteristic of Enlightenment prototypes. In the context of Putin's Moscow, on the newly configured Red Square, facing the luxury shopping precinct with its open-air café terraces and the gaudily rebuild Kazan cathedral, the compactness of the Lenin mausoleum seems to be the result of a process of shrinkage, as if it has been drawn in on itself. During my visit, some young couples took photographs of one another on their mobile phones, foreign tour groups paused to click away dutifully on their way to the Kremlin, which is the main attraction. Nevertheless, people still make use of the chance of seeing Lenin free of charge. Many more, however, watch the dramatic changing of the guard that now takes place at the War Memorial around the corner.

So how could a visit to the mausoleum further an understanding of Russia at this point? Neither leaflets nor posters provided any information, other than the opening times and the need to deposit cameras and large bags for security reasons. There was no attempt to provide any historical context at all. No mausoleum merchandise was for sale either, except for some postcards. The former Lenin Museum on Revolution Square was closed, with official reasons citing restoration work. It seems that the current oligarchy that rules Russia does not depend on ideological justifications, has long abandoned Leninism and does not wish to present any link between the state and this mausoleum, which has become an anachronism and something of an embarrassment. Flags are not flown nearby and the ceremonial changing of the guards has been discontinued. At the 2010 commemorations of the 65th anniversary of the end of the Second World War, which assembled a large number of foreign heads of state and participating former Allied troops, the mausoleum was shrouded behind hoarding. This was because Putin preferred to view the parade from a specially built rostrum, rather than use the mausoleum's tribune, which had been the favoured spot for the holding of parades throughout the history of the Soviet Union. Given the absence of any official line of interpretation, which in itself speaks of the ideological vagueness in which the present Russian government operates, visitors were forced to rely on the impression of the mausoleum and its setting, helped by the cumulative montage effect I have mentioned, that is, on the juxtapositions and sequences that build up an idea, an abstract notion and a strong emotional effect, frame after frame. Without the mediation of official texts, the visitor now encounters the *mies en scène* of the 'immortal Lenin' in a similar way to that when the mausoleum was first put into operation, when nothing needed to be said. For the new generation of Russians who have grown up without exposure to Soviet ideology and without the old narratives of the Revolution, the decontextualized mausoleum and its smartly suited waxen-faced incumbent has no real meaning. Younger Russians leave it to the tourists and the old diehards, while they prefer to shop at the refurbished GUM department store opposite.

The Mausoleum of Ho Chi Minh

> Moscow, January 1924. The Russian winter is at its height. The temperature sinks at times to 40 degrees below zero. A few days ago Lenin died. That morning, a quiet knocking on our door in Lux Hotel aroused me. The door opened and a frail young man entered. He said he was Vietnamese and his name was Nguyen Ai Quoc. He also said he intended to go to Trade Union House and see off Lenin. [. . .] Somewhat around ten at night I heard a soft knocking on the door again. It was Comrade Ai Quoc. His face was blue, and the ears, nose, and fingers on the hands were blue, too, from the fierce cold. Ai Quoc said he had just seen Comrade Lenin. He was trembling from the cold as he explained that he could not wait until tomorrow to pay homage to the best friend of the colonial people [. . .] He finished by asking if we didn't happen to have some hot tea.[19]

The shivering young man who paid his last respects to Lenin on that cold January of 1924 was twenty years younger than the deceased Russian revolutionary. He was born on 19 May 1890 in the village of Hoang Tru, a poor district some 300 km (around 186 miles) north of Hué, in what, since 1885, had become 'French Indochina'. The boy was given the name 'Nguyen Sinh Cung'. His father, Nguyen Sinh Sac, was an educated man who had passed the highest examinations in the still operating Confucian educational system but who found that such qualifications counted for little in the French colony. He therefore not only insisted that his sons had training in classical Chinese but enlisted them in schools where the curriculum was focused on French language and culture. Although the French colonial rule in Indochina found some support among the ruling elite, it was generally resented, especially by peasants who were badly affected by increased taxation and forced labour. Active resistance was first limited to intellectuals but by 1908 had spread to rural areas. Official biographies, trying to trace the radicalization of the young man as far back as possible, claim that young Tanh, as the later Ho Chi Minh was then called, frequented nationalist meetings. In May 1909 he was summarily dismissed from the academy and decided to leave the country. In 1911, aged 21, while working as a cabin boy on a French ship, he began the long journey that would take him to the USA and Britain, where he survived by doing menial jobs. By 1919, he settled in Paris, joined the Socialist Party and adopted the name 'Nguyen Ai Quoc'. In 1920 he was present at the second Comintern Congress. He was a founding member of the French Communist Party and became a spokesman on colonial affairs. Galvanized by Lenin's 'Theses on the National and Colonial Questions', he became convinced that communism was historically and culturally more congenial to Asia than Europe. Invited to Moscow to study Marxism, he arrived on 11 January 1924, just ten days before Lenin's death. Lenin's international perspective made him sympathetic to the cause of colonial oppression in far-off corners of the world. His speech on the occasion of the Fifth Congress of the Comintern, in the summer of 1924, made his position clear:

> I am here in order to remind the International of the existence of the colonies and to point out that the revolution faces colonial dangers as well as a great future in the colonies. It seems to me that the comrades do not entirely comprehend the fact that the fate of the world proletariat, and especially the fate of the proletarian class in aggressive counties that have invaded colonies, is closely tied to the fate of the oppressed peoples of the colonies.[20]

The Comintern eventually sent Nguyen Ai Quoc to Guangzhou (Canton) in China and there he began to organize members of the large Vietnamese expatriate community into an embryonic revolutionary force, the 'Vietnamese Revolutionary Youth League', from 1925 to 1927. However, when Chiang Kai-shek dissolved the United Front, in which the Chinese Communist Party was allied to the Nationalists, and began to persecute communists, Quoc was recalled to Moscow. After a period of convalescence from tuberculosis, he went back to Asia by ship from Italy and spent a year in Thailand before returning to Hong Kong with the remit to organize the fractious Vietnamese left-wing movements. This led to the formation of the Indochina Communist Party (ICP) in 1930. Although the British authorities arrested Quoc, they resisted French pressure to have him extradited, claiming that he had died in custody. He made his way back to Europe in 1933 and spent the new few years in Moscow, teaching at the Stalin School and waiting for his requests to join the anti-colonial struggle in his homeland to be accepted.

The situation in Vietnam had deteriorated and widespread peasant uprisings were brutally suppressed. It was only in 1938 that Quoc was finally permitted to go back to China, where he joined the communist forces that had assembled in Yunan, before moving south to Guangxi province. The National Salvation Office there employed him as a journalist and health cadre and he wrote articles for radical French-language papers that could at that time be published legally in Hanoi as a result of the left-wing Popular Front government having taken control of France in 1936. This also made it possible for the International Communist Party to organize and recruit workers and peasants in Vietnam. In August 1939 Nguyen Ai Quoc moved close to the border with Indochina, now using the new name of 'Ho Chi Minh' ('The one who enlightens'). His mission was to identify a suitable and safe location for the new ICP headquarters and to begin an intensive training programme for new cadres.

In 1940 France capitulated to Germany and the Japanese took over the French colonies in Indochina, which from 1941 onwards the French administered on behalf of Japan, bringing a double colonial burden on the Vietnamese. In 1941 Ho Chi Minh secretly entered Vietnam to preside over the 8th Plenum of the ICP, which led to the formation of the Vietnamese Independence League (Vietminh). Their main aim was to bring about national independence. At that time Ho Chi Minh was hoping to win international support for this cause, especially from Roosevelt, who was known for his anti-colonialist views. Ho was arrested by the Kuomintang (the Chinese Nationalist People's Party) on his return to China and spent two years in prison. In one of hundreds of poems from this time he wrote:

> The grain of rice suffers under the impact of the pestle but once the ordeal is over admire its whiteness! Similar are the human beings in this world we live in: to be man one needs the pestle of misfortune.[21]

He was released in the autumn of 1943 and involved himself again in the Vietnamese Revolutionary League. He was confident that once the Allies had defeated Japan, China would help Vietnam to achieve full independence. But first, on 9 March 1945, the Japanese assumed full control and granted Vietnam only nominal 'independence' under the former emperor of Annam, Dao Dai. Ho Chi Minh designated ten northern provinces as 'liberated zones' and began to implement radical social, economic and political reforms. When on 15 August 1945 Japan surrendered to the USA, the Vietminh used the opportunity to call for insurrection and ousted the 'Japanese puppet-regime' of Dao Dai. On 2 September, Ho Chi Minh stood before a crowd of half a million people on Ba Dinh Square in Hanoi to declare national independence.

> The French have fled, the Japanese have capitulated, Emperor Bao Dai has abdicated. Our people have broken the chains, which for nearly a century have fettered them and have won independence for the Fatherland. Our people at the same time have overthrown the monarchic regime that has reigned supreme for dozens of centuries. In its place has been established the present Democratic Republic [. . .] [W]e, members of the Provisional Government of the Democratic Republic of Vietnam, solemnly declare to the world that Vietnam has the right to be a free and independent country and in fact it is so already. The entire Vietnamese people are determined to mobilise all their physical and mental strength, to sacrifice their lives and property in order to safeguard their independence and liberty.[22]

This was the culmination of Ho Chi Minh's career: he had seized the chance of the moment and led his revolution to victory.

His triumph was short lived. The fates of former colonies were being decided far away, in negotiations after the end of the Second World War. Following Roosevelt's death in 1945, France, under General De Gaulle, was keen to reassert full control over its East Asian colonies. In accordance with the Potsdam Agreement, British forces led by General Gracey landed in Saigon, freed the imprisoned French troops and allowed them to set up a new French colonial administration in Saigon. This was recognized by Britain as the only legitimate authority in South (Cochinchina) Vietnam. 65,000 French soldiers arrived within months to bolster the military power. The situation was also difficult in the north, where Japan's surrender led to the arrival of Chinese Kuomintang troops and the dissolution of the ICP. Ho Chi Minh reacted by making a tactical alignment with France against nationalist China. France duly recognized the Democratic Republic of Vietnam as a free state within the French Union in 1946, but maintained a military presence in Hanoi. The infamous Haiphong Incident in November 1946, when a French cruiser bombarded the port city at the cost of 6,000 civilian casualties, as well as the French commander's orders to disarm the Vietminh, triggered renewed and armed resistance, and a struggle that was to last for thirty years. Ho Chi Minh and General Giap, who had closely studied Mao Zedong's strategies of a 'People's War', decided on the adoption of guerilla tactics; operating like the proverbial tiger 'who brings down the mighty elephant by never allowing him to sit still'. The strategy proved effective and the French realized that superior equipment and firepower were of little use against an enemy who avoided pitched battles. They could hold the main cities but could not pacify the countryside, where the cause of independence was generally supported.

Ho Chin Minh was careful not to push the communist revolutionary agenda above the cause of national independence and this tactic allowed the Vietminh to gain widespread support among the population. Given the military impasse, France decided on a political solution, creating another Vietnamese government (uniting Cochinchina, Tonkin and Annam) under Bao Dai, but with France maintaining control over foreign policy and the economy. This move effectively created two Vietnams, although support for Bao Dai's government rested, as under the Japanese, mainly with the wealthy merchants and bourgeoisie at Saigon.

With China's unification under Mao Zedong in 1949, a new powerful power communist state came into being and thus the fate of Vietnam became even more firmly embedded within the Cold War scenario.[23] Previous efforts by the United States to speed up French decolonization were reversed as President Truman began to give massive military assistance to South Vietnam. On the other hand, the new People's Republic of China and the Soviet Union identified North Vietnam as belonging to their sphere of influence and officially recognized the DRV. Ho Chi Minh's skills of diplomacy were severely tested over the following decades, not least owing to the worsening relations between Stalin and Mao.

Despite U.S. assistance, morale among the mainly colonialist French troops deteriorated. The capture of their fortress at Dien Bien Phu on 7 May 1954 signalled the end of the French presence in Vietnam. The ensuing peace conference at Geneva led to the formal, though officially temporary, partition of the country on 21 July 1954, which was to be followed by internationally supervised elections. Prime Minister Ngo Dinh Diem headed South Vietnam's government and soon assumed autocratic control, while the USA took responsibility for the training and development of the South Vietnamese Army. Although Ho Chi Minh was still hopeful that the promised elections would lead to a political solution and a peaceful unification of the country, he also intensified the military capacity to resist American influence. This led to the creation of the 'People's Liberation Army' (known as the 'Vietcong') and to efforts to infiltrate the South in order to trigger a popular uprising there (under the auspices of the Vietnam Workers' Party). In 1963, when hopes for the political solution were fading fast, armed resistance by the North was stepped up to be met by a u.s.-sponsored counter-insurgency. This involved a massive increase in troops and military hardware, as well as aerial bombardment of targets within North Vietnam. China, while supporting the Vietcong with weapons, did not get involved, threatening to interfere only if the North was to be invaded by American troops. In the resulting so-called limited war (from 1965 to 1968), millions of bombs were dropped on North Vietnam, in addition to the use of defoliants and herbicides. These attacks all caused heavy casualties among civilians and fanned their determination to liberate the country. President Johnson's 'war of attrition' was brought to a close by the so-called Tet Offensive of 31 January 1968, in which the Vietcong managed to attack major centres, including Saigon, in the South. Although the hoped-for popular uprising there did not materialize, it showed the limitations of American control, and mobilized American public opinion against the already unpopular and increasingly costly war. Efforts to disengage the u.s. from Vietnam gained ground under President Nixon, as part of the general détente with Moscow and also later with China.

Ho Chi Minh had stayed in Hanoi during these difficult years, leaving much of the actual business of government to the Politburo. Refusing to live in the former Governor General's residence, he occupied rather spartan buildings, and finally a sparsely furnished modernist version of a vernacular bamboo hut: his famous 'Stilt House', where the elderly president tended his garden and fed the fish in his ornamental lake. Always in frail health – he had suffered from recurrent bouts of tuberculosis and his incarceration in China had also left lasting damage – his condition weakened. He died on 2 September 1969, on the 24th anniversary of Vietnamese independence. His death did not lead to a crisis of succession, as the party maintained control, with Ton Duc Thang, leader of the Fatherland Front, becoming president. Despite ceasefires and the 1972 peace conference in Paris, the war rumbled on, not least owing to the refusal of the South Vietnamese government under Nguyen Van Thieu, to relinquish power. Only when Saigon fell to the Vietcong on

30 August 1975 was Vietnam reunited. One of the government's first acts of was to change the name of Saigon to 'Ho Chi Minh City'.

Throughout the 1960s, Ho Chi Minh had revised his testament, aware of his fragile state of health and the dangers that surrounded him during the war against the United States. Chi Minh was aware of the posthumous cult of Lenin and he stipulated that his own death should not result in spendthrift gestures:

> As far as I am concerned – after my death, big funeral celebrations should be avoided so as not to waste the time and money of the people. I demand that my body be incinerated. [. . .] You should bury my ashes on a hill. It seems that there are very good ones near Tam Dao and Ba Vi. Build above the tomb a simple, large, solid and airy house as a resting place for visitors. A plantation of trees should be planted on the hill. Every visitor should plant a tree as a memorial. And care should be taken that each tree grows well. In time, the trees will form a forest, which will make the countryside more beautiful and profit agriculture.[24]

Ho Chi Minh's efforts to control what should happen to his body after death were thwarted by the Vietnamese Politburo, who began preparations for his eventual demise as early as 1965. In a special meeting on the occasion of Chi Minh's 77th birthday, his body was declared national property and preparations begun for its long-term preservation.[25] Ho Chi Minh was to be 'Vietnam's Lenin' and given the same treatment as the Russian revolutionary leader. In all secrecy, a team of Vietnamese scientists were sent to Moscow to work with the team of specialists at the Lenin mausoleum. Some experts were sent to other countries that had already buried embalmed leaders, such as Bulgaria and Mongolia, to study the funeral procedures and which vehicles were used to convey the body. Another group studied optimal conditions for body preservation at the funeral sites and during transport. Experiments were conducted on several models of glass sarcophagi, and even Chi Minh's famous sandals and their possible deleterious effects were catered for. Specially trained soldiers even drilled for the task of carrying the coffin weighing more than 200 kg (around 31 lb). When he did die, some years later, on 2 September 1969, all was ready.

The Russian and Vietnamese medical experts set to work immediately:

Ho Chi Minh mausoleum, side view.

>It took about two hours to finish the initial stage of medication and preservation of the President's body. The medical experts were very careful with every strand of his hair and beard, and any cells on his face and hands were to be kept so that the President looked as still alive.[26]

Having gone to such great lengths to ensure the preservation of Ho Chi Minh's body, the whole exercise was threatened by the worsening security situation, given that Hanoi was the main target for American bombs at the time. The Central Executive Committee of the CPV decided to move him to a safer place and chose the military base in Ba Vi (code name 'K9'), the secret headquarters for the Central Executive Committee, which provided secure underground shelters, water and electricity. An old air-raid shelter was modified for the purpose. After a perilous journey across difficult terrain and rough roads, using a specially modified truck with reinforced shock absorbers to reduce vibration, the huge, glass coffin was successfully installed early in 1970. However, when in November of the same year, U.S. forces launched a surprise attack on the area, Ho Chi Minh's body was secretly moved back again to Hanoi. He did not stay there long. Late in 1971 he was evacuated again to avoid damage by the unusually high water levels of the Red River and moved back to Ba Vi. The intensification of U.S.

bombing raids deep into North Vietnamese territory in 1972 necessitated yet another move to a safer location. The chosen site was a huge and suitably deep cave by a river, some fifteen kilometres (nine miles) from K9, in the middle of a forest. When in 1973 the U.S. army withdrew from Vietnam, senior Vietnamese officers decide to move Ho Chi Minh's body back to the old place in Ba Vi, where he awaited the completion of his mausoleum. This was the fifth move.

Orders to construct a mausoleum for Ho Chi Minh were issued as soon as the Party Central Executive Committee had decided on the preservation of his body. They also chose the location on Ba Dinh Square, the symbolic centre of old and new Hanoi and the place where Ho Chi Minh had declared Vietnam's independence in 1945. Although the various locations of Ho Chi Minh's coffin were kept secret, the intention to build the mausoleum was communicated to the populace after Chi Minh's death. The Central Executive Committee organized a design competition and invited the public to comment on selected models. The brief for the design stated that it should be 'modern yet traditional, imposing yet simple' and according to official records, some 45,487 people visited the travelling exhibition showing a selection of entries. People liked designs they considered typically Vietnamese, such as one in the form of a huge lotus or an artificial *tumulus* with a mausoleum and pavilion on top 'for poetry recitals'. The official Vietnamese leaflets and books now available about the mausoleum suggest that it was based on vernacular Vietnamese architectural styles. In fact, the building strongly reflects the input of Soviet engineers. The Russians had sent their experts, including the prominent architect Garold Grigorievich Isakovich (1931–1992), who had been responsible for many high-profile architectural commissions, not least the Lenin Memorial in Ulyanovsk,[27] to direct the design and construction. The contribution of the Vietnamese architects involved, Vuong Quoc Ny and Nguyen Ngoc Chai, was restricted to the building's interior planning and decoration. The main message of the exterior was to affirm Vietnam's allegiance to the Soviet bloc. Ho Chi Minh was thereby claimed as an international communist first and only secondly as a patriotic leader and founder of a new state.

The story of the construction of the building, echoing that of the successful preservation and protection of Ho Chi Minh's dead body, now forms part of the heroic national narrative, that of a triumph against all odds in the face of very difficult conditions during the war. In fact, work on site did begin in 1971 but was postponed until 1973, after the Paris peace agreement. The provenance of some of the materials was not just a matter of practicality but had symbolic significance: the grey marble, for instance, originated not only from the hard-won southern provinces below the 17th parallel (the initial military demarcation line between North and South Vietnam) but from Marble Mountain, an ancient holy site, which had also served as an important base for communist operations.[28] Utilizing the labour of 'tens of thousands of volunteers', it was finally completed on 29 August 1975, four months after the victory over the South and six years after Ho Chi Minh's death. The cult of Ho Chi Minh as the great revolutionary leader, which had come into force even during his lifetime, was given fresh impetus through his final installation in the mausoleum.

The main entrance to Ba Dinh Square, a vast open expanse, partly grassed over and large enough to accommodate some 100,000 people, is closed to all vehicle access except on formal state occasions. Tree-lined avenues and art deco mansions in leafy gardens surround the square but the only prominent building is the mausoleum. A single flagpole at some distance in front underlines its importance as a national monument, and guards keep a close watch to ensure that people behave respectfully and stay on the footpaths.

The main building is a cube (21.6 metres, or around 70 feet high) sitting on a concrete block, surrounded by a portico with square pillars. Low walls on either side screen the gardens and subsidiary buildings and provide space for text quotes. The words 'CHU TICH HO CHI MINH' ('President Ho Chi Minh) written in large, dark-red letters (said to be fashioned from rubies) identify the incumbent. The mausoleum looks like countless other Soviet public buildings from the Cold War period, with its stiff portico of grey pillars, such as could be found at any place during the Soviet sphere of influence. Only the slight outwards curvature of the eaves makes a token concession to local building traditions. The three-stepped pedestal topped with a temple-like structure has some affinities with Lenin's mausoleum, but while in the Moscow building the portico at the top is a purely symbolic finish to the ziggurat-like body of the mausoleum, here it constitutes the main part of the structure. The tiered pedestal and eaves, as well as the pillars, are of grey marble in contrast to red granite on the inner facade. The whole elevation is governed by strict symmetry and lacks the volumetric subtlety of Lenin's mausoleum. Imaginative landscaping on either side and behind the building softens the cold and stark appearance of the building, though 79 miniature cycad trees, planted in large pots and placed in a long row in front of the building, symbolize the president's age at the time of his death.

I went to see the mausoleum in July 2010. In the years since 1986, when the Vietnamese government announced reforms (*Doi Moi*) to liberalize the economy, the Communist Party has retained power while officially loosening the ideological commitment to Marxism-Leninism. Economic and military support, provided by the Soviet Union until 1991, now comes from many countries, including the USA. Criticism of the previous allegiance to Soviet Russia is no longer censored, and the general secretary of the Vietnamese Association of Architects Nguyen Truc Luyen, could express reservations about the design of Ho Chi Minh's mausoleum, deploring its 'heavy feel' and 'lack of refinement'.[29] Despite embracing free market liberalism, the political and economic situation in Vietnam is quite different from Russia's and the ruling CPV still relies on party membership and general support. The narrative of Vietnam's long and painful struggle for independence, of the metaphoric tiger crushing the elephant by his cunning and agility, continues to inform national identity. Ho Chi Minh's life, as told in countless hagiographic versions, is one of the founding myths of the state and this ensures that his mausoleum retains its ideological importance for the government, which continues to maintain the full ritual panoply.

At the time of my visit, all visitors were expected to dress 'respectfully' and I had to retrieve my shawl from the hotel to cover my bare arms. Bags were screened and cameras had to be deposited in a locker room located in one of the subsidiary buildings. There was no charge for their safekeeping, and no entrance ticket was required. Since this was the hot season, plastic canopies over metal frames protected visitors from the sun. Most visitors were Vietnamese, including many now elderly veterans in their uniforms, as well as groups of people from the provinces dressed in local folk costumes. Even very small pre-school children were admitted but admonished to keep quiet, which they only were inside the coffin chamber. Visitors entered through the central doorway that faces Ba Dinh Square. Several large wreaths from various provinces and organizations were positioned on either side of the entrance and a delegation was about to present another. While Lenin's corpse is kept in a dark and icy subterranean crypt, Ho Chi Minh's coffin is kept within the temple-like main building on the upper level. The temperature in the interior was much less cold than in Lenin's mausoleum and the interior furnishings have been made to dispel any gloom. The walls of all the internal spaces are lined with light, yellow-tinged marble, honey coloured in places, with a geometrically patterned dado. Wave-like recesses ornament the ceiling and hold concealed lights.

Memorabilia showing Ho and his mausoleum.

Only the six black marble pillars on the side of the stairwell lend an air of sombre solemnity. The coffin chamber is a spacious hall with a high ceiling and dark-red marble walls, ornamented with the hammer and sickle emblem and the golden star of the DRV. The light here was more subdued than in the surrounding corridors but this was by no means a dark space. A square, recessed light fitting set into the ceiling illuminates the centrally placed sarcophagus. Made of dark tropical wood, this is sunk into a lower level, as with Lenin's tomb, so that one looks down at a glass-lidded coffin. Four guards stood on each corner of the coffin recess. The dead president was lying there, both hands stretched along the sides of the body, wearing a dark-grey silk shirt without a collar and his lower extremities draped by a black cloth. His long wispy beard was carefully combed, and he lay there, with an expression of serenity on his thin ascetic face. I remembered the chant 'Ho, Ho, Ho Chi Minh' that echoed during the protest marches I had attended in the 1970s and found myself suddenly in tears.

Visitors exit through another door that gives access to a carefully tended garden, stocked with plants from all provinces of Vietnam. The cameras that had to be handed in beforehand could be retrieved here, and people posed in the gardens with the mausoleum in the background. Many continued their pilgrimage by visiting Ho Chi Minh's last dwelling, the charming Stilt House, and the striking new museum by Isakovich, built close to the old One-Pillar Pagoda.

All of these sites are located within the former grounds of the Governor-General's palace and constitute the symbolic centre of Hanoi. They conveniently juxtapose the remains of a Buddhist temple from the old Vietnamese kingdom, ruled by the eleventh-century Ly Dynasty, with the representative building of the French Colonial era and the long struggle for independence documented in the museum, Ho's headquarters and final resting place. This dense concentration of historical buildings, surrounded by beautiful gardens and amply stocked with refreshment and souvenir stalls, stands in stark contrast to the vast, highly surveyed, controlled and depopulated expanse of Ba Dinh Square.[30] While the various memorial sites, and not least the museum, offer multiple readings of what Ho Chi Minh might mean to contemporary visitors, the square remains a space reserved for highly organized and choreographed government rallies and parades. This spatial dichotomy between the populist and popular, free-market space of the Ho Chi Minh Memorial Site Complex behind the mausoleum and the supervised space in front is characteristic of the ambiguities and contradictions of modern Vietnam.

Ho Chi Minh is still a powerful symbol of the nation and the revered icon of the modern Vietnam. His image is printed on all banknotes, his photographs are prominently displayed, and he remains the acceptable and benign face of the VCP. However, his revolutionary legacy is less emphasized now and the government strongly dissuades people from congregating in the square, where he once declared independence to demand political change. He is increasingly portrayed as a benevolent and kindly sage whose simple lifestyle and love of nature and of children lift him above his now outdated ideological allegiance and also above the overly materialistic values of the present generation. For the generations born after his death, Ho Chi Minh had become a revered ancestor, referred to as '*ngai*': a term reserved for a tutelary spirit or an ancient king who can be appealed to for supernatural help:

> Ho had succeeded in ridding the country of foreign occupation, thus the powers he possessed while alive were transferred to the supernatural realm, where humans can draw upon for assistance and protection. Some [. . .] even asserted that Ho

had supernatural links in his lifetime, saying that he was a living god sent by the heavens to help liberate Vietnam.[31]

There had been attempts to use the term 'comrade' but '*bác*', literally meaning 'father's older brother', stuck.

> He referred to himself as uncle and to the people as 'nephews' and 'nieces' (chain). He said that he never married but that his wife was Vietnam, although he had married at least twice and had children he never publicly acknowledged.[32]

The official Ho Chi Minh 'cult' now emphasizes his image as that of 'a simple man and patriot' by endorsing the populist 'Uncle Ho' image and downplaying the revolutionary persona. Already in 1989, Colonel Bui Tin had made a proposal to honour his body, 'interred into the mother soil of the fatherland'.[33] So far, this has been resisted, although the contents of his last will and testament, stipulating his wish to be cremated, are no longer kept secret.[34] While it is unlikely that the ruling Communist Party of Vietnam will relinquish its hold over Ho Chi Minh's remains, the most powerful symbol of the nation, it has encouraged the celebration of a much older Vietnamese history to be played out against the backdrop of the mausoleum. In 2010, Hanoi celebrated the 1,000-year anniversary of King Ly Thai To's decision in 1010 to move the capital of Vietnam to Hanoi (then known as 'Thang Long'), in colourful and very costly displays involving dragon dancers, goose-stepping soldiers and lavish firework displays.[35] During this occasion of conspicuous, state-sponsored consumption, the sheer size of Ho Chi Minh's mausoleum might have saved it from being hidden behind the hoardings that obscure Lenin's during Putin's extravaganzas. Despite Daniel Hémery's remark in his 1990 biography that 'One can't exclude the possibility' that, if ever Ho Chi Minh's ashes are interred, according to his last wish, they 'will be buried with indifference'[36] more than twenty years later, this is hard to imagine.

Mao Zedong Memorial Hall (Mao Zhuxi Jinian Tang)

> A revolution is not a dinner party, or writing an essay, or painting a picture, or doing embroidery; it cannot be so refined, so leisurely and gentle, so temperate, kind, courteous, restrained and magnanimous. A revolution is an insurrection, an act of violence by which one class overthrows another.[37]

Mao Zedong, born on 26 December 1893, was of the same generation as Ho Chi Minh, and younger by just three years. The political lives of the two men were intertwined in their efforts to free their countries from foreign occupation and to bring about revolutionary change.

Mao was born into a family of peasants from Hunan and this class background was to be of great importance during the Revolution. However, the family was not poor and Mao was able to

> gravitate by stages to higher education and conversance with an urban intellectual-political milieu. This alone separated him from millions of peasant youth living in more remote areas, destined to repeat the timeless cycle of their ancestors. When he reached adolescence, moreover, Mao was a member of a comfortably well-off family, measured against prevailing standards. This fact enabled him to have a secondary education thereby putting him into a very special category among his generation.[38]

By 1911, when the Qing Dynasty had been overthrown and China declared a republic, Mao was attending a teacher training college in Changsha, where he acquired a taste for Chinese classical poetry and Western philosophy. This was because of his tutor Yang Changji, trained in the British educational system, who took the gifted student with him when he was offered a chair at Beijing University.[39] Unlike Ho Chi Minh and Lenin, Mao did not spend his formative years in Europe. Nevertheless, he was in touch with Chinese expatriates and learned about the Russian Revolution from their accounts, which contributed to the formation of his political thinking. His intellectual education continued after he began working as a librarian at 'Beida' (the local term for Peking University), when he began to contribute articles to the radical left-wing journal *New Youth*. He continued to write for similar publications after he had moved back to Changsha in 1919 and, by becoming one of the founder members of the Chinese Communist Party (CCP) in 1921, began his revolutionary career first in Hunan and then in Shanghai, where he joined the Central Party Committee. Following the Soviet-engineered merger of the CCP with the nationalist Kuomintang (KMT), Mao worked in Canton until the terror campaigns against communists forced the flight of the CCP leadership into the remote province of Jiangxi. In the years between 1927 and 1934, he took part in guerrilla campaigns again KMT forces and efforts to educate and radicalize the peasant population. The decision to leave Jiangxi and embarking on what became known as the 'Long March', to the new Communist base in Yunan, proved decisive for Mao's future. At the 1935 Zunyi Conference, the party decided to emancipate itself from Soviet interference and base their power on the support of the peasantry in the countryside. Arguing against Lenin's dictum that the peasantry was not ready for revolution, he used his own peasant background and knowledge of Chinese history to radicalize the countryside. Mao remarked that 'the peasants are the sea, we are the fish, the sea is our habitat'. Just as in Russia, land reforms helped to broaden the support of the countryside for the party.

It was during this period that Mao established his own supreme position in the politburo of the CCP by becoming 'Chairman of the Party' in 1946. When the nationalist regime under Chiang Kai-shek proved unwilling and ineffectual in countering the brutal invasion by Japanese forces in 1937, the Communist Red Army began to be seen as the only force able to expel the occupiers along with the compromised KMT forces. Utilizing strategies of guerrilla warfare, these were pushed southwards and by 1949 Chiang fled to Taiwan and the communists were greeted as liberators in all the great cities of China. On 1 October 1949, Mao proclaimed the People's Republic of China from the Tiananmen Gate of the former imperial palace in Beijing.

The new state faced its first political and military test in the Korean War (1950–53), in which the PRC supported the communist forces. By driving U.S. and South Korean armed forces below the 38th parallel, they secured its border. Mao's hopes to overtake Russia and the USA in steel production led him to push through the enforced and haphazard industrialization of the countryside, the so-called Great Leap Forward (from 1959 to 1961), which not only failed to achieve its objective but resulted in the death of fifteen to twenty million peasants. In the aftermath of the catastrophe, Mao was sidelined by the party leadership and he only regained his power by appealing to the country's youth to 'create disorder under the heavens', in order to create a new order. This revolutionary movement, known as the 'Cultural Revolution' (from 1966 to 1969 by Mao's own reckoning), entailed not only a sustained, if virulent criticism of the party, but an attack on the remaining bourgeois elements in society through enforced re-education. Mao Zedong's *Little Red Book*, a collection of excerpts from his published works and speeches, became the Revolution's primary text and symbol. The Chairman's position was now unassailable: he reigned in the revolutionary fervour when it began to threaten the leadership of the party. In 1967 he sent in troops and began to embark on foreign diplomacy to reduce China's political and economic isolation which had deepened after the split with the Soviet Union, following Stalin's death in 1953. This led to President Nixon's visit in 1972. Deng Xiaoping was called back to take up office and the next years were marked by internal struggles within the party leadership. The so-called Gang of Four (Mao's wife Jiang Qing, along with Zhang Chunqiao, Yao Wenyuan and Wang Hongwen), whom Mao had brought to prominence during the Cultural Revolution, exercised considerable control.

Mao's health had suffered from years of heavy smoking, bad dietary and hygiene habits and although apparently of robust constitution, his heart was affected. According to his physician, he also suffered from motor neurone disease. For the last few years of his life he lived in one of the precincts of the Forbidden City and rarely ventured outside.

In 1976 two important members of the Chinese Communist Party died in the People's Republic: Premier and Foreign Minister Zhou Enlai (8 January) and Red Army Marshal Zhu De (6 July). Both had been founding CCP members and revolutionary 'Long March' heroes. Although they had signed a party policy document dated 27 April 1956 in favour of cremation and simple burials, their mortal remains received rather different treatment.[40]

Zhou Enlai had stipulated in his will that his ashes should be scattered over 'the rivers and mountains of China', possibly a reference to the ancient 'Stone of Rivers and Mountains' on Beijing's Altar of the Country, which symbolized the endurance of state power. This took place after a state funeral presided over by Deng Xiaoping on 15 January. The air force scattered Zhou's ashes over areas of China that were politically sensitive, such as minority areas and the Taiwan Straits, in an act which could be read as a gesture to bind them more firmly into the central state.[41]

The 'Gang of Four' ordered the suppression of all public expressions of mourning in light of widespread grief at the death of a much-respected senior figure that had led to mass protests in many parts of China. Some two million residents of Beijing lined the streets, unhappy with the attempt to obliterate what Zhou had stood for politically, along with his remains. These demonstrations culminated in the first Tiananmen Square 'incident' on 4 April 1976, held on the day of the 'grave sweeping ceremony', when thousands of people congregated in the centre of Beijing to stage a spontaneous and collective display of mourning in defiance of the party's injunctions.[42] One the eulogies that was read out argued that:

> He left no inheritance, he had no children,
> He has no grave, he left no remains.
> His ashes were scattered over the rivers and mountains of
>   our land.
> It seems he has left us nothing
> but . . .
> He has hundreds of millions of children and grandchildren
> And all China's soil is his tomb.[43]

The forceful and brutal removal of protestors by the authorities resulted in a great number of casualties. When Zhu De died a few months later in July, he was also cremated but his ashes were buried, in a 'model reflection of party policy', in the Babaoshan Revolutionary Cemetery near Beijing. Zhu De was 89 years old and had ceased to be an active statesman: he had attended Zhou Enlai's funeral in recognition of the latter's support during the Cultural Revolution. Mao Zedong, though in frail health throughout 1976, decided the manner of burial for his comrades without attending in person.

On 18 July, an 8.3 magnitude earthquake rocked Tangshan, a city north of Beijing, killing hundreds of thousands of people, which for some commentators was taken as ominous sign that Mao's 'mandate of heaven' might be slipping. Mao had consistently put himself above the rules that he expected everybody to follow, and when it came to making preparations for his own death, he disregarded the policy document on cremation that he had been the first to sign. In fact, he had acquired, together with his fourth wife Jiang Qing, a family plot at Babaoshan, which he visited a number of times.[44] His health had deteriorated badly since the beginning of 1976 and he had suffered from coronary and pulmonary heart disease, an infection of the lungs, cataracts, bedsores, insomnia, and also had trouble swallowing food and drink. The Chairman's illness was kept a secret from all but the members of the politburo. The earthquake, considered an evil portent in China, frightened him and he moved to an earthquake-proof building within the Forbidden City. Although his condition improved intermittently and he retained a lucid state of mind, he suffered another heart attack on 9 September that proved fatal.[45] Mao died

> on the grossly inauspicious time of ten minutes past midnight on mid-Autumn festival, the birthday of the 'Great Yin', a peak time for the dangerous feminized yin energy.[46]

While Zu Deh's ashes were buried at Babaoshan and Zhou Enlai left 'no remains' at all, Mao was to have his remains preserved for 'eternity' and put on public display. Exceptionally, among the prominent communist leaders, Mao's corpse was not embalmed by the Soviet experts from Moscow but by a Chinese team.[47] He was laid out for public display in the Great Hall of the People on Tiananmen Square, surrounded by evergreen plants and shrubs to counter the unlucky emanations of death. The number of people paying their respects was markedly inferior to that of the mourners who attended Zhou Enlai's unofficial mourning rites.[48] Mao's widow Jiang Qing had been neutralized in the wake of the Chairman's death – she was only able to send a huge wreath with striking sunflowers. Instead, it was Hua Guofeng (Su Zhu), Mao's political heir, who officiated as chief mourner at the lavish state funeral, attended by a plethora of ambassadors from around the world.

Hua Guofeng had much to gain from the continuation of Mao's cult. He had succeeded Zhou Enlai as premier and was Mao's chosen successor as leader of the CCP and the PRC after the elimination of his rival Deng Xiaoping, who was held responsible for the protests in the wake of Zhou Enlai's demise. Hua's legitimacy therefore rested strongly on direct transmission of power from Mao. On 6 October, after the ending of the official mourning period, he ordered the arrest of the 'Gang of Four' who had been imprisoned in the same underground complex where Mao's body lay. Hua was keen to bring the party back to the Leninist principles of their early republic, with central party control and industrial planning. His decision to turn the wayward and unorthodox Mao into a Soviet-style dead leader was to project the idea of a return to revolutionary beginnings and solidarity with Russia, which Mao's foreign policy had jeopardized. By presenting himself as Mao's political heir, he enhanced his own prestige. In the planning and supervision of the mausoleum he also monumentalized his own succession to the position of 'Great Helmsman'.[49]

The question arose as to where Mao's mausoleum was to be situated. The most prestigious historical burial site on Nanjing's Purple Mountain was already occupied by Sun Yat-sen (see Chapter Three). Nearby Baboashan cemetery was the preferred resting place for revolutionary heroes and was where Mao himself had already secured a plot. However, given Mao's pre-eminence this was not considered sufficiently distinguished. More to the point was the fact that Ho Chi Minh's mausoleum had set a precedent by being built on the spot associated with the birth of the new state. Tiananmen Square was therefore the obvious

Mao Zedong Memorial Hall from Tiananmen Square after visiting hour.

choice as it was from the rostrum of Tiananmen Gate that Mao had declared the foundation of the People's Republic of China on 1 October 1949. Moreover, it was also the entrance to the 'The Forbidden City', built in the early fifteenth century for the rulers of the Ming Dynasty, which been the centre of political power for some 600 years. Mao himself had also inhabited parts of the extensive complex until his death. In the years before China was a People's Republic portraits of Sun Yat-sen, and thereafter Chiang Kai-shek, had been fixed to the monumental Gate of Heavenly Peace in order to suggest the continuing symbolic importance of the old imperial centre for the republican era.[50] After the revolution, the new government of the PRC exchanged Chiang's image for a giant portrait of Mao Zedong. No subsequent Chinese leader's likeness has yet replaced Mao's at this symbolic spot.

While the mystique of the Chinese emperors was maintained by their inviolate seclusion within the Forbidden City, China's modern rulers turned their backs on the old ceremonial centre to face the multitudes assembled before them. A whole swathe of residential and commercial buildings of the old city was demolished to create the Tiananmen Square we see today. Mao had wanted it to be large enough to hold one billion people and although it could only ever accommodate some 600,000, it did become the biggest public square in China.⁵¹ It was the main site for choreographed displays of the state and also, on rare occasions, for public demonstrations against the state, such as the mass gathering of mourners for Zhou Enlai a few months before Mao's death and the more recent, just as euphemistically entitled, 'incident' of 1989.

Tiananmen Gate marks the primary north-south axis that runs through Beijing. This axis determined the layout of the Forbidden City that was built according to geomantic principles (*feng shui*). Although the revolutionary government of the PRC publicly decried such 'feudal superstitions' as irrelevant to the modern age, the planning of Tiananmen Square nevertheless not only respected but continued to emphasize this axis, first by the placement of the flagpole in 1949, and then by the pillar-shaped Monument to the People's Heroes in the 1950s, which was meant to commemorate those who had died in all the revolutionary struggles since the nineteenth century. It was along this axis that Hua Guofeng ordered the mausoleum to be built – between the Monument to the People's Heroes and the imperial southern (Zhengyang) Gate. The main entrances to the mausoleum were also placed north and south. As Cheater observed,

> Mao's body lies fractionally to the south of the exact centre in the square hall, at the point of the most concentrated geomantic force in a tomb. The axis now runs through his body as well as the imperial throne.⁵²

Hua Guofeng, personally supervising the project, mobilized all resources to ensure that the mausoleum was constructed with record speed. Officially, the architectural design was the result of a collective effort of 'people throughout China', although it was effectively executed by a group of seventeen experts under Hua's guidance.⁵³ The Mausoleum formed part of a group of buildings known as 'Ten Grand Architecture', exemplified by the huge public buildings that flank Tiananmen Square – the Great Hall of the People and the National Museum (both built in 1959). J. F. Zhou commented on the elements that characterized their design:

> While some of them used Chinese decorative motives and details, others used the Chinese roof and the outline. Formally, they were a continuation of the first wave of 'Chinese Form'. Strategically or methodologically, they were a continuation of

eclecticism and the Beaux-Arts paradigm, this time reinforced by the Russian influence.[54]

Some 700,000 people from all over the country, so official accounts inform, 'took turns in voluntary labour at the construction site [and] triumphantly completed the work in the short span of only six months'.

> They trekked to Beijing for the spiritually transforming honour of shoveling dirt or laying brick for the glory of Mao's enshrinement. Many of the worker pilgrims brought rocks or pieces of lumber from their home villages to be incorporated into the project. Their gifts of labour and building materials were a kind of ex-voto to the cult of Mao.[55]

Of paramount concern was the need to make the structure earthquake resistant. Reinforced concrete panels, half a metre (around nineteen inches) thick, plus the shear wall of the basement, combined with the floor slabs, form a box frame of great stiffness that is able to withstand even major tremors. The materials, the granite, marble and other stone types, came in unprecedented quantities from all over China, including water and sand from the Taiwan Straits to symbolically emphasize the PRC claims over Taiwan and earth from the quake-stricken Tangshan. A slab of black granite from Mount Tai in Shandong Province, one of the Five Sacred Mountains where Chinese emperors from the Han Dynasty onwards had performed sacrifices in the hope of attaining immortality, was used as the plinth for Mao's crystal, placing him symbolically on Mount Tai.[56] Scores of artists and craftspeople worked on the ornamentation of the mausoleum's interior, on the wall and lacquer paintings, tapestries, and panels of calligraphy in Mao's hand.

On 24 May 1977, exactly six months after the groundbreaking ceremony, Hua Guofeng officially opened the building. His identification with the project – it is in fact the only memento to this transitional Chinese leader – is embedded on the huge sign written in Hua's own handwriting that identifies the building as 'Chairman Mao Memorial Hall'. In his public address, he proclaimed that:

> Chairman Mao will always be with us; he will always be in the hearts of each comrade and friend among us; he will always live in the hearts of Chinese people and revolutionary people the world over.[57]

Millions of Chinese have since been to see the Chairman in his mausoleum, despite the attempts at de-Maoization. When Deng Xiaoping assumed control of the party leadership in the early 1980s and initiated the economic reforms known as 'Socialism with Chinese Characteristics', Mao Zedong's historical importance was up for re-evaluation. The Cultural Revolution in particular was interpreted as a deplorable 'error' and Mao's fallibility was acknowledged in the formula 'seven parts good, three parts bad'.[58] Deng spoke against the personality cult of political leaders and ordered the removal of official portraits of the former Chairman. On 26 December 1983, the 90th anniversary of Mao's birth, additional 'Memorial Chambers' dedicated to other prominent Long March revolutionary heroes and political leaders were opened in his mausoleum. Each of these rooms contains a centrally placed portrait bust on a black stone plinth, surrounded by red flowers in porcelain pots. Glass cases display photographs, documents and items of personal use, relics such as uniforms, and Mao's broken spectacles, for example. Zhou Enlai, Liu Shaoqi, Chen Yun and Zhu De were the first to be given such a chamber, in addition to the one for Mao himself, in a gesture that signalled that Mao was but one of a series of significant personalities. When Deng Xiaoping died on 19 February 1997, aged 92, he was cremated and his ashes were scattered. However, he too was awarded his own Memorial Chamber within the Chairman Mao Memorial Hall. These added facilities not only detract from the previous centrality and singularity of the person whose body the building enshrines, but allow for different visiting rituals by party officials and foreign dignitaries who are shown a more collective and inclusive assemblage of historical memory. Paradoxically, the addition of these facilities made it more difficult to do away with the whole edifice and to remove Mao's body – an idea that has been mooted on various occasions. It seems an ironic twist that Zhou and other comrades, who had had reasons to be wary of Mao's unpredictable behaviour, now safeguard his remains. From 1985 onwards a series of protests against the government took place in Tiananmen Square that culminated in mass rallies in the summer of 1989. Student protestors appealed to the revolutionary spirits of the early leaders commemorated in the mausoleum to inspire their resistance against the repressive and inflexible government of the day, then still presided over by Deng. While the portrait of Mao at Tiananmen Gate was torn down and the famous statue representing the 'Goddess of Democracy' set up instead, the Monument of the People's Heroes served as the central rallying point. As all the fervour of living

View of the North Hall with statue of Chairman Mao.

View of 'Solemn Hall of Last Respects'.

insurrection washed over Tiananmen Square, the mausoleum precinct stood inviolate.[59] Since the violent repression of these demonstrations, security provisions in Tiananmen Square mean that any spontaneous mass gatherings are strictly blocked.

When I arrived at Tiananmen Square at eight o'clock in the morning on a hot summer's day in July 2010, accompanied by a former student of mine from Beijing, long queues had formed in Tiananmen Square. My student commented that nowadays only people from the countryside visit the mausoleum and that she herself had never been. There were many thousands of Chinese in the queue, and a great number had small children who ate ice cream sold by itinerant vendors. Unlike at Ho Chi Minh's mausoleum, no particular dress code was enforced and even girls in very skimpy shorts were freely admitted. A sign posted on the outside of the mausoleum reminded people to behave properly: there was to be no running, no shouting, no talking whilst inside the building. Guards wielding megaphones ensured that people kept moving within the yellow lines painted on the pavement and organized the safekeeping of larger bags, cameras or video equipment. Before gaining access to the mausoleum enclosure, everybody had to pass through a scanning device. Inside the crowded forecourt of the mausoleum yellow chrysanthemums were for sale as offerings. I saw only a few people buy them.

The mausoleum is set on a two-tiered platform, some four metres (thirteen feet) high, on a level above the mundane world, as is customary for sacred spaces in China. The white marble balustrade is ornamented in an auspicious floral pattern that 'is meant to symbolize the Chinese people's determination to keep the red state founded by China firm as a rock and long-living as the evergreen'.[60] Passing between the high granite-faced pillars of the colonnade that surrounds the mausoleum we entered the vast North Hall (19.3 x 34.6 metres, or roughly 63 x 113.5

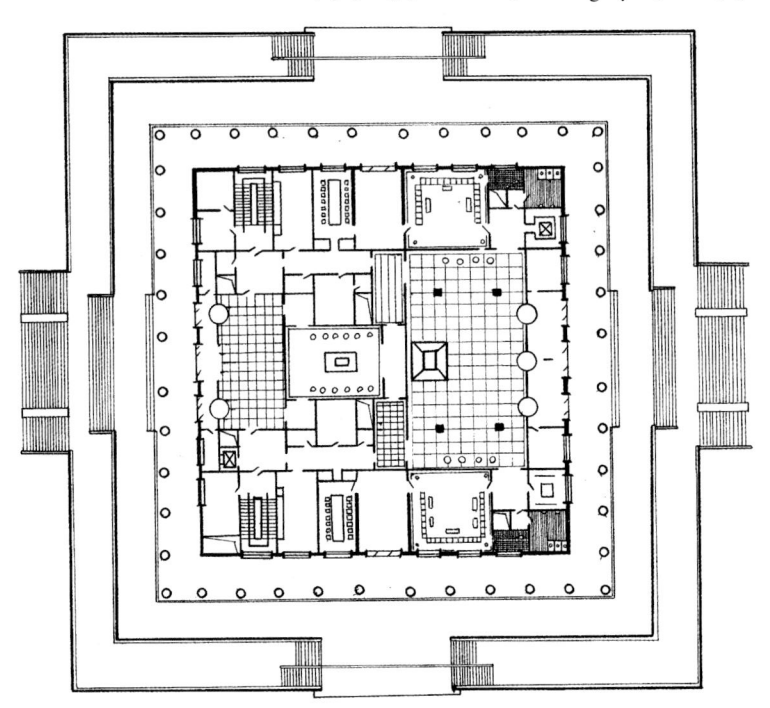

Plan of Chairman Mao Memorial Hall.

feet) to come face to face with the larger-than-life size marble statue of the Chairman, seated in an informal pose, one leg casually crossed over the other. Behind him is a large mural painting depicting a scene of mountains that tower above swirling mists.[61] Masses of chrysanthemum had been laid at the feet of this statue, where they formed a thick layer of bright yellow and filled the air with their bitter smell. Uniformed soldiers motioned visitors to move towards the right into the Central Hall (11.3 x 16.3 metres, or 37 x 53 feet), which, as the official reports says, 'in order to embody the idea that Chairman Mao is always living in our hearts has been designed as to resemble a bedroom'. This is where Mao's body is shown, lying inside a centrally placed crystal sarcophagus, with his face towards the Forbidden City, surrounded by potted evergreen plants.[62] Lit by a strange pink luminescence, he seemed to glow from within. Lee Haiyan once remarked that

> while power may grow out of the barrel of a gun, as Mao famously pronounced, it can only glow by igniting the desires and fantasies of the ruled and by basking in the mystique of popular sovereignty. It must not only intimidate, but also enchant.[63]

The enchantment of coming face to face with Mao is curtailed by the rapidity with which one is urged to pass. One can make out his unusually large head with the still somewhat unruly mop of thick, slightly greying hair and the heavy drooping jowls. He wears a grey 'Mao jacket' that used to be such a common sight in China, whilst the red Chinese flag covers the rest of his body. Golden emblems of the party and army ornament the sides of the coffin base. The Chinese inscription on the green marble on the southern wall behind the sarcophagus in large gold letters reads:

> MEMORY OF OUR GREAT LEADER AND TEACHER CHAIRMAN MAO ZEDONG: FOREVER ETERNAL WITHOUT CORRUPTING.[64]

The visit concludes by passing through the South Hall, which, after the gloomy atmosphere of the coffin chamber, is light and airy. Here too calligraphy forms the main ornamentation: written in gold letters is an excerpt from Mao's poem 'Reply to Comrade Guo Moruo', enlarged from a copy in his own florid handwriting. From there we descended a flight of steps to a forecourt that was lined with small shops offering souvenirs, such as busts, pictures and books, pendants and badges with Mao's picture on the Heavenly Gate. Just outside the enclosure that surrounds the mausoleum precinct was a large multi-figured terracotta sculpture group, representing all minority groups, striding forwards towards the future. This corresponds to a similar group placed outside the north entrance side that refers to the past and depicts major historical episodes from the time of the Revolution.

The sequence of the visit follows the axis from the Forbidden City, past the Monument to the People's Heroes to the sculpture group that stresses Mao Zedong's role in the revolutionary struggle. Once inside the 'sacred precinct', the kindly smiling, fatherly Chairman is encountered; a man of the people, an object of love. Then comes the room where the mortal body, defying corruption in his crystal coffin, lies under the symbolic protection of the national flag, the party and the army, an inner light illuminating the well-known features of the Chairman. The last words of calligraphic ornamentation, written in golden letters in the South Hall, describe Mao as poet rather than revolutionary, as the chosen text is not an excerpt from his political writings but a poem evoking peace after a tumultuous storm, and was perhaps chosen as an apt description for a China that was all the more restful for his passing:

> Four oceans storming
> Clouds, waters raging;
> Five continents rocking,
> Thunderstorm roaring.
> Sweep away all deadly insects:
> No enemy anywhere.[65]

Looking at the mausoleum from other parts of Tiananmen Square, it forms a funerary realm within the vastness of the paved square. The only greenery is its lawns, bordered by pines, cypress, camellia and other trees. Most Chinese and foreign tourists were clustered around the Heavenly Gate, where the huge portrait of Chairman Mao still hangs. So intimate is the connection between Mao and Tiananmen Gate that a Chinese colleague from Hong Kong, whom I had asked to photograph the mausoleum, sent a picture of the Heavenly Gate thinking that this was the mausoleum!

The topographical context of the mausoleum, rather than the merits or failings of the building's architecture, has been subject to several critical appraisals. Ellen Laing pointed to the political symbolism of placing Mao's mausoleum at the south end of the square as signifying 'a closed chapter in the history of the Chinese Communist Party and PRC.'[66] Wu Hung saw the irony of the monument's position but as part of a general pattern to be observed on Tiananmen Square in which changes in the political discourse destroyed the original meaning of monuments:

> Mao's Mausoleum (which was unveiled in 1977 at the anniversary ceremony of the Chairman's death), is again an irony, but its becoming so took no time: by adding this monument to the Square its patrons had unconsciously undermined the symbolic system they had established and tried to perpetuate. The mausoleum changed the map of the Square as it took over the Monument's original role to become the counterpart to the Gate. The opposition and connection between the past and the present of the 'revolutionary history' was then most graphically expressed by this new juxtaposition: while the living Mao's image still hung on the Gate, his embalmed corpse dwelt in the mausoleum.[67]

For A. P. Cheater, the whole mausoleum is redolent of the ambiguity befitting Mao Zedong and his character like that of a mythological trickster, one that defied being tied down to conformity and revelled in playing sometimes very cruel tricks. He allows that, for once, the joke might have been on him:

> Political revenge must be regarded as a possibility in the crafting of some of the embedded symbolism of Mao's mausoleum. Some irony is clearly apparent in the symbolic transformation of Mao into a deified, embalmed, late-twentieth-century emperor's successor, the very antithesis of a revolutionary leader.[68]

Rudolf Wagner is primarily interested in the mausoleum's role as the culminating point of Red Guard pilgrimages, which had been very popular during the Cultural Revolution and which continued well into the period when the mausoleum was constructed.[69] He reads the placing of the mausoleum in the centre of Beijing as a way of attracting pilgrims to a city devoid of revolutionary destinations. Such pilgrims, steeped in the history of the Revolution, hardly exist in today's China. Recent governments have instead developed 'scenic spots' to encourage internal as well as international tourism. It is also interesting that Mao Zedong's birthplace is now a major destination for Chinese visitors. A huge rock-carved face of the youthful Mao is presently being finished, which, as at Mount Rushmore in the USA, projects the features of a historical figure into the landscape. Not unlike the transformation of Ho Chi Minh into a benign ancestral figure able to bestow blessings, Mao has taken his place amongst supernatural spirits and deities. He has become a talisman, hanging from rear-windows of taxis, or even being placed among various Buddha statues in temples or family shrines.[70]

For the millions of rural Chinese who continue flock to Mao's Memorial Hall, they do so for all sorts of reasons, not least because it offers a rare gratis form of entertainment in the now very expensive capital. At the mausoleum they not only see the still imposing face of the long-dead leader but see and experience themselves in the performance of forming the long and orderly queues, with all the variety of minorities. Although no longer wearing the clothes of times past, they can still constitute a collective and one united in purpose. As such, these thousands of people waiting to file past Mao form a vivid contrast to the tourists clustering around Tiananmen Gate and the ceaseless flow of traffic on the huge boulevards that isolate the square from the city. They also form an almost anachronistic solidarity and perhaps a collective defiance of the state-imposed commercialization and competitiveness of the twenty-first century People's Republic. Whether the spirit of Mao, in the form of a revolutionary trickster instead of a benign mascot, will one day inspire a new 'chaos under heaven' that sweeps away the existing order remains to be seen.

Kumsusan Memorial Hall, 'The Sacred Temple of *Juche*: The Mausoleum of Kim Il Sung and Kim Jong Il in Pyongyang

On 17 December 2011, North Korea's 'Dear Leader', Kim Jong Il, died whilst travelling on a train in North Korea. According to official sources, he suffered a fatal heart attack. Kim Jong Il's embalmed body was placed in a glass coffin for a lying-in-state, surrounded by crimson *Kimjongilia* begonias.[71] His son Kim Jong-un was officially entitled 'Great Successor' and given the supreme command over the armed forces. On the day of Kim Il Jong's funeral on 28 December, North Korean TV footage showed the hearse being slowly driven along the wide boulevards of Pyongyang on the way to Kumsusan Memorial Palace, as the mausoleum is called. The Great Successor firmly grasped the car's door handle, walking alongside the vehicle, followed by his uncle. The cameras lingered on the tear-stained faces of the distraught citizens wailing as they witnessed the procession. A few weeks later, on 12 January 2012, the North Korean government announced the decision that the body of Kim Jong Il was to be put on permanent display: 'Great leader Kim Jong Il will be preserved to look the same as when he was alive, at Kumsusan Memorial Palace', 'the official KCNA news agency reported, adding that Russian experts already had arrived to carry out the necessary procedures.[72] This is to date the most recent example of the practice of making a political leader 'immortal' by embalming. Whereas in Russia, Lenin's preserved body is increasingly seen as an embarrassing anachronism, a relic of a now distant past, in North Korea the practice is seen as entirely befitting the sacred remains of the Kims.

Although for much of its history Korea was profoundly influenced by the neighbouring Chinese empire, the peninsula was sufficiently remote to develop a distinct culture and social structure. During the long-lasting Joseon Dynasty (1392–1910) the ruling aristocratic elite held sway over commoners and people classed as 'outcasts' by a system based on Neo-Confucian morality and education.[73] Political independence from China was intermittent and by the nineteenth century Korea paid regular tribute to the Qing emperors. With the expansion of Japan's interest in procuring raw materials and resources to fuel its programme of 'catching up with the west', Korea became a prime target for Japanese imperialist expansion. The Tientsin Concession Treaty allowed foreign powers to establish a presence on territories under Chinese control (1885) and gave Japan the right to station troops in Korea. When a rebellion broke out in Seoul in 1895, the Japanese used this as *casus belli* against China, triggering the First Sino-Japanese War (1894–5), which was essentially fought over Korea. The Chinese forces suffered heavy defeats in Pyongyang, particularly at the Yalu River and Port Arthur. Although the Treaty of Shimonoseki granted independence to Korea five years later in 1910, Korea became a Japanese colony.[74]

Kim Il Sung was born during the early years of Japanese colonial rule.[75] According to his at least partially legendary North Korean biography, the birth occurred on 15 April 1912 in a small cottage at Mangyondae on Taedong River, not far from Pyongyang. He was the oldest of three sons of a Protestant Christian family and his father worked as a Chinese herbal doctor (he died in 1926 when Kim Il Sung was fourteen), while his mother taught at Sunday school. Kim Il Sung's family had moved to Manchuria, but they shunted back and forth between their homeland and China throughout the 1920s. Although the Japanese occupation brought a degree of modernization, the heavy-handed repression of any form of dissent was experienced as a 'national trauma'.[76]

The 1920s saw the beginning of nationalist movements, inspired by those that had sprung up in China. Once the military had established its hold on the Japanese government in the 1930s, a more aggressive imperialism gathered momentum and Korea was transformed into an industrial base to help mobilize the Japanese war effort, with the population pressed into arms factories and mines. Furthermore, Korea was to be totally assimilated with Japan and in 1939, forced to adopt Shinto worship and Japanese surnames. Korean youths were enlisted and recruited to serve in the Japanese army and the general repression was stepped up. To escape these conditions, thousands of Koreans sought refuge in China and Manchuria, where the first anti-Japanese resistance groups operated mainly underground.[77]

Kim Il Sung, already in China, attended school in Yunan and joined such guerilla groups under Chinese control in 1930. He became commander of the sixth division of the 'Northeast Anti-Japanese Unit Army' and was instructed in Marxist-Leninism by Wei Zhengmin, a Chinese professional revolutionary and graduate of the prestigious Huangpo Military Academy. When these guerilla units were destroyed by the Japanese in 1941, Kim and his Korean comrades fled into Soviet territory, where the anti-Japanese units were reorganized under Soviet command as the 88th Special Independent Sniper Brigade of Partisans, which appears to have been primarily an intelligence gathering unit. Although these activities in China and Russia might have had little impact in the short term, they were the formative years for the people who would later assume positions of leadership in liberated Korea in 1945.

On 19 September 1945, Kim Il Sung and 66 Korean officers, most of them 'Partisans', arrived at Pyongyang from Russia. On 14 October, the Soviets introduced the 33-year-old Kim Il Sung at a public rally as a guerilla hero and major political figure. Although he might have fought courageously in the small-scale Chinese Communist-led campaigns during the 1930s, he was practically unknown to the general public and to the communist movement in North and South Korea. He relied on the heavy promotion by the Soviets, who were attracted to Kim because he suited their requirements. As Seiler noted, he was

> an archetypal political-military cadre of the Soviet mould – efficient, unquestioning, obedient and deferential, well suited to ruthless political mobilization and class warfare.[78]

In the middle of the Second World War in 1943, the Allies met in Cairo to decide the future of all territories acquired by Japan since 1894, should Japan be defeated. The United States, China and Britain agreed that Korea would become free and independent after the Allied victory. Although Roosevelt and Stalin had wanted to establish an international trusteeship for Korea at the Yalta Conference of February 1945, no decision was made on the exact formula for governing the nation in the aftermath of Allied victory. The landing of Soviet troops in the northeast of the peninsula on 10 August 1945 compelled the United States government to hastily improvise a formula for Korea. On 15 August, 1945, the day Japan surrendered, President Harry S. Truman put to Stalin the proposal to divide Korea at the 38th parallel and thus into two occupational zones. The next day Stalin agreed, and on 24 August 24 Soviet forces arrived in Pyongyang to transfer power to the local Communist Party Committee. The 'Partisans' assumed control by eliminating or suppressing other communists and opponents. On 18 December 1945, Kim Il Sung became Chairman of the North Korean Communist Party (NKCP) and head of government. Two years later, in 1948, The People's Republic of North Korea was established with Soviet assistance in counterpart to the USA-backed Republic of Korea below the 38th parallel.

The existence of a separate Korean state with a pro-Western ideology under the autocratic rule of Syngman Rhee was a thorn in the side of Kim Il Sung. As soon as the U.S. troops were withdrawn from the South in 1949, he prepared for a military expedition to unify the country. The history of the ensuing Korean War is still a contentious issue, especially the roles played by the Soviet Union and China.[79] Even if the initiative was primarily Kim Il Sung's, as some historians think, he needed the logistical support of the Russians.[80] All parties involved in the initial invasion envisaged a short campaign and underestimated the readiness of the USA to intervene. When North Korean troops invaded the South on 25 June 1950, they made rapid progress, taking Seoul within four days and advancing down the peninsula. The UN Security Council immediately issued an order to stop the fighting. When this was ignored, President Truman committed U.S. troops on the ground. The combination of aerial bombardment and heavy tanks checked the North Korean advance. By October 1949, the UN sanctioned an assault above the 38th parallel in an attempt to unify the whole peninsula, leading to the fall of Pyongyang on 19 October. At this stage China intervened by sending troops to defend North Korea and its own sphere of influence. Heavy fighting continued over the next four years, despite various ceasefires, with very heavy casualties on all sides. As neither side proved more powerful than the other, the ceasefire of 27 July finally re-established the status quo of 1945. A demilitarized zone on either side of the 38th parallel still divides the peninsula.

The political effect of the war for North Korea was the consolidation of Kim Il Sung's power. His leading role in the attempted liberation of South Korea allowed him to neutralize the Korean Workers' Party, which had represented a cross-section of the Korean Communist movement. He replaced it with a much narrower party controlled by Kim's guerilla group, which, as Linter has pointed out, projected their own experiences and modes of operation onto the government:

> hence the post-war ideological and policy framework in the DPRK increasingly came to reflect the tastes, prejudices and experiences of the Manchurian guerilla mindset – militaristic, Spartan, anti-intellectual and xenophobic.[81]

Kim Il Sung was to rely heavily on the Soviet Union to supply investment and technical expertise. However, the Russian government made sure that the investments in North Korean infrastructure and factories also served the enormous needs of a recovering Soviet economy.[82]

By 1958 Kim and his supporters, having achieved complete domination of the party and the state, promoted a new ideology to secure their hold on power. This entailed the rigorous isolation of the population from foreign contact, including that with former allies Russia and China. By blocking all access to the outside world by any means (including printed and aerial media) it became possible to heighten the sense of insecurity among the population. The state of constant anxiety was maintained by the pressure to continue the 'revolutionary struggle' inside the country and by fanning fears of an imminent attack from the outside. High levels of military expenditure and preparedness for war were justified as a necessary means to counter any foreign aggression, but importantly too, to bring about the unification of the peninsula. Kim Il Sung alone was said to guarantee the safeguarding of the revolution and the people, and his personality cult developed into an 'absolutist personal autocracy'.[83] The relatively good conditions in North Korea during the decades it enjoyed Soviet and Chinese support, as well as Kim Il Sung's genuinely outgoing personality, helped him to secure great popularity.

The new ideology, called '*Juche*' (literally 'self-identity'), was developed by Kim Il Sung from the 1960s onwards and formally accepted as state ideology in 1980.[84] Kim used a twelfth-century Korean concept, the philosophy of independence of early Korean rulers, to anchor his system in the depths of Korean tradition and wisdom. He also revitalized the Neo-Confucian acceptance of social order, in which all people have a particular place in society, and which justified the absolute rule of the *suryeong* (leader) 'who serves as the brain to control the body'.[85] Since such a system contradicted the Marxist theory of the primary importance of class struggle, references to Marxism-Leninism were dropped altogether from the 1992 constitution. The practical result of implementing *Juche* policy was the enforced isolation of the PRNK. Given that neither the Soviet Union nor the People's Republic of China were willing to provoke further U.S. retaliation in East Asia and therefore refused to support any further military interventions in South Korea, North Korea had to stand alone, trust nobody and develop its own capacity to sustain itself and at the same time step up its military potential.

Despite the rhetoric of political and economic self-sufficiency, North Korea continued to depend substantially on the People's Republic of China and the Soviet Union for investment, technical expertise and export markets. When the break-up of the Soviet Union put a stop to Russian largesse, Kim Il Sung initiated closer links with South Korea in the late 1980s. Problems emerged in the late 1980s when the Soviet Union ceased to exist and China embarked on economic reforms under Deng Xiaopeng when North-Korean self-sufficiency translated into isolation and steeply declining productivity. Despite such economic woes, Kim Il Sung began to embark on nuclear research programmes.

In the early 1990s Kim Il Sung passed the chairmanship of the national defence to his son Kim Jong Il to smooth the handover of power after his demise. On 8 July 1994 Kim Il Sung, aged 82 years, suffered a sudden heart attack and died. Kim Jong Il succeeded him as supreme leader and the personality cult of the Kims intensified, while economic mismanagement and isolationist policies caused even more hardship for the population and led to severe famine in the early 1990s. Trade agreements with the South were also revoked under Kim Jong Il's more aggressive stance and occasional military provocations.

Since the succession of Kim Jong-un in 2012, following his father's death, there has been no indication of any changes in North Korean ideology. An article published in April 2012, 'The Great Comrade Kim Il Sung is the Eternal Leader of the People', reports that Kim Jong-un

> called for carrying forward the idea and exploits of Kim Il Sung and Kim Jong Il in building the party, state and revolutionary

Kumsusan Memorial Palace, Pyongyang, on a rainy Sunday morning.

armed forces. He underlined the need to take Kimilsungism-Kimjongilism as the unique guiding idea and permanent guidelines of the Korean revolution and construction cause. In the treatise, Kim Jong Un said Kim Il Sung raised the *Juche* (self-reliance) idea, had ingeniously combined the socialist cause with national independence and ushered in a new *Juche* revolution era. It added that under the banner of *Songun* [Military First], Kim Jong Il, who protected the dignity and supreme interests of the DPRK in reliance on powerful arms, had turned the country into a political, ideological and military power and greatly improved its people's living standard.[86]

This rhetoric, backed by the decision to embalm Kim Jong Il and to have him laid out forever next to his father, suggests that the regime is trying even harder to maintain their hold on power through *Juche* and coercion. China's unwillingness to interfere, as well as the threat of using nuclear arms, developed at a terrific cost to the already hard-pressed population, has until now inhibited superpower interventions by force.

The whole of Pyongyang is an embodiment of state ideology. Only privileged citizens can live there and it serves as the showcase for the North Korean identity. Following the complete destruction of the old city in the Korean War, an almost utopian new capital was built with an extraordinary coherence of its spatial and visual programme, linking urban planning, architecture and monumental public art.[87]

One of the most important centres of political power in Pyongyang was a building known as 'Kumsusan Assembly Hall', where the Workers' Party of North Korea originally conducted committee meetings. It was built between 1976 and 1977 in the northeastern periphery of the city centre, above the northernmost bend of the Taedong River. Like other public buildings in Pyongyang the architectural style combines the neo-Classicism of the Soviet era with projecting eaves, the usual token acknowledgement of 'eastern' – here Korean, vernacular forms. The erstwhile meeting place for the party was transformed during the 1980s into the official residence of Kim Il-Sung and a venue for the reception of delegates and foreign visitors. Kim Il Sung died there on 8 July 1994. Millions of people came to see his body lying in state at the Kumsusan Palace.

As soon as Kim's chosen successor, his son Kim Jong Il, had consolidated his position and become Chairman of the WPK, he set out to safeguard the body of the 'Great Leader' Kim Il Sung. First of all this involved the preservation of the corpse by embalming and then by designing a mausoleum to house the remains in a suitably impressive manner. Kim Il Jong immediately declared an official period of mourning, which was to last three years and provided a transitional phase. There was to be a break between the era of the 'Great Leader' Kim Il Sung and the 'Dear Leader', as Kim Jong Il was to be called henceforth. Once the party and the army had rallied behind him, he embarked on the process to transform his deceased father into the 'Sun of the People' and bestow upon him official immortality. The title of 'president' was to be reserved for Kim Il Sung alone, who was thereby 'President Forever'. Another crucial decision was to turn the abode of the Great Leader, the former Assembly Hall, then Kumsusan Palace, into a Memorial Hall and Mausoleum. Apart from the fact that it had been the last abode of Kim Il Sung, the choice to keep him there was also based on practical consideration. The building was suitably remote from the city centre, already surrounded by a water-filled moat filled and protected by high-level security measures. It was situated close to the Martyrs' Cemetery, another very popular and sacred site, dedicated to the Heroes of the Korean War. Kumsusan had already been made grand enough to function as

North Korean visitors who have just completed their visit to Kumsusan Memorial Palace.

a showcase of the regime's opulence. It also needed only comparatively minor structural changes to become a mausoleum.

In contrast to the mausolea of Lenin, Ho Chi Minh and Mao Zedong, Kim I Sung's is not in the centre of the capital and not topographically linked with the declaration of national independence.

While Mansudae Art Studios were officially credited as responsible for the conversion, Kim Jong Il is said to have taken an active part in the design. According to his treatise on architecture, he was fully aware of its ideological importance and his ultimate supervisory role:

> The ideological and artistic qualities of architecture are the characteristics that distinguish architecture from other branches of science and technology; its utility is the feature that distinguishes it from other arts. [. . .] For its high utility and noble and beautiful ideological and artistic qualities, socialist architecture gives people an understanding of the advantages and invincibility of the socialist system, inspires them with national pride and confidence, and educates them

North Korean students at Kumsusan Memorial Palace.

to be unfailingly loyal to the Party and the leader and love their country ardently, thus contributing to the capture of the ideological fortress of communism. [. . .] The leader, with uncommon organizing ability, mobilizes the masses in the gigantic work of architectural creation under a great plan of lasting effect and victoriously guides the difficult and complex struggle to transform the appearance of the country through his skilful operation and direction.[88]

In this case the building had already fulfilled the ideological demands and other than blocking up all the windows the exterior was largely unchanged. A huge granite paved forecourt was added to allow sufficient space for mass rallies to take place. A perimeter wall around the whole compound enhanced security and in 1999 peripheral cloisters and underground walkways were added. Although I was unable to find out exactly which changes had been made to the interior, the previous purpose of a presidential palace was still clearly in evidence during my visit in July 2010.

All foreign tourists to Pyongyang have to follow an officially prescribed routine to ensure that they take account of the buildings and monuments deemed best to embody *Juche* ideology. Kim Il Sung's mausoleum is on this itinerary and my guides, when I told them that I had came especially to see it, remarked that in their experience such a request was unprecedented and pronounced it a recommendable example of interest in the Great Leader. All visits to the mausoleum, by local people as well as foreigners, need to be booked and cleared beforehand and unfold in a strictly controlled and choreographed sequence.[89] Tourists are told to dress smartly and behave respectfully. They are strictly supervised by their guides and kept apart from North Koreans. For these North Koreans, a visit to the mausoleum is a privilege, and only those citizens who have been bestowed the badge bearing the likeness of the Great and/or the Dear Leader, are admitted, which excludes all children under fifteen years of age. This provides a mechanism to monitor citizen's participation in this rite, which for those privileged enough to reside in the capital to begin with, is a serious commitment. A special tram service, which operates on the days the mausoleum is open, connects the city to the monument, and its use is free of charge.

I was there on a Sunday, a day of rest in North Korea, and thousands of people kept arriving. There were groups of young students in their regulation white shirts and black trousers or skirts; groups of soldiers and ex-soldiers; married couples, groups of men wearing the currently fashionable brown polyester suits with an elasticated waist and scores of women in jewel-coloured, voluminous and gauzy *hanbok* (traditional) dresses. All were immaculately coiffed and wore highly polished shoes.

A single gate led to a low-rise reception pavilion and a cloister that form the unique link to the Palace. Cloakrooms and toilets are accommodated here; people can have a last check that their hair and clothes are impeccable. Before the visit, bags and cameras needed to be handed in. The staff in these preliminary areas consisted entirely of young and attractive women, all dressed in long, black velvet, traditional Korean smocks and with identical hairstyles – the hair swept up at the sides and twisted into a long, tight roll, with a free mass of curls gathered at the top of the head. These graceful but stern-looking maidens ushered the crowds towards the covered walkway that links the reception area with the main building.

The first stage of the journey proceeded along the cloister at ground level. The open windows along the corridor allowed a view of the stone perimeter walls with the flying cranes, 'symbols of eternal life', as my guides solemnly declared. The moat that surrounds the whole edifice was also visible from here; it widens to form a lake replete with swans, in which the facade of the mausoleum is reflected. At the end of this corridor a flight of steps led to the subterranean level. Here the 'liminal' stage began and the outside world was shut out as all visitors had to step onto a constantly moving walkway like those in airport terminals. There were two such 'travelators' moving in opposite directions, to and from the main building. No one was allowed to walk on them and people had to stand very still in groups of two, passively conveyed along a distance of 1,000 metres. At the end of this conveyor strip, rolling brushes removed any remnants of dirt from footwear while gusts of air from automatic fans blew dust off the clothes. Thus mechanically purified, people crossed the threshold to the sacred space of the Memorial Palace proper.

Unlike in the mausoleum of Mao Zedong or Ho Chi Minh, where the spatial sequence was quite short and consisted of no more than three or five rooms, the Kumsusan interior is much more complex. With its labyrinthine corridors and stairways, it reminded me of the enchanted castle in Jean Cocteau's *La belle et la bête* (*Beauty and the Beast*). The walls were all lined in polished grey marble – even the architraves of doors were of marble – and the ceilings were very high. Since all the windows have been blocked in, the dim artificial light cast by elaborate chandeliers left the corners in shadow. The scale is palatial and meant to overwhelm.

A very elaborate marble staircase rose from the centre of the hall, but visitors were directed instead to a series of lifts, each carrying ten or so people, to reach the first floor. After this rather mundane ascent, the visit gained momentum. Having traversed another vestibule, we entered a large square hall with a row of green stone pillars on either side. A larger than life-size bronze statue of Kim Il Sung stood within a recess on a plinth, his hands clasped behind his back, bathed in a glowing orange-pink light from concealed lamps behind the skirting board. This was the first 'epiphany' of the Great Leader; people approached the statue and bowed once, and the Koreans deeply, to the waist.

From this radiant vision we passed into the dark and gloomy 'Hall of Tears', where the initial elation at the first sight of the Great Leader changed to despair. Listening devices were handed out, which played a recording of a spoken, or rather intoned, commentary that tried to evoke the deep grief experienced by the Korean people during the three years of mourning after the Great Leader's death. The highly emotive tone of the English-language version was said to match that of the Korean original. It seemed to work equally well in Russian, as a Russian-speaking visitor told me that it had moved her to tears. While listening, we were directed to carefully examine the large bronze reliefs that depict grieving peasants, factory workers, intellectuals and soldiers. Having been so vividly reminded of the terrifying chaos and emptiness the people experienced after the loss of their Great Leader and having relived the period of mourning, redemption awaited in the next room, the main sanctuary. Here, in a darkened and lofty hall, lay the immortal leader in a crystal coffin placed in the centre. White-gloved soldiers were positioned at all corners of the sarcophagus, holding polished machine guns. Visitors in rows of four were invited to step forward to the rope that secures the distance to the coffin and to bow deeply, then proceed around all three sides, bowing each time, though not behind the Great Leader's head.

Loudspeakers played an instrumental version of the 'Song in Praise of Kim Il Sung'. The body of Kim Il Sung was covered up to the chest by a red cloth. He wore a dark suit and tie and his face looked very fresh and rosy. His still shiny, greying hair had been neatly brushed. The Great Leader appeared to be in excellent condition.

After this climax of coming face to face with the 'Sun of the People', visitors were invited to express their feelings in large books of condolence and to gaze at a map of the world that showed all the places he had visited. Foreigners were taken to the Honour Room, where medals and honorary degrees bestowed on the Great Leader by Korean and foreign institutions were displayed, as well as photographs showing him receiving these honours from leaders such as Anwar al-Sadat, Fidel Castro, Muammar Gaddafi, Yasser Arafat and Jean-Bédel Bokassa. An adjacent room that was not open to ordinary North Koreans housed Kim's personal train carriage, complete with embroidered curtains, upholstered chairs and a writing desk. His Mercedes-Benz car was also on display but there were no 'relics', no objects that had been in proximity to the deceased's body, such as spectacles or clothing.

The return journey involved taking the lift back down to the moving walkway, though without passing through the purification machines. Visitors retrieved their bags and cameras and were free to walk to the huge forecourt of the building, to wander around there and pose for photographs.

The facade of the Memorial Palace has also been clad in grey marble panels and was adorned with a large image of the beaming Kim Il Sung. Flowerbeds were stocked with the pink *Kimilsungia* begonia and ducks and swans were swimming on the lake. No recreational activities other than a stately strolling on the forecourt were permitted here. Nor was there any sign of commercialization on the site. There was no souvenir shop, no postcards were for sale; there were no refreshment stalls, no hawkers selling batteries or bottled water, unlike in Tiananmen Square. Walking in the beautifully landscape parkland, where all sorts of deer and peacocks evoke a paradisiacal idyll, was also strictly forbidden.

In terms of its content, Kim Il Sung's mausoleum does not differ from other such establishments. It now houses the bodies of two former leaders here that, as in other communist countries, are preserved 'for eternity' and made visible in the state of non-corruption. It too has a preliminary hall with a larger-than life statue, and exhibits objects and photographs that bespeak of the Great Leader's international recognition. There are some important differences though. The architectural setting is that of a palace rather than a mausoleum, with the grand stairways and long corridors that still evoke the former purpose of a place where high-level diplomacy was conducted and where a potentate resided in imperial splendour. More important than this evocation of the deceased's high status is the 'Hall of Tears', with its emotional multimedia manipulation into abject grief. The subsequent encounter with the remarkably well-preserved body amounts to a revelation, a mystical encounter, and people were not hurried past, but given time to gaze at the radiant face of the Great Leader in his crystal coffin. This coffin too looks more like something from a science fiction movie and is devoid of signs of mourning. Like Melnikov's original sarcophagus for Lenin it emphasis the immortality of the Leader, who, as so many inscriptions in North Korea proclaim, 'will be with us forever'. The mourning has been relegated to the past, a time of collective trauma for the nation bereft of its 'Sun' has been overcome by the efforts of the 'Dear Leader', who ensured, if not the resurrection, the immortalization of his father. He himself is about to become an object of veneration. It is the deeply religious aspect of Kumsusuan that is so striking.

Although officially there are four recognized religions in North Korea (the Korean Christian Federation, The Roman Catholic Association, the Buddhist Federation and the Central Committee of the Korean Chondogyo Association), their activities are strictly controlled and no proselytizing is permitted, which means that whatever congregations do exist, they dwindle, as dying members are not replaced.[90] While the Neo-Confucian acceptance of hierarchy underpins the current social structure, it also underpins 'the direct, mystical and emotional union of followers with a spiritual leader, the source of all wisdom and authority'.[91] A leader to whom, for 'having bequeathed the nation', people are expected to repay this act of benevolence by unquestioning loyalty and devotion.[92]

'Kimilsungism' has several components. It does not only amount to the political philosophy formulated by Kim Il Sung himself, the doctrine of *Juche*, but to a spiritual revitalization movement. This reinterpretation was the work of Kim Jong Il, who made the cult of Kim Il Sung into the mainstay of his own legitimacy. It was under Kim Jong Il that references to Marxism and Leninism were dropped and *Juche* became an article of faith rather than a guide to its practice. The deification of Kim Il Sung also justifies the cult of Kim Jong Il as the supreme interpreter of *Juche* and as the new supreme spiritual guide.[93] A keen film buff and with some artistic pretentions himself, Kim Jing Il personally orchestrated the visual manifestations of his father's cult. In fact, he subordinated all artistic practice and architecture to the mandate of serving *Juche* and glorifying the person of Kim Il Sung. It was he who had chosen the portrait with the benignly beaming face of the Great Leader that is attached to the facade of the mausoleum and can be seen everywhere on public buildings, schools and railway stations. This has been continued after Kim Jong Il's own death, as his successor ordered the manufacture and countrywide dissemination of statues and images dedicated to the departed 'Dear Leader'.

Sonia Ryang explained that a crucial aspect in understanding the way that this new religion became so pervasive in North Korea is that the concept of the exclusive individual attachment to the Sovereign Leader (*suryeong*) supersedes all other social ties. This splitting from the deep attachment to family and kin, which characterized East Asian social values for millennia, was effected through the practice of punishing the whole family for the misdeeds (real or fabricated) of the individual member, which means that 'the self and others exist in a random mixture of insecure commonality and disconnections'.[94] The only certainty lies in the connection between the self and the Great Leader through loyalty and love. A climate of suspicion and fear, as well as carefully graduated rewards and punishments ensure that this loyalty is more than just internalized and constantly put to the test.

The most conspicuous sign of approval and indeed of full citizenship is the little badge with the likeness of either Great or Dear Leader that all those who have been deemed worthy to own must safeguard as their most precious treasured object. For all of these North Koreans who are thus privileged to be allowed into the immortal presence of Kim Il Sung, the visit to the mausoleum is the highest reward. While all over the country there are countless steles that represent *Juche* in symbolic form, obelisks inscribed with the motto 'Our Great Leader Marshal Kim Il Sung will be with us forever' and surmounted by an electrically lit red flame, there is only one Supreme Temple of *Juche* that is his mausoleum.

Destroyed Communist Mausolea

Georges Bataille wrote about 'silencing forms of architecture', cathedrals and palaces that 'oppose the logic of majesty and authority to any confusion.[95] He could have included the monumental tombs of great leaders. They were meant to perpetuate their memories for a distant future and were constructed solidly so as to withstand even major earthquakes. Yet they are vulnerable to ideological change. After 1990, previous satellites of the Soviet Union had to readdress the question of their national and cultural identity. The years under communist governments were suddenly seen as only the most recent and painful episode of a people's *longue durée*, as something that had been imposed from outside. The embalmed erstwhile revolutionary heroes and statesmen whose cult had formed a mainstay of the Soviet imposed etiquette of state rituals and whose revolutionary credentials as freedom fighters had been reinterpreted to fit the ideological narratives of the Eastern bloc could simply become ordinary dead people by being buried or cremated.

Ulan Bator

Mongolia, with its wide grasslands and vast deserts, had for centuries been under Chinese domination. In a highly turbulent period between 1911 and 1921 Mongolia experienced a brief period of independence terminated by Chinese occupation imposed by a force of arms which was ousted by a band of White Russian guards in 1920. The band then declared Mongolian independence again. Mongolian freedom fighters, notably Damdin Sühbaatar (also spelt 'Sukhe-Bator') and Khorloogiin Choibalsan, inspired by Lenin's writings, set up left-wing revolutionary groups and joined in 1920 to set up the first communist party outside Russia (the 'Mongolian People's Party'). A Soviet account of their triumph tells us:

> The First Congress of the Mongolian People's Party, held in March 1921 under Sukhe-Bator's direction, summoned the Mongolian people to rebellion and declared the party's task to be anti-imperialist and anti-feudal revolution. Sukhe-Bator

was elected to the party's Central Committee, and on Mar. 13, 1921, he became a member of the Provisional People's Government, minister of war, and commander in chief of the People's Revolutionary Army. Youth regiments of the army, led by Sukhe-Bator, defeated the Chinese militarists on Mar. 18, 1921, near Maimachen (present-day Altan-Bulak). The army, commanded by Sukhe-Bator, together with units of the Soviet Red Army that had come to the aid of the Mongolian people, defeated Ungern's White Guard forces between May and August 1921. On July 6, 1921, Urga was liberated, and on July 10 the Provisional People's Government was reorganized as a permanent People's Government, in which Sukhe-Bator became minister of war.[96]

Mongolia had become one of the first Soviet satellite states. Sükhbaatar died in 1923 and Choibalsan remained as head of state until his death in 1952. Following Stalin's example, he initiated violent purges in the late 1930s.[97]

Choibalsan happened to die in Moscow and was duly embalmed by the Lenin Mausoleum morticians. A Mongolian blogger expressed how incongruous this felt to a people who do not bury their dead but leave them in the open country 'to be re-united with nature', while the remains of Choibalsan received an official state funeral and the government used film footage of the event to 'teach people how they should deal with their deaths'.[98] Choibalsan was put on public view within a mausoleum that was closely modelled on the one in Red Square, where the remains of the exhumed body of his erstwhile comrade, Sükhbaatar, were also buried.

Protests in the 1990s brought the one-party system to end and Mongolia, like Russia, has embarked on economic liberalization and a measure of democracy. The question of Mongolian identity was much debated:

> Prior to the recent shift toward a reexamination of the socialist past, that period had been largely elided in discussion of Mongolian history. The socialist void had been viewed as a period of 'white noise.' [. . .] For most Mongolians in the early 1990s, history stopped in the early twentieth century (just prior to the People's Revolution of 1921) and only resumed with the protests of 1989–1990. Moreover, to be

Mongolian was seen to be linked to 'tradition,' which was presented as having been repressed but 'kept inside of us' during the socialist period. A key component of this identity as it was being re-remembered and reconstructed was the point that to be Mongolian and traditional was to be not Russian, and not socialist [. . .] Socialism was seen as a foreign imposition.[99]

The occasion of the 800th anniversary of the Mongolian state in 2005 provided a suitable context for the invention of new traditions and the creation of new ceremonial spaces in Ulan Bator. The government decided, after a nationwide opinion poll, to dismantle the mausoleum and rebuild Sükhbataar Square. Our Mongolian blogger gives an account of what happened as events unfolded and notices that at least the officiating Buddhist monks had forgiven their former persecutor:

> The bodies of Sukhbaatar and Choibalsan were removed and apparently the day before yesterday the bodies of Sukhbaatar and Choibalsan have been ritually cremated. There were monks present at the ceremony to bless their last farewell, which especially in the case of Choibalsan was quite remarkable. He is held most responsible for the destructions of more than 900 temples and monasteries and the killing of thousands of monks.

There remain no visible traces of the mausoleum and its incumbents. On the spot of the mausoleum stands a huge statue of Genghis Khan, now recognized as a true Mongolian hero, lawgiver and, importantly, conqueror of China.

Sofia

The last location I used as a meeting place was the mausoleum of Georgi Dimitrov. I did not use it often since I did not live nearby, but it was nonetheless my usual marker for the space in the center of town. In the summer of 1999 the mausoleum was blown up, and today its blank space serves in regular succession as a garden, a summer opera stage, and a location for stalls for the Bierfest (the local version of the Oktoberfest beer drinking festival, which happens at unpredictable times of the year in

Sofia). The square between the mausoleum and the old king's palace (now housing the National Gallery) was formerly called 'September 9' commemorating the government takeover in 1944; now it has been duly renamed 'Battenberg Square,' in honor of Bulgaria's first prince after 1878, the German Alexander Battenberg. There is no physical artifact in place where the mausoleum once stood, nor is there any sign to remind passersby of its long presence. Yet, in a curious way, the mausoleum still exists, and the joking 'Let's meet at / in front of / behind the mausoleum' needs no explanation: even the younger generation knows its ghostly location. It seems to be still there– no longer as a site of historical memory but still as a marker for everyday orientation. To paraphrase Derrida, it is 'the presence of an absence.'[100]

The 'presence of an absence' that Maria Todorova describes here when talking about monuments and statues that have been erased from the fabric of the city can be experienced in many post-Soviet countries and is by no means a phenomenon restricted to ex-communist societies. The mausoleum in the centre of Sofia used to house Georgi Dimitrov (1882–1949). He was a social democrat until he joined the Communist Party in 1919 and his early revolutionary activities resulted in prison terms. Dimitrov was active as a union leader and had been exiled to Yugoslavia and the Soviet Union, where he was a member of Comintern under Stalin from 1934 to 1943. In 1946 he returned to Bulgaria and became leader of the Communist Party; following Bulgaria's incorporation within the Eastern bloc he became premier. When he died in 1949, in a sanatorium near Moscow, rumours circulated that he had been poisoned by or on behalf of Stalin who resented Dimitrov's overtures to Marshal Tito of Yugoslavia. Dimitrov was the second political leader after Lenin to be embalmed by Boris Zbarsky at the Lenin mausoleum laboratory.[101] Subsequently, he was placed in a mausoleum that had been hastily but solidly constructed within days.[102] For 50 years, beginning with the official opening on 11 December 1949, it was a major focus of party ceremonies. As Todorova describes:

> 18 million people passed through the commemorative chamber, among them political figures like Mikhail Gorbachev, Boris Yeltsin, Aleksey Kosygin, Fidel Castro, Indira Gandhi, Angela Davis, and many others. There was a strict protocol

Dimitrov's mausoleum, Sofia.

concerning the laying of wreaths at the mausoleum, the movement of visitors, and the arrangement of the party leaders during public events, and a veritable ritual was created for the military honor guard, specifying everything from their stylized uniforms to their poses and the specific music to be used for different occasions.[103]

After 1989 a non-aligned Bulgaria became a real possibility and the mausoleum served as a gathering place for anti-government demonstrations and was even daubed in slogans and graffiti. In 1990 Dimitrov's body was removed and buried in the Central Cemetery in Sofia. The mausoleum was left standing empty. It was used at times as the backdrop for open-air opera performances, most notably and fittingly, as Todorova remarks, for Verdi's *Aida*. Very suddenly, and without bothering to engage in even a semblance of popular consultation as in Ulan Bator, the government decided to take down the mausoleum on 21 August 1999. The building was packed with explosives but had been built so solidly that it failed to 'even crack'. It took a whole week to dismantle the structure mechanically piece by piece.

The destruction of the mausoleum was not universally welcomed and the obliteration of history from collective memory could be seen as yet another authoritarian intervention. There had been numerous suggestions for what it should become: a library, a national museum, even the largest disco club in the Balkans. Instead there is the presence of its absence.

Prague

Klement Gottwald had been a particularly close ally of Stalin's and propagated the Russian leader's cult with great fervour in Czechoslovakia. Addressing the crowds on the occasion of Stalin's funeral on 5 March 1953, he proclaimed with great emotion:

> I believe that when we stand in front of Lenin's mausoleum – now Lenin and Stalin's mausoleum – in Moscow, we shall be able to make a confident promise to these two greatest geniuses of humanity, in the name of all the people of Czechoslovakia, that we shall follow to the end, the path which they have shown us, and under the banner of Stalin and Lenin, we shall strive onwards towards the goal of socialism.[104]

Gottwald was not a healthy man and had defied his doctors' orders in order to send off his hero. Nine days later, on 14 March, he was dead himself, having suffered a burst artery. Again, a death in Moscow warranted the attention of Ilya Zbarsky and his fellow embalmers and Gottwald returned to Prague as a 'mummy'.[105] He was laid to rest with great pomp and ceremony in Vitkov Hall, which had originally been built as a war memorial for Czechoslovak soldiers who had fought during the First World War. It had been turned into 'The Proletarian Pantheon' after 1948 and was a favoured burial site for high-ranking communist party leaders. It took six months to convert the building into a fully functioning mausoleum, complete with all the necessary facilities to sustain the embalmed body of Klement Gottwald, who lay there in open view from 1953 to 1962. By that time his body had began to show visible signs of deterioration and in any case, the time for his personality cult had passed. His blackened remains were cremated and placed in a common grave at Olšany Cemetery. In 1989, all bodies and remains were removed from the Vitkov monument and buried in simple graves.

While in Bulgaria the government tried to erase the memory of Dimitrov and his mausoleum, leaving a 'space of emptiness' that was nevertheless redolent with memory, the Czech authorities decided to make the former tomb of dead communist leaders into an opportunity to inform a new generation about this period of history. The earlier pantheon and Gottwald mausoleum were reopened as a public memorial in October 2009 and now house a permanent exhibition, entitled 'Laboratory of Power', which in a strange twist, perpetuates Gottwald's memory once more.[106]

In Tirana, the capital of Albania, the former mausoleum of Enver Hoxha, built in 1988 in the form of a glazed pyramid three years after his death, now functions as a shopping and art centre. Hoxha was buried in the cemetery of Tirana in 1992. Moves to demolish the now rather dilapidated structure have so far been resisted by petitions and protests.[107]

We have seen how the 'mummies', the 'greatest communists and stem of the party' in Vladislav Todorov's ironic paean with which we opened this chapter, have formed the core of personality cults that would last beyond the natural lifespan. In order to maintain this fiction that the great leader would never leave and that he's merely asleep, enormous resources of man-power, electricity and water were mobilized just to stave off decay. The mausoleum was not just a grand funerary chapel in which the masses could commune with their everlasting heroes, but a complicated machine to keep the body without organs seemingly alive. Utmost solemnity had to be observed when coming face to face with these effigies, most elaborately staged to this day at Pyongyang. The very efforts that had been taken to make the buildings last forever, as in the case of Mao's Memorial Hall that is said to be indestructible, can contribute to maintain the spectacle even if it has no or little relevance for present regimes. Eventually, as it has already happened in the former eastern bloc countries, the mummies will be returned to dust and visitors, like those in Prague, can take tours to inspect the previously hidden mechanisms of the 'laboratories power'.

CHAPTER THREE

Fantasy and Reality
The Burial Places of Fascist Leaders

Fascist leaders of the 1930s, just like their communist counterparts, considered architecture as 'politics in stone', as Mussolini put it. Hitler made grandiose plans for the transformation of Berlin that remained unrealized while *Il Duce* ('The Leader', as Mussolini styled himself in 1922) managed to cut a swathe of destruction through Rome in order to leave a lasting imprint on the city. The idea to have their own mortal remains entombed in a monumental structure was wholly in keeping with the personality cult that fascist leaders promoted with much enthusiasm. While the idea of exhibiting embalmed remains could not be countenanced as this would have meant following the communist example set by Stalin with Lenin's mausoleum, the possibility of creating a national shrine as a setting for a continuing personality cult would have been entirely in keeping with fascist notions.

Adolf Hitler was impressed by the tomb of Napoleon, which he visited after the fall of Paris in June 1940, and remarked that 'my life will not end in the mere form of death. It will, on the contrary, begin then.'[1] Hitler, whose fascination with monumental architecture is well known, might well have wished to be buried in a suitably grand mausoleum but evidence as to exactly what was planned is circumstantial and contradictory. The state archive in Munich contains a sketch drawn by Hitler himself, dated 21 June 1939, which shows a tumulus-shaped mound of vast size, but there is no proof that it was meant to be his own grave.[2] He had great plans for several German cities, sites where he had experienced personal triumphs, such as Berlin, Munich and Nuremberg.[3] Of particular importance, and increasingly so in the last years of his life, was the Austrian city of Linz, where he had spent his early youth and

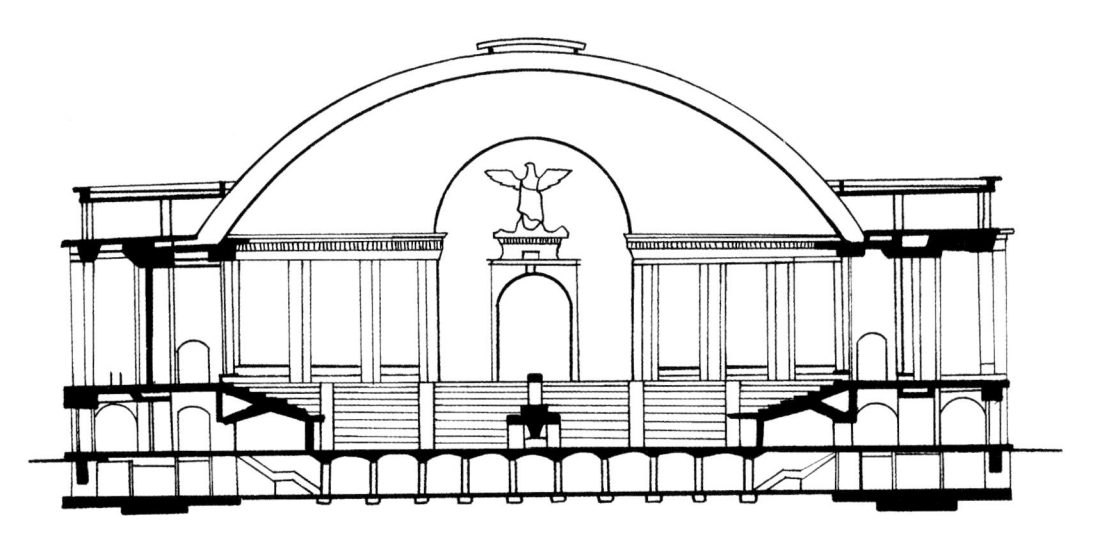

Section of Munich Party Hall and attached mausoleum.

where both his parents had died and were buried. He envisaged Linz as the future epicentre of German culture, having always felt a deep resentment against the cosmopolitan Vienna, where his efforts to be accepted as an artist had been summarily rejected. Linz was to supplant Vienna as the Austrian capital and 'its new prominence should cement the Austro-German bond so vital to the salutary growth of National Socialism'.[4] Following Albert Speer's estrangement from Hitler in 1941, the architect charged with drawing up plans and providing models for his grand schemes was Hermann Giesler (1898–1987). Giesler later wrote a memoir on his time working with and for Hitler.[5] A large portfolio has also survived, containing some 300 architectural drawings that date from 1942 to 1945.[6] The portfolio contains, amongst other proposals, plans for the massive redevelopment of the left bank of the Danube in Linz, to be known as 'Hitropolis'. Some of the drawings, dated to the very period that Hitler spent in the bunker in Berlin, depict the final stages of a scheme that had been interpreted as a possible mausoleum. There is a monumental stairway leading up to the sarcophagus and a rotunda surmounted by two spirits holding up the initials 'AH'. Speer recorded that this building was intended to house Hitler's tomb. Giesler, however, recalled an earlier instance in 1940, when Hitler had asked him to design his tomb for a site in Munich. Giesler provided a section drawing of the proposed structure, a cube surmounted by a dome, which was to be linked to a large Hall of the Party. It is certain that another Giesler design, for a 162-metre-high bell-tower (around 531 feet), situated right on the Danube shore in Linz, pertained to the proposal for the last resting place for

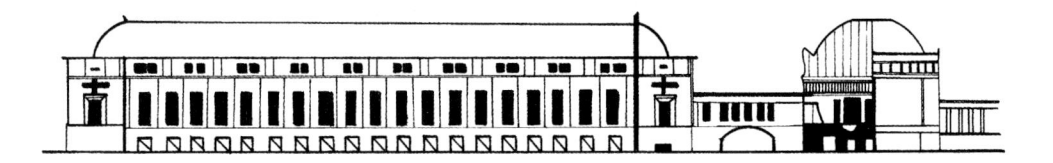

Section of Party Hall, with a possible placement for Hitler's tomb.

Hitler's parents, who as he said 'had done great things for the German nation'. It thus seems clear that Hitler was planning to incorporate a monumental mausoleum for his parents, while having only vague plans for his own memorial site. He himself had designed the headstones for the graves of his mother and father in Leonding, a suburb of Linz.

The architectural fantasies he harboured in his Berlin bunker remained just that, as the Red Army's advance on Berlin sealed the end of the Third Reich. Realizing at long last that all was lost, he gave instructions to destroy his mortal remains by burning immediately after he and his newly married wife Eva had committed suicide on 30 April 1945. Their remains were later recovered, identified and disposed of by the Soviet authorities to avoid their place of burial becoming a site of Nazi pilgrimage. In the absence of any specific memorial site, the graves of Hitler's parents in Linz had in recent years become a gathering place for right-wing extremists until the headstones were removed by order of the local government on 30 March 2012.[7]

Mussolini's Crypt in Predappio

Hitler's erstwhile ally, Benito Mussolini, still has a grave, though by no means a mausoleum. Given his ruthless urban interventions in the historical part of Rome, especially around the Campo Marzio, he might have been thinking of following the example of Augustus but there is no evidence for this at all. When his game was up, he tried to evade capture by fleeing to Switzerland but he was arrested and shot by communist partisans near Lake Como on 28 April 1945. His body, together with that of his companion Clara Petacci, and the corpses of members of his entourage, were taken to Milan and dumped. They were strung upside down on meat hooks at a petrol station as objects of ridicule and contempt, and subsequently buried in an unmarked grave at Musocco, a northern suburb of Milan. Mussolini's body was dug up by neo-fascists in 1946, kept hidden at various secret locations, and eventually recovered by the Italian authorities, who after years of indecision over what to do with his remains finally allowed them to be deposited in the crypt of the

Entrance to Mussolini's crypt at the cemetery of Predappio.

Cimiterio di S. Cassiano in Predappio, near Forlì, where his parents, brother and other relatives had already been buried.

On a rather more modest scale than that envisaged by Hitler for Linz, Predappio Nuova was his 'Mussolinopolis'. It was built from scratch in 1927 by order of Mussolini, who was born in 1883 in a small village nearby. It was to be a model town, based on a combination of rationalist, modern principles and notions of the ideal Italian city. It features a neo-Renaissance church, an over-large piazza and a straight avenue, flanked by rationalist monumental buildings, such as the Casa Littoria by Arnaldo Fuzzi, a project that exemplifies the contradictory aspects of fascist architecture. Diane Ghirardo remarked that

Sarcophagus of Mussolini with his marble bust, the miniature coffin said to contain his brain and a pressed black shirt in the vitrine.

The entire 20-year history of Fascism was marked by vacillation between an apparently adventurous modernism and a recalcitrant traditionalism. Fascism as a concept was advertised as something thoroughly new, the next and better step after the liberal democratic state. On the other hand, it claimed to sink its roots deep in Italian history, especially Roman history.[8]

The trees along the piazza and major avenues are a very dark variety of purple sycamore and look disconcertingly like substitutes for 'Blackshirts' standing to attention. While the present municipal administration does not advertise the connection with the former dictator and has banned pro-fascist displays, the town derives some profit from its association with Mussolini. Several souvenir shops along the main road specialize in fascist and Nazi memorabilia and offer a wide range of goods, from the usual plaques, flags and T-shirts to full-scale uniforms and even bottles of castor oil. They also sell their produce successfully online.[9]

The cemetery of Predappio was designed by the architect Florestano Di Fausto, best known for his works in the Italian colonies in North Africa in a neo-Byzantine-Ravennaesque (that is, from Ravenna) style.[10] The architectural focus is the terracotta mortuary chapel whose crypt was

FANTASY AND REALITY

intended to serve as a dignified burial place for Mussolini's parents. His mother, Rosa Maltoni, who had died in 1905, became a saintly fascist figure to whose memory the schoolchildren intoned a poem entitled *felix mater* (Happy Mother). His father's tomb in Forlì also attracted pilgrims and a suitable monument was needed to unite the bodies of both parents and to serve as 'a sacred site for their veneration'.[11] At present the memorials to the parents are on the ground floor and the crypt, a rather confined space, not only accommodates Benito Mussolini but several other members of his family, including his wife Rachele.

The *Duce*'s grave has been placed in a semi-circular niche behind a metal grille with the initials 'BM'. His larger than life-size marble head, placed in a fasces-framed niche above the sarcophagus gives the startling impression of Mussolini sitting up. Glass-fronted cases set into the wall on either side display a curious assortment of relics: on the left is a stone model of the sarcophagus said to contain the Duce's brain and next to it are his old black riding boots, a black cloth and a handwritten note. The case on the other side contains a neatly pressed black shirt and a rather dusty cockerel-plumed hat. A metal signature 'M' topped the display. A winged iron angel holding an electrically lit torch enhances the funereal atmosphere.

One of the side rooms next to Mussolini's crypt.

At the time of my visit there were facilities on either side for buying and lighting candles, and a box soliciting contributions for the upkeep of the crypt. A little room next door was furnished with a small altar, a kneeling pew and benches; the walls and shelves displayed framed photographs of *Il Duce* and family members, as well as plastic Madonnas and a picture of Padre Pio amidst various memorabilia of Mussolini. Faded floral tributes, such as pot plants and cut flowers, had been placed on special stands or directly on the sarcophagi. The most popular offering, and more resistant to decay, was small bunches of dried wheat, tied with *tricolore* ribbons.

The people, all Italians, who arrived while I was there in June 2010, talked in whispers and signed the visitor book, some took photographs; one man raised his arm in the 'Roman salute'. The visitor book had been renewed on 2 June (a national holiday, to commemorate the day Italy became a Republic in 1946), which seemed to prompt a number of visitors to make the journey to Predappio; most just signed, but quite a few wrote comments such as:

> *Orgogliosi di essere fascisti.*
> *Il Tuo innamorato fidele nell' idea. Non to scorderemo mai.*
> *In tuo onore a te eterno Duce d'Italia.*
> *Sempre presente!*[12]

Although the decorative scheme of stone fasces tried to imbue Mussolini's tomb with some symbolic power, the framed photographs, awkwardly placed on coffins or hung on the wall, gave it an air of an ordinary family vault. Only the once iconic huge marble head, quite out of scale given the small alcove, brooded over this close assemblage of relatives, as if mourning the demise of greatness. Mussolini's tomb is not an official site of national memory but is considered as a private funerary monument. It confines a megalomaniac ruler to the small circle of his immediate relatives, back in the remoteness of his origins. While for some of his devotees this may be a site of pilgrimage, they have little to linger over, other than to give expression to their loyalty in writing, in the perpetually renewed visitor book.

Franco and the Righteous Fallen in Santa Cruz del Valle de los Caídos

Adolf Hitler and Benito Mussolini were swept away by the tides of history; Francisco 'Franco' y Bahamonde on the other hand lived until

1975, having ruled Spain since 1936. Like Philip II, whom he much admired, Franco was obsessed with the idea of collecting bones and relics. His burial place at Santa Cruz draws on the tradition of burying Spanish monarchs in a Catholic church while assembling a pantheon of the 'righteous fallen' who had died in defence of the fatherland. Like a pharaoh, he spent decades of his reign planning and supervising the construction of this monument, saw it completed well before his own death and was therefore able to orchestrate the continuing accumulation of dead bodies in the sacred space of a basilica, supervised by specially installed Benedictine monks. The multiple functions of his monument, apart from being the final resting place of the *Generalissimo*, that of a national war memorial, an ossuary housing tens of thousands of fallen soldiers and a fully consecrated basilica, have ensured that despite much controversy and embarrassment as to the anachronism of maintaining a monument to a 'fascist dictator', it remains an important Spanish patrimonial site. Indeed, after a period of closure, it now continues to be open to visitors.

Unlike Lenin or Ho Chi Minh, Franco reigned for a long period and was in power for a total of 36 years (from 1936 to 1975). Known as *El Caudillo* ('The Leader' in analogy to *Der Führer* and *Il Duce*), he was born Francisco Paulino Hermenegildo Teódulo Franco y Bahamonde Salgado Pardo on 4 December 1892, the son of a naval postmaster in El Ferrol. Franco received a military education at the Toledo Infantry Academy and in 1913 was posted to Morocco, where Spain was engaged in securing its North African protectorate by force. By 1917 he had reached the rank of major and after a stint in Spain, suppressing labour unrest in Asturian coalfields, was sent back to Morocco in 1920 to become second in command to Lieutenant Colonel Millán Astray of the Spanish Foreign Legion (*Tercio de Extranjeros*), where he gained a reputation as a brilliant if ruthless strategist and able administrator.

In the joint French-Spanish war against the anti-colonial forces of the Berber chief Abd el-Krim he was in command of the Spanish army and in 1926, at the age of 34, he had become Europe's youngest general. He was appointed to direct the newly founded military academy at Saragossa. Spain at the time was under the dictatorial rule of Miguel Primo de Rivera, a right-wing officer who with the support of King Alfonso XIII had come to power through a military coup in 1923. His disastrous economic policies nearly ruined the country and he was forced to resign in 1930. The king abdicated and free elections were held in the following year, which were won by the Socialist Party. Franco, who had made no secret of his right-wing and monarchist views, was demoted and sent to the Balearic Islands. However, when a series of strikes broke out in the coalfields in 1934, the government ordered him to suppress the unrest and he was appointed chief of staff by the minister of war. In the national elections of 1936 the coalition of various left-wing parties, known as the 'Popular Front', was opposed by the right-wing National Front, which included the *Falange Española*. The Popular Front advocated the restoration of Catalan autonomy, amnesty for political prisoners, agrarian reform, an end to political blacklists and the payment of damages for property owners who had suffered during the revolt of 1934. After the tightly fought election on 16 February 1936, the Popular Front, having won by 34.4 per cent, formed a government and set about to implement its political programme. They also granted autonomy to Catalonia and made the *Falange Española* illegal.

The turbulent events of 1936, caused by changes in the government and increasing panic among conservatives, led to a series of rebellions that Franco, together with other officers joined. By November of that year he had become leader of the Nationalist Army. When Falangist leader José Primo de Rivera, the son of the erstwhile dictator, was taken prisoner and shot in November 1936 and General Mola died in a plane crash, Franco was left in control of the Nationalist cause. His army made rapid progress in several parts of Spain while the centre remained in the control of the Republicans. At great material cost he had secured military help from Hitler and Mussolini.

> He derived invaluable assistance from the Axis powers and clearly enjoyed being projected as a fascist leader on a level with Hitler and Mussolini. However, Franco was never inhibited by gratitude. Moreover, just as a young man, he had adopted totally the persona of the courageous hero of the Legion, now he believed himself to be the warrior hero restoring Spain's greatness.[13]

The provision of German air power was particularly crucial to the Nationalists' advance throughout 1937 and this success prompted Franco to consolidate his hold on power by ideological means too. To this end, he borrowed freely from the doctrines of National Socialism and Italian Fascism. The Nationalists made much use of the *Reconquista* of Spain from the Moors in order to reinforce the notion that Franco was the heroic leader of a 'Crusade' to liberate Spain from the godless hordes of Moscow. He himself explained to a French journalist in 1937 that

> Our war is not a civil war [. . .] but a Crusade [. . .] Yes, our war is a religious war. We who fight, whether Christians or Muslims, are soldiers of God and we are not fighting against men but against atheism and materialism.[14]

Further strikes against Republican forces in Catalonia, secured here with the help of 6,000 troops as well as aircraft sent by Mussolini in 1938, in addition to France's decision to close the Pyrenees passes, all but sealed the fate of the Republicans, who were now concentrated around Madrid. When Madrid was taken on 31 March 1939, Franco could claim that 'Today, with the Red Army captive and disarmed, our victorious troops have achieved their final military objectives. The war is over.'[15]

Although the Civil War was over, at a cost of more than half a million dead, purges and labour camps for former Republican fighters persisted. Throughout Spain, while the battles of the Civil War were still being fought, Franco had embarked on building numerous memorials, altars and monuments, formed 'in a new aesthetic, which expressed itself in crosses, monoliths and huge monuments, that acquired the connotations as altars dedicated to "divinities" of a new creation.'[16]

Franco propagated the cult of dead martyrs, who, like their medieval predecessors, had given their life to Catholic Spain. Yet they had died fighting not the 'infidels' of yore but the 'red menace' of communism. Fernando Olmeda speaks of 'a whiff of necrophilia' that surrounded the dictatorship of Franco. The Falangist battle cry, after all, had been *¡viva la muerte!* ('long live death!'). During the whole of the Civil War, thousands of people on both sides died and were often buried in mass graves. Lavish funerals for the 'heroes' of the Civil War combined religious devotion and martial fervour as the bedrock of the Spanish Right. The reburial of Falangist leader José Antonio Primo de Rivera is a prime example of 'the integration of the cult of the Fallen into the mythology of National Catholicism'.[17] On 20 November 1939 Primo de Rivera's body, which following his execution by Republican forces in 1936 had been buried in Alicante, was exhumed and his coffin borne on the shoulders of supporters for reburial at El Escorial. Primo de Rivera, 'martyr in the crusade against Marxism', was thereby imbued with a status akin to that of the great Spanish monarchs of the past. Generally, the often brutally enforced separation between 'good Spaniards' (those on the Right) from 'bad' republicans or communists, also affected their mortal remains. Bodies of 'red' or otherwise unworthy 'fallen' were denied honorary reburial.

General José Millán Astray, founder of the Spanish Legion, describes in his memoir on Franco that the latter had shown a keen interested in architecture during his service in Spanish Morocco. Moreover, he had designed various buildings for the Legion. Franco's obsession with architecture was a trait shared with Adolf Hitler, whom Franco admired.[18] Franco was shown models and drawings of Hitler's grandiose projects for Berlin on the occasion of an exhibition on Modern German Architecture in Madrid. This seemed to have triggered a resolution not only to follow Hitler, who had identified himself with Bismarck, but to himself to become a modern day Philip II.[19]

Franco began to conceive of the idea to gather all 'good dead' within a grand, national pantheon to the fallen. On the occasion of the victory parade held to celebrate the first anniversary of his triumph over the Republic in 1940, he proclaimed his wish to build a monument of a scale

> that must have the grandeur of the monuments of old, which defy time and forgetfulness, one that reflects [. . .] the dimension of our Crusade, the heroic sacrifices involved in the victory and the far-reaching significance which this epic has had for the future of Spain.[20]

This new sacred site was close to the traditional symbolic centre, the palace of of El Escorial built by Philip II, but it was to herald the beginning of a new era in Spain's history. Like El Escorial, it was to look towards the capital; like El Escorial, it was to house a monastic order; like El Escorial, it was to include a basilica, and like El Escorial, it was to house the bodies of dead heroes and leaders. In 1940 Franco commissioned José Moscardó Ituarte to search for the exact spot for his Valley of the Fallen.

He chose the site dominated by a freestanding rocky outcrop, the Risco de la Nava, which seemed suitably majestic to Franco, with splendid views over pine-clad mountain ranges. Furthermore, the chosen place was close to the site of a bloody battle fought at Alto de León, one of the first Nationalist victories in the Civil War, and the source of the first consignment of 'righteous' bodies. A ministerial decree issued soon after the official announcement of the project on 1 April

View of the cross at Guadarrama.

1940 concerned the identification of mass graves, especially in Republican zones, for future exhumation and reburial in the 'Pantheon of the Fallen'. This was the first reference that the future mausoleum was to be destined for the dead of the victorious faction.[21]

Franco always stressed that the general concept for the VDC was his own idea. It was he who had thought of placing the fallen in a crypt underneath the Risco rock. The various architects involved, beginning with Pedro Muguruza Otaño until 1949, followed by Diego Mendez, were merely to implement his suggestions.[22] Failing to appreciate the complexities of such an undertaking, he predicted optimistically that the work would be finished in just a year. It took nearly twenty years to complete.

When work began in the early 1940s, the country had been devastated by three years of civil war and the economy was in ruins. There were severe shortages of food and clothing, fuel and building materials. Denouncing the idea of free trade as evil, the regime decided on a policy of self-reliance on its own raw materials and food and of an expansion of exports. Franco held on to the possibility of joining the war on the side of the Axis powers, whose policies and ideologies he supported, and hence sent considerable resources to Germany. Furthermore, Franco's obsession with fighting the 'red menace' of liberal democracy and communism within his own country made the peaceful integration of republicans problematic. Franco decreed that the 'crime' of having resisted should be 'redeemed by work'. Some 20,000 people were employed in the construction of the VDC, a labour force primarily constituted from prisoners convicted for operating on the Republican side in the Civil War or for resisting the new regime. They were temporarily accommodated in the nearby village of Cuelgamuros.

Construction cost the equivalent of £200,000,000, which was a colossal sum to be spent on a single building at a time when the country's population was experiencing severe hardship.

Franco appointed the architect Pedro Muguruza to supply initial plans and oversee the construction.[23] Muguruza was head of technical services in the Falange and in 1939 Franco put him in charge of the General Directorate of Architecture, one of the key positions in the reconstruction of Spain. Muruguza suggested a cruciform crypt large enough for 3,000 worshippers, although he made no specific mention of where to put the human remains. A 120-metre-high (around 393 feet) granite cross was to be placed at the summit of the Risca. He had also planned a monastery and barracks to house guards, a large cruciform lake in the axis of crypt, a cemetery, a pilgrim's way and chapels for the Stations of the Cross. At this stage it was regarded as a military as well as a religious building. As far as the architectural style was concerned, the Falange insisted that the new monument should respect Spanish tradition, best expressed in the architectural style of Juan de Herrera and Juan de Villanueva, the architects of Philip II and Charles IV, who had created El Escorial.

Franco demanded that the crypt, the surrounding walls and all other buildings and gardens should be finished within a year and by 1 April 1941. Excavating the hard granite rock under the Risco, carried out with pickaxes and shovels, proved arduous and dangerous; accidents and casualties caused by falling stones were frequent. Progress was therefore very slow and by the official deadline of 1 April only a small part had been cleared. The malnourished workers eventually received higher food rations, but this hardly accelerated the work, partly because of the considerable technical difficulties of working underground and also because Franco kept altering his mind and demanding changes, which meant that the work dragged on. When he visited the nearly finished excavation in 1954, he was disappointed with the tunnel-like

Longitudinal section of the Risco de la Nava at the Valley of the Fallen.

interior as it did not meet his expectations of a 'cosmic cave'. At this stage Diego Méndez was the architect in charge and he added wider side aisles to the main body of the crypt and also raised the height. The tube-like space was to be divided into four distinct zones: the portico, the atrium, an intermediate space and the main nave. The new crypt attained much grander proportions, with the height of the dome being only surpassed by that of St Peter's basilica in the Vatican.[24] He also found a solution as to where the remains of the fallen should be placed. This was to be at a lower level, with the side arms of the transept terminating in chapels on either side, from which stairwells gave access to the ossuaries.[25]

The crypt of the VDC was finally completed on 31 August 1956, sixteen years after the work had started. It had been a colossal undertaking to excavate a space that was 262 metres long (around 859 feet) and up to 40 metres (approximately 131 feet) high from the hard granite.

The official inauguration of the monument took place three years later on 1 April 1969, coinciding with the twentieth anniversary of the end of the Civil War. Franco and his wife Carmen, seated on special thrones under a canopy near the high altar, watched the solemnities performed by two cardinals, assisted by bishops and archbishops. The press reported the event as the culmination of Franco's victory in 1939, and Franco himself referred to this theme in his inauguration speech, as described by his biographer Paul Preston:

> His speech, about the heroism of 'our fallen' in defence of 'our lives', was triumphant and vengeful. He gloated over the enemy that had been obliged 'to bite the dust of defeat' and showed not the slightest trace of desire to see reconciliation between Spaniards. The controlled press described the inauguration as the culmination of his victory in 1938.[26]

In subsequent years, Franco continued to make full use of the propagandistic potential of the VDC as a stage for mass rallies and commemorative celebrations, especially on the anniversary of the end of the Civil War. In the 1960s, when internal fissions and political struggles began within the ruling party, such celebrations provided an opportunity to ingratiate politicians with Franco. This was the case in 1961, for example, when a massive fascist rally was organized to bring together extreme rightists from across Europe, especially Italy and Germany, to pay tribute for the only surviving right-wing regime. The 25th anniversary of the end of the Civil War in 1964 was another grand occasion to celebrate Franco's victory.

Franco was coy about his wish to be buried in the crypt of the Basilica.[27] The architect Diego Méndez recorded that on the day of the basilica's inauguration Franco indicated a spot by the altar, saying, '*Bueno, Méndez, y en su día yo aquí, ¿eh?*'[28] Other architects involved in the project, such as Ramón Andrada and Antonio Orejas, were also convinced that a vault for Franco had been planned from the very start, at a prominent place near the altar. However, since he had never made any official pronouncements and left no stipulation in his will, when Franco died on 20 November 1975, after a short stay in a Madrid hospital, nobody knew where he should be buried. It was the newly crowned king, Juan Carlos, who sent a telegram authorizing Franco's burial at the VDC on 22 November 1975. Franco's funeral was the last of the great state occasions at the VDC. It was at this point that he finally joined the ranks of the righteous fallen, despite having died in his pyjamas, as some Falangists sourly remarked. The funeral was an occasion of great public mourning and huge crowds went to pay their respects at his grave.

When looking for the possible origins of Franco's tenacious hold on power, Michael Richards suggested that Primo de Rivera's dictatorship in the 1920s 'had opened the way to an excessively radical, even sectarian republic, which in turn led to a conservative reaction.'[29] After the uprising of July 1936, the regime went far beyond what the Right fighting against the republic had intended and Franco was hence a consequence, if not the very cause, of this.

The transition to a revived democracy was not without its difficulties and there remains resistance against the reassessment of Franco's impact on Spain. Valle de los Caídos could be seen as metonymic for the contentious legacy of Francoism. Richards identified its inherent contradictions:

> The popular perception was that the Valle sanctified Franco's victory rather than the sacrifice of thousands of lives. Only reluctantly, and somewhat in contradiction with the triumphalist rhetoric, were Republican dead permitted a resting place there, although very many families, on both sides, were resistant [. . .] But the socially integrating potential was limited because the 'triumph of the Cross' was always, in some part, an obviously ideological proposition in Franco's Spain.[30]

I set out to see this monument with a friend, on a Sunday in April 2010, having consulted the website for the opening hours. On the journey from Madrid, along a busy motorway that skirts the extensive suburbs of the city, the huge granite cross of the VDC was visible on the horizon long before the exit for Guadarrama. In the midst of densely wooded landscape, it hovered incongruously above the hillside, just a massive cross without any architectural context.

When we arrived, access was denied and a steady stream of cars was turned away with the explanation that only 'services' were to be admitted. In 2009 the Socialist government under José Luis Rodríguez Zapatero had decided that the monument should be closed to the public to allow maintenance to be carried out. However, the exact terms of the closure were not spelt out clearly. This decision was preceded by a lively debate in the media and on blogs about whether a monument so closely tied to the memory of the Franco era should be maintained in its present state, demolished or transformed. Determined not to waste the journey, my companion and I climbed over the wall of the adjacent municipal cemetery, and under the cover of the woodland we followed the main road, some seven kilometres long, which leads from the entrance gates to the main site.

The long approach road that led through beautifully kept woodland did not reveal a glimpse of the monument except from the viaduct that spans a small river. When we arrived after a two-hour walk, we found the basilica forecourt deserted and the entrance door cordoned off by security gates. There was no indication of any work being carried out at the time; no building materials or scaffolding were in sight. Normally, the VDC would have attracted many visitors as a place to spend sunny days in the beautiful setting of pine forests.

As we had just visited the sombre but grand abbey of El Escorial, we found the frontal approach to Franco's monument devoid of architectural interest and formulaic in its attempt to echo the monumentality of sixteenth-century Spain. It relies on the woodland setting for effect and consists at first sight of a huge, pyramid-shaped rock, which has a giant concrete cross stuck into it. The whole thing looks like an enormous candlestick.

While this rock with its rough lumps of stone forms the centrepiece of the monument, the artificiality of the setting is enhanced by a series of wide platforms, capacious enough to accommodate thousands of people, which lead towards a semi-circular colonnade. This forms a stony embrace of stiff, cold grey granite, with the vaulted corridors imitating the sparse classical lines of sixteenth-century architectural forms with a mechanical precision. A single doorway in a central arched recess forms the only entrance, set below a monumental sculpture of a Pietà. The figure of heavily veiled mother, bent double in grief over Christ's prostrate body, represents the prototype of all mothers mourning their sacrificed sons and this image sets the tone for grieving remembrance that the whole edifice tries to stimulate.

The monumental cross that rises from the summit of the rock was completely out of proportion to the ensemble of terraces and the colonnade. It serves as a focal point to signal the presence of the monument to the wider landscape below. At the foot of this 150-metre-(just over 492 feet) high stone cross, like ossified giants, are monumental sculptures that are figures of the four evangelists and their symbols. They are by the sculptor Juan de Ávalos who was responsible for the Pietà. Above them, immediately at the base of the shaft of the cross, are four emblematic muscle-bound male figures, representing the virtues of fortitude, temperance, prudence and justice, in their vigorous masculinity. This is a triumphant, masculine counterpoint to the Pietà below them.

Seen from this side, the basilica itself has no architectural presence. The main purpose of the wide terraces is to serve as a gathering place for

The stone terrace overlooking the valley at Guadarrama.

The main entrance to the basilica.

state occasions played out against the rock behind and the open landscape beneath. At the rear of the rock are the buildings that house the Benedictines, the choristers, the research institute and administration offices, which are grouped around a large quadrangle, forming a cloister-like enclosure, suitable for religious processions and assemblies. Here the ordered rectangular courtyards of El Escorial appear exactly like an architectural quotation. On the day we visited it was completely deserted.

The Socialist government under Zapatero drew up plans to diffuse the divisive connotation of Valle de los Caídos by changing it from a site for 'a glorification of the right-wing martyrs against communism' into one setting out the 'meaning of the [Franco] dictatorship and its horrors'. Reports of structural damage to some of the statues on the exterior were used to justify the closure on the grounds of health and safety while some repair works were carried out. The closure of the VDC has led to various protests by righ-wing groups and some members of the clergy.

The basilica was reopened in 2011, perhaps partly to appease critics of the government, which had seen its popularity plummet in the wake of the country's grave economic difficulties. To date, no decision has been made on the future of the monument. Suggestions have included the removal of the huge cross at the top of the Risco, the relocation of Franco's own tomb and even the closure of the whole site. It remains one of the largest ossuaries in Spain and relatives see the site as much as their private memorial place as a national monument. It has also been proposed that it should continue to function as a national war memorial but be made truly inclusive by the addition of substantially more remains from grave sites, especially those with large numbers of republican casualties.

Detail of the stone facade of the basilica, with crucifix.

A commission of experts composed of all the different parties and interest groups (including the Catholic Church of Spain), ordered by the Zapatero government in May 2011 to provide new proposals for the future use of the VDC, suggested the reinterpretation of the memorial and the reburial of Franco's remains.[31] Three out of twelve committee members voted against this and cited the argument that it would be better to leave things as they are rather than stir up old conflicts.

It remains to be seen whether the newly elected Conservative government, given the dire economic situation in the country, will risk upsetting the traditionalists among the electorate. So far the possibility seems remote and the Valley of the Fallen is open to visitors once more. Whether such an over-determined space – the huge hollowed out church with its ossuaries and Franco-era iconography, the oversized cross on the rock above and the series of stone terraces could ever lend itself to reinterpretations is debatable. Even if the bodies of Primo de Rivera and Franco were to be removed, and the bones of communists brought to join those of their erstwhile enemies, would it not persist in being a monumental relic of dictatorial aspirations to complete control and a work of hubris?

In his analysis of the particular features of Francoism, Ismael Saz argued that

> the distinctive feature of the Francoist dictatorship was precisely that it was a nationalist dictatorship. This was in the double sense that the concept had at that time in Europe, that is, both antidemocratic and essentialist. It is correct to say this about Spanish nationalism, national-catholicism, and that we notice the high degree of fascistization of the connected ideology which comes along with it.[32]

The tendency of such a system to conflate the nation, the Catholic Church and historic periods with the personality of the autocratic ruler produced such complicated symbolic tangles that it will take a long time to unravel.

The other Iberian dictatorship, that of António de Oliveira Salazar, whose control of Portugal lasted from 1932 to 1968, was more concerned with colonialism and his 'reign' did not lead to a ferocious civil war. He had no wish for a monumental burial and preferred a simple grave in the cemetery of his native village, Vimieiro. This was a gesture of humility and self-effacement that suited his carefully cultivated image as a man of the people. Franco and Salazar perhaps lived too long and endured too long in power to sustain the momentum of their personality cult and thus Franco may be deemed lucky to have been dispatched by Juan Carlos into his pantheon of the fallen, from which he may be moved one day in order to become, like Salazar in death, a private person.

CHAPTER FOUR

New Nations, New Monuments
Mausolea for Fathers of the Nation

Tertium decimum consulatum cum gerebam, senatus et equester ordo populusque Romanus universus appellavit me patrem patriae idque in vestibulo aedium mearum inscribendum esse atque in curia et in foro Augusto sub quadrigis, quae mihi ex s. c. positae sunt, decrevit.[1]

In these words the Roman Emperor Augustus explains how he was officially proclaimed to become *pater patriae*, 'Father of the Fatherland'. It happened when he was 60, in the year 2 BC. With his famously astute sense for 'spin', he had capitalized on his adoption by Julius Caesar, who had traced his descent to the mythical founder of Rome, Aeneas. Augustus commissioned Virgil to write the great epic of the Trojan hero, who embodied all the great Roman virtues, such as selflessness, honour and loyalty. He also had himself portrayed on coinage as a 'second Numa', the famously pious second king of Rome.[2] Furthermore, in his *Fasti* Ovid highlights the equation between Jupiter and the emperor:

> Sacred Father of the Country, this title has been conferred
>   on you,
> by the senate, the people, and by us, the knights.
> Events had already granted it. Tardily you received
> Your true title, you'd long been Father of the World.
> You have on earth the name that Jupiter owns to
> In high heaven: you are father of men, he of gods.[3]

While in the Republican era the title *pater patriae* had been granted in recognition for saving the city of Rome from great peril, it now cast the all powerful emperor as father of the Roman family and state, and importantly, as one initiating a new beginning. Augustus was a new founder of Rome, a second Aeneas and Nema, ushering in a new Golden Age.[4] The propagandistic value of the title diminished once it was routinely offered to Roman emperors, and some even rejected it.

The notion of the revered Founding Father gained currency again with the emergence of nation states and especially in the context of independence from colonial rule. A new narrative emerged, that of a revolutionary hero leading the struggle for freedom and independence, who having triumphed against all obstacles, declares the birth of a new state, becomes its first president and whose name is forever linked with the very idea of the nation. George Washington, the first president of the United States (from 1789 to 1797), is one of the first examples. He has become a 'secular saint':

> His name is everywhere. His face adorns the dollar bill and the 25 cents coin. Across the modern U.S., 26 mountains are named after him, as well as 740 schools, a dozen colleges and universities, 155 towns and counties, various bridges, parks and forts; not to mention an entire state of the union and the very capital of the country he did so much to found.[5]

Harris Memel-Fotê, the late Ivorian anthropologist, identified the salient ingredients that make up the myth of the Founding Father. Although with particular reference to post-colonial Africa, these 'ingredients' are equally valid in other contexts.[6] By examining biographies and hagiographies of founding 'fathers', he noticed the traits they shared. All were born in the colonial era and the facts of their birth, their personal characteristics and other circumstances of their early lives were recounted from a teleological perspective as portents of things to come. Then followed the second phase, that of initiation into urban practices, often in the form of involvement in labour activism, which would lead to revolutionary engagement. A new name pointed to the heroic third stage, which often began with the creation of a political party (and might include a spell as political prisoner), followed by the taking of arms and the joining of the resistance. The fourth moment was the accumulation of superior tactical skills that conferred a reputation for great wisdom. The fifth and final stage was the official saizure of independence in which the 'Promethean hero as liberator becomes the consecrated father figure'. The subsequent trajectory entailed attempts at consolidating the acquired power by various means, not least through a cult of personality, a single party system and the elevation of the leader's ideological thought to canonical status. We can see how the careers of the leaders so far discussed fitted some of the stages of Memel-Fotê's scheme, but it works better for those engaged in colonial emancipation and the founding of new nations. The familiar narratives of the Founding Fathers' lives underpin the symbolic content of monuments built in their honour and of course, their tombs.

Sun Yat-sen's Mausoleum (*Lingmu*) on Purple Mountain

When Augustus became the first Roman Emperor he did not create a new nation, as such a concept did not yet exist, but he forged a new political identity, a new way of being Roman, and by claiming descent from the mythical founders he stressed the rebirth of Rome and the renewal of old but vital values. Russian revolutionaries also sought to revitalize a state made weak by a corrupt monarchy, though Lenin relied on Marx and Engels, who in communist iconography were to become ancestral figures too.

For the Chinese revolutionary Sun Yat-sen, born in 1886, sixteen years after Vladimir Ilych Ulyanov, Lenin was a role model. Yet Sun Yat-sen had also studied Confucian scholars. Illness and the intractable situation in China in the 1920s prevented him from being publicly recognized as a national leader for but the briefest time. When he died, some fifteen months after Lenin in 1925, it was hoped that he too would be kept 'forever' in a crystal coffin, housed in a suitable mausoleum that would attract innumerable pilgrims and strengthen the cause of the revolution. Even more than Lenin, his subsequent reputation was that of one who 'lighted the way', a torchbearer for the future. The twist in the tale is that Sun Yat-sen is the Founding Father of Taiwan as well the Republic of China, and that he is claimed as having prepared the way both for Chiang Kai-shek's right-wing Republic of China and the communist People's Republic.[7]

In late nineteenth-century China the Manchu rulers of the Qing Dynasty were seen to be just as weak and corrupt as the Romanovs in Russia. They had ceded Hong Kong in 1842 and thereafter allowed other major ports on the east coast to be opened for international trade through a system of treaties. The widely perceived failure of the imperial government to fulfill the Confucian obligation to provide a stable administration and to ensure justice triggered a series of revolts. Chinese nationalists were fuelled by both hatred for the Manchu regime and resentment of Western imperialism. Rebellions, as well as brutal suppression by local government militias, brought devastation and famine to many parts of China. An eyewitness account from 1913 summarizes the situation that led to revolution of 1911, also emphasizing the influence of education:

> In tracing the remote causes [of the revolution] I must say that the general awakening of the conservative Chinese began in the year of 1894 when China was defeated in the Chino-Japanese War. The second period of awakening began in 1900 when the allied troops besieged the capital of the empire. Since then, the tide of new learning has rushed in with full speed until the minds of the scholars have been saturated with the translations from works of Montesquieu and of Rousseau, their brains have been permeated with the accounts of the lives of Peter the Great and of George Washington. It is the education that pushes people ahead. Corruption of the government, however, was not a small contributing factor of this gigantic revolt. Everywhere the people realized the weakness and pessimism of the government, which could never be trusted and would never raise the nation's prestige. Favouritism and bribery were almighty. The sluggish, selfish and oppressive nature of the Manchu government had led us to overthrow it entirely, after gentle appeals were unsuccessfully and ineffectually resorted to.[8]

Sun Wen was of the generation that had grown up in the moribund old China ruled by the Qing Dynasty.[9] He was born on 12 November 1866 into a family of farmers and fishermen in a coastal village not far from Macao. His elder brother Sun Mei had left China for a better life abroad and once settled in Hawaii called for the younger sibling to join him. Sun left in 1878, attended local missionary schools and quickly earned English. When he returned to China after four years, he could no longer stand village life and at seventeen left for Hong Kong to further his education. He converted to Christianity and enrolled at the Canton Medical College, while also learning classical Chinese, earning a 'Licentiate in Medicine and Surgery', which in theory allowed him to work as a physician, using both Western and traditional Chinese methods. In practice his attempts to make a living from his profession in the Westernized coastal cities failed because the Chinese degree was not recognized. Even so he was known as 'Dr Sun Yat-sen' for the rest of his life.

By 1892 he turned his attention to the political state of China. He gravitated first towards the reform movement advocated by the traditional elite but he felt more at home in grassroots revolutionary societies. He began his life as a professional revolutionary by travelling to Hawaii and to raise funds. This was an activity that was to take up much of his time in the coming years, especially after he was banished from Hong Kong for his efforts to organize revolts against the Manchu government in 1895. He gained much publicity when Manchu agents kidnapped him in London, from where the Foreign Office procured his release in 1896. He stayed in London for a year, reading the works of Karl Marx in the British Museum and cultivating contacts with Chinese expatriates. The early 1900s were spent in Japan, where he mingled with the exiled students who had left China after the failed Boxer Uprising and formed new revolutionary organizations. It was there, during his ten-year long Japanese sojourn that he formulated his own doctrine, known as 'Three Principles' ('Nationalism, Democracy and People's Livelihood'). He attracted a strong following among the Chinese expatriates but the Japanese authorities forced him to leave the country, whereupon he resumed his restless wandering around the world, drumming up support and raising money within Chinese communities.

He had been in the United States while the revolution in China gained momentum, leading to the successful uprising in the Yangtze Valley. Dr Sun's name was put forward by revolutionary delegates from fourteen provinces at a meeting in Nanjing, and on 29 December 1911 he was elected provisional president. In this capacity he proclaimed the founding of the Republic of China on 1 January 1912. Since he lacked any previous experience in government, he passed the responsibility of being in charge to Yuan Shih-k'ai, an aristocratic army commander based in northern China and whose support for the Revolution was deemed crucial. Once handed the presidency, he managed to force the Manchu emperor to abdicate, thus ending 270 years of the Qing Dynasty and 2,100 years of the imperial system. However, the new republic relied on the existing bureaucratic apparatus and the old culture, society and economy hardly changed. Dr Sun spent his time devising ambitious plans for a grand, national railway network.

By 1914, through the founding of a new party, the Chinese People's Party (*Chung-hu Kae-ming Tang* or *Kuomintang*, abbreviated as KMT), Sun formalized the functions of undisputed leadership. All party members had to swear a personal oath of obedience and discipline and to pledge themselves to an ideology inspired by scientific developmental principles. On the other hand, Sun understood 'his strategy of revolutionary leadership to be licensed by the ancients and informed by science. Both counseled disciplined obedience to special competence'.[10]

Instrumental in founding the new party, which merged various parliamentary parties, was Sun's ally, Sung Chiao-jen (Song Jiaoren), who also organized the first elections in 1912–13, which brought the new party a parliamentary majority. When Chiao-jen was assassinated soon after, suspicion fell on president Yuan. He not only rejected Sun's demands for justice, but turned the tables by having Sun removed from office, even sending a warrant for his arrest, which forced Sun once more into exile. Yuan also suppressed the Kuomintang. The bitter power struggle led to the second uprising, which proved disastrous for the revolutionary side. Meanwhile, Yuan set up his own power base, and Sun had to watch from Japan as Yuan, having betrayed the Revolution, declared himself emperor and assumed autocratic leadership, from which he was finally ousted in 1916.

During the following decade China disintegrated into mutually hostile provinces, with frequent clashes between warlords and their militias, and generally disastrous effects on civilian life, especially in the countryside.

In Japan, Sun created a new secret society and married his English teacher, Rosamonde. He returned to China in 1916, settling with his wife in Shanghai, lecturing and writing his treatise *The Principals of National Reconstruction*. In 1917 he tried to establish a rival government at Canton, but was soon forced out of office and exiled to Shanghai. Upon the dissolution of parliament on 13 June 1917, Sun became leading champion of constitutional republicanism against attempts to reinstate Manchu rule. In 1918 the Constitution Protection Movement in Canton elected him to the post of Grand Martial of the Military Government, which existed only on paper, and was another role for which he had no training or qualifications. He managed to raise troops to fight in Fukien and revived the KMT on the eighth anniversary of the 1911 Revolution on 10 October 1919. Now, however, it was called the 'Chinese KMT'. The party was to develop a highly elaborate, idealistic ideology based on Sun's Three Principles, and its own military wing. It derived considerable support from the so-called May 4th Movement, which had organized violent protests against the intended redistribution of former German areas of influence in China among the Allies, as set out in the Treaty of

Versailles. It was not the only political movement at the time and the Chinese Communist Party, which had been formed in 1921 with Russian help, also tried to widen their popular support. Sun managed to persuade the communists, who were still few in number, to set up an alliance with the Kuomintang in 1921 and to form the United Front. Sun reorganized his new party along Leninist lines, which gave him a central role, and for the first time in his life he was able to command an efficient political machinery, developing what became known as 'Sunism'. He believed that a period of political tutelage was needed to guide the masses towards the transition to democracy, and that the party should control the state until conditions were right.

He spent the next two years in semi-retirement in Shanghai, writing *Memoirs of a Chinese Revolutionary* and *The International Development of China* (about the railway scheme) and reorganizing the Kuomintang. When the Kwantung army, with Sun's political support, managed to regain Canton, Sun resumed control of the military government and organized a further military expedition. In the summer of 1921 Kwangtung troops invaded Kwangsi (Guangxi). Sun planned a northern military campaign from Kwangsi but his forces suffered defeat and Sun had to escape to Hong Kong. The following year he was back in Shanghai trying to organize the recapture of Shanghai. Looking for more substantial assistance, he finally accepted direct Russian help. Comintern agent Mikhail Borodin arrived to lend the southern revolutionary forces Russian Communist support and to reorganize the Kuomintang along more radical and Bolshevist lines. This was a development that alarmed the propertied Cantonese, who resisted violently. On 23 October 1924 the republican general Feng Yü-hsiang overthrew the warlord Wu P'ei-fu in Peking, which offered the chance to reorganize the Peking government. Sun, at the time near the northern border of Kwangtung, about to launch another campaign, rushed to Peking in an effort to unite the country.

Sun arrived in Peking on 31 December 1924, feeling very weak and ill. A diagnostic operation at the Peking Union Medical College detected highly advanced liver cancer. Sun moved to a private house in Peking. When he became aware that his days were numbered, he wrote his political testament, urging his comrades to follow his Three Principles and to abolish the unequal treaties. This became know as 'The Declaration of Independence of Revolutionary China'. He also signed a private will and a third document, addressed to the Central Executive Committee of the USSR, drafted in English by Eugene Chen, appealing to Stalin for continued help in the struggle for liberation.

Borodin had come to see him just a few hours before his death. He later recalled that Sun had kept saying, 'if only Russia would help', and that he had asked him if he wanted to be buried like 'his friend Lenin'.[11] Sun died on the following day, 12 March 1925, uttering the words 'peace, struggle, and save China'.[12]

As soon as Dr Sun was pronounced dead, the struggle for his remains began, which was to last until 1929. Sun's family resisted Russian proposals for a Lenin-like burial and arranged for a private, Christian funeral service to be held in the chapel of the Medical College on the 19 March. Tuan Ch'i-jui, acting as provisional president of China, had wanted to arrange a state funeral in a manner befitting a nationalist revolutionary. Since the Russians also wished to show their role as partners in the fight for China's independence, a second ceremony was held, transporting Sun's body to Peking's Central Park. Russian's ambassador, Lev Mikhailovich Kharakan, officiated as chief mourner. Sun's corpse could now be shown to the grieving public. Like most 'Founding Fathers', he proved to be particularly popular after his demise and large crowds came to pay their respects. For three weeks his body lay in state in a coffin of Chinese design at the Shejitan, the Altar to Earth and Grain, a site for the celebration of imperial rule during the Ming and Qing dynasties. Sun was not dressed in his trademark *zhongshan* suit with the high collar but a Western suit and draped with the Kuomintang flag. The KMT party leaders were quick to make use of the occasion for political propaganda by placing boards inscribed with quotations from Sun's works on the gates, while an inscription next to his photograph read 'The revolution is not yet achieved: our comrades still need to strive.' After the three weeks were over, the embalmed body was taken to the Buddhist Azure Cloud Temple in the Western Hills monastery, where it immediately became subject to an institutionalized KMT cult:

> Different from the traditional *ji* rite, which allowed individuals to provide offerings to either the body or the spirit of the dead, the *gongji* services redesigned by the KMT created an occasion for the masses attending the rites to receive tutelage from the dead. [. . .] Parks were equipped with phonographs playing Sun's speeches and movie projectors showing documentary footage of his activities. The image of Sun acquired great significance for this feature of the *gongji* service: on the one hand, his frontal photographic portrait, along with is coffin, was the focus and the recipient of the service; on the

other, it represented the teacher himself, who maintained eye contact with the visitors.[13]

The grave in the Western Hills was never intended as Sun's final resting place. His untimely death had made him into a highly important symbolic figure as the Founding Father of a new China and the Kuomintang were determined to make full use of the possibility to present themselves as the only party dedicated to fulfill Sun's vision. Therefore, a much grander setting for the Sun cult was needed. Russia had honoured Lenin by placing his embalmed remains in a mausoleum situated in the new capital and the question arose about what kind of monument would be most suitable for China's first president. Although Soon Ching Ling, Sun's widow, vetoed his wish to be preserved like Lenin, and had insisted on the Christian funeral, she acquiesced in demands made by the Kuomintang to fulfil Sun's other wish, that of being buried on Purple Mountain in Nanjing. Sun had on occasion compared himself to the first Ming emperor, Zhu Yuanzhang, who had overthrown the Manchu Yuan dynasty, just as he himself had helped to oust the Manchu Qing. Zhu Yuanzhang had built himself a splendid funerary complex there. Furthermore, echoing the choice of the Ming emperor, Sun had chosen Nanjing as the capital of the new state, in his case the Republic of China. During his brief presidency in 1912 he had even staged a ceremonial procession to this ancient tomb, informing the spirit of the emperor that 'the alien Manchu tartar had been removed'.[14] The site was clearly important for him. As a Chinese scholar remarked,

> His decision to be buried at Nanjing was an attempt to make a spatial link between himself as a representative of popular sovereignty and Nanjing as the home of the true popular government.[15]

For the Kuomintang, a mausoleum for Sun Yat-sen on Purple Mountain was an ideal site for providing political guidance. They set up a Preparatory Committee for the Funeral of Sun Yat-sen (PCFS) to coordinate the different aspects of the project. During the second meeting of the PCFS on 23 April 1925 they declared that Sun's tomb was to be located to the east of the Ming emperor's tomb, but at a higher level and in the woodland, thus satisfying the principles of *feng shui*. A few weeks later an international architectural competition was launched, the first ever in China, with guidelines in English and Chinese, overseen by Sun's brother-in-law, Soong Tzu-Wen. The committee had decided that the mausoleum was to combine the function of a grave with that of a memorial hall (*jinian*) with a didactic and ritual purpose where there would also be sufficient space for mass rallies. Its architecture was also to convey the spirit of the modern, new China without sacrificing a distinct Chinese identity. The guidelines issued by the PCFS were prescriptive, stating that the Sacrificial Hall be made from solid stone and reinforced concrete rather than brick and wood and that the design of this room be in 'a classical style with distinctive and monumental features'. The Shanghai-based Czech sculptor Bohuslav Koci was commissioned with the task of making two stone statues of Dr Sun that were to be placed in the mausoleum.

Only one of the 40 entries received for the competition met the committee's full requirements. The jury selected the design by Chinese architect Lü Yanzi, who had been to Paris, studied at Cornell University in New York and after his return to China had worked for the American firm Murphy and Dana at their Shanghai office.[16] His drawings show the strong influence of his training in the Beaux Arts; he typically subordinated elements of traditional Chinese architecture to a classical composition.

Lü Yanzi's scheme made full use of the large, 30-acre site. A tripartite gate, and various ceremonial buildings accentuated the platforms and made the whole site resemble the layout of the imperial tomb, of the *lingmu* (rock cut) type, as opposed to the *fenmu* tumulus type on a flat piece of ground.[17] It staggered five large platforms, with the uppermost section able to accommodate some 50,000 people, along a single straight axis cut into the side of the mountain that was linked by 400 granite steps. A retaining wall surrounded the whole complex, including subsidiary pavilions and parkland. It was the outline of the retaining wall that particularly enchanted the jury, as it looked like a bell drawn in elevation. They found the symbolism of the bell 'profoundly meaningful' since Sun Yat-sen's testament began with the sentence 'it is necessary to awaken the mass of our own people'. The whole mausoleum could therefore express the wish to rouse the masses.

Construction work began in March 1926 and proceeded with such urgency that the architect Lü died of exhaustion before it could be completed.[18] The whole project had cost 3.4 million yuan which was a colossal figure at a time when much of the rural population was suffering from famine. Furthermore, it was never made clear where the funds had come from.

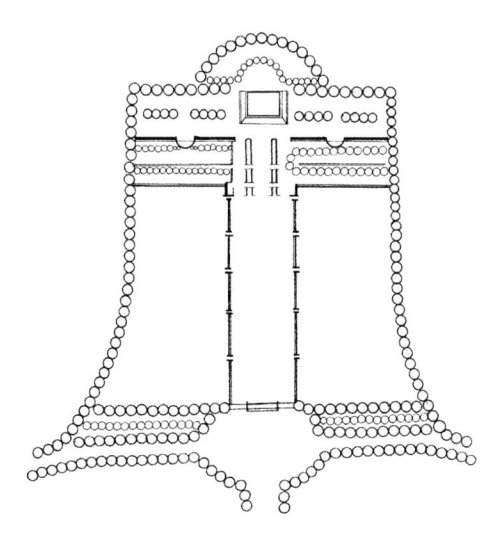

Ground-plan of Sun Yat-sen's mausoleum.

In the four years between Sun's death and his final burial in Nanjing in June 1929, China had become strongly militarized as the country was still divided into rival military regimes. The Kuomintang was also split into hostile factions, partly cause by the radicalization of the party under communist influence, which led to strikes, boycotts and anti-imperialist revolts, especially in Shanghai and other treaty ports. As class conflict grew more acute, Chiang Kai-shek, head of the Huangpu military academy and by 1926 commander of the National Revolutionary Army, tried to appease his wealthy sponsors in the treaty ports by limiting communist influence at the top level of the party. However, he still relied on Soviet expertise and equipment for the relaunched Northern Expedition. The Nationalist government moved its central headquarters from Canton to the Wuhan cities of the Yangtze. In March 1927 Nationalist armies succeeded in taking Nanjing and Shanghai, where a general strike led by communists triggered a conservative backlash, masterminded by Chiang Kai-Shek, which culminated in a bloody repression of unionists in a number of cities. The KMT conservatives then established a rival Nationalist government in Nanjing to that in Wunan, headed by Wang-Chin Wei. This led the Chinese Communist Party to revolt and to stage an uprising in Nanchung and other provinces, which was brutally repressed.

In 1928 the KMT resumed the Northern Expedition and finally managed to take Peking. On 10 October the Nationalists formally established the Nationalist government of the Republic of China, with their old power base Nanjing remaining the capital. This was the beginning of the so-called Nanjing Decade (1928–37). Chiang Kai-shek was the leader of this government, although he presided over a highly factionalized regime and was confronted with persistent challenges by rivals within the party.

Given the widely enforced cult of Sun the 'homecoming' of the Founding Father was seen as a highly significant act, especially for Chiang Kai-Shek, who could declare himself the direct successor to Sun's Republic of China. When the mausoleum was completed, he staged a dramatic second funeral.[19] Sun's coffin was moved from the Western Hills, carried by train bearing his photograph, to Nanjing, while loudspeakers reminded bystanders of his doctrines. In Nanjing, Sun's body was embalmed again and dressed in a long blue satin gown, black silk jacket, ready for another three days of lying in state. On 1 June 1929 Sun was reburied in a lavish ceremony led by Chiang Kai-shek himself. The funerary procession, lasting six hours and involving a huge crowd, was meant to convey the unity of the Chinese people, comprising representatives of all classes, ethnic groups and religions. However, no one but Sun's widow, his son, Chiang himself and his brother in-law Soong Tzu-Ven were allowed to follow Sun's coffin up the 392 steps to the mausoleum.

The Nanjing Decade lasted until 1938, with Chiang Kai-Shek maintaining his authority over the KMT and presiding over the Republican government, which had control over most of China. The growing Japanese encroachments on Chinese territories, however, proved disastrous for the Nanjing government, especially as Chiang Kai-Shek refused to check Japanese advances, focused as he was on his wish to complete the unification of China first and, increasingly with an obsession to

The long ascent to Sun Yat-sen's mausoleum, Purple Mountain.

eliminate the communists, who had regrouped and were much more engaged in fighting the Japanese. From 1937 to 1938 Japan invaded eastern China, annexed Taiwan and controlled almost all major cities, including Nanjing, which suffered a particularly brutal repression in the winter of 1937. The Nationalist retreated to the southwestern provinces and the communists to the northwest. Wang Chin-Wei, a former close associate of Sun Yat-sen's and left-wing member of the KMT, had joined the Japanese and been appointed to head a Japanese supported collaborationist government in Nanjing. He had found out that some Sun's of entrails, which had been removed prior to his embalming, had turned up in Peking, where they had been kept in a temple. Having secured permission for their safe transfer to Nanjing, he had 'the holy entrails' deposited in a grand ceremony on 5 April 1942 and added a new ritual to the customary silent recitation of Sun's Will, called 'showing respect from afar to the holy entrails of the father of the nation.'[20]

By 1939 Chiang Kai-Shek was ensconced in Sichuan, hoping to tough it out until the hoped-for entry of the USA in the Far Eastern zone of conflict, leaving the communists, who had considerably expanded their influence, to mount an effective resistance by organizing peasants and stepping up guerilla attacks.

Following Japan's defeat in 1945, Chiang Kai-Shek rebuilt his dictatorship and the Nanjing government. He celebrated the liberation of the country from foreign invaders at Sun's mausoleum. His claim that only the Nationalist government had the legitimacy to represent China was fiercely contested by the communists in the ensuing Civil War. By 1947 The People's Liberation Army had gained the upper hand and once it had brought Manchuria and Northern China under control and had taken Beijing in 1949, the Nationalist forces were quickly defeated. Chiang Kai-Shek's last resort was Taiwan, where he and some two million Nationalists and displaced people were to take refuge. Here his Republic of China enjoyed financial and military help from the United States, which supported his regime against the People's Republic of China, declared by Mao Zedong on 1 October 1949.

Chiang Kai-Shek continued to use Sun Yat-Sen's cult to legitimize his rule even after the Nationalists had fled to Taiwan. According to some reports, he tried to take Sun's body with him, but it would not have been possible to remove it without damage. Given that Sun's body had to be left behind in the mausoleum inaccessible to Nationalists, he ordered a monumental Sun Yat-Sen Memorial Hall to be built in the centre of Taipei.

Site plan of Purple Mountain in Nanjing, showing the location of Ming tombs and Sun Yat-sen's mausoleum.

In Communist China, Sun was considered a 'bourgeois revolutionary', although one officially recognized as a 'pioneer'. It also helped that the mausoleum was planned and largely built before Chiang Kai-Shek had come to power to impose his own interpretation of the heritage. Zhou Enlai went to visit his tomb at the end of the Second World War. Although it was a prime target as a reminder of Chiang's dictatorship during the Cultural Revolution, it had survived. It subsequently attracted many United Front pilgrims and the memory of the short period of common purpose between KMT and the communists was also invoked for diplomatic meetings between PRC and ROC representatives at the mausoleum. Since 1989, relations between the two countries have improved. In 2005 the KMT's Chairman Lien Chan was the first KMT member to visit the site since 1949.

I went to see the famous Scenic Spot on Purple Mountain on 28 July 2010.[21] The densely wooded hillside (some 400 metres, or approximately 1312 feet high) overlooks Nanjing from the east and is named after the purple clouds that sometimes hover over its peaks at sunset. The designated National Park contains a number of significant archaeological sites from the Ming Dynasty, including the partially restored Xiaoling Tomb of Emperor Zhu, natural beauty spots and lakes, as well as Sun's mausoleum, a Buddhist temple, a pagoda and burial sites for KMT soldiers.

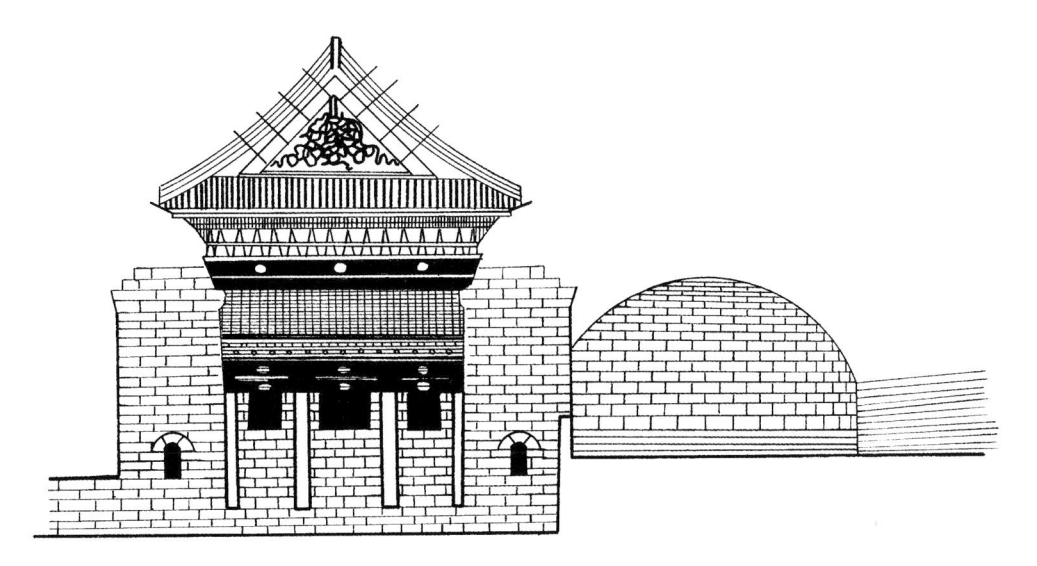

Side elevation of the central memorial hall and tomb chamber of Sun Yat-sen's mausoleum.

Free motorized transport was available but entrance tickets needed to be purchased to gain entry. The whole area is beautifully landscaped and very well maintained. All sites were well visited, but on the day I was there Sun's mausoleum attracted by far the greatest number of visitors, many of whom came from Taiwan.

The path to the Ming emperor's tomb follows the contours of the hillside and so reveals the various gates and stations one by one. The tomb itself remains hidden from view behind a massive wall. In contrast, Sun's mausoleum has a strictly axial layout. The path and the 392 granite steps lead steeply up the wooded slope. All the buildings, including the two gates, have gleaming white walls set off by the azure-blue glazed roof tiles, in keeping with the symbolic colours of the KMT. I was surprised that no security checks were carried out and bags and cameras did not need to be left with security personnel.

The whiteness of the wall was almost painful to look at in the strong sunlight. There was something disconcerting about these buildings that looked as if their construction had been costly in their stiff alignment and relentless colour coding. The exegesis to their elaborate symbolism was supplied by the bilingual English and Chinese notices posted alongside each feature, though few people bothered to take notice of them, as climbing the steep slope on a hot morning demanded considerable energy.

The general succession of gates and pavilions follows the imperial precedent. The triple arched gateway is succeeded by the Stele Pavilion that contains an eight-metre-high (around 26 feet) stone stele inscribed by one of the Kuomintang founders in attractively rendered calligraphy. This serves as a Nationalist equivalent of the Tablet of Great Merit found in the Ming tomb. A pair of bronze tripods attracted much attention from visitors, who looked for the holes left by Japanese bullets from the 1937 bombardment. Finally, the last stage, the 'Sacrificial Hall' loomed into view. Apart from the kiosks selling bottled water, snacks, memory sticks and souvenirs, there was also a stall selling flowers. The large terrace afforded a splendid view over the long approach route, the wooded hill and the city below. Three arched doorways led into a square hall with four rows of columns supporting the flat ceiling that depicts the KMT symbol (a white sun on a blue background). This is where one comes face to face with the seated marble figure of Sun Yat-sen, dressed in a traditional robe and holding a scroll. The architect had been much impressed by the Lincoln Memorial in Washington and suggested a similar solution for the mausoleum, which was later, as we have seen, taken up again in Mao's Memorial Hall. In keeping with the didactic function of this Sacrificial Hall and accommodating the rituals developed at the Beijing cemetery, several large panels of writing, including Sun's Three Principles and the Final Testament were attached to the walls on each side.[22] Furthermore, the plinth of the statue depicted various iconic scenes from Sun's life. Vases of flowers and potted plants stood before the statue.

    It is quite a jolly looking room; enlivened by a pink stone above the black marble panelling along the wall and a frieze inlaid with mosaic tiles. The high ceiling prevented any stuffiness and the high windows let in an agreeably subdued light. People milled about freely, taking pictures of Dr Sun's statue and of each other. A single guard officiated but he was not a soldier, did not stand to attention, and made no effort to instil a sense of reverence or discipline.

    Bronze doors led to a short vaulted passage and from there three steps gave access to the coffin chamber. This, the inner sanctum, was the most un-Chinese space in the whole complex. It was circular in plan, with a shallow central dome and a sunken rotunda, obviously inspired by Napoleon's tomb chamber at the Dôme des Invalides in Paris. Only the coffin was rather different, as instead of the plain red porphyry sarcophagus with its Empire-style scrolled edges, I was rather startled to find the carved likeness of Dr Sun as a dead man, lying straight on his back, dressed in his characteristic high-collar tunic, his hands folded at his breast. He seemed to be like a substitute for an embalmed Sun – placed on a bier, a pillow supporting his head. According to a notice on the wall,

Sun's statue in the memorial hall.

his actual remains are buried five metres (around sixteen feet) below in the earth. Glazed square recessed niches allowed a diffuse light to enter and although there were also lamps concealed behind the rim running along the base of the dome, this was a suitably sepulchral and gloomy room. Written signs indicated that that photography was not allowed but almost all visitors took pictures of Sun's coffin, before filing out into the Sacrificial Hall again.

At the back of the domed annexe was a permanent exhibition documenting the history of the monument's construction. As with all the other signs at the complex, explanations were both in Chinese and English. The flowers sold near the mausoleum and the many available souvenirs allowed private offerings to be made and mementoes to be taken home. Many visitors availed themselves of these facilities.

The most immediately striking aspect of Sun Yat-sen's mausoleum was its dazzling visual presence and prominent position on the hillside. This was a particularly assertive possession of an old sacred site. The straight slash of the steep stairway serves as a radical reordering of topographical meaning and presents a new interpretation of the concept of *lingmu*. This could be seen as an expression of confidence, a no-nonsense revolutionary bluntness or as an arrogant disregard for tradition. This ambiguity is characteristic of the whole mausoleum complex and its uneasy relationship between tradition and modernity, radicalism and reactionary conservatism.

The decision to place Sun's mausoleum on Purple Mountain was based on the desire to declare the first president of Republican China as equal in importance, if not more so, than the first Ming emperor buried nearby. The architect made conscious references to the Xiaoling

Sun's effigy on the sarcophagus in the tomb chamber.

Flower offerings at the entrance to Sun Yat-sen's mausoleum.

Souvenirs on sale at Sun Yat-sen's mausoleum.

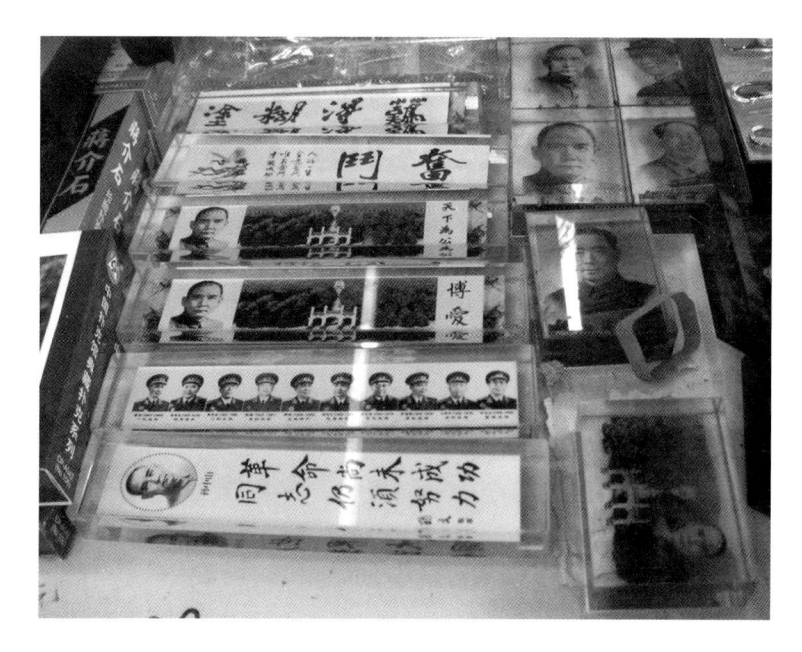

Tomb. For instance, he copied the linear sequence of the memorial archway, tomb passage, entrance, stele pavilion, sacrificial hall and tomb. On the other hand, modernity was suggested by simplifying this sequence. While the Ming emperor respected the local topography and allowed his processional path to deviate from a single axis, being 'respectful of nature', the modern straight line to the top approach proclaimed the overcoming of old superstitions. At the same time the site of Sun's tomb enjoyed even better *feng shui* properties. This was an aspect that was not publicly acknowledged at the time it was built but is freely commented on now. Instead of being buried within the darkness of an earth-covered tumulus, Sun lies within a freely accessible, light-filled, round coffin chamber. The two lifelike sculptures made in the European tradition also cast Sun in different aspects. First he is shown as a teacher and 'Chinese Lincoln', gazing benevolently across time and space, while the recumbent statue on the coffin serves as a simulacrum of an embalmed revolutionary leader.

The whole monument is a mixture of European and Chinese elements, with the references to Chinese traditional architecture concerning primarily the exterior (the trapezoid elevations, overhanging eaves and the glazed tiling of the roofs) and in a very restrained manner, some decorative elements. Meanwhile, the interiors are handled much more freely: the flat-roofed pillared hall is followed by a pantheon-like rotunda.

Of particular importance, and this follows the ancient precedent, is the prominence of the written word. The buildings are all inscribed on the outside and feature panels with calligraphic texts inside. This allows Sun's words and message to be directly associated with his tomb, which became a medium of indoctrination. An important aspect of the mausoleum was its function as a site of public ritual and pilgrimage. Sun's cult, as instituted by the KMT in the late 1920s and '30s, was ostensibly meant to 'inculcate' his doctrine, The Three Principles, through constant repetition. It also elevated Sun's *persona* to the level of a sage, a founding father, as well as a powerful ancestor. At that time a visit to his shrine was not just a demonstration of acquiescence in the political programme of the KMT, it was also an opportunity to make a pilgrimage, to evoke the blessings of the nation's ancestral spirit.

Since the recent relaxation of entry for Taiwan nationals to the mainland, the mausoleum attracts many thousands of Taiwanese tourists. As part of the Purple Mountain 'Scenic Spot' it is also heavily promoted as an attractive site for PRC tourists. Sun, claimed by both as a 'founder of the nation', provides a common bond of shared history for a generation of young Chinese tourists for whom strife and turmoil is as ancient and remote as Emperor Zhu Yuanzhang next door.[23]

Anıtkabir: The Memorial Tomb of Mustafa Kemal Atatürk

It was Atatürk's mausoleum that sparked my fascination with such monuments. I was married to a Turk at the time and when we visited his father in Ankara, who was an officer in the Turkish army, we would go to Atatürk's grave together. Despite the rather stiff ceremonial at the site and the exaggerated nationalist sentiment that it was meant to inspire, I was unaccountably moved by the experience. This was a reaction that subsequent visits did not change. Although at the time I knew very little about Atatürk, the tomb and the whole setting at the mausoleum triggered an emotional response, even a feeling of reverence, in me. I kept thinking of a sentence by the Viennese architect Adolf Loos in which he describes the feeling of solemnity (*Feierlichkeit*) upon coming across a burial mound in a forest clearing. He was later to proclaim that in architecture 'only the tomb and the monument belong to art'.[24] I began to look at the mausoleum more carefully, trying to understand how it could exert such a powerful impact. It also made me want to understand Atatürk better and how he ended up in such a fascinating place.

Although Atatürk died a long time ago, in 1938, he still commands a strong visual presence in Turkey. His face features on Turkish banknotes, framed photographs of him hang in every classroom, in all public offices, in countless coffee houses, shops and houses. Schoolchildren line up before his bust in every schoolyard, as do recruits in barracks across the country. Atatürk's image is ubiquitous, and tentative attempts by political parties sympathetic to Islamic principles to challenge this personality cult have so far been met with widespread resistance. The Turks seem to want Atatürk to watch over them.

His mausoleum, completed in 1953, functions as one of the most important national monuments and as a prime site for the performance of state rituals on public holidays. All official visits by foreign heads of state comprise the laying of a wreath at the cenotaph of Atatürk. Images of 'Anıtkabir', as the mausoleum is called in Turkish, are widely disseminated and footage of a montage of Atatürk and the mausoleum terminated national television broadcasting each night until the 1990s.[25]

The mausoleum is open all year, can be visited free of charge, and attracts some 4,000 visitors daily. Given the continuing symbolic importance of Atatürk as the heroic defender of the nation and founder of modern Turkey, it is not surprising that his monumental burial site has become a 'sacred national site'. I would like to show, however, that the continuing popularity of Anıtkabir owes as much to its architectural and spatial qualities as to the personality of its esteemed incumbent.

Atatürk, literally 'Father / progenitor [of all] Turk[s]' is the name its bearer chose for himself, when in 1934 he had made it a legal requirement for every Turk to adopt a surname.[26] He was born simply as 'Mustafa', son of Ali Riza, sometime in 1881 in Salonika, at that time part of the Ottoman Empire. Since the exact day of his birth was not recorded, he also chose an official birthday, 19 May, in remembrance of the day he had landed in Samsun to begin the Turkish War of Independence in 1919. One of his teachers gave him the name 'Kemal', which he kept until 1934 when be became 'Atatürk'.

Atatürk, as he would be known, opted early for a military career and graduated from the Military Staff College in Constantinople in 1905. He was deployed in various provinces of the Ottoman Empire and distinguished himself in the Italian-Turkish War fought in North Africa. He also took a keen interest in politics, which, given the dire situation of the empire under Sultan Abdulhamid II, was shared by many people of his class and background. He joined the progressive Committee of Union of Progress and was involved in the 'Young Turks' Revolution of 1908, which forced the abdication of the sultan and the establishing a unionist government. In the First World War, which the Ottoman Empire entered on the side of Germany, Colonel Mustafa Kemal was put in command of the Dardanelles campaign against the British and Australian forces, where he won great acclaim for his victories. Promoted to the rank of General, he commanded Ottoman troops in eastern Turkey, Palestine and Syria. Before the war had ended, the Entente powers had made a series of treaties which divided the territories previously under Ottoman control between themselves. Reacting against the acquiescence of the reestablished Sultan to what was perceived as a humiliating dismemberment, Mustafa Kemal began to mobilize resistance against the forceful implementation of these plans. He rallied a liberation army in the eastern and central provinces of Anatolia and initiated the political process to create an alternative Turkish government. On 23 April 1920 he inaugurated the Grand National Assembly as its president. Commanding his new army and drawing on all the reserves of willpower and equipment, he succeeded in defeating French, Italian and British troops at various fronts. In what is known in Turkey as the 'Liberation War' he led the armed resistance to an invasion of Greek forces in 1922. In a mood of gratitude for his victory at the battle of Sakarya, Mustaf Kemal's appointment as commander in chief was extended, though he faced opposition from other assembly members. The decisive victory at Dumlupinar led to the wholesale retreat of the Greek army and negotiations with the Entente powers. On 24 July 1923 a new national government, having abolished the sultanate, signed the Treaty of Lausanne. Great Britain, France, Greece and Italy thereby recognized Turkey as a completely sovereign state.

By this stage the country was ravaged after ten years of almost continuous warfare, seriously depopulated and deeply impoverished, but free from foreign interference. Mustafa Kemal consolidated his position of power in the new government as the leader of a newly created political party (the People's Party), dissolved the assembly and put himself in charge of the government. When the Turkish Republic was officially proclaimed on 29 October 1923, Mustafa Kemal became president and General Ismet Inönü prime minister.[27] Ankara had been declared the new capital two weeks earlier. One of the first acts of the new government was to abolish the caliphate and to adopt a new republican constitution.

Mustafa Kemal was 42 years old when he achieved his ambition and became the first president of the Turkish republic. But the challenge to his power had not been removed. Mustafa Kemal strove for personal power, but power was not an end in itself. It was a means to refashion the country, to make it civilized in the way that France and other major Western states were civilized. He was convinced that only he alone was capable of doing this: what was good for him was good for the country [. . .] He believed that his people had the potential to create and sustain a civilized state: though many were still burdened with ignorance, they could be educated, and he would be their teacher.[28]

He used his powers to push through a wide range of reforms. He was determined to turn the still primarily rural, poorly educated and mainly Muslim Turks into modern citizens and to reverse the long decline, which had reduced Ottoman Turkey into a backward and under-developed country, by making it decidedly more European. He adopted the Swiss civil and the Italian penal code, introduced the European calendar, the European alphabet, the use of surnames and European dress codes (notably the abolishment of the *fez* and the head-scarf). Most controversial was another decree, modelled on the French post-revolutionary constitution, which was the separation of state and religion. Rebellious movements by Kurdish nationalists were suppressed. The Law on the Maintenance of Order was used to close down news-papers and to subdue the opposition, the Progressive Republican Party, thus assuring Mustafa Kemal's position of complete control. From 1925 to 1945 Turkey was a one-party state under the autocratic rule of Atatürk until his death, and thereafter under his successor Inönü.

Atatürk's political thinking, known as 'Kemalism', was publicized in very lengthy speeches in parliament, and written versions were widely distributed. The cult of Atatürk, spread by countless photographs that showed the Father of the Country in all varieties of modern dress, from English-made sportswear and a tweed cap to black tie, were distributed, and despite the abhorrence of pious Muslims against depictions of living beings, he insisted on placing busts and lifesize statues of himself in every town and village.

Atatürk died on 10 November 1938, having been ill for some months. His death was the result of overwork and a seriously damaged liver from heavy alcohol consumption. He was only 57 years old. He died at the Ottoman Dolmabahçe Palace in Istanbul and his coffin was taken by train to Ankara amid great public mourning and temporarily deposited in the Ethnographic Museum. It was highly unusual in an Islamic society for a body to be left unburied for any length of time. In the case of Atatürk it took fifteen years. Although it was a matter of urgency to find a suitable place and manner of burial, this was not resolved immediately, not least because of the Second World War.

A day after Atatürk's death, the National Assembly elected the Acting Prime Minister Ismet Inönü, also a Hero of the Liberation War, to be president of the Republic. He managed to steer Turkey through the war years by retaining neutrality at the cost of raising a potentially defensive military force (from 120,000 to 1.5 million men), financed through raised taxation. He continued the policies of Atatürk and exercised the same autocratic rule behind a facade of a one-party assembly. The economy stagnated and there was high inflation. By intensifying the cult of Atatürk, Inönü hoped to derive legitimacy as the best person to carry forward his former comrade's political programme of reform and modernization; he also prohibited any expression of discontent by the populace. By the end of the war the government was so hated that Inönü decided on a degree of liberalization and consented to the formation of other political parties. In 1946 this led to the transition from dictatorship to democracy. Parliamentary elections followed in 1950 and Inönü lost to the newly formed Democratic Party. Three years later there was a renewed assumption of autocratic government rule, with the Democratic Party seizing the assets of the Republican Party in 1953. The inauguration of Atatürk's memorial and his final burial on the fifteenth anniversary of his death were a solemn occasion that officially reaffirmed the government's commitment to Atatürk's political programme. Throughout the turbulent years of the 1970s and '80s Atatürk's centrality remained a constant element and grew even more important after the 1982 constitution was passed. This

> allowed the State to be easily embodied in a single individual, Atatürk, whom some Kemalists revere as a semi-sacred purveyor of the modern Turkish state [. . .] Indeed, one of the most intense demonstrations of state fetishism has been a startling intensification of devotion to Atatürk and his memory [. . .] Very often these representations [of his images] are accompanied by a famous speech or proverb, most commonly his saying, *"ne mutlu Türküm diyene* (What happiness to those who can say "I am a Turk"). Atatürk's likeness is regularly reproduced on large banners, it has been carved into hills and near a Black

Sea village, and a mountain range draws visitors because it casts a shadow that once a year mystically resembles Atatürk's profile.[29]

Atatürk had died in Istanbul, which is the most cosmopolitan and largest of Turkish cities. His tomb, however, is in the city he had chosen as the capital of the new Republican Turkey. The city lies on the Anatolian plateau at an important crossing of ancient trade routes and has a long history of occupation, going back to the Paleolithic period. In the second millennium BC the Hittites fortified the rocky outcrop that overlooks this crossing. In the first half of the second millennium it served as an urban centre of the Phrygian kingdom and another 1,000 years later the Romans made Ancyra (Ankara) the capital of the province of Galatia. Thereafter, the city fell into a decline, although the Byzantines and later the Seljuks continued to make use of the fortress. Atatürk chose this sleepy market town for its central position in the heart of Turkey. Sufficiently remote from Istanbul, Ankara was to be made in his own image and populated with citizens supportive of his ambitions. When Atatürk died in 1938, his new capital was still in the process of becoming a modern city. German and Austrian architects, some of them exiled by the Nazi regime, were enlisted to design functionalist yet dignified ministries, a parliament, a university, administrative offices, as well as housing for the new government employees within the city plan set out in the 1920s by Hermann Jensen. Ankara in the 1930s and '40s became the only large-scale example of modernist planning and architecture in Turkey. These sturdy Bauhaus-type buildings, many of them built with red-brown sandstone from surrounding mountains, are still in use today.

The site chosen for Atatürk's mausoleum was an alluvial hill rising in the flat, previously marshy depression just outside the new residential neighbourhoods. It used to be known as 'Besh Tepe' ('Five Mounds'), a name that refers to the ruin mounds at its top. After a weather station was installed, it was called 'Rasat Tepe' ('Observation Mound'). Here the Phrygians, whose own capital was situated some 100 kilometres (62 miles) further west, had buried some of their elite in large tumuli.[30] Since the hill was uninhabited, offered good visibility and had an ancient tradition for use as a burial site, it appeared to be the ideal location for Atatürk's mausoleum. In a moment of poetic inspiration, the president of the committee in charge of the project commented that

Site model of Anıtkabir.

since the shape of present and future Ankara reminds one of the shape of a crescent, Rasat Tepe is like the star in the centre. If Atatürk's memorial were built on this hill, it would embed Atatürk in the centre of our flag.[31]

İnönü ordered an international architectural competition, specifying that the design should 'symbolize the achievements and personality of Atatürk and through him the Turkish nation'. Altogether 49 designs were submitted over the following year. The winning entry was a project jointly submitted by the Turkish architects Emin Onat and Orhan Arda. They described their concept as follows:

> Atatürk rescued us from the Middle Ages and showed us our real history resided not in the Middle Ages but in the common sources of the classical world [. . .] we wanted to reflect this new consciousness [. . .] and decided to construct our design philosophy along the rational lines of a seven thousand year old classical civilization rather than associations with the tomb of a sultan or a saint.[32]

Lenin's Tomb Chamber.

Ho Chi Minh mausoleum from Ba Diem Square.

Steps leading to the Hall of Honours, Anıtkabir, a customary destination for high school graduates.

Roof construction and circulation at Ziaur Rahman's mausoleum in Dhaka.

opposite: Mohammad Ali Jinnah's Illuminated mausoleum, Karachi, at nightfall.

Arafat's mausoleum in Ramallah at night.

Ghanaian schoolchildren visiting the Founding Father's grave at Nkrumah Memorial Park, Accra.

Hastings Banda Mausoleum in Lilongwe.

The Road of Lions walkway to Atatürk's mausoleum at Anıtkabir.

North-west access to Anıtkabir, with one of the pavilions ('Liberty Tower') and Hall of Honour in the background.

The 'Middle Ages' evoked in this passage is a veiled reference to Islamic (Seljuk and Ottoman) Turkey. Given Atatürk's adoption of a secularist constitution, the architects were keen to stress a more European architectural ancestry. However, given its role in the War of Liberation, they avoided mentioning Greece. The celebrated Turkish architect Sedat Hakki Eldem, who had worked with Onat on several projects, characterized the policy for nationalist architecture current at the time as 'Stone Age' and one that relied on the

> inevitability of stone to sustain the desired monumentality and classicism, to be achieved through symmetry, use of giant orders and heavy cornices and dramatic impacts of light and shade.[33]

View of the porticoes, with *kilim* patterned ceiling mosaics.

These were the exactly the qualities that autocratic rulers generally admire in architecture. The neo-Classical idiom of the design also marks both a distance from the earlier modernist public buildings in Ankara and the prototype of Lenin's mausoleum. Perhaps to avoid any reference to the tomb of the Communist leader, Anıtkabir is clad in golden hued travertine with subtle striations of sandy tones rather than the red sandstone commonly used for Ankara's 1930s buildings.

I went to see Atatürk's monument again in April 2011. 'Anıtkabir very nice! Atatürk number one man in Turkey!', enthused the taxi driver who took me to the mausoleum. The city has grown at a fast pace from the 500,000 citizens it was originally planned for in 1923 to the 4.5 million inhabitants that now live there. Despite the many new highrise buildings in the centre, Anıtkabir's distinctive silhouette on the green hill remains visible from afar. Two roads lead to the monument. Official visitors in limousines are swept to the western circular plaza and from there ascend a grand stairway set into the bastion-like retaining walls of the terrace. A giant flagpole, the only one at Anıtkabir, stands at the top of these steps. I took the slower, ceremonial access route on the northwestern side of the complex. It is the one that allows individual visitors to experience the full aesthetic narrative of a pilgrims' route.

View of Ceremonial Area with Hall of Honour.

Two tower pavilions on either side of wide stone steps were guarded by soldiers still dressed in heavy woollen winter uniform, their guns resting at their sides. Looming over them were three monumental stone figures, males to the left, females to the right. These rather stiff stone statues are the only human sculptures in the round at Anıtkabir and represent peasants, soldiers and intellectuals. The single rooms in each tower contain exhibits documenting the history, construction and meaning of the mausoleum complex. Every architectural element has a name that refers to a concept or historical incident, beginning with the two pavilions, named 'Tower of Independence' and 'Tower of Liberty'. This nomenclature and its exegesis only transpire if one either takes the time to study the exhibitions, read the official leaflet or listen to the explanations of a guide. There are no identifying signs on the buildings themselves. The casual visitor can admire the seasonal planting and vistas over the city, the well-laid masonry, the impressive scale and proportions of the architecture without being constantly reminded of their ideological message.[34]

The figurative sculptures face towards the visitors on their journey up the Lions Road, named after the six pairs of crouching lions on either side. They are said to have been inspired by Hittite lions that were excavated in the 1940s. Indeed, Atatürk encouraged archaeology to demonstrate the *longue durée* of Anatolian civilization. This road is nearly a quarter of a kilometre (273 yards) long and paved with rectangular slabs of limestone. Gaps between these slabs made walking on them somewhat difficult, and one is forced to a slower, processional pace. The dark foliage of densely spaced junipers screened the surrounding park and further enhanced the aspect of 'liminality', that is, of a transitional space before the full extent of the Ceremonial Area, a wide-open plaza – large enough to accommodate some 15,000 people – and the actual mausoleum building is revealed. The very first sight, however, was that of a tall flagpole set at the opposite side of the square, and that of a wide view over the city, the hills of Çankaya, and the tall office buildings that have sprung up in Ankara's business district in the last twenty years. The Ceremonial Area is the site for mass rallies during official festivities in the national calendar. This is the main space for state rituals, where politicians and high-ranking military take up positions halfway up the steps leading to the mausoleum, while the populace is gathered on the square below, waving flags and joining in the singing of patriotic hymns. At the same time army representatives perform military choreography. All of these elements are meant to engender a heightened emotional response of 'national feeling' and *communitas*.[35] As this was a normal day and the square was fairly empty, the *kilim* patterns of the paving resembling modern wall-to-wall mosque carpets, were clearly visible.

Symbolic Coffin of Atatürk.

Interior of the Hall of Honour.

The peristyle around the square and the single-storey 'towers' are all built of the same travertine stone and establish a set of proportions against which the mausoleum asserts its monumentality.[36] Seen from the plaza below, the pillars – with neither bases nor capitals – are thrust

Anatolian women before Atatürk's Symbolic Coffin.

upwards in overbearing verticality. The architects had originally wished to place a large box-like superstructure above the colonnade, but they never planned a classical triangular pediment. The absence of such a pediment makes the mausoleum look like a ruined classical temple, one that might have lost its roof to an earthquake or the ravages of time but endures in solid perseverance. The retaining walls, on either side of the wide, central stairway, depict in low relief and the stylized manner of expressionist Turkish modernism crucial moments in the War of Independence. A low wall halfway up the stairs, inscribed with the motto (in Turkish) 'Sovereignty belongs to the State', serves as podium for political leaders on state ceremonial occasions. Having climbed these steps to reach the main 'sanctuary', known as the 'Hall of Honour', a shaft of sudden sunlight struck the gold letters inscribed on the entrance wall, the only ornament on the facade.[37] The hall is open at both ends of the main axis and as there are no glazed panels this affords a view straight through the building to the city beyond. This is where the huge dark red marble monolith (the 'symbolic coffin') has been placed, before the large window opening with its geometrically patterned bronze grill. The

North-west retaining wall showing scenes from the Liberation War and Atatürk.

rest of the interior was in sombre darkness, with the funereal torch-like lamps giving only a little artificial light and the recessed windows set low into the thickness of the walls. The high ceiling showed the transverse concrete beams, just like those found in the Seljuk Pillar mosques, but here they were overlaid with a red-and-gold mosaic as in Byzantine churches. The shallow barrel vault above the sarcophagus was also covered in mosaic tiles but they were of pure gold to signify the special sanctity of this space. Visitors stood and bowed before the symbolic coffin under the golden vault and posed for photographs. Some raised their hands in the gesture of prayer. Smartly dressed young men acted as guides inside, while uniformed, ceremonial guards of honour stood at either end of the pedestal. The ritual of their hourly relief involved a sharply stepping ascent of the stairways.

    Right opposite the Hall of Honour, but well below, on the level of the Ceremonial Square, stands the symbolic coffin of the only other person who had been granted the right of burial at Anıtkabir, that of Ismet İnönü, who succeeded Atatürk as national leader and president.[38] Here too the portico was widened to allow a sweeping view over the city.

From the beginning, Anıtkabir combined the function of a mausoleum with that of a memorial museum. The galleries exhibited relics, such as clothes, walking canes, cigarette cases, coffee-sets and personal photographs that belonged to Mustafa Kemal as a private individual, and also objects associated with his status as head of state, such as documents and gifts from foreign rulers. There were also two wax figures of Atatürk dressed in his original clothes and shoes. The 'Tower of Victory' still holds the cannon carriage that transported Atatürk's 'holy corpse' from Dolmabahçe Palace to Ankara; his official Lincoln cars are kept in the Tower of Peace and his private Cadillac in the 23rd April Tower. The museum was redesigned in 2002, in the wake of the new government headed by the Justice and Development (AK) Party. The exhibits are now placed in modern, sleek, wall-mounted glass cases, lit by LED spotlights, with explanatory notes in Turkish and English. This replaces the earlier, far less mediated forms of display, although the contents seem to have changed little. During my visit people walked through these darkened halls rather faster than they used to do, when they could see it all in broad daylight.

In recent years another museum space has been opened in the vaulted spaces beneath the Hall of Honour. This adds a more didactic element to the Anıtkabir experience. The exhibits aim to provide information about the historical events of the War of Liberation, as well as the founding of the modern republic. The rooms and corridors contain large-scale three-dimensional installations, composed of wax figures, painted backdrops and actual old guns and other props in order to recreate iconic scenes of the battles commanded by Mustafa Kemal. Audiotapes provide a soundtrack of heroic film music, simulated thuds of exploding shells, the clatter of steel on steel and horses neighing. The exhibition makes a case for Atatürk's historical role as the saviour who rallied the nation to resist foreign occupation. At the same time, the many portraits of other officers and the row of portrait busts along the corridors stress the fact that the Turkish army ensured victory. Even in the panoramas it is the common soldiers who dominate the forefront and one has to make an effort to spot Atatürk in the background, surrounded by colleagues rather than heroically isolated and dominant. The rest of the exhibition shows the formation of the Turkish Republic and the various 'reforms' instigated by Atatürk but it does not address the history of Turkey after the founder's death.

The opening up of the lower galleries does not allow public access to Atatürk's actual burial crypt, situated some seven metres (around 22 feet) below the monumental marble sarcophagus in the Hall of Honour. However, its placement is indicated by an arched niche in one of the corridors, with a bronze relief of Atatürk's face built into the wall. During my visit a plasma screen relayed live footage of a CCTV camera panning the octagonal chamber. The footage showed a plain red marble coffin surrounded by bronze urns, which, as text panels in Turkish and English explained, contains earth from all Turkish provinces, as well as Northern Cyprus and Azerbaijan. A window set into the wall opposite was to allow the incumbent, so the guide told his charges, 'a glimpse of his beloved Cankaya Hills'. A plaque nearby records what had happened to Atatürk's corpse after fifteen years of lying embalmed in the present Museum of Ethnography. The texts states that when the embalming materials were removed, his body was shrouded according to Islamic traditions and buried directly in the soil of his country with his face towards Mecca. Having paused at this, the most sacred space closest to Atatürk's body, the visit continued to the first floor, through Atatürk's newly reassembled private library, and concluded, just like in any Western museum nowadays, in the new gift shop installed in the 'Tower of The Defence of Rights'.

Although the architectural concept conforms to the programme of the neo-Classical 'Stone Architecture' mentioned above, it has the redeeming feature of an open and fluid spatial concept. Unlike at many other mausolea, where the order of the visit is strictly proscribed, at Atatürk's tomb visitors – except on official occasions – can choose their mode of access and what they wish to see and in which order.[39] The spatial configuration of access routes and architectural planning is such that it allows permeability of access, as well as wide vistas across the surrounding urban landscape. Even the 'inner sanctum', the symbolic centre with the symbolic sarcophagus, is open on both sides along the main axis rather than just being contained by the massive walls. There is also an interesting variety of scale. The height and size of the 'towers' and the peristyle relate to a human scale, only the proportions of the Hall of Honour are truly monumental and are clearly meant to be awe-inspiring.[40]

The steps leading to the mausoleum were a popular vantage point to observe others or for being observed; people liked to sit on them, took photographs of each other and enjoyed walking up and down. The tawny colour of the limestone is pleasant to look at in the harsh light of high summer and lends a sense of warmth on the bitter cold days of winter.

Portico with views over Ankara and patterned paving.

The official leaflets and the website now draw attention to the various cultural references embedded in the design, such as the 'Hittite' lions, the 'Seljuk' cornices, the 'nomadic' tents and textiles. These features also alleviate the rather stark purity of the stone surfaces. Some of these architectural effects were the result of tectonic and engineering concerns, which influenced scale and proportions. Others were because of financial constraints and the need to keep the monument simple. Nevertheless, they all make the whole site more open to diverse interpretations and experiences.

The Ministry of Culture managed Anıtkabir until 1980, when the General Staff of Turkish Military Forces assumed control. The army still runs the monument and it is effectively a military installation. The personnel consists of recruits doing their military service, as well as officers, some civilians, researchers and library staff. The most conspicuous representatives on normal visiting days are the guards of honour which are positioned at particularly elevated spots, where their silhouettes stand out against the sky, guns at their feet. In recent years, a greater number of recruits has been drafted to serve at Anıtkabir as security guards and guides. Dressed in well-cut dark suits and ties, wielding walkie-talkies, their status as soldiers was not obvious. They seemed to embody Turkey's new identity as a successful service-oriented country with a neo-liberal managerial ethos. The 'guides' offered assistance to groups, as well as to individuals. Some were fluent in French, or German or English. They also volunteered to take people's photographs in front of the symbolic tomb.

At times of national crisis, for example when the more pro-Islamic Welfare Party first achieved political success and Islamism became prominent in the 1990s,

> The state added to the many thousands of likenesses of Atatürk, including placing more images in religious conservative Sincan and similar neighborhoods that had largely voted for the Welfare Party in the 1995 elections. The increase in the prevalence of Atatürk images seemed to be the Kemalists' direct counter to the expanding visibility of women in veils, as the two symbols – Atatürk and the veil – have become those of competing cultural identity for the Kemalists and the Islamists respectively.[41]

Anıtkabir served as a focal point to demonstrate support for the Kemalist ideology that was perceived as threatened. Some protesters, during actions they described as 'complaining to Atatürk', voiced concerns over the government's attempts to challenge the interpretation of secularism or the constitutional role of the army. Silent protests by pro-Islamic supporters of the government, holding up copies of the Koran, have also taken place. In 1997 the police reported to have foiled a plot by Hezbollah to destroy Anıtkabir by means of aeroplanes.[42] The more recent proliferation of security guards, however, was motivated by domestic political protests, which, as one guard told me, were now 'forbidden'. He pointed out that all visits were monitored and counted, that some '4,000 people visit a day, one and half million a year', and concluded that the mausoleum was 'becoming more popular every year'.

The notice outside Atatürk's crypt, which emphasized how Mustafa Kemal had been buried according to Muslim practice, after having lain embalmed for fifteen years, could be seen as a gesture of accommodation to the changed self-understanding of many Turkish citizens under a government that encourages traditional values and displays of piety.

Tellingly, the leader of the AK Party, Recep Tayyib Erdogan, hoping to secure another term as prime minister in the general elections in June 2011, used a poster referring to the 100th anniversary of the foundation of the Turkish Republic in 2023, which showed the Süleymaniye Mosque in Istanbul together with Anıtkabir.

Although some governments were at odds with the military over the interpretation of Atatürk's legacy, none have as yet tried to abolish his cult altogether. His mausoleum is firmly anchored in the national psyche as the place most closely associated with Atatürk and continues to be not only a highly effective site for the performance of state rituals but a place that attracts an increasing number of visitors. The actual visit of the mausoleum allows the ordinary citizen to experience a heterogeneous spatial and personal encounter with the ancestral figure of modern Turkey, to learn about the violent and heroic collective struggle that marked the 'birth pangs' of the republic. The mixture of solemnity and informality, of military precision and a freedom to explore and wander at will, the spatial dissociation from the city and the generous views of it, all allow multiple emotional responses in the course of the same visit. The spatial dynamics create tension and relaxation, intimidation and comfort, exposure and enclosure. Despite the efforts of successive governments to determine the content of the Anıtkabir and to proscribe the nature of its enchantment, the qualities of the space and its architecture elicit emotionally powerful but personal reactions.

Mazar-e-Quaid-e-Azam, 'The Mausoleum of the Great Leader', Muhammad Ali Jinnah, in Karachi

This was the second mausoleum built for a founder of a new nation state in a predominantly Muslim country. Muhammad Ali Jinnah was born in 1876, five years before Atatürk, and he died in 1948, ten years after the Turkish leader. He had to wait even longer for his mausoleum – 23 years – until his tomb was officially opened on 18 January 1971. Atatürk had insisted on the strict separation between religion and the state and although the issue of Turkey's secular constitution has been much debated since the arrival of new Islamist governments, this issue proved to be much more contentious in Pakistan. Jinnah's idea was to create a homeland for Indian Muslims, which he defined as a nation. This definition, despite Jinnah's own secular interpretation, meant that religion was to remain a central and divisive factor in Pakistani politics. We have seen that the design of Anıtkabir codified Turkish nationalism while eschewing references to Islamic traditions. At the same time, the dominant ethos of secular modernity was expressed by the stark modernist neo-Classical architecture which relegated 'Turkish' identity, until then defined by Islam, to a subordinate register. With Jinnah's mausoleum this proportion was reversed. It is immediately recognizable as a modern version of a long line of Islamic mausolea, surrounded by geometrically laid out parkland, with channels and cascades of flowing water, just like the famous tombs of Mughal potentates. Here aspirations to modernity and even to secularism can only be detected in the secondary register, in the choice of construction methods and materials, in the ornamentation, and especially in the use of artificial lighting.

Muhammed Ali Jinnah was born in Karachi on 25 December 1876, the son of a Shia businessman. When the British disbanded the Mughal Empire in 1858 and brought all the lands previously controlled by Mughal rule under their administration, the local elite adjusted to this state of affairs by sending their sons to be educated in England. Young Muhammad was also dispatched to London to make useful contacts and to gain experience as a future businessman but he chose to study law instead. He was called to the Bar in 1895 and two years later he returned to the subcontinent to establish a legal practice in Bombay, where he quickly acquired a reputation as a skilled lawyer and advocate. He had become interested in politics during his stay in Britain, rallying to the call of Indian nationalism. In 1905 he joined the Indian National Congress, where he held a position as 'ambassador of Hindu-Muslim Unity'. At that time Muslim Indians were less concerned with achieving independence from British rule than with safeguarding their economic, social and political interests after the eventual, inevitable departure of the British. Although Jinnah joined the All India Muslim League in 1913, he persisted in being committed to the objectives of Indian nationalism and therefore continued to be a member of the Indian National Congress. When, with the rise of Gandhi's Congress Party, politics in India became more polarized in terms of religion, Jinnah despaired of this state of affairs and returned to England. However, Jinnah, urbane and articulate, with a lawyer's grasp of complex issues, was deemed too valuable to the Muslim cause as their best-known figurehead. As pressure mounted he gave in and returned to India in 1935. It was in these years that he elaborated on the 'two nations theory', arguing that Hindus and Muslim had 'two different religious philosophies, social customs and literatures' and that they belonged to 'two different civilizations'. The only way to guarantee protection for Muslims was to create a 'homeland'.[43] Thus the idea of Pakistan as a state offering a safe haven for all Indian Muslims was born, articulated in the Muslim League's 'Lahore declaration' of 13 March 1940. It found enthusiastic reception among Indian Muslims. Jinnah's influence as the only official spokesman for Indian Muslims rose accordingly and it was owing to sensitivity and political 'genius' that the various, widely heterogeneous Muslim populations of British India found a common cause and unity.[44] In the provincial elections of 1945–6 the share of Muslim voters for the Muslim League rose to 75 per cent. It was also an idea that appealed to the British, who were keen to disengage from the Raj in the aftermath of the Second World War. They announced the decision to partition India along religious lines on 3 June 1947. Soon afterwards, on 14 August, Pakistan, divided into an eastern and western wing, was the first country to become a new state after the Second World War and Karachi was declared the capital.[45] Stephen Cohen points out some of the long-lasting effects of the partition for Pakistan:

> Partition and the horrific violence that accompanied it had important consequences for both the idea and the state of Pakistan [. . .] First came a mass migration that changed the power balance in what was to become West Pakistan. Support for the Muslim League and a separate Muslim state had been strongest in North India, where Muslims had been in a minority. However, Pakistan was established on the periphery of the sub-continent, where Muslims were in a majority but support for Pakistan was weak [. . .] The upshot was that the strongest supporters of Pakistan migrated in huge numbers to the new state [. . .] These individuals were more educated, urbanized, professionally qualified, and experienced in the ways of the British Indian bureaucracy than the local population; the incoming trading communities possessed significant capital as well. The refugees thus gained control of the government, bureaucracy, and business in the West Wing, while the traditional Punjabi and Pathan leadership – the descendants of the Unionists who had controlled the politics of pre-independence Punjab –were frozen out. Also taking shape was the 'triad' consisting of the army, the bureaucracy, and the feudal landlords that came to dominate the politics and social life of the Indus basin, and that today 'continues to exercise inordinate influence over public and economic affairs.'[46]

By the time Ali Jinnah assumed power as Governor General under the British Government of India Act, while his close associate in the Muslim League and fellow lawyer Nawabzada Liaquat Ali Khan occupied the more ceremonial office of prime minister, he was already very ill. He suffered from tuberculosis, a fact that had been kept a secret. He died on 11 September 1948, barely a year after having assumed leadership of the newly independent Pakistan. His death was a great shock and the country was to suffer in various ways from this premature departure. The most damaging part of his political legacy was that of leaving the ramifications of Pakistan's Muslim identity undefined. The ensuing fundamental uncertainty has beset the country's fate to this day. Jinnah was buried in Karachi after the funeral, attended by thousands of grieving Pakistani citizens, many of whom had left their homes in India to begin a new life in the new state.

Muhammad Ali Jinnah, like Sun Yat-sen (ten years his junior), had received a Western education and pursued a professional rather than a military career. He had lived abroad for years and was, like Sun, able to see the political developments of his place of origin with a critical distance. This allowed him to rise above factional or sectarian disputes amongst his fellow activists and made him stand out from his rivals. Jinnah was no freedom fighter, though in some Pakistani hagiographies he is called precisely that, and was never imprisoned or forced into exile. He had, together with other founders of the Muslim League, sought a solution for a potentially disastrous clash between Muslims and Hindus after the withdrawal of the British and had been able to secure one as an acceptable figurehead of the movement. Sun had been president of a united China only very briefly and had died in the middle of a violent revolutionary and anti-imperialist struggle that would continue for another twenty years. Jinnah died thirteen months after the declaration of independence, before unresolved internal conflicts led to the loss of East Pakistan, to rapid changes of governments, to successive military coups and endemic internal violence.

The brief Jinnah reign was in retrospect a golden era of hope and promise, when millions of Muslims arrived from all over India to build new lives. He was honoured with the titles of 'Great Leader' (*Quaid-e-Azam*) and 'Father of the Nation' (*Baba-e-Qawm*).

The very uncertainty about Pakistan's political and cultural identity, its contradictory aspiration towards modern nationhood, yet one based on the profession of a particular faith, and the ensuing and so far unresolved question of what sort of Islam this might be, is reflected in the story of how Jinnah's mausoleum came to built.[47]

After Ali Jinnah's sudden death, the political elites were left with the problem of deciding and then ratifying the constitution, which in turn hinged on the question whether this was to be an Islamic constitution and if so of what type of Islam.[48] Liaquat Ali Khan, who had finally emerged as the main holder of power, was assassinated in 1951 while addressing a public meeting in Rawalpindi, having served under two years in office. Amid the general political instability in the 1950s Jinnah's legacy was still a matter of contention. Pakistan's first constitution was promulgated in 1956 and it was during the reign of General Muhammad Ayub Khan, who had ousted President Iskander Mirza and had declared martial law, that plans were first made for a monumental memorial dedicated to the Father of the Nation.[49] The decision might have been a gesture of atonement for the demotion of Karachi as the capital in favour of the new foundation of Islamabad (which had not, after all, as had been suggested, been called 'Jinnahbad') in the northern Punjab. Furthermore, by honouring Jinnah with a mausoleum (which was also to accommodate the assassinated Liaquat Ali Khan), the beginning of the new nation and its founders could be celebrated, and the general's own status as a safeguard of its continuing strength legitimized. Ayub Khan's military rule brought a measure of calm and prosperity to Pakistan, at least until 1965, when the second war with India over the issue of Kashmir drained the state's resources again.

The general's first move was to commission an Indian engineer, Nawab Zain Yar Jung, from Hyderabad, whose 'Islamic' design was rejected as too commonplace. The committee entrusted with the task of building the mausoleum then asked the Turkish-based, originally Swiss, modernist architect Ernst Egli, only to reject his 'ornate and magnificent' scheme as too expensive. In 1957 it was decided to hold an architectural competition in order to elicit high-quality responses from the international architectural community. Zahir-ud Din Khwaja, a Kenyan-born Indian architect who had trained in Bombay and Liverpool, was asked to select the jury. The brief was ambitious: 'to submit designs for the construction of a mausoleum on the site of the sarcophagus, and to landscape and plan roads, parking areas, footpaths and gardens within the site.' Only the mausoleum and gardens were to be executed at the time, but the design 'also had to site a mosque for 25,000 people'.[50] The jury consisted of six prominent European modernist architects (Robert Matthew, Giò Ponti, Eugène Beaudouin, Pier Luigi Nervi and Georges Candilis), plus two nominees from the Pakistani government. The jury unanimously selected the entry from the British firm Raglan Squire &

Partners. The design of the mausoleum, with soaring sail-like wings stretching out on all sides, was reminiscent of Eero Saarinen's work, although the garden design by William Whitfield was said to be 'in the best tradition of Muslim architecture'.[51] The decision was met by an uproar in the local press (someone claimed that the design copied a railway station in the USA) and categorically rejected by Fatima Jinnah (Muhammad Ali Jinnah's younger sister). The condemnation of this 'European design' was not surprising, as foreign architects had rarely been entrusted with the politically sensitive task of building the tomb of a national leader of such importance. Indeed, to select a British design for the Quaid-e-Azam would have been seen as giving in to neo-colonialist paternalism. The government decided to retreat at this point, and Ayub Khan left it to Fatima Jinnah to decide who was to design and build her brother's mausoleum. She called upon the Indian architect Yahya C. Merchant, who had developed a reputation for industrial and commercial designs and who claimed to have designed the Quaid-e-Azam's house in Bombay. His much more conventionally 'Islamic' scheme' found general acceptance and was built with public funds throughout the 1960s.[52] However, the mosque and all the other buildings, which were specified in the 1957 brief have not been realized to this day.

Fatimah Jinna, by then recognized as the 'Mother of the Nation', was nominated by the Combined Opposition Party as a candidate for the presidential elections in 1965 and campaigned vigorously against the Ayub Khan's 'guided democracy', as he preferred to call his regime. A few years later, in 1969, Ayub Khan was ousted by General Agha Mohammad Yahya Khan, who thus became Pakistan's second military president. It was Yahya Khan who presided over the official opening ceremony of the mausoleum on 18 January 1971 and who allowed Fatima to be buried near her brother in the secondary burial site close to the mausoleum itself, when she died in 1967. Two prominent members of the Muslim League, Sardar Abdur Rab Nishtar (1899–1958) and the Bengali Nurul Amin (1893–1974), were also granted the privilege of burial near the Quaid-e-Azam, highlighting the fact that the origins of the Pakistani state arose from the collective effort of the Muslim League.

I was in Karachi at the beginning of the New Year in 2011, when tensions were high. In December 2010 reporters for the *Small Wars Journal* reported that

> Over the last month, Karachi – Pakistan's largest city and the center of its commercial and financial life – has witnessed

its worst ethnic violence in years. On October 16 a wave of targeted ethnic killings began rolling across the city; four days later, more than 60 people were dead and Karachi had come to a standstill. Since then, the city has been teetering on the brink of even more bloodshed.[53]

Groups of armed soldiers were stationed at regular intervals along the main thoroughfares and flyovers and all guests staying at international hotels had to pass through security screens. Riding in a moped-taxi along the traffic-choked boulevard that leads from the harbour of Karachi, I could see the mausoleum built on a natural plateau from afar. Its gleaming white tower appeared to float in immaculate purity above the densely packed, ramshackle houses and glass-walled office blocks. I was deposited at the entrance to the 63 acres of parkland that surround the mausoleum. Surprisingly for a national monument, everybody had to purchase an entrance ticket. What appeared to be a nominal sum to me (ten Pakistani rupees per person) must surely deter impoverished citizens (the majority of the population in fact) from visiting. Even more surprising, given the state of high alert elsewhere in Karachi, where almost every fast food outlet had a armed guard, was the complete absence of security checks. There were also no restrictions on luggage or cameras. The whole atmosphere was carefree and relaxed and apart from the guards of honour at the tomb itself, no security personnel were visible. A cafeteria provided tea and simple snacks, which people consumed under trees in the open air. Several paths led to the gleaming white mausoleum building that was placed at the highest elevation of a gently sloping hillside. There were no signs forbidding anyone to step off the paths. The landscaping consists of informally grouped trees and shrubs, as well as axially placed water conduits of white marble. These form gradual cascades down the central access routes on all four sides of the park, descending from the wide terraces below the mausoleum. Arriving at noon on a Sunday, I noticed that the park was a popular destination for families, couples and groups of young men. Although there was no prescription on what could or could not be

The marble water cascade (without water in January) at Ali Jinnah's mausoleum, Karachi.

worn, people were smartly dressed: the women and girls in brightly coloured *shalwar kameez*, and men in either the male versions of the traditional clothes – long shirts over trousers made of the same material – or Western combinations of trousers or jeans, with pressed shirts. People sat on the patchy grass or on rugs on the grass, or on the benches that lined the main pathways and posed for photographs at especially scenic spots. There were also no hawkers selling drinks or snacks; they must have been barred from entry at the main gates. The grounds were kept very clean; there was no litter. A central, ceremonial axis led up towards the mausoleum that crowns the summit of the hill. This was a gentle slope, quite unlike the steep ascent to Sun's tomb on Purple Mountain. Formal pools (at this time of year they were still without water), ran down the middle of the path into a series of shallow cascades. The mausoleum sits on a wide terrace of smooth light pink marble. The green-and-white Pakistani flag was hoisted on a flagpole on the west side. At the steps leading to the top-level terraces shoes had to be removed. The sun had made the stone pleasantly warm to the touch and it felt very agreeable to glide over the soft surface in bare feet. Seen from the terrace, the building (on a 27-metre square or 90-foot square footprint) loomed like a fortress, with its tapered solid walls and steeply projecting parapets at each corner. The semi-circular dome rose above on a smooth white drum. The whole exterior is clad in white marble, ornamented all over with a slightly raised pattern of L-shaped brackets brought into sharp relief in the strong sunlight. Early Islamic facades were often covered with designs recalling embroidered textiles; here the effect was one of machine-printed cloth. The pattern relieved the monotony of the walls but also drew attention to the modern method of construction with reinforced concrete. This was even more apparent in the huge, parabolic-arched doorways, disconcertingly reminiscent of McDonald's 'golden arches', which pierce each of the four tapered facades of the mausoleum.[54] The doors were held wide open at all sides and allowed air and light into the high-domed space of the mausoleum, as well as views over the city. The interior plan consists of an octagon, since secondary walls placed against the four corners have been built to conceal service areas, such as the stairways to the gallery and the crypt. As at Atatürk's mausoleum, Jinnah's actual tomb has been set into the earth below the main hall. The floor was paved with black-and-white marble tiles. The interior walls had a similar abstract pattern as the outside – rectangles enlivened by small oblong panels of green onyx. The clerestory was covered in plain white mosaic, while the dome had a blue tile facing. This

Visitors thronging the grounds of Ali Jinnah's mausoleum on a Sunday afternoon.

Author with Pakistani
visitors at Ali Jinnah's
mausoleum.

Main access to
the mausoleum.

Facade of Ali Jinnah's
mausoleum.

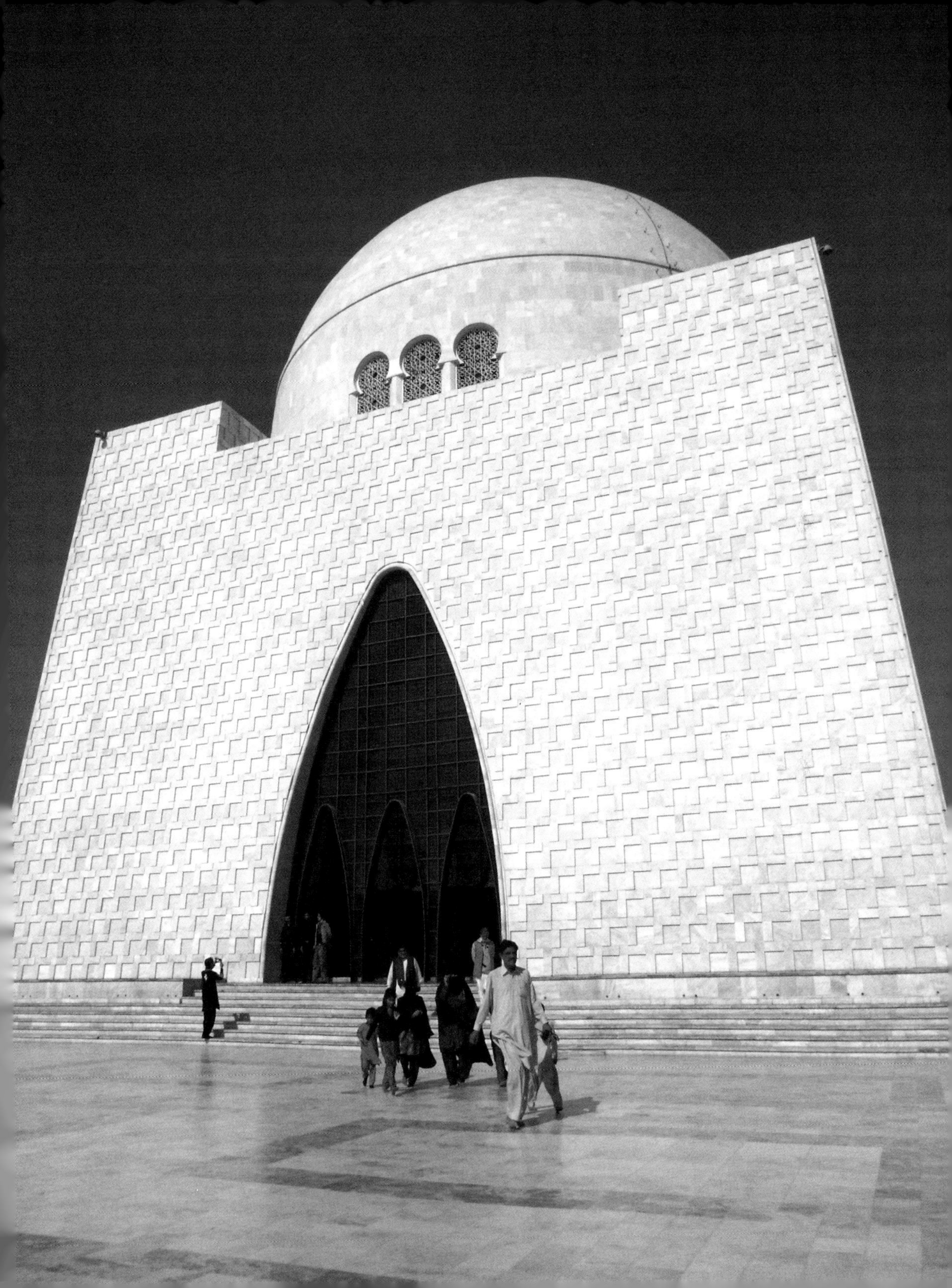

Symbolic sarcophagus of Ali Jinnah.

Interior of Ali Jinnah's mausoleum.

Crypt with Ali Jinnah's real sarcophagus.

was meant to impart 'heavenly solemnity, well deserved by Great Leader buried here', according to the official publication. A double waist-high balustrade with a delicate floral pattern surrounded the marble sarcophagus, ornamented with carved flowers and bearing the name and dates of the deceased leader. An ornate blown glass chandelier hung above the sarcophagus, a gift from the Muslim community of the People's Republic of China.

There was no other inscription and no state ensigns within the tomb chamber, and there were no religious emblems or texts either. In addition to the four guards of honour stationed outside at each corner, four more were positioned around the sarcophagus enclosure. They changed position every five minutes to the sound of a bugle. Their captain explained to me that members of each unit of the armed forces spend four months on guard duty at the mausoleum. They wore a red plume in their headwear and were very handsome; their drill was not executed with much precision. In the main room people milled around, posing for photographs in front of the coffin. A few raised their hands in prayer but this did not seem to be a site for displays of piety. There were also no flowers or any other offerings, such as rose petals, that are a popular offering at shrines in Pakistan. The captain volunteered to show me the real sarcophagus in the crypt below, a place normally only accessible to VIPs, he stressed. The proportions of this room were on a much more intimate scale then the great hall above and the furnishings, such as the silver rails around the coffin and the white marble wall cladding, showed an almost feminine intricacy. Built into the lower level of the mausoleum, but accessible only from the outside, was a flat-roofed annexe that houses the simple marble coffins of Fatima Jinnah, Liaquat Ali Khan and the two original Muslim League members.[55] Next to this modest room was the so-called Relic Chamber, dedicated to house the personal effects of Ali Jinnah. It displays items such as photographs, clothes, tableware, his famous astrakhan peaked hats, as well as two official cars.

Outside this annexe I discovered the only stall in the whole complex. It sold water and snacks, as well as souvenirs such as mugs with a picture of the mausoleum, key rings, fridge magnets and even table lamps made of plastic or onyx in the shape of the mausoleum.

I came back again in the evening. As dusk descended over the city the mausoleum began to glow in an ethereal lilac light. The walls that had looked so impenetrable during the day now became like the transparent veils that women like to wear here. The whole park now thronged with people; one teenage boy, keen to practise his English, said that he enjoyed coming here during weekend evenings to watch girls and 'hang out'. Couples were strolling arm in arm; groups of families sat on rugs and shared snacks they had brought with them. Children were sliding across the smooth and still warm marble on the mausoleum terrace, or were turning cartwheels. Many lamps dotted about the park illuminated the pathways and benches but left areas of shadow and darkness, while below twinkled the lights of the big city. The mausoleum stays open until nine p.m. and for many people in Karachi this was a safe and enjoyable place to spend Sunday evening, at least for those who were able to afford to pay for the entrance ticket. The luminescence that seemed to emanate from the mausoleum itself (in fact, there are up lights cleverly concealed at the perimeter outside) threw a soft glow that bathed the whole terrace in a gentle light, which in the fading redness of the sunset, turned the whole terrace into a dramatically lit stage set. Later on, as darkness had descended, those plastic or onyx lamps sold at the kiosk made sense. Like a child's night lamp, the mausoleum glowed reassuringly over the troubled city.

Playing and socializing outside the mausoleum.

In comparison to Raglan Squire & Partners' modernist scheme, Yahya Merchant's design is recognizably an Islamic tomb monument, with its prominent dome and battered walls, corner projections and arched doorways. As such, it looks like a modern version of a traditional form of a common building type in the area that is now Pakistan. The landscape design that combines axial pathways and straight water channels with informal planting also refers to ancient patterns. So in this respect, as well as in the equally traditional floral ornamentation of the sarcophagi, the demands for Muslim identity to be acknowledged are amply fulfilled. The architect himself wanted to do justice to the famously slim and elegant silhouette of Jinnah through the design of 'the tall and slender arches [that] remind the viewer of the Quaid-e-Azam's tall and slender figure'. Furthermore, 'the majestic steps leading up to the vast platform and mausoleum . . . serve to protect his forceful character'.[56] He even sought to bring out certain stereotypes of provincial inhabitants who live in areas that surround Karachi, thereby contrasting 'the massive, masculine edifice [that] blends with the mountainous character of the people of Beluchistan', with 'the feminine grace of the arches [which] reflects the docile nature of the Muslims of Sind.' Downplayed in the architect's own account is the forward-looking, modernizing and secular agenda of the Great Leader. This aspect is stressed in the glowing endorsement of the building in the publication by Ahmad Hasan Dani, from the Quaid-i-Azam University in Islamabad,[57] who stressed the fact that modern technology (particularly the use of reinforced concrete and cement) had allowed the architect 'to vary the traditional design, to construct a massive tomb chamber with highly exaggerated walls and take in the dome without undue emphasis on the phase of transition'. He commended the decision to have the mausoleum 'stand alone in silent majesty', which he considered an 'entirely new concept whose sole aim is to impart sanctity to the building'.

This sanctity is conveyed by architectural means alone. Although the outer form of the building signals continuity with Islamic architecture, this is not a religious Muslim site, unlike the many tombs of various Muslim 'saints' in and around Karachi which attract large numbers of primarily Shia pilgrims. The political context is equally vague; the design makes only subtle references to modernity and secularism and there is little in the way of state symbolism. This reticence may well have contributed to the popularity of this monument. Its discreet or underplayed ideological message made it more immune to the frequent and often violent changes of government and policies. All subsequent governments have maintained the upkeep of the site and some have contributed further embellishment. Separated from the volatile centre of power after Islamabad became the capital, Jinnah's tomb remains a sacred and symbolic site and a reminder of the original aspiration to national unity.

My own experience of the site, at least on this particular day, a normal Sunday and not one of the official days of remembrance, suggested that the real success of the architectural programme lies less in the subtle subversion of its traditional Muslim form by daring technology than by the configuration of the public spaces around the monument: the generous terraces of smooth marble, the stepped walkways with central water cascades and the landscaping that evokes gardens of paradise. Even people who cannot afford to pay the entrance fee can at least look at the hillside and watch the glowing tower at night.

The Mausoleum of Shaheed President Ziaur Rahman in Dhaka

An article in a Bangladeshi newspaper describes the complex itinerary of various political leaders as they celebrated Victory Day by visiting specific monuments and mausolea in Dhaka:

> President Zillur Rahman laid wreaths at 7:40am at the National Mausoleum in Savar to pay respect to over three million Bangladeshis who laid down their lives to free their motherland from the clutches of Pakistani occupation forces 38 years ago. A few minutes later Deputy Leader of Jatiya Sangsad [parliament] Syeda Sajeda Chowdhury went to the National Memorial and placed a floral wreath on behalf of Prime Minister Sheikh Hasina who is now in the Danish capital Copenhagen attending the UN Climate Summit [. . .] Leader of the Opposition in parliament Begum Khaleda Zia reached the National Mausoleum at around 9am and placed floral wreaths at the alter of the huge monument to pay homage to the martyrs who gave their lives for the sake of their motherland [. . .] Later, Khaleda went to the *mazaar* of Shaheed president Ziaur Rahman who was a valiant freedom fighter and a sector commander during the 9-month-long Liberation War in 1971. [. . .] LGRD Minister and Awami League's General Secretary Syed Ashraful Islam also laid floral wreaths at Savar Memorial Wednesday morning along with a huge number of party leaders and workers. Later, the Awami League General Secretary went to Dhanmondi Road No 32 to place floral wreaths and pay homage to the portrait of the Father of the Nation Bangabandhu Shaikh Mujubur Rahman.[58]

This exemplifies not only the bipartisan nature of Bangladeshi political life but the manner in which each of these monuments is implicated in the vexing question of what it means to be Bangladeshi.

We have seen that although Sun Yat-sen's mausoleum had become 'tainted' because of its association with Chiang Kai-shek, it had escaped destruction during the Cultural Revolution and now serves as a symbol of the fundamental unity of China. This is because Sun's role in the creation of modern China is recognized by Taipei and Beijing alike. For its part, the Turkish army ensures that Atatürk's tomb in Ankara functions with the same panoply of military ceremony as it did when it was first opened. It also continues to be the most sacred site of secular Turkey and a genuinely national shrine. Jinnah's status as the Founding Father of Pakistan was never contested and although it took 23 years to build him a mausoleum, this is now a national monument where politicians from the different parties assemble on days of remembrance to demonstrate at least a token unity.

The situation is very different in Bangladesh. Ever since the birth of the nation in 1971, the question of national identity has been especially fiercely contested by all the major factions that dominate the political life of the country. No fewer than three different monumental tombs have been built for national leaders in Dhaka since the 1980s. Whilst all are in a strikingly modern design, they reveal very different attitudes towards the role of their incumbents in shaping the identity of the nation.

The first monument, known as the 'National Martyrs' Monument', lies at Savar, some 35 kilometres (22 miles) outside the city of Dhaka, and is a war memorial for those who fell in the 1971 Liberation War. Construction began soon after the war, in 1972 and finished in 1982. It is the least partisan of the 'national' monuments. In the 1980s President Ziaur Rahman, under whose auspices the war memorial was completed, also built a mausoleum in Dhaka, on the grounds of the former Dhaka Racecourse, near the ruins of a former Hindu temple destroyed by Pakistani troops in 1971. He chose to commemorate three pre-liberation politicians (Fazlul Haq, Hussain Shaheed Suhrawardy and Khawaja Nazimuddin), rather than the first post-independence president and reputed Father of the Nation, Sheikh Mujibur Rahman, who had made an impassioned speech on this very spot on 7 March 1971, which is held as the unofficial declaration of independence. Instead of honouring Mujibur, Zia, himself representing the rival Bangladesh National Party (BNP), ordered that the three politicians from an earlier era should be taken from their respective graves and be reburied in the newly erected Three Leaders Mausoleum (*Tin Netar Mazar*), referred to as the 'National Mausoleum'. The architect in charge was Masud Ahmed, who symbolized the three leaders by three huge parabolic concrete arches that form a billowing silhouette.[59] Few people in Dhaka know what it stands for now, even my well-educated friend could not remember what this somewhat dilapidated structure was meant to commemorate.

Since 1991, two women, both related to previous presidents – one, Sheikh Hasina the daughter of Sheikh Mujibur Rahman, the other, Begum Khaleda Zia the widow of President Ziaur Rahman – have won majorities in general elections and exercised power alternatively. It was Khalida Begum, representing the Bangladeshi National Party (BNP), who built a grand mausoleum for her husband right opposite the National Assembly as soon as she took up office as prime minister in 1991 (this is the *mazaar* mentioned in the article above). Her rival, Sheikh Hasina, the leader of the Awami League (AL), reacted by having the remains of late father reburied in a grand tomb adorned with his portrait, opposite the house where he was assassinated, which she had converted into a museum.

The term 'Bengal' derives from the ancient Sanskrit name for the alluvial plains formed by the Ganges and Brahmaputra rivers before they flow into the Bay of Bengal. The old word 'Vanga' became 'Bangla', hence the name of the present country 'Bangladesh' is literally 'Land of the Bengalis'. Although in subsequent centuries Hinduism and the caste system were widely adopted, Eastern Bengali Hindus were regarded as having a distinct character and were alienated from the Hindus in the rest of India. It was therefore in East Bengal that many people converted to Islam at the beginning of the thirteenth century. The conquest of Nadia, the capital of the Bengali kings, in 1202 by the Muslim Ghurids from Afghanistan, marked the beginning of Muslim rule in Bengal that would last until the transfer of tax collection rights to the English East India Company in 1756. Several Bengali Muslim sultanates managed to obtain independence from Delhi, with the Hussain Shahi Dynasty (1494–1538) being considered the golden age of the Bengali sultanate. By the seventeenth century, however, under the rule of the Mughals, East Bengal became incorporated into their vast empire until 1858, when the British took over.

Since Bengal was considered the most advanced province of British-controlled India, it benefited from the setting-up of higher-level elected bodies meant to give Indians experience in government. However, the British administration favoured the appointment of Hindu personnel over the erstwhile Muslim ruling elite, a practice which led to Muslims not only distrusting the colonial power but Hindus in general. A response to this situation was the Two Nations Theory represented by the All-India Muslim League, which proved popular with the Muslim middle classes. The predominantly Hindu bureaucrats and entrepreneurs supported the Congress Party, while the left-wing parties could not compete with the two main factions defined by religion rather than ideology.

In 1905 Lord Curzon, Viceroy of India, applying the principle of 'divide and rule', decided to divide the province of Bengal into two halves. This was welcomed by the predominantly Muslim population of the newly created province of Eastern Bengal and Assam (with the capital in Dhaka) but nationalist protests by Hindus led to reunification in 1911. When the Government of India Act of 1935 allowed elections to be held for new legislative assemblies and councils, two Muslim parties (the Muslim League and Fazlul Haq's KPP, or Farmers' People Party) stood against the Congress Party and various minor and independent parties.[60] Since the assembly elections did not lead to clear victory by any one party, the Muslim League merged with the KPP and formed a ministry under Fazlul Haq. Haq, along with many ministers, resigned in 1939 over the fact that Indian ministries had not been consulted about Britain's entry into the war with Germany.[61] Various coalition governments operated during the war years, which brought famine and deprivation, especially to the rural population of East Bengal. Since much of the cultivated land had been turned over to the production of textile fibres, especially jute, the country depended on rice imports from Burma, which came to end when the Japanese took Burma in 1942.

After the end of the war, the newly elected Labour government in the United Kingdom was committed to abandoning imperial claims to India. 15 August 1947 saw the creation of a new country for Indian Muslims, Pakistan, that was itself divided into a western and an eastern component. East Pakistan did not benefit greatly from this arrangement. Although the jute that was grown in the east was the export staple of the whole country, little of the earnings returned. Furthermore, West Pakistanis, posted from Sind and West Punjab, took the top positions in government and the economic sector.[62] Other divisive issues were Ali Jinnah's insistence on Urdu as the national language throughout Pakistan, as well as the under-representation of the east wing in the national parliament.[63] Most contentious was the constitutional definition of the state as Islamic, which was an idea that was much more widely supported in West rather than in East Pakistan. These tensions deepened after the deaths of Ali Jinnah (1948) and Liaquat (1951), leading to the development of democratic movements demanding greater parity and provincial autonomy for the east. There, Fazlul Haq renamed his Farmers' People Party (KPP) as 'Krishak Sramik Party' (KSP: Peasants' and Workers' Party) and formed a coalition with Hussain Shaheed Suhrawardy's rival to the Muslim League, the Awami (People's) Muslim League, to form the opposition United Front. However, their efforts to reach an agreement with the military leaders of Pakistan proved futile. In 1970 East Pakistan was struck by a devastating cyclone that claimed a quarter of a million lives.

In the elections held early in 1971, Mujibur Rahman, representing the Awami League, won by a large majority in East Pakistan, while Zulfikar Ali Bhutto's Pakistan People's Party won 81 of 138 seats in the West. When talks about a new constitution broke down on 25 March, Mujibur Rahman was arrested, tried for treason and condemned to death (which President Yayha Kahn deferred). Exactly who had made the first official declaration of independence is still a matter of intense debate between the two major parties in Bangladesh today. Mujibur's speech on 7 March in Dhaka had not called for independence as such, although it galvanized mass support for a campaign of civil disobedience. According to the Alwawi League's historiography, official calls for independence came from inside Mujib's cell on 25 March. The Bangladeshi National Party (BNP) favours the version that independence was first declared in a radio broadcast and stresses the involvement of Major Ziaur Rahman. At any rate, Yahya Khan reacted to the announcement by sending the army into East Pakistan. In the ensuing violent civil war, Bengali *mukhti bahini* guerillas were backed by Indian troops dispatched by Indira Gandhi. On 16 December 1971 Pakistani forces surrendered in Dhaka; India declared a ceasefire and Bhutto took over from Yahya to form a civilian government. Bhutto released Mujib, who as head of the prospective government of Bangladesh, travelled first to London and New Delhi, where he thanked Indira Gandhi for her support. He arrived in Dhaka on 10 January 1972 to an enthusiastic reception and assumed the presidency.

The inheritance of Pakistan's non-democratic state structure, dominated by the bureaucracy and the military, posed a considerable challenge to the new nation. Mujibur Rahman and his party drew up the constitution, which was closer to that of India than Pakistan. The main principles (known as '*Mujibbad*') were nationalism, socialism, secularism and democracy. The bitter civil war had devastated the country and many problems associated with the legacy of the two Pakistani states. There was a shortage of trained administrative personnel and too many weapons still in circulation. Mujib generally distrusted people who had remained in East Pakistan and favoured 'freedom fighters'. He also banned the Muslim League and other parties who in the past had advocated the union with Pakistan. His personal popularity was high – he became known as '*Bangabandhu*', 'friend of Bengal' – and in the 1973 election the Awami Party won easily if not quite fairly.[64] However, Mujib's standing fell as the economic situation deteriorated in the wake of a widespread programme of nationalization and rampant corruption. When severe floods and famine hit the country in 1974, he declared a state of emergency. In January 1975 he amended the constitution to establish a presidential system, making himself president and setting up a single-party system, thus assuming dictatorial rule. Half a year later, on 15 August 1975, Mujib and most of his family were assassinated in a coup organized by disgruntled army officers; only his two daughters, who were in India at the time, survived. The army selected Mustaque Ahmed to become president, who promoted General Ziaur (Zia) Rhaman to Chief of Staff. This was a position Mujib had always denied him, despite his reputation as a freedom fighter and able officer. Zia was briefly placed under house arrest during another abortive army coup but was reinstated in the ensuing revolt instigated by the National Socialist Party. He quickly formed a new government under his control (with A.S.M. Sayem as president), but delayed presidential and parliamentary elections while assuming responsibility for the ministries of home affairs and finance. He gradually transformed himself from a military to a political figure, travelling widely throughout the country and building up a reputation as somebody 'who got things done'. When Sayem resigned on health grounds in April 1977, Zia made himself president and thus held all major positions in government. In order to distinguish his ideology from that of Mujib, he stressed the Islamic nature of Bangladesh and pursued anti-Indian policies. He amended the 1971 constitution to expunge secularism and thus established Islam as the foundation of Bangladeshi, as opposed to Bengali, nationalism.[65] When order returned after further rebellions in 1977, he announced that he would run in forthcoming elections as a National Front (JAGODAL – National Democratic Party) candidate. His victory in the election consolidated and to some extent legitimized his position. He changed the JAGODAL Party into a new party, the 'Bangladesh National Party' (BNP), headed by his vice president Abdus Sattar. The country's economy improved under Zia's rule but he failed in building the new party into an effective organization.

On 30 May 1981 Zia was assassinated by Major-General Muhammad Manzur, the army commander of Chittagong, while he was on a visit to the city. Zia's chief of staff, Major General Ershad, quelled the rebellion; Vice President Sattar became president and announced elections. Facing a divided Awami League, he was duly elected but there was trouble with the army, and on 24 March 1982 Ershad assumed full powers under martial law. He dissolved cabinet and parliament and initiated a new period of military dictatorship that lasted until 1986.

Ershad continued the anti-secular policies of Zia and declared Islam the state religion. He intensified the push for free-market reforms to make Bangladesh one of the most economically liberalized countries in South Asia. He pledged to hold elections in the near but unspecified future but banned political activities. His intention to create a new constitution based on Sharia law led to protests and the arrest of political leaders, which included Begum Khaleda Zia, the widow of Ziaur Rahman, the former president and leader of the BNP, and Sheikh Hasina Wajid, the daughter of Mujib, leader of the Awami Party. Both women were released after a month but continued to agitate against Ershad, which led to further intermittent terms of imprisonment for both. Although they were united in their opposition to Ershad, they were intensely hostile to each other. Finally, mass demonstrations in October 1990 forced the resignation of Ershad. He was arrested in December, and under an interim ('caretaker') government the country went to the polls on 27 February 1991.

The main contest during this election was between the Awami League and the BNP. The former campaigned for a parliamentary system but otherwise adhered to the policies of nationalization, secularism and socialism that Mujib had promoted. Awami League leader Sheikh Hasina was also adamant about bringing her father's murderers to justice. The BNP under Begum Khaleda favoured free-market policies, Islamic identity and the continuation of the presidential system. In the end, the BNP won most seats, though just short of a majority, and Begum Zia was sworn in as prime minister on 20 March 1991. She took the credit for single-handedly defeating the autocratic regime of Ershad and vowed to continue the political programme of her late husband.

Over the next ten years, the two women took turns as head of state in Bangladesh. Indeed, this has continued to the time of publication in 2013. The other party always puts up an implacable opposition and both parties deny the other's right to rule. Whichever party is in opposition, it resorts to calling crippling strikes and frequently refuses any cooperation.[66]

In 1996 it was Sheikh Hasina's turn, then Khaleda Zia had another stint from 2001 until the last elections in 2008, when Sheikh Hasina and the Alawi Party were put firmly back in power.

Ziaur Rahman's notion of Bangladeshi nationalism, based on the affirmation of its primarily Muslim identity, went hand in hand with modernization. He saw the potential of architecture and public art to foster national pride in well-functioning and modern-looking cities.

The National Parliament of Bangladesh by Louis Kahn.

The new international airport he commissioned still bears his name. Rahman also ensured the completion and inauguration of the greatest, costliest and most symbolic of the major architectural projects, that of the National Assembly Complex, designed by the famous American architect Louis Kahn. The initial idea for such a building to house the permanent federal legislature of East and West Pakistan was proposed by President Ayub Khan and construction work started in 1961. The National Assembly Complex was much praised as an outstanding example of 'regionalist' architecture, fusing modernism with local traditions to create a 'timeless' construction.[67]

The decision to build a grand monument to the relatively obscure pre-liberation leaders was also typical of Zia's attitude of denying Mujibur Rahman's role in the early years of the new nation. This pointed omission of the *Bangabandu*, Bangladesh's first president, from the canonical founders was seen as particularly insulting to the Awami League. The rehabilitation of her father's memory obsessed his daughter, Sheikh Hasina, who as leader of the party derived much of her own credibility and legitimacy from being his political heir. At the first session of parliament in July 1986, when Ershad was still president, she proposed a motion to have Mujib officially acknowledged as the Father of Nation, to include his name in all school textbooks, to have his photograph inside parliament and public offices, as well as to have a mausoleum erected on his grave.[68] However, since it was not Sheikh Hasina who won the 1989 elections but her rival, Zia's widow Khaleda Begum, Mujib's rehabilitation had to wait.

Since Khaleda Begum's credibility as a politician derived from the fact that she took over the BNP after her husband's assassination, it was in her interest to foster a Zia cult, presenting Zia (and the military) as the saviour of the 1971 war. She therefore commissioned the Public Works Department to construct a proper mausoleum for her murdered husband (including a small museum and a prayer hall, as well as two gatehouses). It was finished in 1991.

Zia Rahman was assassinated in the early hours of the morning of 30 May 1981 in Chittagong. His body was transferred to Dhaka and a huge crowd attended the burial of his coffin in 'Moonlight Park' (*Chandrima Uddan*), close to the National Assembly in Shar-e-Banglanagar. More than twenty years later (in 2002), during Begum Khaleda's (Zia's widow) third term in office, plans were made for the construction of a proper mausoleum above his original tomb.[69] The Department of Architectural and Public Works announced an open architectural competition, and of the 25 entries received, the Dhaka firm Bashat Architects & Engineers were chosen to design the mausoleum. Their proposal was to 'respect the master plan of Louis Kahn' for the whole site of the National Assembly and to insert the new subsidiary buildings in the existing parkland with minimal disturbance. Construction lasted from January 2003 until November 2005. The simple marble grave was to be embedded within a new geometrical configuration of a pyramid. However, this was not to be a hermetically sealed container but a permeable, freely accessible space and open to the light.[70] To achieve this, reinforced concrete walls, open at each corner, were surmounted by a steel-framed, glass pyramid roof structure. While the interior sides of the concrete walls were clad in marble, earth was shored up against the external sides to be grassed over and to thus form a green slope arising seamlessly from the surrounding lawns. An important addition was the bridge spanning Crescent Lake to form a ceremonial access point and to stress the connection of the axis to the Assembly Building. The bridge's platform was made of glass over steel trusses and the whole structure was suspended from reinforced concrete arches. The entire

Concept sketch by Masud Bashat, the architect of Ziaur Rahman's mausoleum, showing the connection to the parliament building.

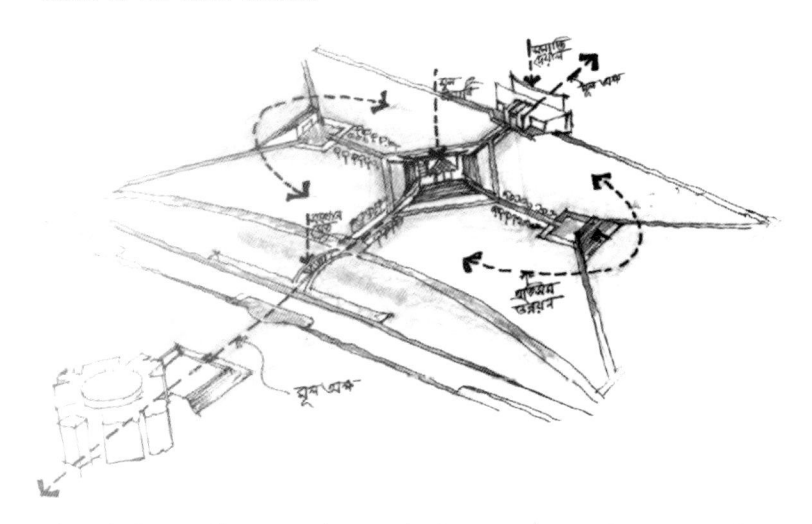

glass deck was illuminated at night from underneath, conceived as 'conceptually [. . .] acting as [a] way of light, [symbolizing] the lifestyle of Late Zia, and way of prosperity of the nation'.[71]

In a further acknowledgement of Kahn's Assembly Building, the arches were also pierced by triangular openings and the north-south axis, which aligned the parliament with the bridge and the mausoleum, was extended by another walkway that terminated in a two-storey memorial hall and mosque building. The grave was thus situated exactly in the middle between the Assembly Building and the Mosque and also between a subsidiary east-west axis leading to the courtyards at either end, which provided public toilets, food outlets and general seating and gathering spaces. While the bridge and the main mausoleum were built of steel and concrete, these secondary structures were built of baked brick. Indeed, the bricks were just like those used for the administrative blocks that surround the concrete Assembly Building in Kahn's master plan. All of these references are intended to tie Zia's mausoleum visually and metaphorically to the national parliament.

When I went to Dhaka in January 2010, Begum Khaleda's rival, Sheikh Hasina of the Awami League, was again in power following her landslide victory in 2008. Since her government takes no interest in this mausoleum, associated with the BNP, signs of neglect were evident. Flowerbeds were untended, lights broken and litter was strewn. The prayer room and exhibition space were also closed. No national flags were hoisted, although a soldier was on duty to look after the tomb and surrounding park. Furthermore, the mosque and the exhibition spaces underneath had been closed to the public. The glass footbridge that spans the shallow Crescent Lake, suspended from a rather fussy white painted steel and concrete structure, was defaced by political posters. This footbridge allows a view towards the looming massive bulk of Kahn's parliament on one side and Zia's tumulus on the other. The decision to construct an earthen burial mound open to the sky may hark back to early Bengali open-air tombs but the low silhouette makes it look self-effacing, and about to sink into the ground. Although the form suggests a dark and enclosed earthen cavern, the interior of Zia's mausoleum confounds such an expectation, revealing light-filled space, open at the four corners of a square. The floor and the walls are lined with white marble, which adds to the brightness and contrasts with the black marble panels inscribed with Arabic quotations from the Koran that serve as a reminder of Zia's promotion of the Islamic nature of Bangladeshi nationalism. In the centre, sheltered from the elements by an elaborately engineered system of struts holding a glazed pyramidal canopy, is the original tomb. Within a chest-high circular marble enclosure, paved inside with shiny black tiles, sits the white marble sarcophagus. Instead of a lid there is a little expanse of lawn on the coffin, neatly shorn and well watered. Here too posters had been pasted to the walls, especially in the four short corridors that give access to the tomb.

The 'Memorial Hall', with a prayer room on the first floor, had not been open since the accession of Sheikh Hasina. The two gatehouses at each end of the transverse axis that used to provide accommodation for guards and public toilet facilities had been taken over for quite different purposes. A family was squatting in the western gatehouse; I saw a woman cooking *roti* on an outdoor oven built into the entrance. A washing line with clothes drying and a few goats completed the domestic set-up. The gatehouse on the eastern side was not inhabited but served as a storage area for hawkers' carts.

Young men were practicing kickboxing moves in one of the entrance passages of the mausoleum, but most people who came by took a look at the sarcophagus, leaning on the wide marble balustrade. Asked why they come here, some said that they liked the park and that they liked to see the mausoleum. Others mentioned that it was a pleasant place for sporting activities and indeed, the parkland around the mausoleum was being as a cricket practice ground. One man said that Zia had been a good president but those in the present government were 'all bad'. As in Jinnah's mausoleum in Karachi, the park here provided a quiet and shady place in the middle of a polluted and overcrowded city. Here, though, the absence of a perimeter fence made it

Ziaur Rahman's mausoleum from Bangal Nagar.

The glass bridge across Crescent Lake.

Inside view of the mausoleum.

Sarcophagus of Ziaur Rahman.

even more accessible. Since the Dhaka mausoleum is not enclosed and had no facilities to charge for admission, anybody could come, whether they were rich or poor, and at any time. People did not seem to display any particular reverence at the mausoleum. Indeed, some sat on the enclosure of the coffin area, with their backs to the coffin, chatting with friends, joking around. The very openness of the design allows or even encourages this sort of behaviour, and the 'high-tech' canopy lends it a secular atmosphere, as in a stadium or railway station. There were also no guards to enforce decorum.

I returned to the mausoleum after dark, expecting it to be as populated as Jinnah's mausoleum was in Karachi. There was more activity than during the day, but being dimly lit by just a few spotlights and neon tubes suspended from the roof canopy, the mausoleum did not look very inviting. My Bengali companion said this state of affairs differed greatly to the situation when Begum Khaleda was in power. Under her rule, the whole place was brilliantly lit, especially the bridge and the walkways.

Since the majority of Dhaka's huge population (estimated at some twenty million people), are under twenty years old, they have no memories of Zia. His mausoleum is still visited by some loyalists but also attracts visitors because it happens to be situated in the popular 'Moonlight Park'. The proximity to the parliament is a constant reminder of the parlous state of Bangladeshi democracy. Zia's mausoleum's position is unlike that of the Founding Father's *mazar* complex in Karachi on a lofty hillside elevated above the city, well removed from the centre of power, where people can be nostalgic about the 'good old days' full of promise. In its present state of partial closure and neglect Zia's mausoleum also demonstrates the bipartisan nature of Bangladeshi politics, highlighted by the posters stuck on the footbridge and the walls.

The other political shrine in Dhaka, the one dedicated to Mujibur Rahman, presently (in 2013) has all of the state support. As soon as Sheikh Hasina became prime minister in 1996, she implemented long-planned policies to rehabilitate the memory of her father. In 2010 his image was everywhere, usually combined with that of Sheikh Hasina. She had Mujib's body moved from the village grave and had him interred on a lakeside spot opposite the house in which he had been killed. This house was converted into the 'Bangabandhu Sheikh Mujibur Rahman Memorial Museum' in 1997. The grave has been given a monumental aspect by a marble framework that forms an open, modern interpretation of the ancient Bengali open-air tomb. The legal pursuit of those who perpetrated the murder continues to absorb the attention of the prime minister and given the lively cult of Mujibur Rahman, she may not remain content with the simple lakeside tomb for long, unless Begum Khaleda were to thwart such ambitions by achieving another turn in office, which would see the lights turned on once more on Zia's mausoleum and leave a temporary solution for Mujib.[72]

These four mausolea that were built for the Founding Fathers of new states are strikingly different from the communist examples which all relate to Lenin's mausoleum prototype. The architects involved in the individual projects tried to give expression to the idea of a new beginning to supersede the backwardness and lack of modernity of the old social and political structures. These buildings made use of new construction techniques, especially of reinforced concrete and steel. At first sight Sun Yat-sen's mausoleum may look like a Ming tomb but also like a much improved, twentieth-century re-interpretation – with a concrete dome rather than an earthen mound, a no-nonsense straight to the top ascent instead of picturesquely winding paths. In Jinnah's tomb chamber the tall parabolic arches piercing all four sides of the slightly inclined walls also subvert the traditional form of the building, which at night, when the lighting turns the marble walls into transparent veils, is even more pronounced. The Turkish mausoleum in Ankara has something of the lofty openness of a railway terminus with its soaring pillars and exposed concrete beams. The steel framework of the cantilevered roof structure at Ziaur Rahman's mausoleum emphasizes a 'high-tech' contemporaneity that challenges the archaic forms of Louis Kahn's Assembly across the road.

The question of national and cultural identity was also addressed much more directly in these monuments to Founding Fathers than in those for communist rulers. The architects selected architectural elements or forms characteristic of the textbook periods of historical greatness to suggest the renewal of such former vitality. Hence we found 'Hittite' lions in Ankara, an evocation of early Ming Dynasty imperial tomb architecture at Nanjing, elements from the Hussain Shahi Dynasty at Dhaka and the pre-Mughal era at Karachi. Another important aspect is the desire to underline the personal qualities of the Founding Fathers in the design of the building. This is most pronounced in the Pakistani example and Yaha Merchant's attempt to allude to Jinnah's 'tall and slender figure'. In Dhaka the open roof was to suggest Zia's simplicity and openness while Atatürk's almost superhuman aura of authority finds expression in the overbearing scale of the mausoleum's main hall. At Nanjing Sun's wisdom

Grave of Mujibur Rahman in Dhaka.

is shown in a much more literal manner in the panels of textual quotes on the wall and the statue depicting him as a Chinese sage and 'Lincoln' all in one.

The nature of the modern state, that is, its constitutional structure, was another point of reference that these buildings tried to communicate by architectural means. The strictly secular nature of Kemalist Turkey is suggested by a robustly modernist interpretation of pre-Islamic tradition, while the 'Homeland for Muslims' idea for Pakistan needed a clear expression of its Islamic identity by making it look like the splendid tombs of its early Muslim rulers. Sun Yat-sen's tomb corresponded more to Chiang Kai-shek's vision of a modern China and ruled with the same autocratic power as that of the previous empires. Indeed, the references to the 'alarm bell' are only apparent when one looks at the plan. In Zia's mausoleum the BP's emphasis on the Islamic nature of Bangladesh is shown in the Koranic verses inscribed on the marble panels and the unadorned simplicity of the grave beneath the open sky. Of course, Zia's status as a Founding Father is contested. While the structure of Mujibur Rahman's tomb, much smaller in scale than Zia's, also recalls the early

Bengali open-air tombs, it features a large portrait of Mujib and avoids religious references, in keeping with the Awami League's preference for Bengali nationalism.

However eloquent the architects have tried to make the final resting places of these national heroes the message only gets across to subsequent generations when there is no break in the transmission of its ideological content. In Turkey, for the time being, schoolchildren are still being taught about Atatürk. In Pakistan, Jinnah's achievement as the creator of the nation is also undisputed, despite the perennial confusion over what this nation is intended to be. At Nanjing the original meaning is now so irrelevant that like in a museum written notices explain the symbolic meaning of every detail. In Bangladesh, after decades of bipartisan politics, people are used to decoding the messages of politicians and can read the language of monuments, at least the 'codes' of those that have been built recently.

In of all the examples discussed here we can see that the spatial and decorative programmes of the mausolea, including the settings and landscaping, are as redolent with meaning and allusions, as self-consciously assembled from a variety of references, as the monuments dating from the start of the Augustan era in Rome. While the communist mausolea were often the main sites for the rituals of state, even serving as tribunes to address the people, those dedicted to the *patres patriae*, while also functioning as spaces for collective celebrations, were meant to be read as a form of architectural heroic narrative, a history lesson and an ideological tract in one.

CHAPTER FIVE

Not the Final Resting Place
Temporary Mausolea

Normally a mausoleum is a final resting place. We have seen that when the corpses of dead leaders had to wait for such a building to be constructed, they might be placed in a preliminary place for quite a long period. But once ensconced in the proper mausoleum, they are expected to remain there 'forever'. In this chapter I will look at situations where the political aspirations of the politicians have yet to be fulfilled. Although they have been placed in a mausoleum with full state recognition, they officially remain in a state of limbo. Hence they stand for the as yet unrealized hopes for and dreams of a fully free or united nation. While the memorial sites so far discussed celebrate the revolutionary, glorious beginning of the nation, the teleology of these temporary mausolea is their obsolescence because in the 'fullness of time' the Great Leader will be laid to rest elsewhere.

Chiang Kai-shek at Chihu, Taiwan

> Ever since his arrival in Taiwan in 1949, President Chiang has worked and planned continuously for the day when he could return to the mainland. When that day comes his body will be moved one last time to Nanking where he will be laid to rest. Only then will the Chinese people say a final farewell to the man who led them through one of the most dynamic periods of Chinese history.[1]

Chiang Kai-shek, president of the Republic of China, died in Taipei on 5 April 1975, the same year that Ho Chi Minh was finally placed in the completed mausoleum in Hanoi. Chiang had often expressed his desire to be buried in Fenghua, his native village, on the Chinese Mainland. Fenghua, however, belonged to the People's Republic of China. Even in the unlikely event of Mao Zedong consenting to have his old adversary buried there, it would have been seen as a sign of defeat for Taiwan to allow their leader to be buried on the mainland that was still in the hands of 'communist rebels'. Chiang might have wished for a grand monument in his hometown, perhaps like the one he had ordered for Sun Yat-sen, but it turned out that Mao Zedong, who died eighteen months after Chiang Kai-shek, rests embalmed in his mausoleum in the centre of Beijing, while Chiang's own similarly embalmed body still lies 37 years after his death in its temporary sarcophagus in Taiwan, where it continues to symbolize the contentious issue of Chinese unification.

Taiwan, claimed by Chiang Kai-shek as a haven for the Chinese fleeing the revolution, came to represent the only legitimate China for the non-communist world during the Cold War period. The Chinese identity of Formosa, however, had shallow roots.[2] When Spanish and Dutch traders established their first footholds in the sixteenth century, the population consisted of many different ethnic groups. The island had only a brief period of being an integral part of China, when it became a province of the Qing Empire in the late nineteenth century. Following the First Sino-Japanese War, it was ceded to the Japanese Meiji Empire in 1885. The Japanese enforced policies of modernization in keeping with the Meiji project of catching up with Western technological development. As in Korea, they invested in infrastructure and rationalized rice production. Although their harsh rule improved living standards and education (in Japanese) on the island, they were widely resented by the indigenous population. When the Allies met in Cairo in 1943 to discuss the fate of the Japanese occupied parts of China, it was decided that they should be handed over to the Republic of China (ROC). After the defeat of Japan in 1945, American warships conveyed ROC troops to Taiwan to accept the formal surrender of the Japanese on 25 October. General Chen Yi established the administration of Taiwan as part of the ROC. This was followed by a large influx of Han Chinese fleeing the war-torn mainland. When the Taiwanese, who had not been consulted, perceived these events as another new foreign occupation and mounted a resistance, Chen Yi declared martial law and brutally suppressed any opposition.

Meanwhile, Chiang-Kai-shek was still presiding over the Kuomintang administration of the Nanjing government of the Republic of China. However, given the steady advance of the Communist People's Liberation Army following the withdrawal of Japan, the position of the

ROC became increasingly precarious.³ Finally, on 21 January 1949, Chiang announced his decision to resign as president of the Republic of China, leaving his former vice president Li Zongren to negotiate terms of surrender with Mao Zedong. Chiang made a last ceremonial visit to Sun Yat-sen's mausoleum to mark his departure from office and from China:

> With the aid of walking stick, he climbed the white steps he had ascended nineteen years earlier behind the coffin of the founder of the KMT. He bowed three times before the marble statue, spent some time looking over the capital city, then walked down the steps between thick ranks of guards, followed by a posse of generals. He drove to airport and flew with his son to Hangzhou.⁴

Chiang Kai-shek did not intend to retire from political life just because his troops could no longer hold out against communist forces at the time. Nor did he leave the mainland straight away. Instead he made a tour of the coastal cities that had not yet fallen to the People's Liberation Army with the aim of extracting as much money, gold and art treasures as possible to bolster the administration in Taiwan, which he intended to take over himself. He organized the transfer of hundreds of thousands of troops, most of his personnel, as well as the gold and silver reserves of the ROC to the island. While this provided a practical support system, Chiang also needed to secure international military and political backing. He paid visits to other right-wing governments in the Philippines and South Korea, where he made much mileage of the 'Domino Theory', which was to become a mainstay of U.S. foreign policy in the 1950s and '60s. The gist of this idea was that without strong resistance and Western support communism would spread inexorably across East Asia.

After Mao Zedong declared the foundation of the People's Republic of China (PRC) on 1 October 1949, the executive body (Executive Yuan) of the ROC voted to move the capital from Nanjing to Taipei. Two days later, on 10 December, Chiang Kai-shek flew to Taiwan. From there he continued to lead the nationalist government in relative security and prepared for future military expeditions to win back the mainland.

The declaration of the People's Republic of China in 1949 meant that there were henceforth two separate Chinese republics, with the older ROC now restricted to Taiwan. However, given the context of the Cold War, it was Chiang Kai-shek who signed the United Nation's Charter on 24 August 1945 as the sole representative of 'China'. Assisted by his glamorous and u.s. educated third wife, Soong Mai-ling, who had addressed Congress in 1943, he became a Cold War icon during the 1950s, making the title page of *Time Magazine* no fewer than ten times. He was seen as a staunch bastion against communism and was supplied with substantial military and economic support by America. Taiwan became a model capitalist economy under the increasingly dictatorial rule of Chiang Kai-shek and his single party, the KMT. However prosperous Taiwan became, he never gave up the hope of taking back the mainland. He saw a chance in the 1960s, during the chaos and famine that followed Mao's Great Leap Forward, but Washington blocked his plans for an invasion of the mainland and declined to supply him with nuclear warheads. In 1971 the United Nations finally admitted the PRC as only legitimate representative of China, and following Nixon's visit in 1972, the USA finally established full diplomatic relations with communist China in 1979. This recognition of the PRC and the acceptance of the official position of the PRC to the effect that 'there was only one China and that Taiwan is part of China'[5] made the issue of Taiwan more opaque and more open to different interpretations by successive governments on either side of the Taiwan Straights.

Chiang Kai-shek went into retirement after he contacted pneumonia in 1972. His state of health did not improve and he died of a heart attack just before midnight on 'grave sweeping festival' day, 5 April 1975. As Mao's death followed an earthquake, an unusually heavy storm seemed to be a heavenly announcement of Chiang's death, in the words of the local newspapers:

> As midnight approached, the clear starlight was suddenly darkened with clouds. Rain fell, and many people in Taipei were awakened by the peals of thunder and flashes of lightning. It was as if Heaven itself was pouring out its anguish and grief. Those who had been awakened wondered at the sudden change in weather. No one knew that at 11:20 the president was stricken with a heart attack. Emergency treatment was administered to no avail; by 11:50 Chiang Kai-shek, leader of the Republic of China for half a century and the last of World War II's 'Big Four', was dead.[6]

When his body was taken from the hospital to the Sun Yat-sen Memorial Hall in Taipei hundreds of thousands of people lined the street, braving the heavy rain. Before the official funeral began, 2.5 million

Merchandise at Chihu's souvenir shop.

mourners had passed through the Hall, 'one sixth of the entire island population'.[7] The public grief over Chiang's loss allowed the Nationalist government to enforce the regime's ideological commitment to its main principles, which were anti-communism, efforts to recover the mainland, and to further economic development. Newspapers praised Chiang for his dynamic leadership of Taiwan, but above all, for having been close to Sun Yat-sen and for having fought the Japanese and resisted the communists.

The party asked Chaing's son, Chiang Ching-kuo, to take on the presidency. After a first refusal out of 'filial piety', he acquiesced. Since his father's wish to be buried in his native Fenghua on the mainland could not be fulfilled, it was decided that he should not be buried anywhere, and that his body should be embalmed and kept in a sealed sarcophagus in his former residence at Chihu. This was superficially converted and Chiang was conveyed there after a lavish Christian funeral, attended by tearful masses. The funeral cortège was witnessed by thousands of people lining the streets. The parents of my former Taiwanese student, who accompanied me to Chihu, said that they remembered being made to kneel by the side of the road as the hearse was passing by.

While Chiang Ching-kuo and his successor were in office, Chihu was a major site of pilgrimage and thousands of people visited daily. When the KMT lost its hold on power, and the Democratic Progressive Party under Chen Shui-Bian was swept into office after the 2000 elections, the cult of the Chiangs became officially irrelevant but formed a still powerful symbol for the KMT in opposition. During the last stages of Chen's DPP presidency, between December 2007 and May 2008, he closed the whole site down but it was reopened when the KMT won the last election later in 2008.

When my Taiwanese hosts drove me to the mausoleum in July 2010, it took some one and a half hours from Taipei. The site was prominently signposted in Chinese and English and we bought entry tickets at the Tourist Information Centre. The building also housed a small exhibition about Chiang and his son Chiang Ching-kuo, who died in 1988 and is buried in a separate mausoleum nearby at Touliao. Various relics were on show, such as photographs, documents, medals and other artefacts, as well as the wedding clothes worn by Chiang Kai-shek and Mei-ling. In the adjacent souvenir shop one could buy baseball caps and T-shirts emblazoned with the portraits of Chiang Kai-shek and his son, which have been designed by Chiang's grandson, a professional designer.

The official narrative on Chihu reports that Chiang Kai-shek had come across it by accident when his motorcade got stuck on a visit to a tunnel project in 1950. He was so taken with the pretty site, which reminded him of native village in Zhejiang, that the owner of the plot had little alternative but to donate the land to the government. The site was originally called 'Piwei' but Chiang renamed it 'Chihu' in memory of his mother, Madame Wang. He spent his vacations in a simple single-storey house that he built there but the secluded location also lent itself to military purposes. During the 1960s, when Chiang Kai-shek still harboured plans for an attack on the mainland, it served as a command centre.

In 2010 the path from the visitor centre wound past the decaying remnants of military barracks towards a small natural lake surrounded by tropical forest. This was indeed a charming and secluded spot and one that conforms to traditional Chinese ideas of an ideal landscape with perfect *feng shui* – high mountains at the back, a stream and a lake in front. The single-storey brick house was set at some distance from the shoreline, while the flag flying the banner of Taiwan indicated that this rather modest building has national importance. Since the site itself had been chosen for nostalgic reasons, the architecture of the house was also meant to evoke the Southern China of Chiang's childhood. It is a four-section compound around a central courtyard, given a grand exterior by an overhanging porch supported by wooden columns. My impressions were that it still had a rustic appearance, with plain red-brick

Lake Chihu.

Entrance to Chihu Presidential Burial Ground with statue of Chiang Kai-shek.

walls and a red-tiled roof. The main courtyard has been paved over and all of the walkways timbers surrounding the courtyard have been painted blue in keeping with the KMT colour scheme.[8] The sarcophagus, made of shiny black stone, had been placed in what seems to be a Western-style sitting room, distinguished by an open fireplace surrounded by marble. Blue silk curtains, small flags, and framed photographs of the deceased decorate the area around the coffin. Here, in this clearly domestic setting, the temporary nature of the mausoleum was most conspicuous, suggesting a lying-in-state just after death. Having just entered, we were told to leave for the changing of the guard, a reminder of the fact that although this was just a provisional resting place, it was a publicly maintained nationalist site. The soldiers, one representing the air force, two the navy and two the army, changed guard, presenting fixed bayonet guns amid much twirling and saluting. Their performance was avidly filmed and photographed by a throng of visitors. All the while recorded music, a song called 'Memories of Chiang Kai-shek', was relayed on loudspeakers. A man, who proclaimed himself an official guide, gave explanations to anyone who wanted to listen. He mentioned that Chiang Wei, Chiang Kai-shek's brother, was also buried there, in the second room, following traditional spatial patterns, though his grave is not shown to visitors. He also pointed out that the song played was not the national anthem but one dear to Chiang and deplored the fact that young people did not know the words.

    The authorities had made various attempts to enhance the appeal of the site for tourists. The paths were lined with flags and there were little bridges made of concrete and painted to look like bamboo over rivulets, little waterfalls and other such 'scenic' spots, where people posed for pictures. The most extraordinary site, however, was the sculpture park next to the car park. Here the previously marshy ground had been drained, grassed over and now provides a sanctuary for effigies of Chiang Kai-shek, which had been rescued from various dumps and depots around the country after the Taiwanese nationalist Democratic Progress Party had come to power. Rows of busts line the pathways, with one smiling head of Chiang next to the other, while dotted about the meadow are a few huge equestrian statues and many life-size figures of Chiang in various outfits. These figures seem to greet each other. The leaflet mentions that this was the only sculpture park in the world dedicated to a single person. Some of the bronze sculptures showed signs of damage and some have been carefully repaired. The whole site, from the private house serving as the 'holding station' for the dead president,

Crowds of visitors outside Chiang Kai-shek's temporary mausoleum.

Changing of the Guard outside Chiang Kai-shek's temporary mausoleum.

Chiang Kai-shek's coffin.

to the salvaged vestiges of his cult, appeared to be a lesson in the limits of autocratic aspirations.

Most poignant and perhaps the most ideologically pertinent point about Chihu was the oxymoronic status of the place: it is a temporary mausoleum, and so reminds the immigrant Han Chinese sector of the population of their own separation from the mainland. Wakeman says of the site that 'it symbolically represented filiality, inner family life, and retirement to the mainland itself.'[9]

The body of the country's founder is not below ground in the soil of the fatherland, but packed like a parcel in a coffin in his old house. It is still a powerful statement of the fundamental displacement of many Taiwanese people and a symbol of their fraught national identity – that of a primarily refugee nation that has now become prosperous and begun to doubt the desirability of integration with the mainland. The Chihu mausoleum site is 'grounded' in Chiang Kai-shek's nostalgia for the homeland and his continuing presence there suggests that his most cherished project, the unification of China, just like that of final burial on native soil, is suspended in time.

Sculpture park with decommissioned and re-assembled statues of Chiang Kai-shek.

To make up for the lack of a proper mausoleum to rival that of Sun Yat-sen in Nanjing, Chiang Kai-shek's successor, his son, Chiang Ching-kuo, immediately decided to construct a substitute shrine in Taiwan. This is the monumental Memorial Hall in the centre of Taipei. The precedent for such a building was the Memorial Hall for Sun Yat-sen, which Chiang had constructed in 1972 to facilitate the public cult of the Founding Father whose Nanjing mausoleum was inaccessible for Taiwanese citizens. This building included educational facilities, lecture halls, a library and exhibition spaces. Chiang Kai-shek's Memorial Hall was to incorporate these facilities on an even grander scale to document the general's role as the defender of the real China and to provide a monumental setting for his continuing, fully institutionalized personality cult. The architect Yang Zhao-cheng was commissioned to design the structure. The building was officially opened on 5 April 1980, the fifth anniversary of Chiang's death. A huge area in central Taipei had been cleared for the memorial set within a landscaped park, fronting a vast open space wide enough to accommodate a multitude of people on ceremonial occasions. The aesthetic programme of Chiang's memorial is highly evocative of the Sun Yat-sen mausoleum in Nanjing. The ornamental gardens create a natural and verdant setting. The flight of granite steps rises as steeply but places the hall itself at the summit. The interior is dominated by the seated statue of Chiang and so duplicates the Lincoln-like figure of Sun, making an iconographic link between the KMT's founder and his chosen successor.

In view of the improved relations between the PRC and the ROC, previous restrictions on visiting the mainland have now been relaxed. Large numbers of Taiwanese visit the homeland of their forefathers and engage in business ventures there. As the nostalgic yearning for the old China is being replaced by more pragmatic views, Chiang Kai-shek, like Sun Yat-sen, is on track to becoming a revered but increasingly dimly remembered ancestor.

Yasser Arafat at Ramallah

> And we have a land without borders, like our idea
> of the unknown, narrow and wide.
> . . . so we shout in its labyrinth: And we still love you, our love
> is a hereditary illness.[10]

Kim Il Sung had lived and died in his sumptuously appointed presidential palace, which was subsequently converted into 'the sacred shrine of *Juche*' to display his embalmed remains. Yasser Arafat too was buried in the compound where he had spent the last years of life, although the makeshift and battered *Muqata* headquarters of the Palestinian National Authority) could not have been more different from the marbled halls of the Korean leader's palace. On the other hand, unlike Kim Il Sung, Arafat did get a purpose-built, architect-designed and expensively built mausoleum. Yet just like that of Chiang Kai-shek's at Chihu in Taiwan, it is officially a temporary resting place, awaiting the time when burial in the 'homeland', in this case Jerusalem, will be possible. In 2013 Palestine is a nation without a state. Arafat's mausoleum anticipates his as yet unfulfilled hope for an independent Palestine that includes Jerusalem.

Like other charismatic leaders whose early lives are shrouded in mystery, Arafat chose to obfuscate the narrative of his birth and childhood. Even the appearance of a birth certificate would have been unlikely to settle the matter once and for all. Indeed, myths tend to create their own truths.[11] Arafat was born Mohammed Abd al-Rahman Abdel al-Ra'ouf Arafat al-Qudwa al-Husseini on (or around) 24 August 1929 in Cairo. The alternative version, propagated by Arafat himself, was that of his birth in Jerusalem in a house close to the *al-Haram al-Sharif*, one of the holy Muslim sites in Jerusalem.[12] Arafat's father, Abdul Raouf al-Qudwa, belonged to a family of merchants from the Gaza area, and al-Qudwa and his wife's first children were born there in the 1920s. The situation after the break-up of the Ottoman Empire and the subsequent division of the Middle East into European-controlled protectorates prompted the family to move to Egypt. Al-Qudwa left early to safeguard his business but moved frequently between Gaza and Cairo. His family occupied a large house in West Cairo, and here the young Rahman, as he was then called, spent his early childhood. It when his mother suddenly died in 1933 that the four-year-old and his younger brother were sent to Jerusalem to live with their maternal uncle. They returned to Egypt after Arafat's father had remarried in 1937. Rahman, who was raised mainly by his older sister, attended local schools and acquired the nickname 'Yasser' (meaning 'carefree' or 'easygoing'). In 1945, when Arafat was sixteen, he became involved in smuggling arms to Palestine. Meanwhile, the discovery of the full extent of Nazi persecution of Jews was used to give greater urgency to demands for a Jewish homeland. In 1947 the United Nations proposed a plan to partition Palestine into two states, one for Arabs and one for Jews, and passed a resolution to this effect. The initial resistance by the local Arabs, followed by open warfare in 1948, led to their utter defeat, and to what became known in the Arab world as the '*Nakba*' ('Catastrophe'). Armed Zionist groups, supported by British, European, and American Jews defied the UN Partition Resolution and forced hundreds of thousands of Palestinians out of Palestine, into adjacent countries and further afield. On 14 May 1949 David Ben-Gurion declared independence from the British Mandate in Palestine and the foundation of the state of Israel. Arafat had tried to join the war but was prevented from actual fighting on account of his youth and lack of training.

Returning to Cairo, he enrolled at the university there to study engineering. He became active in student politics and was made leader of the Egyptian Student Union in 1949. When Gamal Abdel Nasser seized power in 1952 Arab resistance against the British gained momentum and the energetic young Arafat became not only a spokesman for the Palestinian community but trained students in guerilla tactics. After he graduated in 1956 however, he left Egypt for the Gulf to work for the Kuwaiti Public Works Department as a contractor and architect.[13] He was able to raise funds to found and support an underground organization, Fatah, which began to carry out acts of sabotage against Israeli water installations from bases in Jordan. Such attacks were stepped up after the defeat of the Arabs in the 1967 Six Day War. In 1969 Arafat was elected chairman of the PLO's executive committee, a position he held until his death in 2004. The initial goal of the organization was the armed struggle against Israel to regain the Palestinian homeland. Fatah continued its operations from Jordan until a violent showdown with King Hussein led to their expulsion in 1971. Arafat and his men moved to Beirut and he shifted tactics towards negotiations with Israel, a position he maintained following the defeat of the Arab states in the 1973–74 war. The stay in the Lebanon was brought to an end by the invasion of the Israeli Defense Forces (IDF) in 1982, when Arafat was forced to seek a new refuge in Tunis.

It was the first *intifada* ('Uprising') in the West Bank and Gaza in 1987, which had developed from the frustrated Palestinian population in Israel, that put pressure on the PLO to push for official recognition of its right to represent Palestinian interests. Arafat was prepared to 'renounce terrorism' to pursue the Two-State Solution, originally envisaged in the 1947 UN resolution. When the Israeli government under Yitzhak Rabin pushed for mutual recognition between Israel and the PLO, the Oslo Accords were signed in Washington on 13 September 1993 and Rabin and Arafat were both awarded the Nobel Peace Prize in 1994. A separate Palestinian Authority (PA) was set up and Arafat was allowed to enter Israel and to take on the government of territories awarded to PA control.

Matters deteriorated as negotiations with Israel over various contentious issues, such as the fate of Jerusalem, the return of exiled Palestinians to their homeland and the building of Jewish settlements in the West Bank remained unresolved.

In the mid-1990s, acts of violence, such as the assassination of Yitzhak Rabin (by a non-Palestinian Israeli) and of Hamas leaders, the Hebron massacre and Palestinian suicide attacks deepened mutual distrust and all but halted the fragile 'peace process'. Israel continued to ward off the perceived danger of the 'demographic time-tomb' as a result of the much higher birthrates of Palestinians by encouraging Jewish immigration and providing the newcomers with well-equipped, high-security 'settlements'.[14]

Arafat, leader of Fatah, Chairman of the PLO, and by then in charge of overseeing the Palestinian Authority, was not able to exert much influence. He had been away for so long that he found the political reality in the West Bank and Gaza beyond his control. Islamist groups, such as Hamas and the Palestinian Islamic Jihad Movement (PIJ), who had always urged for a military response and violent uprising as a means to establish a Palestinian state, challenged Arafat's legitimacy and authority. To what extent he condoned, authorized or deplored their tactics is still a matter of dispute. As the second *intifada* in 2000 degenerated into a series of suicide attacks on Israeli civilians it was met by intensified Israeli reprisals, resulting in the destruction of Palestinian governmental infrastructure. In an attempt to capture the men thought responsible for masterminding suicide attacks, the IDF besieged the PA headquarters in Ramallah. Arafat's compound, the *Mulqata*, came under attack on 12 December 2001 and a month-long siege ensued.[15] Arafat survived, not least because of the intervention by President George W. Bush, but he remained under house arrest, cut off from communication and in internal exile. As his health began to deteriorate, he was finally airlifted to Paris on 29 October 2004 to undergo medical checks.[16] On 3 November he fell into a coma from which he never awoke. He was pronounced dead on 11 November 2004.

The living Arafat embodied many of the contradictions and tensions which beset all of the Arab communities in the Middle East during the twentieth century, particularly the Palestinians. He was born in Egypt, and although he never lost his strong Egyptian accent he became the iconic Palestinian leader who attempted, with varying success, to speak for all Palestinians in the diaspora and in Israel. He presented himself as a devout Muslim but his party, Fatah, was not Islamist. He cultivated the image of a militant freedom fighter – always wearing some form of battle dress and his *kaffiyeh* (headdress or scarf) arranged in such a way to resemble the map of Palestine – but most of his political activities consisted of endless rounds of diplomacy (primarily with Arab heads of state, European and U.S. representatives, Israeli government officials and UN envoys). He could be pragmatic in his recognition of Israel and then pull back from signing final agreements. He attracted fierce loyalty among his supporters but alienated many Palestinians with his autocratic style of leadership. More used to operating at the margins, waiting to seize the right moment and then to stage highly theatrical appearances in front of the world's media, he found the actual business of administration irksome. Although he received a Nobel Peace Prize he is still regarded by many Israelis as a terrorist. Such conflicting modes of operation and ambiguities were to be reflected in the manner of his burial and the question of his legacy.

After his death in the Parisian hospital, Arafat's coffin, draped with the flag of Palestine, was taken to a military airfield. There a solemn ceremony befitting a head of state took place. This involved guards of honour, the playing of national anthems and the conveyance of the coffin on to an aeroplane witnessed by Arafat's distraught widow Suha, the then French Prime Minister Jean-Pierre Raffarin and Palestinian Foreign Minister Nabil Shaath. It was then flown to Cairo, where the military funeral took place on 12 November, beginning with prayers at a mosque in the Cairo suburb of Heliopolis. Mahmoud Abbas, who had assumed the leadership of the PLO, greeted the international dignitaries from around the world. Here too, Arafat was honoured as a statesman by other statesmen.[17] On the other hand the event also showed concern for the political implications of the ceremonies, as a *Guardian* reporter pointed out:

> Mr Arafat's 25-minute funeral at a military club near the airport, scheduled for late Friday morning, reflects concern for security at an event that will draw dozens of statesmen and foreign ministers. Analysts say Egypt also sought to avoid an outpouring of public emotion that might either get out of control or show that the late Palestinian leader enjoyed more support than other Arab leaders.[18]

Hosni Mubarak, then president of Egypt, followed the horse-drawn hearse behind a gun carriage and a military band to the nearby Almaza Air Base, from where Arafat's body was taken to Ramallah by helicopter.

While the Cairo funeral was seen as a military funeral and an opportunity to assemble international heads of state, the inhumation was to be a more intimate ceremony for Palestinians only. Ariel Sharon (then prime minister of Israel) had vetoed Arafat's long-held and oft-expressed wish to be buried near the Muslim holy sites in Jerusalem. Two Israeli helicopters accompanied the two Egyptian ones to ensure that there was no deviation from the route to the *Muqata* in Ramallah.[19] The Palestinian Authority had wished to stage a solemn and dignified state ceremony, but the huge crowds who awaited the arrival made this impossible. Martin Asser, a BBC journalist, described the tumult that followed:

> With an earth-shaking clatter, they flew low over the roof
> I was standing on and even lower over the three-storey building
> between us and the compound.

People clung on to anything within reach to prevent themselves being blown off the roof as a thick cloud of dust engulfed them. The two pilots unflinchingly took the helicopters down into the spaces cleared of people for them in the Muqata compound, which from my vantage point looked almost impossibly small. Volleys of gunfire rang out as members of the security forces and gunmen in the surrounding streets greeted the return of the dead Palestinian leader in their own way. The helicopters' rotor blades stopped quickly and the huge crowds surged forward to the foot of the aircraft.

Then came the real tumult of this hot afternoon. It took an age for the flag-draped coffin to emerge, but when it did, from the right-hand helicopter, it quickly started moving this way and that, pushed inexorably by the huge crowd. It soon disappeared completely from view, swamped by frantic security men in green uniforms and civilians with black and white chequered scarves. Sometimes the police had to fire over the heads of the crowd to make space, a seemingly lethal measure in this crowded environment. But the truth is that Palestinian people had taken over this 'ceremony' – whose organisers had planned a dignified lying-in-state, prayers over the coffin and a burial before sunset.[20]

Palestinian observers saw that the crowds, having torn down the barbed wire around the compound, had actually managed to get hold of the coffin, 'exuberantly trying to take it to Jerusalem'.[21]

Only with great difficulty did security forces manage to redirect the dense flow of mourners back towards the *Mulqata*, where the coffin was buried hastily. Four sacks of earth, taken from the grounds of the al-Aqsa Mosque in Jerusalem, had been emptied into the hole before the body was lowered. The crowd dispersed at nightfall and any hopes or fears that the occasion could spark another uprising were quelled. As Khalili pointed out in her analysis of these events, while the PA had wished to 'tell a story of the Palestinian nation as a narrative ending in the creation of a state [. . .] militant Palestinians had wanted to commemorate a man who was in their view not so much a founding statesman but an icon of nationalist resistance.' Yet it ended up confirming the reality of the Israeli occupation, which had 'made itself invisible for three days but had ultimately set the parameters of the ceremony and subsequent burial'.[22]

The contradictory legacy of political leaders whose appeal to present and future generations lies in their status as revolutionary fighters that is 'branded' in such a way as to make them relevant to the evolving political situation after their demise often causes great difficulties for their successors. The building of a mausoleum is therefore often an attempt at consolidating a particular reading of their lives within a national narrative. The PA leadership had already decided on the construction of a mausoleum before Arafat was taken to Paris and had approached the architects Jafar Tukan and Partners in Amman (Jordan) to come up with a suitable design.[23] Tukan had already designed a mausoleum for Abdul Hamid Sharaf, a prime minister in Jordan in the 1970s. In this case, there was a simple flat-roofed hall that featured a central opening to reveal the view of an olive tree, with the white facade enlivened by decorative bands of calligraphy from excerpts of the politician's speeches.[24] Tukan Jafar had also built a strikingly simple and modern mosque in Beirut. By choosing this architect, the PA made clear that they thought such modernist, even 'minimalist' restraint in architecture to be most appropriate for Arafat's tomb.

For the Ramallah mausoleum, Jafar recycled the design concept he has used for Abdul Sharaf. However, in response to the brief that stressed the provisional nature of Arafat's monument, he constructed the base of the mausoleum and the promenade that leads up to it to appear 'as if floating above the ground'. Construction was due to start in 2005 but was delayed because of lack of funds until 2006. It was finished in 2007 and officially inaugurated and dedicated by President Mamoud Abbas on the third anniversary of Arafat's death. Furthermore, Abbas announced the decision to build a museum in the reconstructed remains of *Muqata*, also to be designed by Jafar and financed by public funds.

I went to Ramallah in April 2011 in a public minibus from Jerusalem. After passing the Qalandia checkpoint (between Jerusalem and Ramallah), the huge concrete separation wall that divides Israel from the West Bank revealed its graffiti-covered Palestinian side. The very first image of a series of wall paintings, taking up the whole height of the wall, was that of a youthful and glamourized Yasser Arafat.

The *Muqata*, the former headquarters of the Palestinian Authority, where Arafat had spent the last three years of his life, was a bustling building site. It was one of many in Ramallah, a city experiencing a major construction boom. Arafat's mausoleum was built right in front of the battered and shell-marked compound. At the time of my visit it was hidden behind scaffolding and the shuttering works for the planned museum building, which were announced on a billboard at the mausoleum's perimeter wall. The tall, sharply delineated minaret with a folded-over top looms over the low-rise mausoleum complex and forms a vertical accent, echoed by three flagpoles and, on my visit, the contractors' cranes operating on the building site behind. There was no formal security check and no need to deposit bags or cameras. The mausoleum and the coffin were immediately visible from the single entrance gate and through the full-length glazed windows. The building, a simple cube, with large glazed openings on all four sides side has the form of a pavilion, not unlike that of a nearby showroom for luxury cars. It was obvious that the desired effect of this mausoleum was not to overwhelm the viewer with monumental grandeur but to look 'businesslike', straightforward, and at the same time elegant in the manner of many Middle Eastern upmarket business premises. A simple prayer room, referred to as a mosque, had been discreetly semi-interred and inserted into a landscaped garden on the eastern side of the mausoleum. All the facades of these steel-framed structures, as well as the perimeter walls and the paving inside and out, are finished with slabs of pale Jerusalem limestone – in itself a symbolic reference to the contested Palestinian capital. This gives coherence to the architectural ensemble. The ramped forecourt was not designed to hold a large crowd and there is no podium to address an assembly.

Hoarding showing the planned Arafat museum to be built behind the mausoleum.

Arafat's mausoleum at Ramallah seen from the entrance.

In the single-room mausoleum the architect has referenced the date of Arafat's passing (11 November 2004) in the measurements: 11 x 11 metres x 11 metres (around 36 x 36 feet x 36 feet). The arrangement of the limestone cladding slabs inside is on a smaller scale, so as to allow 11 x 11 slabs on each wall, again revealing the symbolic numbers. The interior was very bright as light streamed through the three large windows and the fully glazed doorway. The windows are all the same size and take up two thirds of the wall and rise directly from the floor. The architect described the effect he intended in an interview:

> Behind the grave is a water surface, a reflecting pool symbolizing life and the continuity of life for the Palestinian people. There's also a lot of light inside the space, symbolizing optimism and the insistence of the Palestinian people to go on living and to establish their state. The abstract and minimalist aspects of this design were intended to reflect the conceptual simplicity of the case of the Palestinian people – that this is a displaced people that is fighting to regain its

General view of the previous PA headquarters in Ramallah and Arafat's mausoleum compound.

country and homeland. This in itself is a very simple, straightforward and clear case, though it has become surrounded by complex issues.[25]

Dancing reflections that bounced off the water-filled channels surrounding the pavilion animated the interior walls with a suggestion of constant movement. Arafat lies beneath a white marble slab, placed in the centre, and inscribed with his name in black calligraphy. As in all the Islamic tombs so far discussed, there was no image of the incumbent. The window behind his simple tomb revealed a sturdy, gnarled old olive tree that has been planted behind the pool. This is meant to serve as a metaphor for the land of Palestine, the resilience of its people and its defunct leader.

The two presidential guards, wearing green uniforms and sashes, took up position whenever someone approached the mausoleum; at other times they walked around. Once every hour they were relieved by their comrades who ascended the low ramp from the entrance with some effort at martial rigour.

Guard of Honour at Arafat's sarcophagus.

The second pavilion to the west serves as a space for prayer and meditation. It consists of simple rooms, with one completely glazed wall on the south that overlooks a sunken garden indicating the direction of prayer. The minaret stands separately, rising in a straight line from a square plan and ending in a triangular kink that points towards Jerusalem. The three structures form the 'symbolic cluster' around the mausoleum pavilion.

The limestone cladding of all the reinforced concrete structures that make up the walls, pavilion, minaret and mosque have been left plain and smooth and are precisely fitted. The only concession to ornamentation was the band of incised, elegant calligraphy of Koranic verses in the space above the windows of the mausoleum and on the mosque wall facing the access ramp. Lines of a poem by the famous Palestinian poet and author Mahmoud Darwish are inscribed on a separate marble slab. The lines say that Arafat was a spark or resistance and that each Palestinian has a part of him in them.

Trees, shrubs and flowers have been planted in the spaces around the mosque to soften the stark contours of white walls. Just outside the western wall of the pavilion the carcasses of three dead trees have been

Ancient olive tree and construction works, seen from inside Arafat's mausoleum.

left standing. The gardener working there was not sure whether these withered trees were there for a reason. In response to my questions, he also said that their roots might have been damaged by the construction work. According to a Palestinian web posting however, their form was supposed to 'spell out the name of Allah' and furthermore, they were meant symbolize the three funerals held for Arafat (in Paris, Cairo and Ramallah).[26]

The serenity of this space was compromised by the activities on the building site right behind it. Once completed, the carcass of the original bullet-hole riddled compound will be incorporated into the ramped memorial museum. This will then house relics such as Arafat's *keffiyeh*s, pistols, fatigues and sunglasses, amongst other personal items.

The mausoleum has not been commercialized so far. No leaflets were available, no postcards, no souvenirs. This may change once the museum becomes operational. At the moment, like so many places on the West Bank, it was and continues to be 'work in progress'. During the time I spent observing the mausoleum, on a Monday, two German tour groups arrived with their German guides and admired the architectural qualities of the site. A few Palestinian visitors came in small groups or in couples. Seemingly pressed for time, they walked straight to the sarcophagus, offered a brief prayer, took a few pictures and left. After dusk, when the artificial lighting was turned on, the box-like container of Arafat's tomb gleamed like a magic lantern amid the chaos of construction work, while a red laser beam shone towards Jerusalem.

By dying in such unexplained circumstances, and having spent three years confined in the *Muqata*, Arafat now embodies the condition of Palestinians under occupation. Whereas he was once a controversial figure, he has become a unifying symbol, uncontested even by Hamas and other parties who now all claim credibility by showing respect and reverence for the departed Chairman of the PLO. But it was Fatah and especially the quite uncharismatic President Abbas who had most to gain from the cult of Arafat. The construction of the memorial museum will further cement this link and thus anchor Fatah's Ramallah as a symbolic centre of resistance to the detriment of rival Hamas. The minimalist aesthetic of the mausoleum, with its almost subliminal Islamic architectural references (the chimney-like minaret, cubic pavilion without a dome and calligraphic decoration) could be seen as distinguishing the more secular oriented Fatah from the Islamist Hamas and PIJ. Indeed, had it been built in Gaza, it might have looked more in keeping with traditional forms. It could also be seen as expressing aspirations for a pragmatic,

View of flagpoles from the mosque at Arafat's mausoleum.

Arafat's mausoleum at dusk

Posters and sign on the outer wall of Arafat's mausoleum.

unfussy modernity and one that can make a virtue of the 'provisional'. As such, it is in keeping with Arafat's cultivated informality and spontaneity, or indeed the conceptual simplicity of the cause of 'the Palestinian people', which the architect expounded in the interview cited above.

I found that despite the main pavilion's resemblance to a sleek corporate Middle Eastern car showroom, the whole ensemble communicates an expression of desire and longing for what it still denied to Palestinians and which, in the context of the mausoleum, centres on Jerusalem. As Mahmoud Abbas said during the opening ceremony of the mausoleum in 2007, the denial to grant Arafat his wish for burial in Jerusalem has wider relevance for Palestinians:

> We will continue on the path of the martyred President Yasser Arafat to be reburied in Jerusalem, which he loved [. . .] Jerusalem, which he tried to make, and which all our people are trying to make, the capital of the Palestinian state.[27]

Several features of the mausoleum are meant to keep this aspiration alive. Apart from the slanted ramp that runs from the mausoleum to street level that suggests how easily the coffin could be pulled away, there are several other devices that have been incorporated into the structure. A rail track was buried underneath and earth from the al-Aqsa Mosque was placed in the grave. The natural spring on the site itself, channelled to form a pool and conduits, refers to the fact that water always finds its way to its destination. Finally, at night, from the top of the minaret, a laser beam is directed towards Jerusalem. All these devices not only stress the temporality of the present entombment but seem to serve as quasi-magical mechanisms to bring the transformation into effect. Given the military occupation and the isolation of the West Bank from other Palestinian enclaves, it is ironic and sad that it is now mainly groups of foreign tourists, such as the serious minded Germans I observed, who ponder the complex messages of Arafat's mausoleum.

CHAPTER SIX

Appropriated Traditions

Our next three mausolea, the family tomb of Indonesia's General Suharto, that of its first president, Sukarno, and the memorial mosque of the Ayatollah Khomeini, do not fit into any of the categories established so far. Neither Suharto nor Khomeini founded a new nation, nor were they revolutionaries. As for Khomeini, whilst he did help to unleash a revolution in Iran, he did so as a cleric and from exile. Sukarno was both a Founding Father and a revolutionary but none of the three mausolea function as national monuments or as sites for state ceremonies. All of them, however, continue to attract thousands of visitors. What is interesting about these monuments is the way they refer to a specifically religious context of displaying status and power that draws on historical precedent rather than contemporary realities. I understand this as a form of appropriating traditions to bolster the credibility and status of the person buried there. In the case of Khomeini's mosque this appropriation was enforced only in the second stage of construction, as the earlier version was a much more radically modern building. The Javanese tombs are both self-consciously styled as a synthesis of traditional architectural forms taken from various sacred monuments but equipped to meet the needs and demands of modern tourists / pilgrims.

Sukarno and Suharto in Java

Centuries of exposure to Hindu, Buddhist, Confucian, Islamic and European influences, re-interpreted and integrated into the traditions of the various islands, have shaped the history of the Indonesian archipelago. This complex intermeshing of such varying cultural traditions also characterizes Indonesian modernity. As the main source of much-coveted pepper and spices, the islands had attracted European traders early on. In 1602 the Netherlands established the Dutch East India Company and in 1800 the Dutch Colony, which existed until the Japanese invasion in 1942. Nationalist resistance against Dutch rule began earlier in the twentieth century. One of the pro-independence leaders was Kusno Sosrodihardjo (later known as 'Sukarno'), who was born in 1901 in East Java. He obtained a degree in engineering, practised briefly as an architect, and became active in the pro-independence movement, forming the Nationalist Party (PNI) in 1927. Having studied Marxism as well Islamic philosophy, he formulated a programme to seek a united and independent state, based on social equality, religious tolerance and self-sufficiency. The Dutch had him arrested and sentenced to four years of prison in 1930 as his political activism had gained widespread support. Although he was set free after just one year, the colonial administration disbanded his party and forced him to retire from politics. Sukarno, together with fellow activist Mohammad Hatta, presented Indonesian interests to the invading Japanese, who used local nationalist aspirations to further their own colonialist intentions. On 29 April 1945 the Japanese allowed the setting-up of an Indonesian legislative authority and this prepared the way for the declaration of independence on 17 August 1945, following Japan's defeat in the war. Sukarno became Indonesia's first president. He had also drafted the new constitution, based on the notion of *Pancasila*, which entailed respect for the major religions, nationalism and social justice.[1] However, the Dutch were not prepared to give up their colony without a fight, and it was only after waging a bloody liberation war that the complete transfer of Dutch sovereignty to Indonesia was finally declared on 27 December 1949.

 Suharto was twenty years younger than Sukarno (he was born on 8 June 1921) and came from a more humble background, having been raised in a small village some fifteen kilometres from Yogyakarta on Java.[2] After graduation from high school, he entered the Dutch colonial army and joined *Peta* ('Defenders of the Fatherland'), a Japanese-sponsored defence corps, in the 1940s. Following independence, Suharto was incorporated into the newly formed national army in which *Peta* officers assumed superior positions. He spent the war years in the district of Yogyakarta and after 1949 was promoted to the rank of lieutenant colonel. Not having displayed much interest in Indonesian politics before, he seized the moment in 1965, when a coup attempt by the '30th September Movement' resulted in the killing of senior military personnel. Although the coup was subsequently blamed on the communists, it is likely to have originated from the military. Sukarno was forced to hand over power to Suharto (on 11 March 1966), who kept his predecessor under house arrest for the rest of his life.[3] Widespread protests against his assumption of supreme command of the army and of the presidency were violently repressed. Suharto then demonstrated a particular hatred of communists and instigated large-scale purges, persecutions and mass killings. Given that Suharto's rise to power coincided with the height of the Cold War and the beginning of U.S. military engagement in Vietnam, such a radical demonstration of his virulent aversion to communism made him a useful Southeast Asian ally of the Western powers. He benefited from the oil boom in the 1970s, which helped him overcome the political crisis of 1973–74 and financed lavish public spending sprees. He also instigated the invasion and annexation of East Timor in 1975. Despite the controversial nature of his assumption of office, the brutal repressions of his early years and the illegal occupation of East Timor, Suharto managed to consolidate his hold on power for more than three decades by carefully projecting an image of an ultimately benevolent leader. Building on Sukarno's 'guided democracy', which held that the Indonesian people were not ready, not educated enough for Western liberal democracy and needed to be 'guided', he formulated the even more paternalistic 'New Order' system, which rested on a neo-liberal oil-based economy and a one-party government (Golkar) under presidential control. However, in the wake of the Southeast Asian currency crisis, rising unemployment, rampant corruption and increasing discontent with his authoritarian rule, student demonstrations and riots erupted, which forced the aged president to retire in 1998.

Suharto was an unlettered man and did not leave any writings other than a self-serving autobiography and early diaries. Unlike Sukarno, who spoke several languages and was widely read, he had little interest in Western thought and adhered to no political ideology. According to his biographer Robert Elson, he ascribed to general ethical precepts of Javanese tradition, such as loyalty and duty to the nation.[4] Moreover, like many other Javanese Muslims, Suhartu remained attached to traditional beliefs such as *Kejawen* (the word means 'Javanism' and refers to various spiritual practices and beliefs that are held to be specifically Javanese). He cultivated a mystical aura to uphold the widespread belief that to retain power one needs to enjoy cosmic assent. He would visit caves and other sites associated with supernatural powers and he was much concerned with the 'symbols and attributes of cosmologically defined legitimacy.'[5]

Also in keeping with Indonesian custom, he had married a woman from a higher social stratum than himself, Siti Hartinah (known to Indonesians as 'Ibu Tien'), who was, albeit distantly, related to the Mangkunegaran royal dynasty of Solo (Surukarta) in central Java.[6] This was 'the second most insignificant of the small central Java principalities instituted by colonial authority in the late eighteenth and early nineteenth centuries', which had lost all but its social status in the War of Independence.[7] Ibu Tien exerted considerable influence on Suharto during their 49 years of marriage and assiduously cultivated the public *persona* of an aristocratic First Lady. Some Javanese believed Suharto had special powers, derived at least in part from her mystical bequest (*wahyu*), and that after her death in 1996, he was deprived of this force and lost power.[8] He subsequently retired to lead a quiet inner-city life. He survived several strokes and other serious ailments which allowed him to avoid being publicly held to account and to face criminal charges.

When Suharto was finally dying in January 2008, there was much speculation in the Javanese media on how long his magic powers would last, and it was believed that:

> His *ajimat* [an invisible talisman inside his body] must be withdrawn totally from the feeble body before Suharto can be allowed to die – the mystical force that kept him at the top is now refusing to let him go, some say.[9]

Suharto's belief in supernatural powers was at least one factor that prevented him from granting the last wish of his predecessor. Sukarno had left instructions not be given an elaborate tomb such as the one Nehru built for Gandhi.[10] According to another version of his funeral directions, he wished to be buried in his garden at Batu Tulis, close to a stone bearing an ancient inscription dating from the fifteenth century which was said to have magical powers. Suharto feared that Sukarno's burial place might become a place of pilgrimage and perhaps galvanize political protests. He therefore refused these requests and insisted that Sukarno be buried next to his mother in an anonymous grave at Blitar, a remote location in eastern Java, on 22 June 1970.

Sukarno's mausoleum at Blitar.

By that time, Suharto had begun to think about his own funerary monument. He might have been reluctant to leave such arrangements to his political successors and wished to secure a more ostensibly private final resting place that would stress his connection to his wife's more illustrious lineage. The chosen place was close to the cemetery of the Mangkunegaran royal line and considered auspicious in terms of its closeness to one of Java's sacred mountains. Without Ibu Tien's connection to the Mangkunegaran court he would never have gained access to such a site. Although she was too distantly related to the royal family to gain admittance to the royal burial grounds at Mangadeg itself, Suharto and his wife were able to secure a tract of land very close to it. Nevertheless, it was specifically stipulated that their cemetery was to be situated at a lower level. They formed a foundation (*Yayasan Bangun Mangadeg*) that was officially devoted to the upkeep of the cultural legacy of the royal house of Mangkunegaran, but which entailed the building of a new graveyard for Ibu Tien's and Suharto's family.[11] The president officially opened the new complex, called 'Astana Giribangun'

('The Palace of the Arisen Mountain'), in 1976. At that time it only contained the remains of Ibu Tien's father that were moved there from a previous grave. The architecture of this new complex was in keeping with the aesthetic principles of his New Order policies:

> The New Order's adoption of a cultural discourse routinely anchored in constructs like 'tradition', 'origins' and 'ritual' – and its subsequent cooption and promotion of 'traditional' forms of cultural expression was part of an elaborate privileging of stability and order as dominant characteristics of not only Javanese culture but also the 'Indonesian culture' of the New Order.[12]

Sukarno had trained as an architect and was a self-confessed modernist. He wanted Indonesia to become a modern nation and preferred reinforced concrete and glass structures. Suharto's 'New Order' policy on the other hand emphasized the concept of 'stability' and looked to tradition rather than revolution. One of the projects he spent a significant sum of money on was the 'Beautiful Indonesia in Miniature Park'. This was an initiative dreamt up by Mrs Suharto in 1971 that opened to the public in 1975.[13] The 'Beautiful Indonesia in Miniature Park' was a huge theme park designed to show the cultural diversity of the archipelago and was filled with replica 'traditional' houses. The project triggered nationwide research projects on 'traditional building', but rather than document the rich variety of the local architectural vernacular, it provided homogenized materials that served to construct a transregional national culture and style to suggest a 'national tradition'. While Astanga Giribangun was not meant to be a public building and was hidden away in a remote mountainous region north of Solo, it was entirely in keeping with Suharto's aspirations for a conservative neo-traditionalism achieved with modern technology.

In early January 2011 I took a taxi from Solo to visit Suharto's tomb. As we drove north through the verdant and fertile countryside, billowing clouds partly obscured the mountains that shield the plains of central Java. From the steep roadside, a sign saying 'Suharto Park' indicated a large, empty car park. All visitors had to register at the reception area, where papers were checked but bag searches were not carried out. A paved footpath led towards the top of the hill, where a heavy metal gate gave access to the complex. A glazed cabinet contained an architectural model of the site. It showed the division of the space into three elements: a prayer-room, a courtyard and the mausoleum itself, as well as subsidiary low-rise buildings. The timber-built, flat-roofed prayer room is on a lower level, almost hidden amongst densely spaced trees. A covered seating area allowed special guests to overlook the main gate of the mausoleum.

A bronze gate, heavily ornamented with swirling floral patterns, opened onto the platform on which the mausoleum has been erected. At first sight, it looked like a type of upper-class Javanese dwelling known as '*Joglo*'. With their wide eaves and pyramid-shaped roofs supported by interior columns, they were the prerogative of the higher strata of society. At Astana Giribangun the roof was considerably higher than is common in such buildings and resembled most remarkably the very tall and pointed 'sacred peaks' (*took*) of Sumbanese clan houses. On the other hand, it also looked like the roofed tombs of so-called *Wali Songo*, the nine missionary Muslim saints who propagated Islam in Java. They too are typically set on an elevated platform reached by a series of steps, while a veranda shaded by the overhanging roof surrounds the centrally placed tomb chamber whose importance is signalled by the

Main building at Astana Giribangun.

Pillared portico at Astana Giribangun, showing the doors leading to the inner burial chamber.

peaked roof gable. However, unlike the standard simply constructed tombs, everything at Astana Giribangun is made to look expensive. The main tomb chamber structure is fashioned from tropical hardwood. The floor of veranda-like portico is marble. The inner tomb chamber (82 square metres) was entirely enclosed by wooden screen walls with elaborate carvings.

The interior of the main tomb chamber was kept quite dark because the only natural light came through the opened gate. The wooden ceiling had a coffered recess or 'dome', and a large flower-shaped chandelier was suspended from the centre. A line of identical marble tombs was placed against the wall opposite the main doorway. The framed photographs that showed a likeness of the people buried underneath these coffins were an unusual feature for Muslim tombs. In the Suharto photograph he was depicted in uniform whilst a separate frame displayed his medals.[14] Several flower wreaths on special stands were placed next to the coffins and in front of each tomb was a tray of offerings of incense and rose petals. The floor was covered with wall-to-wall carpet.

Main burial chamber at Astana Giribangun.

A group of Javanese visitors arrived and squatted down in front of Suharto's sarcophagus. A photographer who plied his trade here asked them if they wished their photos to be taken next to the coffins. They sat for a while, listening to their guide, had their picture taken and then left. I was asked to sign the visitor book and when I showed an interest in doing so, the guard brought out another volume. The book recorded the name and place of origin of each visitor, the date of the visit and the number of people in the party. In the months before my visit, groups of several individuals, but also parties of 40, 80, even 100 people were listed. The next book he showed me, covering the period from January to December 2010, showed a similar pattern. The average number of visitors per day was about 50. However, this is a steep decline from the days when the mausoleum was at the height of its popularity, following Ibu Tien's death and just after Suharto's demise. This falling interest is also borne out by the long line of decayed booths along the footpath. They used to sell snacks, votive offerings and souvenirs to the numerous pilgrims. After my visit, I saw a few women brandishing printed T-shirts in the car park but a wider selection of memorabilia had

Memorial plates showing the mausoleum are on sale at the Astana Giribangun gift shop.

now been made available in the reception kiosk. On sale were framed photographs, plates, clocks, key rings that depicted the faces of Mr and Mrs Suharto against the backdrop of Astana Giribangun.

A short distance away was the site of Mangadeg, the burial ground of the Mangkunegoro royal family from Solo.[15] This dynasty had established itself in the mid-eighteenth century and the main architectural structures of the burial grounds date from this period. A very simple timber pavilion sheltered the royal tombs, where the kings are buried in marble sarcophagi set within small chambers and shielded from sight by net curtains. There was no ostentatious display of riches here, no elaborately carved wooden panels and ceilings, no costly metal doors, no flaunting of wealth, unlike Astana Giribangun. A small wooden pavilion, set on a path in a forest clearing, allowed a view over the countryside below, where there were terraced paddy fields, meandering streams and villages. Towards the north, loomed the peak of Gunung Lawu. This is a volcano that has long been considered a sacred mountain. The cemetery was built into its western slopes, since Javanese thinking holds that tombs on mountains are places of power. The mausoleum built by Suhartu, despite his efforts to make it look like a *kraton*-type palace or a Muslim saint's tomb, gave rise to comments that it was rather too 'Chinese' in character and perhaps displayed some of Suharto's 'irrational' impulses all too clearly.[16] Such criticism did not deter thousands of Javanese from visiting. According to a current tourist website,

> Astana Giribangun is religious tourism site [. . .] Today this place has become a destination of pilgrimage for people from different areas of Indonesia [. . .] People feel very comfortable in the complex. Pilgrims go in and out. They come to pray and put flowers on the second president's graveyard.[17]

Spiritual tourism had became a phenomenon of the Suharto years, partly because people had higher disposable incomes than before and because government agencies, such as the Archaeological Service, had taken over the administration of sites, including the *Wali Songa* tombs. According to anthropologist James Fox,

> Javanese people visit tombs at appropriate times for various reasons, including 'to *nyekar*, offer flowers (and incense), to pray, to make requests or to fulfill a vow after having made a request (*nyadran*) and, in the process, to gain the blessing (*berkah*), possibly even the potency (*kesakten*) of the sleeping one.[18]

The fact that not only saints but politicians or people close to them, especially those credited with supernatural powers, were thought to be able to transmit blessings and potency explains the popularity of Ibu Tien's grave first and then that of Suharto's. In recent years though, this has been eclipsed by the appeal of Sukarno's last resting place.

We have seen that Suharto had buried his predecessor in an anonymous grave in East Java. Nine years after Sukarno's death however, when he saw fit to allow a limited rehabilitation of Sukarno, Suharto ordered the construction of a proper mausoleum, known as 'The Grave of Brother Karno' (*Makam Bung Karno*). Suharto inaugurated the mausoleum in June 1979. Since I was not able to visit the place myself, I have relied on the description and interpretation by Pier Paolo di Giosia, who went there in 2008:

The *Makam Bung Karno* area was divided into three levels following Javanese adaptations of Hindu-Buddhist and Islamic principles: the courtyard, the terrace, and the mausoleum symbolizing the Javanese mystic vision of life as Alam Purwo (prenatal period), Alam Madyo (life on earth) and Alam Wasono (after death) [. . .] A magnificent gate, sited in the south of courtyard, indicates the boundaries and the access to a revered space. Pilgrims have to pass through the main gate and between two banyan-trees afore a large open pavilion, a refined copy of a Javanese traditional Joglo house, where Sukarno is buried side by side with his parents [. . .] Behind the grave, there is a dark marble tombstone showing a simple epitaph commemorating Sukarno as the proclaimer of independence, first president of Indonesia and mouthpiece of the people.[19]

Although more than a million people had visited the mausoleum within a year, fences and other obstacles all but prevented the site from functioning as a pilgrim centre. This was only possible after Suharto's death and it was especially once Sukarno's daughter Megawati, leader of the Indonesian Democratic Party (DPI), who was president from 2001–2004, made it into a veritable sacred site. During her election campaign in 2004 she made the pilgrimage to her father's grave no fewer than seven times.[20] Although it did not help her win another term, Sukarno's mausoleum, now equipped with a library, a museum and a statue of the first president surrounded by reliefs depicting scenes from his life, attracts huge numbers of tourists and pilgrims. It operates, as de Giosia observes, as

> an epicenter which attracts both secular and sacred pilgrims from the entire country, with different social statuses and faiths. The grave of Sukarno gives the opportunity to experience the 'pilgrimage' in different ways, emphasizing that 'unity in diversity' (*Bhinneka tunggal ikka*) is the Indonesian political, social and cultural mindset.[21]

Suharto made the mausoleum look superficially like his own, again drawing on the precedent of saints' tombs, although it was rather less sumptuously decorated. With Megawati's patronage, it was then enlarged and augmented so as to serve pilgrims' needs and to make a point about Sukarno's political importance as Father of the Nation. While Suharto has been subsumed into his wife's clan in the relative privacy of the mausoleum, Sukarno's tomb serves as one of the new major sites of spiritual pilgrimage and a national memorial.

The Mausoleum of Ayatollah Khomeini in Tehran

Iran has a much longer tradition of monumental tomb architecture than Indonesia, going back to the sixth century BC in the case of the well-known Tomb of Cyrus the Great at Pasargadae. However, it was during the early Islamic period that mausoleum building in Iran really took off, when the aristocratic leaders of nomadic tribes (such as the Samanids, Seljuks, Ilkhanids and Timurids, who one after the other exercised power in Iran), were buried in splendid, brick-built mausolea. The architectural forms of these tombs, either round, squat towers or barrel-vaulted cubes, as well as the ornamentation on their facades that often imitated finely textured wickerwork or embroidery, hark back to funerary tents that were made of felted or woven fabrics.[22]

As more stable dynasties established themselves in Iran, rulers began to be buried in or very close to mosques. This was a process that began in the early sixteenth century, when Ismail bin Haider (d. 1524), leader of the Safavid order of Sufis, created an empire that would last until 1722. He was the first Iranian leader to adopt Shiism as the official religion of the new state. None of the Safavid shahs were buried in separate mausoleums; they preferred to be laid to rest within existing or newly founded religious complexes. Hence, only 'holy men' or saints were to be honoured with a mausoleum and these sites became destinations for Shia pilgrimages. The most important of these sites were in Mesopotamia: Ali ibn Abi Talib (considered by Shiites to have been the Imam) was buried in Najaf, his son Hussain in Karbala, whilst the tenth Imam, Ali Hadi, was buried in Samarra.[23] The Ottoman conquest of Mesopotamia in 1556 largely prevented Iranian pilgrims from accessing these shrines and led to the demand for alternative holy sites within the Iranian borders.

One of these sites was the mausoleum of Sheikh Safi in Ardabil, dedicated to the founder of the Safaviya order of Sufism and hence also the ancestor of the Safavid Dynasty.[24] It had been built soon after his death in 1334 in the shape of a domed tower. Under the patronage of Safavid rulers this tomb became the centre of a vast complex, comprising several courtyards, each with tall, niched recesses (*iwans*).[25]

Of equal importance were the shrines around the tombs of Imam Reza in Mashhad and that of his sister Fatima Ma'suma in Qum. Built over centuries and benefitting from the largesse of shahs, they were sumptuously decorated, distinguished by golden domes and polychrome wall ornamentations. According to Kishwar Rizvi,

> such commemorative monuments were crucial sites for the construction of an imperial iconography and for the dissemination of ideology [. . .] The past was amended in order that the shahs were presented as both direct descendents of the sixth Shi'i Iman Musa Kazim, giving them both spiritual and familial authority,[26]

and hence political legitimacy.

As Shiism thereafter remained the official religion in Iran, this close link between state and religion survived the demise of the Safavid Dynasty in the eighteenth century and was revived after the Revolution. Only two shahs were buried in a purpose-built mausoleum. The first belongs to Nader Shah, who wished to make an economically weakened Iran more competitive with its Mughal and Ottoman neighbours and tried to pave the way for reconciling Sunni and Shiites. When he was assassinated in 1747, his sister had him buried in a mausoleum in Mashhad, which he had made his capital. Despite the original religious controversy it has survived and is still a popular pilgrimage site.

The other mausoleum belonged to Reza Shah Pahlavi, who had assumed power after overthrowing the Qajar Dynasty in 1925 in a coup. His son Mohammad Reza had his father buried in a concrete mausoleum (not unlike that of Jinnah's in Karachi), in Ray, south of Tehran, in the 1960s. As a potent symbol of the hated Pahlavi Dynasty it was, with some difficulty, bulldozed and dynamited during the Revolution in 1979.[27]

The contemporary mausoleum of the Ayatollah Khomeini near Tehran can thus be fitted into the long tradition of burying first charismatic tribal leaders and later those with primarily spiritual authority. The changes that have been made to the building since it was first opened show a shift in emphasis from his political relevance in favour of his sanctity. A substantial investment is being made to turn the mausoleum complex into a fully-fledged religious complex. As such, it will be the twenty-first-century equivalent of Sheikh Safi's shrine.

Ruhollah Musavi Khomeini was probably born on September 24 1902, in the village of Khomein in central Iran.[28] He was from a family of *sayyids* (people claiming descent from the Prophet Muhammad) and issued from a long line of Islamic teachers and clerics.[29] He was brought up by his aunt because his father, a senior member of the clergy, was killed six months after the child's birth in 1903. He had, by his own accounts, a happy childhood and was enrolled at a religious school at the age of four. He was thus set early on the path to becoming a scholar and studied at theological colleges, first in Isfahan and then in Qum. He obtained his diploma in the early 1930s, which allowed him to teach Islamic jurisprudence, philosophy and religion. By that time Reza Shah Pahlavi had deposed the last king of the Qajars and set about the transforming Persia into a modern state along the lines of Atatürk's republic in Turkey. Like Atatürk, the Shah instigated a radical programme of modernizing reforms and relied on a powerful secret police to stifle dissent.

Khomeini had married in 1930 and with the dowry he purchased a farm near his native Khomein. He began to give lectures on ethics at the Qum seminary, which attracted many followers with its outspoken criticism of the Shah's policies.

Reza Shah openly admired Adolf Hitler and procured German investments in Iran's infrastructure. In 1941 Soviet and British troops invaded Iran, which remained under occupation until the war was over. In 1944 Reza Shah abdicated in favour of his son Mohammad Reza. In a weak position after the withdrawal of foreign troops and with rampant inflation damaging the economy, the young Shah reversed many of his father's most oppressive policies. He allowed the press greater freedom, and even the formation of a Marxist party. The clergy was divided between those favouring abstention from politics and those demanding the introduction of Sharia laws. Khomeini himself had attacked the former Shah in lectures and pamphlets and intensely disliked his successor.

When oil was nationalized in the 1950s, an arrangement that was seen to benefit the British owners of the Anglo-Iranian Oil Company much more than Iran, Islamic militants backed the violent demonstrations by Iranian nationalists led by Mohammad Mosaddeq. At that time Khomeini, while remaining loyal to the appeasing Grand Ayatollah Borujerdi, felt deeply drawn to the uncompromising policies of more radical Islamic activists such as Navab Safavi. This tendency grew stronger in the 1960s when Iran became a key U.S. ally in the context of the Cold War, which led not only to communist purges but to a deepening secularization and strong American cultural influence. Combined with the Shah's mismanagement of the economy this provided ample ammunition to Khomeini, who from his pulpit in Qum inveighed against the Shah with greater freedom after the death of the moderate Ayatollah Borujerdi in 1962. His sermons found a willing audience and when he was arrested after a particularly fiery speech held on 3 June 1962 on the occasion of *Ashura*, the ritual commemoration of the martyrdom of Hussein, rioting erupted in the major cities of Iran. In turn, on the Shah's orders there were violent army clampdowns. Khomeini was released after some weeks, having been told to steer clear of politics. In reality, this was a lenient warning because of his status as a high-level Shia cleric.[30]

The incident only enhanced his standing amongst the populace angered by the Shah's secularist and pro-Western policies. His position as the most vociferous critic of the regime in Iran came to an end on 4 November 1963, when SAVAK officers bundled him into an aeroplane that was to take him into exile to Turkey. Finding the Kemalist country an uncongenial place, in 1965 Khomeini managed to get permission to settle in the Shia holy city of Najaf in Iraq.

He would remain there for sixteen years and spent his time teaching and writing about the 'crimes' of the Shahs and arguing for Islam as the instrument for the overthrow of the regime. He developed the blueprint for an Islamic government based on Sharia law and cultivated links with Amal, the Shiite party in Southern Lebanon, as well as the Palestine Liberation Organization.

Meanwhile, the Shah continued to alienate his people through his pursuit of an arguably overblown personality cult (he wanted to be known as 'The Light of all the Aryans'), the workings of his repressive secret service and the staging of such costly extravagances as the 2,500 anniversary of the Persian monarchy in the ruins of Persepolis in 1971. When the Shah imposed the single-party rule, Khomeini banned his followers from joining it. Many leading clerics in Iran produced *fatwas* to the same end, which were countered by the imprisonment of many prominent religious figures. Other underground resistance groups were also galvanized, including some with left-wing organizations. Despite the crackdown by SAVAK agents and the hard punishment meted out in Iran's prisons, demonstrations continued. They gained momentum in 1977 after the visit by President Carter and in the face of the economic recession in the West that hit oil revenues.

When Khomeini's son Mostafa died in mysterious circumstances, demonstrators in Qum called for Khomeini to be allowed to return.[31]

Khomeini himself bided his time. He set up the Society of Militant Clergy to disseminate his taped speeches among the masses and organize strikes and meetings. When a government newspaper attacked Khomeini as 'a foreigner, a British agent and an alcoholic homosexual', riots erupted and he became the figurehead of popular uprisings. As the only leader who had consistently denounced the Shah he had the support of millions. Indeed, support for the ayatollah grew even stronger in the face of violent repression by the security forces.

When the Shah, his political judgement possibly impaired by the deteriorating state of his health, put pressure on Iraq to terminate Khomeini's stay in Najaf, Khomeini chose to go Paris. In Europe he could count on links with Persian expatriates and gain full access to means of communication and the media. This enabled him to coordinate the Revolution from afar, which compelled the Shah to leave Iran on 16 January 1979.

On 1 February Khomeini made his triumphant return to Tehran, where millions were waiting to catch a glimpse of their long-exiled leader. Ten days later the monarchy was officially abolished. Khomeini quickly consolidated his own political position, appointed Mehdi Bazargan, a veteran of 1950s pro-democracy campaigns, as prime minister to oversee an interim government under the supervision of the Revolutionary Council. With the help of Hezbollah, he suppressed the still active left-wing guerilla groups and formed the Revolutionary Guards (*Pasdaran*) to enforce the new ideology.

> In the few weeks since his return to Iran he had become not just the leader of the revolution: he was the revolution. He achieved almost mystical status amongst the people, and even experienced politicians such as Bazargan thought of him as a 'saint', an image Khomeini did not exactly seek to dispel. As far as the masses were concerned, he was the man who had single-handedly triumphed over the forces of darkness and freed the country so that a new generation could take over the reins of government.[32]

A referendum held to offer the choice between a monarchy and a republic resulted in overwhelming support for the latter, which led to the establishment of the Islamic Republic of Iran in March 1979.

Khomeini then retired to Qum, where he worked on the proposed new constitution to be ratified by the newly elected Assembly of Experts.

This stipulated that while the president was to be elected and his service restricted to two terms of office, a 'Supreme Leader' (*velayet-e Faqih*) was to have the highest official and clerical authority. This position was the one Khomeini created for himself, based on his own theory of supreme power; it allowed him full control without the day-to-day duties of government. It also confirmed his ideas of the state as

> an administrative arrangement to implement the Sharia guided by the just leader, in the model of the philosopher ruler, with a wisdom and knowledge that is higher than the law.[33]

At the same time, quite unprecedented in the history of the Islam, the title *imam* was bestowed on him, with all its connotations of unchallengeable spiritual and political authority. He thus presided over the establishment of absolute Islamic rule in the capacity of a theological jurist and spiritual leader. As Imam of the Muslim Community worldwide he also committed himself to spread his form of revolution to other parts of the world, most notably in the Lebanon, which Israel had invaded in 1982.

The defining conflict of Khomeini's term of office, however, was the war with Iraq from 1980 to 1988. Saddam Hussein had sought to exploit the initial instability of the new regime in Iran to gain control over the oil fields of Khuzestan, but the Iraqi invasion met with fierce resistance. Saddam's purges of the Shia community and the execution of Khomeini's friend and Shia leader Mohammed al-Sadr had already infuriated the Ayatollah, who now declared that 'The war that the Iraqi Baath wants to ignite is a war against Islam [. . .] the regime is attacking Iran, attacking Islam and the Koran.'[34]

The war helped to consolidate the authority of Khomeini, who in turn was able to galvanize the population into united efforts to defend the country. Such was the gain to be made from this conflict that Khomeini, rather than accepting the ceasefire brokered in 1982, opted for a counter-offensive to invade Iraq and thereby prolonged the war for another six years. Drawing on the Shia tradition of holy martyrdom, he urged the youth of Iran into battle, in which they launched wave after wave of suicidal attacks against Iraqi positions. In his earlier writings Khomeini had used the term *shahid* ('martyr') only in the conventional sense of those Shia saints who had died because of obeying God's will. However, during the Revolution anyone killed on the streets became a revolutionary 'martyr'. Especially during the war with Iraq, the *Basij* militia, 'volunteers' who were often unemployed or poorly educated youths recruited by the clergy who died in the massive 'human wave attacks', were assured of the heavenly rewards of martyrdom.[35] It was only when Saddam Hussein resorted to aerial missile attacks on Iranian cities and after the naval clashes with U.S. warships that Khomeini could be persuaded by members of his council to sue for peace. A million Iranians had lost their lives and more continued to die from the effects of chemical weapons deployed by Saddam Hussein in the last year of the war. The economy was severely damaged, not least because of the destruction of oilfields.

Less than a year after the war ended, on 3 June 1989, Khomeini died. After suffering a heart attack in 1986, his health had deteriorated. He was 86 years old. His chosen successor to the position of Supreme Leader, Ayatollah Khamenei, together with other members of the government, issued a statement in which the dead leader was described as 'the most divine personality in the history of Islam after the Prophet and the Imams'.[36]

Millions of people turned out for his funeral, which led to such incontrollable overcrowding that the coffin had to be airlifted to his final resting place near the Behesht-e Zahra cemetery south of Tehran.[37] Ahmad, Khomeini's son, who had served as chief of staff, and who had hoped to succeed him, became the overseer of the mausoleum. When he himself died of a heart attack in 1995, he was entombed next to his father, and Hasan, Khomeini's grandson, became the new superintendent.

A week after Khomeini's death his tomb was surrounded by a provisional structure of green fabric. A gold painted dome placed above the temporary cladding around the coffin emphasized the sanctity of the grave. Meanwhile, a Tehran-based architect, Mohammed Tehrani, set to work on the designs for the mausoleum. This was to consist of a main shrine containing the tomb, flanked by lateral wings on either side, each built around a large courtyard.

Construction started straightaway, beginning with the central shrine. In the initial phase, which lasted until *c.* 2010, the burial hall of around 200 feet square consisted of a single-storey, flat roofed, hangar-like, brick-walled structure, with a facade pierced by 24 doors suggesting a freely accessible space.[38] The plain walls of the main facades contrasted with the gold sheathing that covered the four minarets and the dome. The dome, with a diameter of 27.5 metres (around 90 feet) and a height of 68 metres (223 feet), was the tallest in Iran and the most eloquent symbol of the incumbent's charismatic status.[39] The interior was very simple, not unlike that of halls used for trade fairs, lit by daylight through three clerestory zones and by neon tubing. The flat, prefabricated metal roof was supported by a grid of 12 x 12 columns and held together by a system of struts and trusses, which were left exposed.

The use of modern, even inexpensive materials and modern construction methods, was to 'transform a traditional commemorative type into a contemporary monument'.[40]

The mausoleum was left in this condition until a few years ago, when substantial alterations to the main shrine room were begun, and when the completion of the lateral courtyards was given new impetus. When I went to see this with an Iranian friend in June 2011, construction work was still going on.

The mausoleum lies directly on the motorway that connects the capital to the Persian Gulf along the north-south axis. On a clear day it is visible from the northern suburbs of Tehran. The mausoleum is within easy of the nearby Ayatollah Khomeini Airport. The location between the holy city of Qum and the political capital traces Khomeini's trajectory from spiritual to political power. At the same time it places him even closer to the many thousands of 'glorious martyrs' who are buried in the vast funerary complex Behesht-e Zahra ('Paradise of Zahra'). This municipal urban cemetery, built in 1950, became the main burial place for the victims of the Iran-Iraq war and contains some 1,300,000 graves. The same underground station serves the cemetery and the mausoleum.

Large signs on the motorway indicated the mausoleum. Despite the building works — several large cranes were installed and parts of the building were under the scaffolding – the mausoleum was kept open 24 hours a day. It was said to attract thousands of visitors daily, especially on religious festivals. One of the officials there said that on 3 June 2011, a week before our visit and the anniversary of the Ayatolloah's death, some two million people had come. Most of the available parking spaces (there are enough for some 20,000 cars) were filled on the Friday afternoon we arrived.

The construction works concerning the main area of the mausoleum will significantly transform this part of the building. The whole facade is to be extended to double-storey height and to follow the pattern of Safavid-type *iwan* portals, while the previously existing and modern 'high tech' interior structure will be replaced by a more traditional-looking space with concrete vaulting.

Forecourt of Ayatollah Khomeini's mausoleum, Tehran.

Owing to the ongoing building works, a temporary entrance (with one for men and one for women) had been set up at the side of the main gateway. Bags were screened, shoes deposited, before all visitors went through security screening. Posters in English and Farsi reminded women to keep on their *hijab* headcover. However, the full *chador* (body-cloak) was not required to be worn. Given the temporary subdivision of the interior space by plastic hangings, it was difficult to work out the spatial layout. The bare concrete walls were covered with thick plastic drapes, and the marble floor was protected by machine-made carpets. Little flags, in the colours of the Islamic Republic, were strung from the pillars and metal supports, as well as strings of LED lights.

The tomb chamber is a modern version of the traditional glazed and latticed caskets in Islamic shrines. It looked like a metal cage on a marble plinth, enclosed with green-tinted glass at the bottom and clear glass at the top. A band of Koranic verses runs around the upper

Makeshift entrance to Ayatollah Khomeini's mausoleum.

rim, and rather tawdry vases and ornaments had been placed at the top. Green velvet cloths were draped over the two-tier, flat-topped coffins. The Ayatollah's coffin was larger than that of his son Ahmad. Green-tinted lamps on the ornate glass chandelier hanging above the coffins cast a dim, green light. The metal grill was unglazed, allowing people to toss banknotes inside, where they lay piled up like autumn leaves. People held on to this grill and touched it with their lips and forehead. Many said their prayers in the direction of the tomb. A separate enclosure was reserved for women. I was surprised to observe that the majority of visitors were women, mostly draped in full black *chadors*, and that they walked about the whole space, alone or in small groups, with and without children of all ages. They moved with great assurance while the men huddled to the spaces close to the pillars or the walls. All the women we talked to had come to visit the grave of a son or

Facade of the lateral wings at Ayatollah Khomeini's mausoleum.

grandson or a brother at the cemetery and to pray for them at the Imam's shrine.[41]

Outside, the construction of the new *iwan* entrances to each of the lateral courtyards had been finished; green domes surmounted the high, arched portals. The front parts of these buildings accommodated fast food outlets, several banks, marble-clad and very spacious washrooms and toilets, religious souvenir shops and supermarkets.[42] Painted hoardings hid much of the facades, showing a green, idyllic landscape behind double height arches, as well as huge portraits of Khomeini and his son. The double-arcaded facades in the interior of the courtyards had been completed and were clad with marble panels. These huge buildings should in due course provide accommodation for pilgrims, a clinic, as well as theological seminaries, just like the shrines at Qum or Mashhad.

The grounds around these structures were divided into gridded plots of gardens with trees and shrubs. Many families ate their meals seated on rugs spread on the ground, rather than use the concrete picnic tables, painted to imitate wood. There were several play areas, with swings and roundabouts. People had come here to spend the whole weekend, and plastic tents had been set up at random, under trees or even on the tarmac.

The atmosphere was welcoming, especially to children, who were free to run around even inside the shrine. I had the impression that the whole mausoleum was to be experienced as a place that celebrates life and looks to the future rather than as a solemn place of remembrance and death. Kindly smiling, rather than the familiar stern-looking portraits of the Ayatollah had been chosen for the exterior walls. It seemed that at this stage he was being promoted as a benign father figure rather than the uncompromising revolutionary leader. This was a change of image similar to the case of Mao Zedong's statue inside his memorial hall.

Inside Ayatollah Khomeini's mausoleum.

Officially, the Khomeini mausoleum is a holy site of pilgrimage. To some pilgrims it is even more important than Mecca. It did not promote a nationalist agenda – there were just a few republican flags and no flagpole with the associated ritual of hoisting and lowering the national emblem, and there were no uniformed guards present. A new memorial mosque is currently being built in Tehran and its huge, concrete, arched entrance is already visible. This may become the official site for commemorating Khomeini's role in the formation of the Islamic Republic, which would leave the religious significance of the imam to the mortuary site. Such a move may contribute to efforts by the current president,

Offerings of banknotes; visible here is the coffin of the Ayatollah's son, Ahmed.

Ahmadinejad, to assert greater independence from the Supreme Leader. This is an office still held by the now elderly and reclusive Khamenei. It would also anchor the disastrous if valiant Iran–Iraq War to the memory of Khomeini, buried at Behesht-e Zahra, who had sent so many of the country's youth to their graves.

The remodelling of the mausoleum is an interesting development and one that may signal a new interpretation of Khomeini's legacy. The transformation of the current configuration of the main mortuary space from a startlingly modern and modest interpretation of a traditional architectural form into yet another pastiche of a generic 'Safavid' shrine, built in concrete and surfaced with computer-generated tile patterns on the walls, could be read as an effort to remove the revolutionary and populist references of the building. Bland neo-Safavid constructions proliferate in present Iran, not just in the holy cities and Tehran. Golden domes, once a signifier for great sanctity, have also become almost commonplace. When the buildings will eventually be finished, Khomeini's mausoleum will look just like them, that is, part of a unified and sanctioned apparatus of sacred spaces, and like the pilgrimage sites of previous centuries, fully equipped to suit the spiritual and bodily needs of visitors. Interestingly, no museum on Khomeini, let alone on the war or the Revolution, has been envisaged. Since it suits the present government to derive legitimacy from his legacy and while the constitution and the position of Supreme Leader is upheld, the cult of Khomeini will continue to be a rallying point for popular support for the Islamic nature of the republic. The more secular middle classes might well be grateful for the increasing sacralization of Khomeini, if it contributes to prepare the way for a separation of state and clergy.

Across the border from Iran, in Turkmenistan, the erstwhile dictator Saparmurat Niyazov (1940–2006), better known as 'Turkmenbashi', used much of the wealth generated by the exploitation of natural gas to finance his personality cult.[43] In preparation for his death he had built a huge modern mosque and a mausoleum near Ashgabat in 2004, where he now rests, next to the ashes of his mother and brothers who all died in the 1948 earthquake. Some of the finest Seljuk tombs are in Turkmenistan, and although Turkmenbashi's mausoleum is intended to recall the architectural prototypes of these monuments, he only managed to produce a rather vulgar 'post-modern' edifice made of concrete, consisting of a large, saucer-shaped golden dome, surrounded by arched porticoes and pillars.[44] Known as the 'Mausoleum of the Eternal Leader', it was to serve as an everlasting memorial and cult centre. Since 2006, however, his successor has slowly whittled down the numerous mementoes of his predecessor. The refurbished 'Safavid' mausoleum of Khomeini will be as much a pastiche as Turkmenbashi's 'Seljuk' tomb. Yet I surmise that were the present Islamic Republic to be replaced with another form of government, Khomeini's tomb would continue to be visited by the mothers, sisters and daughters of the 'martyrs' whom he dispatched to paradise in such great numbers, while Turkenbashi's memorial would remain as a reminder of his overinflated ego.

These four mausolea, although quite different in their socio-political contexts, were constructed for the leaders of countries with a Muslim majority. Furthermore, they were erected in places where Islam coincides with the practice of venerating saints, as well as with the idea of deriving blessings from the dead. All of these places have become destinations for spiritual tourism or pilgrimage. In the case of Sukarno, it combines political and religious importance. The architecture of each of these buildings shows a conscious turning back to established prototypes, to the shrines of saints. Thus it appropriates the status of such places for the dead politicians. The blurring between personality cults and religious veneration, which we saw most clearly in North Korea, is embedded in a long tradition of local practices in this present case.

The example of the relative decline in popularity of Suharto's mausoleum shows that by becoming yet another sacred site amongst many others, the specific historical memory looses validity as the incumbent becomes 'saint'. As such, their powers to bestow blessings may wax and wane.

CHAPTER SEVEN
Political Mausolea in Africa

African colonies achieved independence later than those in Asia as European powers clung more firmly to the African remnants of their former empires. This meant that decolonization was played out within the context of the Cold War rather than resulting from the restructuring of world order that followed the Second World War. Liberation movements in sub-Saharan Africa were thus not only trying to throw off colonial rule and to unite people divided by ethnic and linguistic differences. They also had to make choices about ideological alignments. All charismatic leaders of liberation struggles used personality cults as a powerful means to instill national unity, along with the panoply of statehood, such as flags, anthems and parades. In the 1970s monumental memorials and statues also became popular. The mausoleum however, as a building that enshrines both the mortal remains and the public memory of a political leader, was slow to gain currency in Africa. This may have something to do with the unstable political climate of the post-independence period. Many of the freedom-fighting founders of nations did not remain in office for long, having being ousted by coups or assassinated. The more enduring regimes were often those of autocrats or dictators. If they managed to die in their own country, nobody wished to perpetuate their memory. Some leaders preferred not to disclose the location of their graves to prevent any abuse or 'sorcery'. It was therefore in hindsight, sometimes with a considerable delay, that at least some of the early leaders were officially entombed in publicly accessible mausolea by governments who wished to reconnect to the ideals of the pioneers of African democracy, to an era of hope and optimism. As such, they are belated tributes to the Founding Fathers and their architectural forms owe little to classical or historical precedents. Instead they are attempts at narratives about national identity and the life of the rulers buried there. They are therefore radically different from other political mausolea and deserve to be discussed in the context of the particular trajectory of African history.

North African Mausolea

The first political mausoleum in Africa was built in Cairo in 1936 for Saad Zaghloul (1859–1927), the Egyptian revolutionary leader who fought against the British occupation. He served as prime minister for less than a year, from 26 January to 24 November 1924, after Britain had issued the nominal, so-called Unilateral Declaration of Independence in 1922. Soon after his death, the nationalist Wafd Party (Delegation Party) he had created and led decided to turn his house in central Cairo into a museum. Today, it is known as 'The House of the Nation'. They also purchased some land opposite on which to build his mausoleum. The architect Mustafa Fahmy designed this in a neo-Pharaonic style and it was opened in July 1936.

> This is not merely a decorated shed with ancient Egyptian references only applied to the surface. Fahmy combined contemporary design elements (art deco) along with a modern reinvention of ancient Egyptian form and motifs to create a modern building. In plan, this is a symmetrical building with a central axis where two doors (west and east) face one another and lead in and out of the central space where a solid unmarked sarcophagus is located. Along the north–south axis there are two smaller side spaces. The interior space is reached by steps leading to a symbolic pylon gate set between two red granite columns rising around 15 metres [around 49 feet]. A shallow portico leads to the entry doors decorated with re-imagined ancient Egyptian iconography such as the snake, the sun disk and the lotus flower. The tall interior hall is flooded with light from twelve large clerestory windows that separate the lower part of the central hall from the ceiling above. The two side galleries also have three tall slender windows allowing more light into the space. Twelve red granite columns similar to the four on the outside (a pair at each door) line the interior space.[1]

Bourguiba's mausoleum, Monastir, Tunisia.

It is interesting that the first mausoleum in a Muslim country to be dedicated to the memory of an independence leader, should look like an ancient Egyptian temple. It is therefore an early indication of a trend we shall find in later sub-Saharan mausolea that connects to a distant past, to a time when the country was thought to have been truly independent from foreign influence.

Tunisia's first president, Habib Bourguiba (1903–2000), had his mausoleum constructed during his lifetime, just as an Egyptian pharaoh did. Although he professed to admire Atatürk and like the Turkish leader had instigated many radical reforms, he did not wish to be buried in a mausoleum as 'secular' in appearance as Anıtkabir. He preferred a 'neo-Arab' golden domed, marble-clad shrine, flanked by two 25-metre-high (82 feet) minarets. He instructed the Tunisian-born French architect Olivier Clément Cacoub to tour the country to find inspiration for the mausoleum, which turned out to be an eclectic pastiche of elements from various older Islamic monuments.[2] Members of Bourguiba's family were buried there before he himself was laid to rest in his magnificent white 'wedding cake' sarcophagus when he died at the age of 96 in 2002. At the main entrance to the complex, Bourguiba had his own epitaph inscribed in golden letters: 'The supreme combatant, builder of modern Tunisia, liberator of women.'[3]

While the Egyptian nationalist decided to make Zaghloul's tomb look like an ancient temple rather than an ancient tomb, Bourguiba made the connection to the eighteenth-century Husseinite Dynasty whose rulers were entombed in the vast and splendid mausoleum called 'Tourbet el-Bey' in Tunis. It was a dynastic monument and not a destination for spiritual pilgrims, such as those in Shia Iran.

Ahmed Ben Bella (b. 1918), the first president of Algeria, died at the age of 92 in April 2012. Perhaps because of his age and because he was thought to have little relevance to contemporary Algeria, he was buried in a simple tomb within the martyr's section of El-Alia Cemetery in Algiers.[4]

Sub-Saharan Mausolea

An important factor in the process of decolonizing Africa was pan-Africanism, which in the late nineteenth century began as a call for African unity and the return of the African diaspora. It engaged in the re-evaluation of African history and indigenous cultures to counter the effects of imperialist oppression and slavery. Many of its proponents adopted the cause of anti-colonialism and the struggle for political independence, which gained momentum after the Second World War.[5] Some of the prominent U.S. pan-Africanists, such as George Padmore and W.E.B. Du Bois, emphasized their commitment to Africa by emigrating there (in both cases to Ghana) and becoming African citizens. Although African political unity, as envisaged by some activists and thinkers, did not materialize in the aftermath of decolonization, the ideas and ideals of pan-Africanism retained at least some currency, as one can see in the design of many sub-Saharan mausolea. Many feature lions as symbols of African pride and strength and almost all incorporate star emblems. References to indigenous architectural forms or to folk customs are also popular.

In the mausolea built in countries aligned with the Soviet Bloc during the Cold War period, ideological commitment was expressed by the embalmment of the leader or the Soviet-style architecture used in the design.

The earliest sub-Saharan mausoleum was built in Nairobi for Jomo Kenyatta, the first president of Kenya, which had won independence from Britain in 1963. By exercising autocratic presidential powers, he presided for over fifteen years of general stability and economic prosperity, while the West rewarded his pro-capitalist alignment with substantial aid. Kenyatta was still in office when he died in his sleep on 22 August 1978.[6] Vice President Daniel arap Moi was sworn in as president for an interim period of no more than 90 days. Having been

Entrance to Kenyatta's mausoleum in Nairobi.

an associate of Kenyatta's from the days before independence, he vowed to continue the former president's policies and swiftly went about canonizing Kenyatta as the Father of the Nation. By building him a mausoleum, he not only expressed the nation's respect and gratitude but his intention to consolidate his own bid for power.[7] It was a strategy that worked and Moi lasted well beyond his preliminary three months. Indeed, he retired from office in 2002. It had been a smooth succession, which was unusual in post-independence Africa.

Kenyatta's mausoleum, though a modest structure in the form of a simple pitched-roofed pavilion, stands in the centre of Nairobi next to the parliament in Uhuru ('Freedom') Park, where the celebrations following the declaration of independence had taken place. It is a simple pavilion with a pitched roof above the monolithic sarcophagus. A round perimeter wall, like those enclosing Kenyan villages, surrounds the tomb. It is symbolically guarded by a pair of large sculpted lions and protected by the red-coated guards of honour. A row of flagpoles flying the national colours lines the short path that leads to the grave. The mausoleum is not at present accessible to the public, and the closure of the monument to all but members of Kenyatta's family suggests that the coalition government that has been in power since 2002 wishes to distance itself from the Kenyatta cult encouraged by Moi. At the same time the status of the mausoleum as a national monument has been preserved.

President Marien Ngouabi (1938–1977) of Congo was not a 'founding father' like Kenyatta, but the third post-independence ruler since the former French colony became a state in 1963. However, since he had founded the Marxist-Leninist *Parti Congolais du Travail* (PCT) and aligned himself closely with the Soviet Union, he was the first African political leader to warrant being buried in a Russian style mausoleum. He had come to power in 1969, taking over from Alphonse Massamba-Débat. After he was assassinated on 18 March 1977, the military Committee of the Party, under Joachim Yhombi-Opanga, formed an interim government. Massamba-Débat, who was accused of the murder, was executed. Ngouabi's funeral took place on 12 April and he was interred in the compound of his residence and headquarters at Brazzaville. Under Opango and his successor, Dénis Sassou N'Guesso, the site was turned into a 'Leninist mausoleum', which was opened in 1981. This government derived legitimacy by continuing the murdered president's policies and strongly promoted a cult of Ngouabi.[8] The mausoleum, still a single-storey concrete house that has clearly been converted, bears the inscription 'MAUSOLÉE PRÉSIDENT MARIEN NGOUABI'. The tomb is inside a dark chamber, curtained with red silk. A bust of the defunct president, flanked by flags of the republic, stands behind the marble sarcophagus.[9] Although Ngouabi's cult is still prevalent in Brazzaville, the government's decision to build a much more monumental, purpose-built mausoleum for Pietro Paolo Savorgnan di Brazzà caused some controversy. It is not without irony that the Italian-born French explorer, who had opened the way for the colonization of what was later French Central Africa in the 1870s, now has a grander mausoleum than the erstwhile 'freedom fighting' postcolonial leader. Brazzà, who died in Dakar in 1905, was buried in Algiers. N'Guesso had him exhumed from his grave in 2006 and conveyed to the new mausoleum

Kenyatta's sarcophagus at the mausoleum in Nairobi.

in Brazzaville, where he was solemnly reburied later that year in the presence of senior French diplomats.[10]

Angola's President Agostinho Neto visited Brazzaville on 28 June 1979 and was shown Ngouabi's mausoleum, then under refurbishment.[11] Angola had been a Portuguese colony and as long as Salazar was in power in Portugal, decolonization was out of the question. The case for Angolan independence was made by the two ideologically distinct groups: Dr Agostinho Neto's Marxist-inspired *Movimento Popular da Libertação de Angola* (MPLA) and Holden Roberto's pro-Western and pan-Africanist *Frente Nacional de Libertação de Angola* (FNLA). It was Neto who declared independence in Angola on 11 November 1975 and he was proclaimed president. The country, however, was embroiled in a long civil war between the Soviet and Cuban supported MPLA, the Mobutu-backed FNLA and the South-African-supported UNITA. Neto went to Moscow to seek treatment for cancer but he died there on 10 September 1979. As he had been an ally of the Soviet Union his body was embalmed by the experts at Lenin's mausoleum.[12] His Russian biographer reported on the grandiose plans and vast scope of the project:

> According to the design plans, the project will include, in addition to the mausoleum, a political-administrative complex, which will house the Presidential Palace, the central Committee, the Council of Ministers, and the Ministry of Defense, the security organs and the courts. The entire complex will occupy 152 hectares in Luanda [. . .] The mausoleum will be surmounted by a tower 110 metres high [around 360 feet]. There are also plans to erect a chiming block, whose chimes will be accompanied by extracts from Neto's poems. In front of the mausoleum there will be a Demonstration Square that will be used for popular meetings. The grandiose complex will symbolize the boundless love and gratitude of the Angolan people to Agostinho Neto, who is known in Angola as the immortal leader of the Angolan revolution.[13]

Soviet designers and engineers began to construct the tower straightaway but soon all work stopped. There were several reasons for this. Not only did the vicious civil war, which claimed at least 300,000 lives, destroy the economy, but UNITA leader Jonas Savimbi remained in power for 30 years. He had been an implacable enemy of Neto's and had no desire to spend money on building his mausoleum. Neto's

Agostinho Neto's mausoleum in Luanda.

embalmed body could be visited once a year; only his Portuguese widow had free access. After thirteen years, in 1990, the government decided to grant his wife's wish to have him buried. Following the breakup of the Soviet Union, the Russians were no longer interested in financing Neto's memorial. It was only when another MPLA government was elected in 2008 and oil revenues began to flow that the completion of the Founding Father's mausoleum became a matter of political urgency, although on a significantly smaller scale than had been envisaged. It was finally inaugurated 17 September 2012, the nineteeth anniversary of Neto's birth.[14] Known locally as 'The Big Rocket' (*o foguetao*), it looks like a spaceship from a 1950s sci-fi movie. The architectural form is unique amongst all the mausolea I know: it is a 120 metre-high (around 393 feet) spire on a conical pedestal and lacks any specific African references, unless one takes into account the circular enclosure wall. Amid the frantic development boom in oil-rich Luanda, this rocket-shaped tower, on which the government has lavished millions of dollars and which at one time dominated the skyline, has become all but obscured from the coast by the recent construction of highrise buildings.

Dr Kwame Nkrumah Memorial Park in Accra

The rich gold mines of Ghana, hence formerly called the 'Gold Coast', have attracted European traders since the late fifteenth century. In the course of the nineteenth century, the British steadily advanced their control and established the Gold Coast Colony in 1874, to which in 1901 they added the hitherto Asante heartland (known as 'Ashanti') and then a year later, the British Protectorate over the northern region between the White and Black Volta Rivers. Missionary activity was greatly encouraged to provide moral guidance but more importantly, schooling, since the British administration relied on 'educated natives'. It was in such a (Catholic) missionary school that Kwame Nkrumah, born 1909 in Nkroful, a village in the Western Region, received his primary and secondary education. Segregated housing, the issue of land ownership and the excessive commercialization of land (cocoa farming had been introduced around 1910) proved deeply unpopular. The pan-Africanist lawyer, Joseph Ephraim Casey Hayford, advocated that Nigeria, the Gold Coast, Sierra Leone and Gambia become a 'united West Africa'. The Great Depression of 1929 hit the colony hard as most of the revenue depended on cocoa export and the prices had collapsed. The British authorities responded by raising taxes and passing laws to stem the flood of anti-imperialist ideology. This caused widespread protests and even led to a truce between the traditional chiefs, who had gained status and influence under British rule and the rebellious intelligentsia, as they combined forces to form the Central National Committee (CNC) in an effort to influence the British government.

In 1935 Kwame Nkrumah decided to further his studies, not in Britain but in the United States, where he enrolled at Lincoln University in Pennsylvania and read sociology and economics. He stayed there throughout the period of the Second World War and graduated in 1945. In the same year he moved to London to study law and philosophy at the London School of Economics but soon became actively involved in the West African Students' Union. He also worked closely with the West Indian pan-Africanist George Padmore as joint secretary for the fifth Pan-African Congress held in Manchester. From these positions he emerged as an outspoken critic of British colonial rule in Africa.

In his homeland cocoa prices had collapsed again in 1937, and the outbreak of the war saw the mobilization of thousands of Africans for military service.[15] After the war, demands for greater participation of Africans in government led to some changes in the constitution. The United Gold Coast Convention (UGCC) pressed for a new constitution to be drawn up, which would replace the chiefs on the Legislative Council with 'educated commoners'. They sent for Kwame Nkrumah to act as a full-time organizer. Once he had arrived in the colony, he drew up an action plan that would lead to self-government and independence, not just in the Gold Coast but also in Ashanti, the Northern Territories and Trans-Volta Togoland, calling for a coordinated, three-step strategy of mass mobilization. In order to spread the message of nationalism beyond the educated elite of the coastal areas, he travelled all over the country, setting up hundreds of local branches. The second phase involved constant mass demonstrations, to be followed by the convening of a national assembly and further strikes and boycotts to exert pressure on the government. Nkrumah's action plan worked. In the aftermath of the civic disturbances in 1948 the government arrested six of the leaders of the UGCC, including Nkrumah, who then appeared before a commission set up to probe the causes of the unrest. One of the resulting recommendations was that an all-African committee be set up to draft up a new constitution. Nkrumah established a newspaper, the *Accra Evening News*, to disseminate his Positive Action programme, split from the overly careful and elitist UGCC and in 1949 launched the Convention People's Party (CCP), whose slogans 'Freedom' and 'Forward Ever, Backward

Never' resonated widely amongst the population. His calls for a general strike on 9 January 1950 brought the country to a standstill. The government reacted with a crackdown on CCP activists, the closure of newspaper offices, a ban on all political meetings and finally the arrest of Kwame Nkrumah himself on 23 January. He was charged with incitement to strikes and sedition and sentenced to two years' imprisonment. He managed to maintain contacts with the CCP and to mastermind the strategies for the forthcoming general elections scheduled for 8 February 1951 in which the CCP won 34 out of 38 seats. Kkrumah was released the next day but although the people of Ghana had made their wish for immediate independence clear, the process of decolonization was slow and painful. Finally, on 5 March 1957, Nkrumah, dressed in a traditional *kente* cloth, stood on the grounds of the former Polo Club before a cheering multitude and declared the independence of Ghana.

In one of his books he speaks of his frustration that the full implementation of his ideas, especially the strategy of socialist economic development, should face grave difficulties:

> Immediately after Independence, while wishing to proceed on a socialist path of economic and social development, it was considered advisable, in view of the circumstances operating at the time, to pursue a 'shopping list' approach, estimating how much we could afford, and allocating it to projects drawn up into a list according to priority. But it soon became clear that this approach was not producing results quickly enough [. . .] Bourgeois economic interests were too deeply entrenched to be removed entirely, or overnight. Ghana inherited almost total trade dependence on the West. Our economy was almost entirely foreign or local capitalist owned.[16]

He was a charismatic diplomat who met with all the major political players of his time, from Kennedy to Mao Zedong, but he resisted the temptation to align himself openly to either of the Cold War power-blocs. However, his book *The Last Stage of Imperialism*, published in 1965, a scathing critique of Western control over Africa, was seen as proof of his slide towards communism by the Atlantic powers.

An attempt was made on his life in 1962 and again in 1964. After holding a referendum in 1964, Ghana became a one-party state. When reviewing what had been achieved in eight years since independence, Nkrumah could point out that we have built some of the finest roads in the world; we have provided medical and health services for the large majority of our people; we have built universities; secondary schools, training colleges, and provided opportunities for free education for the great mass of the population.[17]

The economy, however, worsened in the 1960s, owing to falling cocoa prices and high inflation. Discontent with the government grew. On 21 February 1966 Nkrumah left the country on a peacemaking mission to help end the war in Vietnam. Three days later, on 24 February 1966, the 'Operation Cold Chop' brought in troops who took control of Accra and Kumasi. The coup was said to have been welcomed 'with far more enthusiasm than had been the case for independence'.[18] Nkrumah's statue outside Government House, which proclaimed him the founder of the nation, was smashed to pieces. Two days after the coup of 1966 the army and police established the National Liberation Council (NLC) under Chairman J. A. Ankrah, who embarked on a policy of national austerity and the reversal of Nkrumah's socialist policies. After parliamentary elections in 1967, Kofi Abrefa Busia inaugurated Ghana's Second Republic and implemented market liberalization under IMF control. There were calls for Nkrumah to be allowed to live in retirement in his own country and a series of strikes further crippled the economy. Another coup on 13 January 1972 brought back a military government under Colonel Ignatius Acheampong, who formed a new government, the National Redemption Council (NRC), and espoused a 'vague kind of socialism'.[19]

Nkrumah spent the remaining six years of his life in exile in Guinea, writing and cultivating roses. His friend, Ahmed Sékou Touré, Guinea's revolutionary president, made him honorary co-president. Suffering from cancer, Nkrumah sought treatment in Bucharest where he died in hospital on 27 April 1972.

Nkrumah's embalmed corpse was first flown to Conakry, where Sékou Touré prepared a state funeral for his co-president. The Ghanaian leader, Colonel Acheampong, who wished to be seen as conciliatory towards the now deceased Father of the Nation, requested that the body be buried in his homeland. Sékou Touré initially refused and then contended that Nkrumah be buried with all the honours due to a former head of state. Other African leaders, especially General Gowon of Nigeria, also pleaded 'that Nkrumah's body should not end up in a mausoleum in Guinea, but should be returned for final burial in Ghana.'[20]

View of Nkrumah's mausoleum in Accra from the main gate.

After two months of negotiations the body was first flown to Accra, where it lay in state for ten hours and was visited by thousands of grief-stricken mourners.[21] At the end of a Catholic burial service in Nkrumah's home village of Nkroful, attended by his mother and his widow Fatiha, as well as over 20,000 people, Nkrumah was laid to rest in a 'modest mausoleum' in his hometown of Nzima, close to the border of Côte d'Ivoire.[22]

On 31 December 1981, after several military governments and the short-lived Third Republic (1978–91), Jerry John Rawlings came to power through yet another armed coup. After initial calls for revolution and not much more than moral support from the Soviet Union and Eastern European countries, Rawlings bowed to the implementation of IMF- supervised 'structural adjustments'. Enjoying considerable popularity, he lifted the ban on political parties in May 1992 and presented himself as a candidate for the forthcoming presidential elections. He consciously drew on the old CCP slogans and chants of the pre-independence era and generally wished to be seen as the true heir to Nkrumah's vision, especially the aspect of Pan-African Unity.[23] The reburial of Nkrumah's body in a sumptuous new mausoleum in the middle of Accra was meant to demonstrate the continuity between the first years of the new republic and the revitalized Ghana of the early 1990s.[24] Rawlings opened the mausoleum with great pomp and ceremony two months before the election on 1 July 1992 and emphazised the themes of nationalism and self-determination in his official address. It was a strategy that worked as Rawlings won 58.3 per cent of the vote.[25]

This marked the final stage of Nkrumah's rehabilitation. Ever since, in what has become the Fourth Republic, he has been publicly recognized as Founder of the Nation and revered leader of Ghana.[26]

Nkrumah Memorial Park was built on the grounds of the former colonial Polo Club, where Nkrumah had proclaimed independence in 1957. It lies on the High Street that sweeps down to the coast of the Atlantic and faces the Supreme Court of Ghana. Railings surround the whole complex and visitors need to purchase a ticket at the gatehouse. When I went to see the memorial in July 2011 no other security measures were in place. The grounds are laid out in rectangular patches of neat lawns and this formal composition is enlivened by shrubs, flowerbeds with annual plants and flowers and a great a variety of trees, many of which had been planted by visiting dignitaries. The main entrance to the mausoleum on the High Street is generally only opened for special occasions and visitors are admitted through a gate at the western side. An open-air exhibition that consists of posters mounted on plinths in the shape of oversized open books (put up by the Pan-African Association) serves as an introduction to the mausoleum visit by referring to the many books Nkrumah wrote and outlining the main points of his political thinking. This lateral approach from the west is at odds with the original layout of the Memorial Park. Here the gate immediately revealed the sight of the main building, set towards the rear of the park, at the end of a highly dramatized vista evoking the rituals performed for traditional Ghanaian chiefs. Seven pairs of life-size sculptures of kneeling hornblowers emerge from two shallow water basins. The memorial's official leaflet explains their significance:

> Hornblowers form part of the tradition peculiar to Southern Ghana. When there is a festival or durbar, at the point when the chief is about to appear in state, the hornblowers herald and announce his arrival. When a prominent person dies, the horn is always blown by court personnel of the chieftaincy to announce his death. So basically, the hornblowers are blowing

the horns to announce his death as well as publicly acclaim his good works. Traditionally, hornblowers don't stand in or near water. The significance of water as a source of life in Ghanaian belief is merely montaged on the horn for brevity of style. However, as the water flows continuously it also represents eternal life. Though Osagyefo is dead, his spirit lives.[27]

His effigy dominates the forecourt of the mausoleum in the form of a larger-than-life-size bronze statue, placed high on a stone plinth on the very spot where he declared the independence of Ghana. He is portrayed in the act of making this famous speech, raising his right arm and pointing forwards in a gesture that illustrates the CPP slogan 'Forward ever, backward never'. Several flagpoles mark the site as one of national importance.

The mausoleum looks more like a very large abstract sculpture than a building; a series of bundled pillars clad in grey marble. My guide explained that it symbolizes the large trees under which people like to be buried in the countryside, but according to the brochure, it is 'like a truncated tree that represents Nkrumah's unfinished works [. . .] it is not in bloom which reiterates the disappointments in his unfulfilled dreams', while also evoking the idea of 'Nkrumah resting under a tree after a hard day's work'. Furthermore, the structure of the mausoleum also looks like a reversed state sword. Traditionally, if a sword is raised upwards, it stands for war. When it is turned upside down, it stands for peace.'

Statue of Nkrumah in the pose of declaring national independence.

The architect of the mausoleum was Dr Don Arthur, who had studied in London and Moscow in the 1970s, returned to Ghana and became a minister. He took all sorts of factors into account when he designed the building:

> Arthur re-read Nkrumah's autobiography and focused on four key facts: Nkrumah admired Gandhi and his non-violent philosophy; he was inspired by the French Revolution; and by the

October Revolution in Russia; as an African he took pride in Egyptian civilisation, going so far as to marry an Egyptian, Fathia. Arthur then looked to prominent architecture in these diverse cultures and realised that with the exception of the Great Wall of China they contained the 'seven wonders of the world'. He developed design principles based on the Taj Mahal in India, the Eiffel Tower in France, the Pyramids of Egypt, the Hanging Gardens of Babylon, the Alexander Tower and the Mausoleum for Lenin in Moscow. As events in his lifetime and surrounding his death had proved, Nkrumah, in the minds of his adherents at least, was a global figure deserving of a globally significant monument. The challenge was how to express this sense of monument in an architectural vocabulary that was fundamentally African.[28]

I thought that the actual tomb chamber was a highly original building and rather beautiful. The three soaring pillars are set quite close together and form an overarching rhythmical structure. At ground level, three high and narrow vaults form a processional way on either side of the central space in which Nkrumah's low granite sarcophagus has been placed.[29] The concrete *brise soleil* slats (to shade from the sun), set high between the pillars and the lateral narrow openings at the sides, modulate the light and bring out the striations of different shades of grey marble that covers the whole structure inside and out. This form of all-over cladding unifies the various architectonic elements and provides a sumptuous and sensual architectural skin, warm and smooth to the touch. The sound of the water fountains emptying into the pools that surround the mausoleum on all sides, the breeze that enters freely through the slits between the pillars and the scent of flowers all contribute to a heightened sense of being alive.

Gardens and fountains around Nkrumah's mausoleum.

At the rear of the mausoleum, a gently curved footbridge leads to the sunken, single-storey museum with its striking Egyptian-African reliefs depicting Ashanti proverbs. The single-room museum keeps mementoes and photographs of Nkrumah and strangely, under plastic

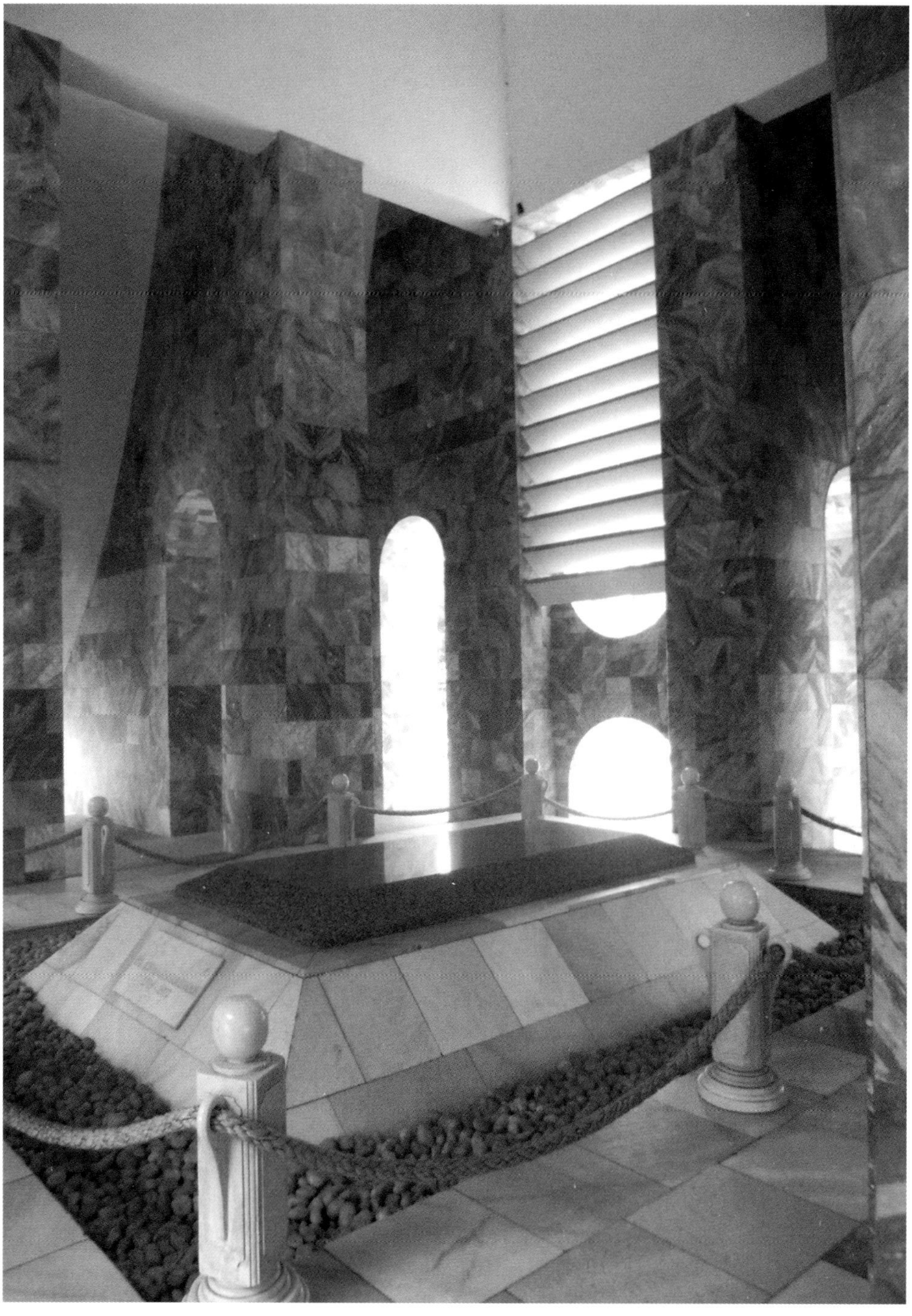

Nkrumah's coffin.

Schoolchildren crowding around the coffin.

sheeting, some of the cheap furniture from his lodgings during his stay in Pennsylvania. There is his collection of books, battered spectacle cases, penholders and the cloak he wore when he declared independence.

In a further demonstration of his rehabilitation, one of the life-size statues of Nkrumah the Redeemer ('*Osagyefo*' in Twi language) that had been smashed after the coup has been re-erected. Its severed head has not been replaced but sits on the ground next to the statue.

The Nkrumah Memorial Park is on the official tourist itinerary and I could see that it was also much visited by Ghanaian schoolchildren. Foreign heads of state are taken there, and every year on 5 March the

A group of school-children and their teacher at the statue of Nkrumah.

declaration of independence is re-enacted right underneath Nkrumah's statue, with an actor embodying the *Osagyefo* for jubilant crowds.[30]

The mausoleum, clearly visible from the surrounding area, does suggest a grove of trees from afar, although the closely spaced, upward battered pillars are sturdy and strong and suggest solidity, though of a very different kind than that of the nearby old slave fort, Osu Castle. The mausoleum manages to look like a monumental abstract sculpture in a figurative and rather kitsch evocation of traditional customs. The black star, the symbol of Ghana as part of the pan-African aspirations, has been placed high up on the front of the central pillars. While the whole memorial park is meant to celebrate the achievements of the *Osagyefo*, in reality it expresses an ambiguous relationship to Ghana's Founding Father. The image of the beheaded tree devoid of branches and leaves seems to suggest a dead end and unfulfilled aspirations, yet it stands in sparkling pools of water that are signs of life. The immobility of the stone slab above the grave contrasts with the forward stride of the statue right outside. The evocations of traditional chiefly customs appear like an ironic reminder of his autocratic rule in the face of Nkrumah's well-known

Damaged statue of Nkrumah behind the mausoleum.

antagonism to Ghana's chiefs. By allowing such ambiguities rather than repressing them into an officially sanctioned formal consensus, this memorial park invites critical reflection while stimulating the senses. However, what excited the schoolchildren most was Nkrumah's official car, a sky-blue 1966 Cadillac, which now sits devoid of its wheels under some trees at the rear of the mausoleum.

The Mausoleum of *M'zee* Laurent-Désiré Kabila in Kinshasa

Laurent-Désiré Kabila (1939–2001), or *M'zee*,[31] president of the Democratic Republic of Congo, was shot by one of his bodyguards in the office of his official residence, the *Palais de marbre* (the 'Marble Palace'). His son and political successor, Joseph Kabila, had his father interred in front of the Democratic Republic of Congo's parliament building in a newly built mausoleum. In such a high-security zone recreational visits to the site are deterred. Yet, just as Kumsusan Memorial Palace in Pyongyang, built to immortalize the Korean leader who had also died in his presidential palace, with its introverted, window-less sepulchral splendour fits the general atmosphere of artificiality of the North Korean capital, Kabila's star-shaped concrete tent, also the result of a team effort by various artists and engineers, seems equally well suited to the much more chaotic and vibrant city of Kinshasa in post-Mobuto's Congo.

Given the great complexities of Congolese history and the general greater relevance of the city to the mausoleum, I will focus this historical introduction on the capital Kinshasa. It used to be known as 'Stanley Port', after Henry Morton Stanley, the Victorian explorer. Stanley had originally set out to trace the course of the Congo River, an arduous undertaking that revealed the extent of the Congo's navigability. King Leopold II, the Belgian monarch, who was keen to acquire a slice of the proverbial 'African cake', approached Stanley to help him set up the so-called Independent State of Congo in 1885, of which he made himself sovereign.[32] Stanley Port was founded in 1887 as a small trading port on Pool Malebo (where the Congo stops being navigable), but it was renamed 'Léopoldville' soon afterwards. Following the construction of the railway, it became an important point for controlling the passage of goods between the Atlantic coast and the Upper Congo and, its population having grown rapidly, was made the capital instead of the coastal city Boma.[33] Local resistance against the Belgian occupation began early, in 1892, and there were various rebellions and uprisings in subsequent years, all of which were brutally suppressed by the *Force Publique* (FP). Although the establishment of Belgian Congo as a formal colony of Belgium in 1908 replaced the Congo Free State, the country continued to be exploited rather than governed. Education was left entirely to missionaries.[34] Patrice Lumumba (1925–1961), just like Kwame Nkrumah in Ghana, received his education at such missionary schools. Lumumba co-founded the *Mouvement National Congolais* (MNC) and was the first Congolese leader to call for independence at a rally in Léopoldville in

December 1958. The city became the centre of radical popular politics and rioting spread to Stanleyville (now known as 'Kisangani') in January 1959. Lumumba was arrested but released to attend the Round Table Conference in Brussels at which the fate of the colony was to be decided. At this stage Belgium was as keen to be delivered of the costs of running the colony while securing the rights to resource extraction and to keeping the Belgian senior administrators in place. Although the MNC did not win an absolute majority in the elections of May 1960, Lumumba became prime minister and declared independence on 30 June 1960. One of his first actions in government was to pay civil servants but not the army, which still primarily had Belgian officers. The military reacted with violent protests and the mineral-rich province of Katanga seceded under Moise Tshombe. Lumumba was dismissed by President Kasavubu and placed under house arrest. Martial law was decreed, and the head of armed forces, Joseph-Désiré Mobutu, announced the 'neutralization' of the government for six months. On 17 January 1961 Lumumba left Léopoldville for Stanleyville but he never arrived. The exact circumstances of his death remain mysterious and Lumuba's body has never been recovered.[35]

On 24 November 1965, during a similar crisis between Kasavubu and Prime Minister Moise Tshombe, Mobutu took power in a bloodless *coup d'état*.[36] He said that he would only govern for eight months, but then dismantled parliament and ruled by decree for another 32 years. He renamed the country 'Zaire', invented a new national flag and made Lingala the official language. Léopoldville was renamed 'Kinshasa' in 1966.[37] The city was Mobutu's main power base and almost the only place in the Congo to be developed. It experienced an enormous population growth and was the one city with relatively high levels of education. Kinshasa was also the main centre of mass culture, as all newspapers, televisions stations and popular music studios were concentrated there. During the Cold War Mobutu positioned himself firmly in the capitalist camp, and his repressive and kleptocratic regime was supported by the USA and other Western powers. During the 1990s, when the civil war in Angola provided almost untrammelled access to the diamond mines in the north of Angola, the city became inundated with money and Kinshasa was a city where anything was possible and anyone could be bought.[38] The production of counterfeit money, made with the complicity of the authorities, meant that billions of false notes were put into circulation, which created hyperinflation. Living costs rose sharply in 1997. By this time Mobutu had become an embarrassment to his erstwhile backers and when he imposed brutal deflation many of his supporters deserted him.

Resistance to Mobutu's regime had started early but was concentrated on the eastern border region. One of the guerilla leaders was Laurent-Désiré Kabila. He was born on 27 November 1939 in Jadotville, the son of a clerk in the colonial administration.[39] He had a difficult childhood and spent most of his time with his mother, who was separated from his father. Although he could not receive an education beyond the first few years of secondary school, he was reputedly an avid reader. Living in Katanga, he opposed the secession of the province and supported the nationalist Lumumba coalition after the president's assassination. He joined the Balubakat youth group and was politically active in the North Katanga provincial government. In the early 1960s he travelled to various left-leaning African countries, China and Eastern Europe to enlist support. Kabila subsequently began his not very successful career as a *maquisard* rebel-leader near the Tanzanian border. From April to November 1965 some Cuban military, directed by Ernesto 'Che' Guevara, attempted to set up an effective rebel force but Kabila's almost continuous absence abroad made them give up.[40] In 1967, having attended political education sessions in the PRC, he formed the *Partie Revolutionaire du Peuple* to put what he had learned into practice. However, he directed his movement from a distance in Dar-es-Salaam, where he pursued lucrative business interests. In the late 1970s he engaged the PRP in a political rather than a military programme, but did launch some military strikes in the mid-1980s. When his own officers rebelled against him in protests over his leadership, he devoted himself entirely to his businesses in Uganda and Tanzania. An open letter he was said to have written on the occasion of Mobutu's 1993 National Conference he called for the elimination of Mobutu and brought him to the attention of the international community. On 18 October 1996 the PRP joined with three other parties to form the *Alliance des Forces Démocratique pour la liberation du Congo-Zaire* (AFDL). A few weeks later on 31 October he launched an offensive against Mobutu, backed by Rwanda, Uganda and Burundi, which by 17 May 1997 ended in the exile of the seriously ill Mobutu and brought Kabila to power. He was sworn in as president and announced national elections to be held in 1999. Kabila declared his wish to reject the heritage of Mobutu and changed the name of the country from Mobutu's 'Zaire' to the 'Democratic Republic of Congo'. Another symbolic move was to reintroduce the old flag of Lumumba's first republic. He failed to obtain the support of major Congolese opposition leaders, in particular Étienne Tshisekedi, and as a result formed a government composed of young technocrats. The atmosphere in Kinshasa changed as public austerity was introduced. Kabila surrounded himself with intellectuals from the diaspora and foreign fighters who had fought alongside him, which alienated the population who perceived him as too close to his Rwandan and Ugandan allies. He strenuously cultivated the image of a bush-hardened nationalist leader and alarmed Western governments by announcing that China should serve as a model for Congolese development and furthermore, that Congo's mineral riches should not be subject to foreign control. An attempt to emancipate himself from Rwanda and Uganda led to the second Congo war breaking out in 1998, which ended in the enforced peace agreements at Lusaka in July 1999. On 16 January 2001, Kabila was shot by his own bodyguard in the 'Marble Palace' in Kinshasa. The gravely wounded president was taken to hospital and pronounced dead. However, together with clinical staff, he was then whisked onto a flight bound for Harare (in Mugabe's Zimbabwe). At a meeting of the Security Council in Kinshasa, assembled ministers were told that the wounded president was in intensive care in Harare and that his son, General Major Joseph Kabila, would secure the situation for the time being. Only then was the news of Laurent-Désiré Kabila's death publicly announced.[41] The mystery of this death, like that of Patrice Lumumba, remains unsolved. If it was an assassination, on whose behalf was it carried out?[42] Taking stock of Kabila's period in office one of his biographers remarked that

> the failure of the ldk regime seems also like the truth of the 1970s rebellions: it showed up the absence of a political vision endowed with a minimum of realism to make things happen, and the vanity of an administration which rewarded loyalty above competence.[43]

Ten days later, on 26 January 2001, the 29-year-old Joseph Kabila became the fourth president of the Democratic Republic of Congo. The funeral of his father took place on 24 January, after the body had been flown back from Zimbabwe. Attended by President Robert Mugabe of Zimbabwe, President Eduardo dos Santos of Angola and President Sam Nujoma of Namibia, the coffin was laid to rest in a small, white, stone chamber outside the Palace of the Nation. Given that Joseph Kabila was so young and that he had spent much of his life away from the centre of power, his legitimacy derived mainly from the dynastic succession from his father, who in turn had always proclaimed to have carried on from the nation's founder, Patrice Lumumba. It was a situation in which a mausoleum built to secure the remains of another murdered president in a setting to stress the ideological links between the first republic and the present, would provide a lasting reminder of the continuity of Congolese aspirations for independence and proclaim the son's legitimacy to succession. On the other hand, France, Belgium and the USA, moved by their own geopolitical considerations, were also ready to endorse the young Kabila. As noted by Emmanuel Nashi, they made

> some gestures of goodwill: the UN asked Rwanda to retreat from Congo [. . .] and by attributing to JK the image of peacemaker, they wanted him to play a role that escaped his attention [. . .] Paris, Washington and Brussels had found in the 30 year old president a blank sheet on which they could write their own wishes.[44]

While the disappearance of Lumumba's body had increased anxiety and the sense of loss, the body of the M'zee was at hand and during his funeral procession was exposed to view.[45] An architectural commission was announced for the design of a mausoleum. The winning entry was by the sculptor Christophe Meko and the construction company 'Homeconstruct', with its main engineer Bonaventure Mutonji, executed the project, which was finished in 2002.[46]

When Kabila's body was returned to the capital for the state funeral, it was decided that he should be buried in the most symbolic and historic site in Kinshasa, the Place de la Nation. The Belgians had built the colonial governor's palace there, intending it to be the official residence of the king's representative. A statue of King Leopold II stood prominently in the square facing the city and it was at this spot that the independence of the Congo was declared on 30 June 1960. The governor's palace then became the seat of the Congolese parliament and still functions as such today.[47] Mobutu had the statue of the Belgian king demolished in 1967. Kabila's coffin was placed in exactly the spot once occupied by the symbolic presence of the colonial ruler. In Hanoi, Ho Chi Minh's mausoleum is sited on Ba Dienh Square, where colonial and republican histories similarly overlap. In Kinshasa, given the disappearance of Lumumba's body and the ignominious ousting of Mobutu,

Laurent Kabila was to be the only candidate for a founder of the nation memorial complex.

The *Place de la Nation* was conceived as a semi-circular space from which main roads radiated south, east and west. Directly in the axis of the central southern avenue lies another nexus, the *Place de l'Indépendance*, built along the pattern of the *Place de l'Étoile* in Paris. This urban plan has been altered to accommodate the mausoleum. When I was there in July 2011 only the southern avenue and the segment of a circular road linked the parliament precinct to the city. For security reasons, soldiers barred any unauthorized vehicles from driving onto the *Place de la Nation* and all pedestrians had to explain their presence. Having presented the soldiers with a token payment for their trouble, I was allowed to proceed.

Kabila's extraordinary and exuberant mausoleum is placed in the architectural context of bland, functionalist 1970s buildings that house the national bank and government offices. The *Palais de la Nation* is not as palatial as its name implies; it consists of a low rise, wide-winged late 1950s modernist block. Its deeply recessed central hall is surmounted by a flat pudding-bowl dome. In sharp contrast to all this rationalist linearity, the star-bedecked mausoleum looked at first site like a circus tent made of concrete. This was an impression that worked even better at night, when the artificial illumination had been turned on.

Approaching the mausoleum from the wide *Avenue des Monts Virunga*, the symbolic axis linking the *Place de la Nation* with *Place de l'Indépendance*, I came face to face with the huge bronze statue of Kabila, which reminded me strongly of Kim Il Sung's statues in Pyongyang.[48] It shows the portly Kabila wearing a loose shirt, in the pose of swearing the oath on becoming president. His right arm is raised high and he points his index finger 'to indicate the unity and indivisibility of the Congo',[49] while his left hand clasps a booklet, presumably the constitution. A pair of gaudily painted plaster lions stride vigorously forward, right behind the bronze effigy of the president.

The area behind the statue was taken up by two paved enclosures with a circular fountain pond, one on each side of the mausoleum, in a layout that recalled a public square in Brussels or Paris. In another contrast, this classic geometrical configuration was encircled by a low fence redolent with symbolism: the balusters took the form of burning candles (their red 'flames' even flickered at night) and the metal grill between them has been worked into a spiky palm branch motif, as well as equally spiky rays of a rising sun, thus 'symbolizing the end of mourning'.

Place de la Nation in Kinshasa, with the statue and mausoleum of Laurent-Désiré Kabila.

The mausoleum itself was raised on a star-shaped pedestal clad with white marble and in the shape of a tent. The corner points of the grey painted concrete walls were not fixed by mundane pegs but held taut by five huge fists (three right and two left hands). These hands, made from concrete and painted uniformly dark brown, arise from shackles that have just been broken.[50] They held what looked like a sturdy rod from close up but which revealed itself on the exterior surface of the 'tent' as a single, white-painted frond of laurel. This motif of a celebratory decking continued: a large golden five-pointed star was placed high on the frontal side of the 'tent', another silver star formed a lid-like cover between the five prongs at the top, itself originally surmounted by a finial representing a burning flame.[51] The timber frame at the bottom edge of the canopy had been painted to look like the stamp-printed wax textiles with which Africans like to decorate their houses for celebrations.

Three steps led up the platform. Here the intention of the commemorative building was revealed. The original marble-lined tomb chamber has been left intact but given additional protection by a glazed steel-frame. It now became clear that the symbolic tent had been erected above the coffin like an eternal place of *funérailles*, the mourning ceremonies performed before or after a burial. The coffin is placed at a lower level that is reached by a few steps. It was draped with the blue-starred flag of the DRC. A few visitors arrived and having recompensed the soldiers on duty, posed for pictures and some even left fresh flowers. Directly behind the tomb chamber, almost like a headstone, was a large open book made of plaster. A bronze lion face has been affixed to the vertical side, above the motto 'NE JAMAIS TRAHIR LE CONGO'. While the exterior of the mausoleum suggested a tent that evokes the camps in the *brousse* (the bush) from which Kabila as guerilla leader used to direct his operations, the interior revealed this to in fact be a solid architectural structure. The steel frame that holds the star-shaped concrete roof together had been left exposed, though the pillars that form an additional support were clad in black tiles. The contrast between the rigid, crystalline configuration revealed by the inside and the sweeping, smooth surface of the exterior reminded me of the similar configuration in Ziaur Rahman's Dhaka mausoleum. In the latter example, the outside was a soft turf mound, while the interior displayed the rigid engineering holding up the glazed

Congolese soldiers on duty at the mausoleum.

Roof construction of the mausoleum from inside.

pyramid. In both cases one could say that the outside appearance evoked the past of both incumbents as well as metonymically and the whole nation, as well as the rural countryside. The interior, on the other hand, referred to modernity, technology, the city and the future.

At the rear of the mausoleum were two additional sculptures, clearly made by yet another artist. They seemed also to symbolize the future, represented by white-painted and therefore somewhat spectral, figures of youths. The boy, dressed like a scout in shorts and tie, joyfully raised another laurel branch, while the girl majorette held aloft a dove of peace.

A group of presidential guards in camouflage fatigues and red berets were on duty at the mausoleum. They did not formally stand to attention but said that they did do so on formal occasions, such as the anniversary of Kabila's birth and death, or during official visits by foreign heads of state. Several tall flagpoles surrounded the mausoleum. The paving and even the flowerbeds repeated the all-pervasive motif of the five-pointed star. While a little black star had been placed discreetly at the top end of the symbolic 'tree trunk' of Nkrumah's mausoleum, the one in Kinshasa abounded in starry configurations. The platform it is built on is star-shaped, so is the main tent-like structure, and in addition a silver, five-pointed star has been placed inside the central opening at the top while a much larger yellow star has been affixed on the front face above the entrance.[52] Surrounded by the fluttering flags of the Democratic Republic of Congo, the stellar imagery refers to the history of this country, from the pan-African aspirations of Lumumba to the still troubled period of rule by Kabila and his son Joseph that followed the dictatorship of Mobutu. Laurent-Désiré Kabila had not only put an end to Mobutu's dictatorship but saw himself as fulfilling the aspirations of Lumumba. By replacing Mobutu green flag with the original post-independence blue-starred banner, he proclaimed this continuity. Kabila in this sense stands in proxy for Lumumba but as an *ersatz* Founder of the Nation, and one cut short in his ambitions by a violent death.

The multiple signals around the mausoleum, from the lone 'Korean' statue flanked by plaster-cast lions, the burning candle fenceposts, the *kitsch* statues of the children with their symbols of joy and peace, the open book with the ambiguous words promising or admonishing never to betray the Congo, can all be read like so many empty slogans. Only the mausoleum itself, with the tent held up by clenched fists, bedecked with laurel fronds and ornamented with wax print cloth has some of the vitality and originality of Congolese popular art. Like Nkrumah's mausoleum, it mixes metaphors and allows contradictions and ambiguities to emerge. Erik Kennes and Munkana N'Ge write in their biographical essay that he

> left the impression of things unfinished [. . .] he was neither a revolutionary nor a real bandit, not a 'warlord' nor a properly responsible president. His ideas, like fireworks, were not followed by lasting implementations because of his limitations (his authoritarianism, his obstinate and hard-headed character, his inability to distinguish the desirable from the workable), but also because of circumstances that were particularly unfavourable for him.[53]

Boy-scout sculpture in the mausoleum precinct and flame-shaped lanterns.

The mausoleum has none of the pomposity of many others; it does not aspire to be a building or even a work of public art as Nkrumah's does. In its mix of naivety, clashing signs of violence and longing for peace, it summarizes the city itself that is vibrant, venal and despite all, hopeful.

The Mausoleum of Hastings Kamuzu Banda in Lilongwe, Malawi

Malawi, formerly called 'Nyasaland', had been a British colony since 1891 and was granted full independence in 1964. Hastings Banda, whose official year of birth was 1906, was educated by Scottish missionaries. After working in South African mines, he got a scholarship and studied medicine in the United States, Glasgow and Edinburgh and Scotland. Hastings Kamuzu Banda set up practice in London and after a personal scandal escaped to Ghana, where he made the acquaintance of Nkrumah and threw himself into African politics. Hearing of the violent protests against British efforts to force Nyasaland to become part of the so-called Central

Mausoleum of
Laurent-Désiré Kabila.

African Federation with Northern and Southern Rhodesia, of which the white settlers were in favour, Banda returned in 1958 and negotiated terms with Britain.

Independence followed swiftly with Banda inheriting Nyasaland in 1966, which he renamed Malawi. Shortly after he became president he turned on his former colleagues, sacking and imprisoning them. After that he was the most totalitarian ruler in Africa. No decision in Malawi was taken without his consent. Like an enthusiastic colonial officer he wanted to impose on Malawi his idea of education and progress, but no colonial officer would have dared treat Africans in Banda's patronising and imperious manner. He regarded them as children to be guided with a firm hand.[54]

Banda was declared president-for-life of Malawi in 1971, imposed a one-party rule and his own idiosyncratic ideas on the country while appeasing the former colonial masters instead of demonstrating any pan-African solidarity, or protesting against apartheid. After many years as an iron-fisted dictator, violent protests and under pressure from Western aid donors, he was forced to allow multiparty elections in 1994. He was heavily defeated at the polls by his former protégé Elson Bakili Muluzi. Hastings Kamuzu Banda died a few years later of pneumonia in South Africa on 25 November 1997. His body was taken to Malawi for a state funeral, where Bakili Muluzi had the eccentric dictator's body placed in a simple grave, thereby helping to put an end to the Banda personality cult. However, despite the ruthlessness of his regime, subsequent generations of Malawian politicians saw fit to reclaim Banda's legacy and celebrate the self-styled *Ngwazi* ('emperor').[55] After Bingu wa Mutharika won the election in 2004, he decided to honour Malawi's Founding Father with a mausoleum above Banda's original grave, which was reputed to have cost some $750,000. A report on the official opening in May 2006 describes how President Bingu wa Mutharika inaugurated the building:

> 'We Malawians have finally given our first head of state and government the respect that he deserves. [. . .] it is befitting that we remember him in this way,' Mutharika told the cheering crowd that witnessed the unveiling of the mausoleum. Mutharika [. . .] observed that there were previous attempts to obliterate the name of Kamuzu Banda from the minds of Malawians and history. He was apparently referring to his predecessor Bakili Muluzi, who promised to build the mausoleum after Banda died in November 1997 at the age of 99, but plans were held up for lack of funds. Muluzi was a strong critic of Banda who referred to his rule as a legacy of brutality, torture and gross abuse of human rights. 'My government will continue to honour this true Malawi hero,' Mutharika said. The Malawian leader hailed Banda, saying during his 30-year rule Malawi was able to feed itself and that the country started begging for food after Banda left government in 1994.[56]

The architect, Knight Munthali, described his scheme:

> 'You can see the chamber which houses the original tomb where Kamuzu is resting,' he says. 'It is on two levels. The lower level is the chamber. The upper level is a public area with a replica of the tomb and lighting that will make it visible even at night.'[57]

Stone walls enclose the original tomb on all sides while the upper storey is an open-frame pavilion surmounted by a truncated pyramid roof, topped a timber cupola painted white, not unlike those in some cricket pavilions, but with a cross instead of a flag at the top. The squat, grey-painted columns at each corner do not fulfil any load-bearing function but each is inscribed with one word from Banda's motto 'Unity, Loyalty, Discipline and Obedience'. A flight of wide steps leads from the foreground to the upper storey, where an archway bearing Banda's portrait gives access to the space with the symbolic coffin, behind which hangs another image of Kamuzu in a smart suit, brandishing his trademark flywhisk, an old symbol of a chief's power.

During Mutharika's period in office the Banda cult was greatly revived, with the airport and a large sports stadium named after him and statues commissioned. During the 2009 election proximity to the Founding Father's values was an important asset:

> In the campaign for last month's national election, Malawi's political parties competed to claim the legacy of Banda. 'Each party is trying to get closer to the name that has suddenly become associated with high standards', a writer in *The Nation*, a daily newspaper, commented during the race [. . .] Incumbent Bingu wa Mutharika, who won re-election, built the Banda monument and mausoleum to forge his own link to the autocrat.[58]

He has since ordered that the mausoleum should have a library and a lecture theatre for virtual tours of the Banda's life. Malawi has thus acquired a national symbolic centre, complete with grave, relics and associated rituals, which, by emphasizing the greatness of the Founder, reflects some of his glory on his successors.

The Tomb of Dr John Garang de Mabior, Juba, South Sudan

Arafat's mausoleum was built in anticipation of a free Palestinian state. Since 29 November 2012 Palestine has been recognized by the UN as a Non-Member Observer State, but remains, however, a political entity occupied by the state of Israel.

John Garang's tomb was also built before there was a state of South Sudan. However, on 9 February 2011 people voted for the formal separation of Sudan at an open field next to his very simple mausoleum. Six months later, on 9 July 2011, on the very same ground, the Rt Hon James Wani Igga, Speaker of the Southern Sudan Legislative Assembly (SSLA), read the Declaration of Independence of South Sudan. The ceremony began with the unveiling of a bronze statue of John Garang, placed opposite his tomb. Then the flag of the Republic of South Sudan was raised while the flag of the Republic of Sudan was lowered, and the new president, Salva Kiir Mayardit, signed the Transitional Constitution of South Sudan.[59]

I went to Juba on 23 July 2011, two weeks after independence was declared. The temporary tribunes next to the mausoleum were still there. John Garang's statue stood on a plinth on a vast expanse of bare brown earth, separated from the tribunes and the mausoleum by a wide, newly paved road. The former freedom fighter is shown in the pose of a teacher, wearing a suit and clasping a large book to his chest and calling people to attention by raising a stick. Flagpoles lined the road, flying the flags of the African Union countries on one side and of many other nations on the other. An arched gate led to the mausoleum compound. The facade had been freshly painted white and the cornices around the roof picked out in bright yellow. The mausoleum is little more than a raised platform shaded by a star-shaped timber canopy (it refers to the star symbol in the SPLA flag). According to the project's chief engineer, Alikaya Aligo Samson, 'the entrance hall symbolizes all of Sudan and the exit hall the new Sudan John Garang promised would come with peace'.[60]

Some reviewers have made disparaging remarks about this unassuming grave and its crumbling tiles but for the occasion of Independence Day it had been not only spruced up and repaired, but decked out in the draperies of blue, white, red and black, colours of the new national flag.[61] These were wrapped around the supporting poles and stretched between them to form cheerful looking walls. Another canopy shielded the path from the entrance to the tomb platform and a red 'AstroTurf' carpet, with the motto 'Welcome to South Sudan', protected the steps. A group of soldiers were lounging under a stretched canvas at the side of the steps leading to the platform. No bag checks were required and photography was permitted.

John Garang's body has been interred in the earth below the platform. A two-tier symbolic slab, clad with the same grey ceramic tiles as the surrounding surface, marked the grave, on which two framed photographs showing Garang's face had been placed. They bore the legend: 'John Garang de Mabior. He was an icon, Freedom fighter and a Hero.'

At the back of the platform, in a continuation of the main axis from the entrance, was a concrete, rectangular pool, filled with stagnant water. Terracotta pots with young palm trees surrounded the pool, the only attempts at landscaping at this stage. The surrounding ground consisted of hard-baked, yellow earth. My guide said that important government buildings were going to be constructed nearby. At the time of my visit, this modest mausoleum, the statue of Garang and some simple buildings to one side were the only fixtures on the otherwise empty land, just beyond the main streets of Juba. In July 2011 there were no buildings taller than six or eight storeys. All the people I spoke to said this is bound to change soon, with the influx of new investment, foreign aid and oil revenues.

The brand new banknotes of the South Sudanese pounds issued on 11 July 2011 bear two images. One side shows a group of the gracefully horned Nilotic cattle, which until recently constituted the main form of wealth for the tribes inhabiting the region.[62] On the front of the notes, as well as on the watermark, is the portrait of Dr John Garang de Mabior. The same portrait can be seen in public offices and on many

Entrance to John Garang's mausoleum, Juba.

South Sudanese guards at John Garang's mausoleum.

posters. Wearing a pinstriped suit, a checked shirt and tie, with his beard greying and a bald pate edged by remaining thick hair, he stares fixedly at the viewer from his deep-set eyes.

On 30 July 2005 John Garang was killed in a helicopter crash. Two years later on 30 July 2007 President Kiir decreed this day to be an annual public holiday known as Martyrs' Day. From then on all of the other fallen heroes and heroines of South Sudan's liberation struggles were to be remembered together with Garang, the 'Founding Father of South Sudan' on the anniversary of his death. The decision to place his image on the new currency sealed the official endorsement of his status as national hero.

John Garang de Mabior was born on 23 June 1945 to a Christian family in Wanglukei village in Twic East district in southeast Sudan. Like most members of the Dinka tribe, his father herded cattle and his mother cultivated fields of sorghum. At that time Sudan formed part of the Anglo-Egyptian Condominium (1899–1955). The British administrators had set up centres for tax collection and tried, with varying success, to stop the habitual inter-tribal warfare and cattle raiding and

John Garang's coffin.

encouraged Christian missionary activities, which also provided some rudimentary schooling. It was a Muslim Dinka, Ali Abd al-Latif, who in the 1920s had formed the first nationalist movement, the United Tribal Society, which was repressed at the time.

After the Second World War, the new political fate of the vast region under joint British-Egyptian control began to take shape. Egyptian independence was secured first, in 1953, following the overthrow of King Farouk by Muhammad Naguib. The Sudan Administrative Conference of 1946 had determined that Sudan should be administered as one country, despite significant cultural, ethnic and religious differences between the mainly Muslim and Arab- controlled north and the Black African, primarily Christian or 'animist' south. Even before Sudan officially achieved independence in 1956, the South rebelled against northern control in the Torit Mutiny of 1955.[63]

After decolonization, a new movement, known as *Anya Nya* ('snake venom'), or 'Anya-Anya' took up the cause. The seventeen-year-old John Garang, who had been orphaned at the age of ten, joined this group in the ensuing civil war, which broke out in earnest when a military coup in 1958 took power in Khartoum.[64] He did not fight for long but took up the offer of a family member to pay for his education. Garang de

John Garang's coffin with his photographs.

Mabior attended secondary school in Rumbek, and then in Tanzania. He was a good student and gained admission to the University of Dar es Salaam. In 1964 he spent a year living and teaching in Kenya, before winning a scholarship to study agriculture in the USA in 1966. Like Nkrumah before him, Garang de Mabior went to the United States, where he gained a bachelor's degree from Ginnel College, Iowa, in 1969. He also did a company commander's course at the Military Academy in Virginia.

In 1971 he returned to the University of Dar es Salaam, and then, in 1971, moved back to Sudan to join a rebel camp. Garang de Mabior had to overcome the suspicions of his comrades, since he was carrying a camera, before being admitted to their ranks under Commander Joseph Lagu.

In 1969 Gaafar Nimeiry had obtained power in Khartoum. Three years later, in 1972, he signed peace accords with the Anya-Anya, giving the south a large degree of autonomy. The rebels became integrated into the regular Sudanese forces and Garang was promoted to the rank of captain. He took leave of absence in 1974 to continue his military training at Fort Benning, Georgia (USA), before starting a PhD. thesis on Sudanese agriculture at Iowa State University, which he finished in 1981.

When he returned to Sudan in 1981, Nimeiri had changed tack, broken with the communists and had allied himself to Muslim fundamentalists instead. They insisted on the nationwide adoption of Sharia law and enforced conversions to Islam. These measures were greatly resented and violently resisted in the south. Garang, now a colonel, was teaching at the university and the military academy at Khartoum.

In 1978 oil was discovered in Southern Sudan, which fanned the flames of resistance towards the North. Deputed to repress a mutiny of 500 soldiers of the Bor garrison, Garang seized the opportunity to put himself in charge of the mutineers and invited other southern garrisons to join him. He formed a movement and called it the 'Sudanese People's Liberation Movement', with its armed wing titled the 'Sudanese People's Liberation Army' (SPLA). It was supported, sometimes with arms, by the neighbouring countries of Uganda, Kenya, Eritrea, as well as by the USA. The most significant ally, however, was Mengistu Haile Mariam of Ethiopia whose Marxist regime was hostile to the ex-communist and now pro-Islamic Nimeiri.[65]

Thus began the long and bitter civil war that was to last 27 years at a cost of more than two million lives. Garang was constantly on the move, frequently in Uganda, where Yoweri Museveni, another alumnus from Dar es Salaam University, had overthrown the military regime. He also stayed for periods of time in Kenya and Ethiopia. In Sudan he moved from one SPLA camp to another, where his charismatic and impressive presence – like many Dinka, he was very tall (1.93 metres or 6.33 feet) – clutching an AK-47, inspired his troops, many of them very young, the 'Red Army' or *jesh a mer* (child soldiers).[66]

Throughout this time Garang favoured and trusted members of his own tribe, the Dinka. This led to fissures in the movement into various rival factions, such as those led by Riek Machar's (Nuer) and Lam Akol (Shilluk), which fanned and revived endemic inter-tribal warfare that was now much more deadly because of the freely available firearms.[67] Garang never formulated a clear ideological basis for his liberation movement, although he was said to enjoy reading classical and contemporary texts on war strategy, and for a while, perhaps to please Mengistu Haile Mariam, pursued a crude Marxism.[68] After the end of the Cold War and the fall of Mengistu, he avoided alienating the Western powers, which had begun to supply the SPLA with arms. Nor was his objective very clear, as he could not decide whether he wished to achieve a united Sudan in which the south played an equal part or to pursue separation and independence. He had broken off peace negotiations with the leader of the first democratically elected president of Sudan, Sadek el-Mahdhi (in power from 1986 to 1989) and refused to join the government of Omar al-Bashir, who like Nimeiri had gained power through Islamist support.

In the late 1990s and especially after the attacks of 9/11, the U.S. government became openly hostile to Khartoum.[69] In March 2002 Garang was invited to Washington, where he met Colin Powell, Paul Wolfowitz and other members of President Bush's entourage. A ceasefire was signed between the Sudanese government and the SPLA for the Nuba region in 2002 and negotiations began in Kenya. However, the uprising in Darfur in 2003 and its brutal repression thereafter, which led to a terrible humanitarian crisis throughout 2004, all but stopped the movement towards a negotiated settlement.

Finally, in January 2005 the Comprehensive Peace Agreement was signed at the Nyayo National Stadium in Nairobi, which included a ceasefire for all parties concerned, power sharing and a referendum allowing the inhabitants of the South to decide whether they wished a union with or separation from the North. The UN imposed sanctions on the government for continuing the violence in Darfur. On 9 July 2005 John Garang was sworn in as a first vice president.[70] Yet less than a month later, on 30 July, he perished, along with fourteen other occupants, when the helicopter that was carrying him back from a meeting with Uganda's president crashed near the border with South Sudan.[71]

Garang's body was first taken to one of the SPLA camps near the site of the accident and from there to Juba, to the Provincial Legislative Assembly, the predecessor of the legislature for the autonomous southern zone over which Garang was to have been president. The place was also chosen because its slight elevation affords a view over the flat plain on which Juba was built. A white bull was sacrificed according to Dinka custom and traditional chiefs read out the names of his ancestors.[72]

Although Garang's widow, in an effort to calm the situation, declared that the crash had been an accident, rioting broke out between southerners and Arabs in Khartoum. Salva Kiir Mayardit, also a Dinka, took on the leadership of the SPLA. He managed to unite and reconcile the various factions that had been hostile to Garang's autocratic rule and formed an autonomous government in October 2005. Relations between the SPLM/A and the government under al-Bashir continued to be fraught. As the violent attacks by militia forces continued in Darfur, the SPLM temporarily suspended its participation in the national government in 2007. While UN peacekeepers took over the policing of Darfur (in 2008), tensions rose in the Abyei region, the source of the newly found oil, leading to armed clashes which continued throughout the following year.

At long last, in December 2009 northern and southern leaders agreed on the date for a referendum to be held in the south in 2011. Al-Bashir vowed to accept the result even in the face of a vote for separation. In the event this was the overwhelming decision in January 2011. Despite continuing border disputes in Abyei, the south gained its independence on 9 July and President Kiir promised to form an 'inclusive government' which he may succeed in doing more easily than John Garang.

We have seen how Garang has been made into an icon and a symbol of unity between North and South. A new image of Garang is now being presented, that of the Founding Father, paternally benevolent and no longer the fearsome military guerilla leader brandishing a Kalashnikov, as he was previously portrayed (and as can still be seen in the huge statue outside the SPLA headquarters). He is now shown as the intellectual, armed with a book and pointing a stick instead of a gun, wearing a pinstriped suit rather than fatigues. Like other former revolutionary leaders, he has been tamed in death, made more amenable to a retelling of the state's narrative. When I visited in 2011, the still makeshift grave with its attending SPLA guards in camouflage uniform evoked a temporary camp rather than a mausoleum. The new country faces countless challenges to overcome the legacies of its war-ravaged past, to secure a tenable coexistence with the north and its neighbours, to unify across tribal division and to be able to function as a state at all. The new government began by neutralizing the potentially still divisive, if not corrosive, influence of John Garang by making him into an icon that drives conciliation. They may eventually build him a proper mausoleum but they may also prefer to keep him there, under the star-shaped canopy, with the dust blowing over his grave, just as it does on the resting places of the millions of his compatriots, many of whom never had the luxury of a grave at all.

Reinventing the Political Tomb in Africa

Given the long and painful history of colonialism in Africa and the equally difficult and painful process of decolonization, the project of forming viable nation states when their borders had been drawn with a straight ruler was particularly difficult. Most of the political leaders, who had campaigned for independence and became the first presidents, were educated in Europe or the United States and had absorbed ideas about development, democracy and modernization, as well as pan-Africanist ideals. Most, like Kwame Nkrumah, John Garang, Jomo Kenyatta and Patrice Lumumba did not last long in office before they were driven into exile or assassinated. Others transformed themselves into veritable tyrants, eliminating and suppressing any opposition, and becoming, like Hastings Banda, self-styled emperors. Their successors could at times derive credibility by declaring themselves loyal to the political vision of the nation's founder and by honoring his memory. That's why Daniel arap Moi buried Kenyatta in the centre of Nairobi and perpetuated the link between Kenyatta and Kenya's independence. More often the new party and the new leader wished to distance themselves from the failures and weaknesses of the first presidents and tried other ways to project a national identity than the cult of the founding father. It was after some time, when memories had faded, that the tarnished glamour of the first leader, especially if he had been a victim of violence, would be polished once more to shine on those who were now proclaiming themselves as political heirs. New and flashy mausolea, often built by Chinese contractors, were to become sacred national sites where new generations would learn the heroic narrative of the first leader.

Almost all of the mausolea I saw in Africa, in spite of the schoolchildren attending and the odd curious visitor turning up, were lonely places and ignored by the bustling crowds. There were certainly no queues waiting for admittance and they were not considered pleasurable environments in which to spend an evening. This indifference may stem from the general distrust of politicians and their empty promises, as well as from a widespread reluctance to visit graves other than those of one's own ancestors. There is no tradition of pilgrimage to dead saints' lasting resting places and no entrenched state rituals of promoting the mausoleum as there is Turkey or in communist countries. The architecture of the African sub-Saharan mausolea stresses that the fact that there is nothing to hide. They evoke trees or tents or at best a pavilion which allow the sarcophagus to be kept in view. The formally inventive ones, most notable so Neto's 'rocket', suggest an ad-hoc modernity, a bricolage of motifs and emblems, juxtaposed with narratives and 'branding'. Some fit well into the chaotic vibrancy of the surrounding cityscapes, others remain a tawdry token of presidential vanity, a redundant piece of junk architecture or a poignantly makeshift simple grave.

In other parts of the world, locally classical precedents – European, Islamic, Chinese or Soviet – determined the architecture of the mausoleum and we saw many variations of a few general themes. It is only in Africa that the genre of the mausoleum could be reinvented. Quite a few have been built very recently and are true mausolea of the twenty-first century, and we can look forward to many more.

References

Preface

1 Originally 'pouche'. There is no etymological connection with Buch (book).
2 Benedict Anderson, *Imagined Communities: Reflections on the Origin and Spread of Nationalism* (London 1983).

1 Enduring Signification: Mounds, Monuments and Mausolea

1 Katherine Verdery, *The Political Lives of Dead Bodies: Reburial and Postsocialist Change* (New York, 1999), p. 27.
2 See Robert Sala Ramos and Isabel Boj Cullell, 'Atapuerca: un proyecto de socialización de la evolución y la ciencia', *Aula-Historia Social*, 15 (Spring 2005), pp. 14–36, especially 24–5.
3 Philippe Descola, *The Spears of Twilight: Life and Death in the Amazon Jungle* (London, 1997), p. 381.
4 Peter M.M.G. Akkermans and Glenn M. Schwartz, *The Archaeology of Syria: From Complex Hunter-Gatherers to Early Urban Societies (ca.16,000–300 BC)* (Cambridge, 2003), p. 52.
5 See Ian Hodder, *The Leopard's Tale: Revealing the Mysteries of Çatalhöyük* (London, 2006).
6 Miles Russell, *Monuments of the British Neolithic: The Roots of Architecture* (Stroud, 2002), p. 38.
7 Ibid., p. 176.
8 Dominique Charpin, 'La mort du roi et le deuil en Mésopotamie paléobabylonienne', in *L'État, le pouvoir, les prestations et leurs formes en Mésopotamie ancienne*, ed. Pétr Charvát, Bertrand Lafont, Jana Mynářová, et al. (Prague, 2006), p. 99.
9 Gwendolyn Leick, *Mesopotamia: The Invention of the City* (London, 2001), pp. 112–17.
10 See Janos Fedak, 'Tombs and Commemorative Monuments', in *Studies in Hellenistic Architecture*, ed. Frederick E. Winter (Toronto, Buffalo, NY, and London, 2006), pp. 71–95.
11 Pliny the Elder, *Natural History*, Book XXXVI Chapter 4(4) pp. 62–70, www.perseus.tufts.edu, accessed 18 May 2012.
12 Kristian Jeppesen and Jan Zahle, 'Investigations on the Site of the Mausoleum 1970/73', *American Journal of Archaeology*, LXXIX/1 (January 1975), pp. 67–79.
13 Jane Clark Reeder, 'Typology and Ideology in the Mausoleum of Augustus: Tumulus and Tholos', *Classical Antiquity*, XI/2 (October 1992), pp. 265–307 Quotation from p. 300.
14 Suetonius, *Vita Divi Augusti*: 100 2-4, http://penelope.uchicago.edu, accessed 22 January 2011.
15 Cristina La Rocca, 'Perceptions of an Early Medieval Urban Landscape', in *The Medieval World*, ed. Peter Lineham and Janet L. Nelson (London and New York, 2001), p. 417.
16 Georgia Sommers Wright, 'A Royal Tomb Program in the Reign of St Louis', *The Art Bulletin*, LVI/2, Medieval Issue (June 1974), p. 224.

17 W. Eugene Kleinbauer, 'Charlemagne's Palace Chapel at Aachen and its Copies', *Gesta*, IV (Spring 1965), pp. 2–11.

18 Wright, 'A Royal Tomb Program in the Reign of St Louis', p. 226.

19 See A. Jahn, *Das Haus Habsburg Vol. 2/2: Die Grabstätten der Habsburger und der mit ihnen verwandten Häuser in Österreichs Kirchen* (Vienna, 2001).

20 Guy Lazure, 'Possessing the Sacred: Monarchy and Identity in Philip II's Relic Collection at the Escorial', *Renaissance Quarterly*, LX/1 (Spring 2007), pp. 58–93 and p. 65.

21 Richard A. Etlin, *Symbolic Space: French Enlightenment Architecture and its Legacy* (Chicago and London, 1994), p. 172.

22 See Philip Ward-Jackson, 'Carlo Marochetti and the Tombs of Napoleon at the *Dôme* des Invalides, Paris and the Duke of Wellington at St Paul's Cathedral, London', *Church Monuments*, XIX (2004), p. 114 and pp. 115–29.

23 James Stevens Curl, *Death and Architecture* (Stroud, 1980), p. 192.

24 'The Obsequies: Funeral of Abraham Lincoln', www.nytimes.com, accessed 29 May 2012.

25 See William J. Hosking, 'Lincoln's Tomb: Designs Submitted and Final Selections', *Journal of the Illinois State Historical Society*, L/1 (Spring 1957), pp. 51–62, and Nancy Hill, 'The Transformation of the Lincoln Tomb', *Journal of the Abraham Lincoln Association*, XXVII/1 (Winter 2006), pp. 39–56.

2 Safeguarding the Immortality of Revolutionary Leaders: Mausolea in Communist Countries

1 Vladislav Todorov, *Red Square, Black Square: Organon for Revolutionary Imagination* (Albany, NY, 1995), p. 95.

2 'Second All-Russia Congress of Soviets of Workers' and Soldiers' Deputies', www.marxists.org, accessed 14 October 2011.

3 For a description of Lenin's death and funeral, see Catherine Merridale, *Night of Stone: Death and Memory in Twentieth-Century Russia* (London and New York, 2000), pp. 146–51.

4 Vladimir Mayakovsky, *Vladimir Lenin*, trans. Dorian Rottenberg (Moscow, 1967).

5 James von Geldern, 'Lenin's Death and the Birth of the Lenin Cult', www.soviethistory.org, accessed 14 October 2011.

6 Quoted in Valentino Garretano, 'Stalin, Lenin and "Leninism"', *New Left Review*, I/103 (May–June 1977), pp. 59–71.

7 As quoted by Ilya Zbarsky, in *Lenin's Embalmers*, trans. Samuel Hutchinson (London, 1998), p. 14.

8 Nina Tumarkin 'Religion, Bolshevism, and the Origins of the Lenin Cult', *Russian Review*, XL/1 (January 1981), pp. 35–46 For a recent study of the God-building movement, see John Gray, *The Immortalization Commission: Science and the Strange Quest to Cheat Death* (London, 2011), pp. 33–76.

9 *Pravda* (30 January 1924), quoted in Edward H. Carr, *The Interregnum, 1923–24* (Basingstoke, 1964), p. 349.

10 Zbarsky, *Lenin's Embalmers*, p. 24.

11 See S. Strigalev, 'On the History of the Design of the Wooden Mausoleum of V. I. Lenin; Architect: A. Shchusev' (original in Russian), *Arkhitektura SSR*, 2 (February 1974), pp. 18–25.

12 Nina Tumarkin, *Lenin Lives! The Lenin Cult in the Soviet Union* (Cambridge, MA, 1983), p. 189.

13 See N. N. Stoyanov, 'The Architecture of Lenin's Tomb, Moscow; Architect: A. V. Shchusyev' (original in Russian), *Stroitel'stvo i Arkhitektura* (January 1948), pp. 8–11.

14 Inter-titles to Dziga Vertov's *Three Songs About Lenin* [1934], *October*, LII (Spring, 1990), pp. 40–51, www.jstor.org, accessed 8 June 2012. For the film itself, see John MacKay, 'Allegory and Accommodation: Vertov's "Three Songs About Lenin" (1934) as a Stalinist Film', *Film History: An International Journal*, 'Documentary Before Verité', XVIII/4 (2006), pp. 376–91.

15 Tumarkin, *Lenin Lives!*, p. 255.

16 Ibid., p. 258.

17 Victoria E. Bonnell, *Iconography and Power: Soviet Political Posters Under Lenin and Stalin* (Berkeley and Los Angeles, CA, 1997), p. 149.

18 According to Nina Tumarkin, the draft inscription was to read '1927 USSR to Vladimir Ilich Lenin' but Bonch-Bruevich, one of the members of the Funeral Committee, crossed this out, leaving only the name 'Lenin'. See Tumarkin, *Lenin Lives!* p. 190.

19 As reported by the Italian socialist and writer Giovanni Germanetto, quoted by William Duiker, *Ho Chi Minh: A Life* (London, 2000), pp. 96–7.
20 Quoted by Duiker, *Ho Chi Minh*, p. 99. Ho Chi Minh also translated Sun Yat-sen, *Three Principles* during his confinement.
21 Daniel Hémery, *Ho Chi Minh. De l'Indochine au Vietnam* (Paris, 1990), p. 158.
22 'Declaration of Independence of the Democratic Republic of Vietnam', Ho Chi Minh, *Selected Works*, vol. III (Hanoi, 1960–62), pp. 17–21: http://historymatters.gmu.edu, accessed 25 October 2011.
23 In the same year the Soviet Union demonstrated its nuclear arms capability and a year later North Korea invaded the south of the peninsula.
24 From his will dated 15 May 1965, quoted in full in Hémery, *Ho Chi Minh, pp.* 163–5 (my translation from French original).
25 Ba Ngoc, *Memorial Site of Ho Chi Minh in Ha Noi* (Hanoi, 2006), p. 1.
26 Ibid., p. 10.
27 He was awarded the honour of 'Hero of Labour' by the Vietnamese government in 1976 in recognition of his efforts. See William S. Logan, *Hanoi: Biography of a City* (Sydney, 2000), p. 194
28 Hue-Tam Ho Tai, 'Monuments of Ambiguity: The State Commemoration of Ho Chi Minh', in *Essays into Vietnamese Pasts*, ed. K. W. Taylor and John K. Whitmore (Ithaca, NY, 1995), p. 280.
29 Logan, *Hanoi: Biography of a City*, p. 253.
30 On the role of Ba Dinh Square as a potential site for political protest, see Mandy Thomas, 'Spatiality and Political Change in Urban Vietnam' in *Consuming Urban Culture in Contemporary Vietnam*, ed. Lisa B. W. Drummond and Mandy Thomas (London and New York, 2003), p. 176.
31 Shaun Kingsley Malarney, *Culture, Ritual, and Revolution in Vietnam* (London and New York, 2002), p. 201.
32 Patricia Pelley, *Postcolonial Vietnam: New Histories of the National Past* (Durham and London, 2002), p. 158.
33 Hue-Tam Ho Tai, 'Monuments of Ambiguity', p. 281.
34 According to Georges Boudarel and Nguyen Van Ky, the will was made public fifteen years later, when Hoang Van Hoan defected to Beijing and publicly charged Le Duan with having falsified Ho Chi Minh's testament. See Georges Boudarel and Nguyen Van Ky, *Hanoi: City of the Rising Dragon* (Lanham, 2002), p. 142.
35 See for instance, Margie Mason, 'Hanoi throws lavish 1,000 birthday bash', www.thejakartapost, accessed 14 November 2010.
36 Hémery, *Ho Chi Minh*, p. 127.
37 Mao Zedong, 'Report on an Investigation of the Peasant Movement in Hunan' (March 1927), *Selected Works of Mao Tse-tung*, (Peking, 1965), p. 28.
38 Robert A. Scalapino, 'The Evolution of a Young Revolutionary – Mao Zedong in 1919–1921', *The Journal of Asian Studies*, XLII/1 (November 1982), pp. 29–36; p. 29.
39 For the influence of Yang Chanji, see Liyan Liu, 'The Man Who Molded Mao: Yang Changji and the First Generation of Chinese Communists', *Modern China*, XXXII/4 (October 2006), pp. 483–512.
40 Douglas James Davies and Lewis H. Mates, eds, *Encyclopedia of Cremation* (London, 2005), p. 121.
41 A. P. Cheater, 'Death Ritual as Political Trickster in the People's Republic of China', *The Australian Journal of Chinese Affairs*, XXVI (July 1991), pp. 73–4.
42 Frederick Teiwes and Warren Sun, 'The First Tiananmen Square Incident Revisited: Elite Politics and Crisis Management at the End of the Maoist Era', *Pacific Affairs*, LXXVII/2 (Summer 2004), pp. 211–35.
43 Quoted in Cheater, 'Death Ritual as Political Trickster', p. 76.
44 Ross Terrill, *Mao: A Biography* (Stanford, CA, 1999), p. 455.
45 For an account of Mao's last illness and the controversial role of his wife Jiang Qing, see the reminiscences of his personal physician Zhisui Li, *The Private Life of Chairman Mao: The Inside Story of the Man Who Made Modern China* (London, 1994), pp. 620–25.
46 Quoted in Cheater, 'Death Ritual as Political Trickster', pp. 81–2.

47 See Li, *The Private Life of Chairman Mao,* p. 630. However, the author does not reveal which procedures were followed. Philip Short reports that a variation of the formaldehyde treatment was used. The heart, lungs, stomach, kidneys and all inner organs were removed first. A tube was inserted into Mao's neck to allow extra formaldehyde to be pumped into the visceral cavity from time to time. As a backup the Institute of Arts and Crafts ordered a wax replica of the Chairman to be made. See Philip Short, *Mao: A Life* (London, 1999), p. 457.

48 According to Philip Short the official wording in the New China News Agency report was changed from the original 'last respects' to just 'respects'. See Short, *Mao: A Life,* p. 457.

49 Hua was ousted as Premier and Chairman in the early 1980s. He died during the Beijing Olympics in 2008. He was buried in his native area on Bei Gua Hill northwest of Jiaocheng County, Shanxi province, in a special cemetery covering an area of ten hectares. Set on a huge mound and with a steep long stepped access way, it looks very much like the tomb of Sun Yat-sen in Nanjing. See 'Hua Guofeng cemetery built', discussion forum on www.sinodefenceforum, accessed 4 July 2011.

50 This name referred originally only to the massive entrance gate that gave access to the imperial palace precinct. The older and fuller name referred to the bestowal of the 'heavenly mandate', the divine sanction of Chinese imperial power. See Hung Wu, 'Tiananmen Square: A Political History of Monuments', *Representation,* xxv, Special Issue: 'Monumental Histories' (Summer 1991), pp. 84–8.

51 See Hung Wu, 'Tiananmen Square: A Political History of Monuments', p. 90. See also, Hung Wu, *Remaking Beijing: Tiananmen Square and the Creation of a Political Space* (London, 2005), p. 23 The actual dimensions of the square are 880 x 500 metres.

52 Cheater, 'Death Ritual as Political Trickster', p. 90.

53 *China Pictorial,* Issue 9 (1977). For some of the 50 alternative designs submitted 'by the public', see also *Architectural Journal Peking,* 4 (1977), pp. 1–47. Most of them feature the flat roof and double cornice solution of the final project; some have only a single cornice roof and look like modernist Chinese railway stations. It is striking that they all envision the memorial to be open to Tiananmen Square and freely accessible and that they did not emphasize the separation and the cemetery-like enclosure of the final design. Perhaps the existence of memorial halls in Taipei, dedicated to Sun and Chiang, continue to hinder such a change of use, as it would appear that the PRC government imitates Taiwan.

54 J. F. Zhu, 'Contemporary Chinese architecture: A Cultural and Ideological Perspective', *City: Analysis of Urban Trends, Culture, Theory, Policy, Action,* xii/ 2 (December 2008), p. 75. Ellen Laing drew attention to the 'unified political statement' which the ensemble of buildings around Tiananmen Square formed by the end of the 1950s, with Tiananmen Gate signalling the proclamation of the new state, the History Museum displaying artefacts from the past which justify the PRC, and the Great Hall of the People, where the National Congress is held, to 'substantiate the dictatorship of the people'. See Ellen Laing, *The Winking Owl* (Berkeley, Los Angeles and London, 1988), p. 92.

55 From *Architectural Journal Peking,* xliv (1977), p. 1. See also, Linda Kay Davidson and David Martin Gitlitz, *Pilgrimage: From Ganges to Graceland: An Encylopaedia* (Santa Barbara, CA, 2002), vol. 1, p. 367.

56 Laing, *The Winking Owl,* p. 95.

57 Translation in Geremie Barmé, *Shades of Mao: The Posthumous Cult of the Great Leader* (Armonk, New York and London, 1996), p. 26.

58 As specified by Deng Xiaoping himself in a document released by the party's Central Committee in 1982. See also Rebecca E. Karl, *Mao Zedong and China in the Twentieth-century World* (Durham, NC, 2010), pp. 166–8.

59 Haiyan Lee, 'The Charisma of Power and the Military Sublime in Tiananmen Square', *The Journal of Asian Studies,* lxx/2 (May 2011), pp. 397–424; especially pp. 419–24.

60 *Architectural Journal Peking,* xliv (1977), p. 4.

61 Wagner quotes remarks made by Lothar Ledderose at a lecture in Berlin about the original scheme

that was intended for this, which was to have shown a huge red sun behind Mao's head, but owing to changes in the political centre it had become more favourable to show the Chairman as a friendly, smiling teacher, a 'reduction of Mao from blazing red sun'. See Rudolf Wagner, 'The Implied Pilgrim: Reading the Chairman Mao Memorial Hall', in *Pilgrims and Sacred Sites in China,* ed. Susan Naquin and Chu Yuan-fang (Berkeley, CA, 1992), p. 406. According to Ellen Laing, the significance of the artistic programme of the mausoleum consisted in its rejection of Jiang Qing's 'repressive art policies'. See Laing, *The Winking Owl,* p. 95.

62 Or, as sceptical visitors maintain, what passes for Mao's body. Given that wax replica figures were also fashioned, no one passing at the enforced speed can know if they file past an artifice or the actual remains.

63 Lee, 'The Charisma of Power and the Military Sublime in Tiananmen Square', p. 399.

64 The original Chinese is '*Yung-ch'ui pu-hsiui*'. This is the translation by Frederic Wakeman given in 'Revolutionary Rites: The Remains of Chiang Kai-shek and Mao Tse-Tung', *Representations,* 10 (Spring 1985), p. 3. Rudolf Wagner renders it as 'be handed down forever without decaying'. See Wagner, 'The Implied Pilgrim', p. 398. The same phrase has been placed above the north-facing entrance. The official translation on leaflets and websites reads more blandly: 'Eternal Glory to the Great Leader and Great Teacher Chairman Mao Zedong.'

65 Translation from Laing, *The Winking Owl,* p. 94. Mao had had a keen interest in Chinese traditional poetry from his youth, when he had worked at the Peking University Library of and continued to compose poetry throughout his life. The poem was written in 1963 and has been related to Sino-Soviet tensions.

66 Laing, *The Winking Owl,* p. 93; but see also Wu, 'Tiananmen Square'.

67 Wu, 'Tiananmen Square: A Political History of Monuments', p. 105.

68 Cheater, 'Death Ritual as Political Trickster', p. 94.

69 Wagner, 'The Implied Pilgrim', pp. 378–423.

70 Karl, *Mao Zedong and China in the Twentieth-Century World,* p. 182.

71 See the article by Kazuhiro Sekine, 'Russians arrive to embalm Kim Jong Il's body, 30 December 2011, http://ajw.asahi.com, accessed 7 January 2012.

72 'Kim Jong-Il's remains to go on permanent display', www.france24.com, accessed 7 January 2012.

73 In the following analysis I rely on the study by Adrian Buzo, *The Guerilla Dynasty: Politics and Leadership in North Korea* (London and New York, 1999).

74 In 1907 the Japanese forced the last ruling monarch, King Kojong, to abdicate the throne in favor of his feeble son, who was soon married off to a Japanese woman and given a Japanese peerage. See 'Korea under Japanese Rule', http://country studies.us/south-korea/7.htm; accessed 30 January 2011.

75 His name at birth was 'Kim Song Ju'. When he was in Manchuria, he changed it to 'Kim Il-sung', which means 'Be the Sun'. See Sydney A. Seiler, *Kim Il-song 1941–1948: The Creation of a Legend, the Building of a Regime* (Lanham, MD, 1994), p. 19.

76 Buzo, *The Guerilla Dynasty* p. 31.

77 Some 870,000 by 1936, according to Buzo, in *The Guerilla Dynasty,* p. 43.

78 Seiler, *Kim Il-song,* p. 90.

79 See for instance 'The Korean War, 1950–53', http://countrystudies.us/south-korea/10.htm, accessed 30 January 2011; or 'The Korean War (1950–1953)', www.sparksnotes.com, accessed 30 January 2011.

80 Kathryn Weathersby, 'The Soviet Role in the Early Phase of the Korean War: New Documentary Evidence', *The Journal of American–East Asian Relations,* 2 (Winter 1993), pp. 431–2.

81 Bertil Lintner, *Great Leader, Dear Leader: Demystifying North Korea Under the Kim Clan* (Chiang Mai, 2005), p. 44.

82 The Western view is that 'it was the Soviet occupational forces' active and pervasive efforts to sovietize North Korea that made Kim's rise and consolidation of power possible'. See Seiler, *Kim*

Il-song, p. 3. North Korean historiography tends to minimize the Russian influence.
83 Buzo, *The Guerilla Dynasty*, p. 57.
84 On the meaning of '*Juche*' see Lintner, *Great Leader, Dear Leader*, p. 41. Linter suggested this translation instead of the more widely used 'self-reliance'. Closely associated are three concepts: *chaju*, 'political independence'; *charip*, 'economic self-sufficiency', and *chawi*, 'self-defence'. The word '*ju*' means 'man, person' and '*che*' means 'body'. Sonia Ryang's reading of the term is that 'people are the subject of their own society as well as subjected to society.' See Ryang, 'Biopolitics or the Logic of Sovereign Love – Love's Whereabouts in North Korea', in *North Korea: Toward a Better Understanding*, ed. Sonia Ryang (Boulder, CO, New York, Toronto, Plymouth, 2009), p. 78.
85 Paul French, *North Korea: The Paranoid Peninsula: A Modern History* (London and New York, 2005), p. 41.
86 'Kim Jong Un: DPRK to carry forward revolution', www.china.org, accessed 20 July 2012.
87 See Philipp Meuser, ed., *Architekturführer Pjöngjang* (Berlin, 2011), 2 vols.
88 Kim Jong Il, *On Architecture* (21 May 1999), see www.scribd.com, p. 11 and 16, accessed 22 August 2011.
89 There is an official video made by North Korean TV on YouTube which gives an idealized impression of the visit. It does show the main gate with the golden door lockers which open as if by magic and allow a straight view of the mausoleum facade and the picture of Kim Il-sung. The Korean voice-over gives a very good impression of the emotional delivery of all commentaries on the mausoleum. See 'Kumsusam Memorial Palace', www.youtube.com/watch?v=jweownb1fig, accessed 27 August 2011.
90 'Religious Organization in the DPNK', *North Korean Quarterly*, LXXVI/LXXVII (Winter 1995), pp. 40–42. See also J. E. Hoare and Susan Pares, *North Korea in the 21st Century: An Interpretative Guide* (Folkstone, 2005), pp. 88–90.
91 Vincent S. R. Brandt, 'North Korea: Anthropological Speculation', *Korea and World Affairs*, VII/4 (1983), p. 620.
92 French, *North Korea*, p. 36.
93 This extends to the ancestors of the Kim family back to the nineteenth century. Their birth places, actual or 'imagined', are shrines, and their deeds subjects of books, films and visual images. See also Jasper Becker's comparison between Reverend Moon's Unification Church in South Korea and *Juche*. Both Kim Il Sung and Moon interpreted the suffering of Koreans in the twentieth century as part of a divine plan, both used existing religions (Christianity for Moon, Neo-Confucianism for Kim) to further nationalism, the aim of unifying Korea, and ultimately a 'self-serving religion': Jasper Becker, *Rogue Regime: Kim Jong Il and the Looming Threat of North Korea* (Oxford and New York, 2005), pp. 80–85.
94 Ryang, 'Biopolitics', especially p. 59.
95 Quoted in Denis Hollier, *Against Architecture* (Cambridge, MA, 1992), p. 46.
96 A. T. Iakimov, *The Great Soviet Encyclopedia*, 3rd edn (New York, 1979), available at http://encyclopedia2thefreedictionary.com, accessed 24 August 2011.
97 Helmut Braun, 'Historische Wurzeln spezifischer Transformations– und Entwicklungsprobleme der Mongolischen Republik', *Vierteljahrsschrift für Sozial- und Wirtschaftsgeschichte*, LXXXVI/4 (1997), pp. 512–43; also C. R. Bawden, *The Modern History of Mongolia* (London and New York, 1989), chap. 5.
98 'Corpses of Choibalsan and Sukhbaatar cremated', www.mongolianmatters.com, accessed 25 October 1012.
99 Christopher Kaplonski Blame, 'Guilt and Avoidance: The Struggle to Control the Past in Post-Socialist Mongolia', *History and Memory*, XI/2 (Fall / Winter 1999), p. 107.
100 Maria Todorova, 'The Mausoleum of Georgi Dimitrov as lieu de mémoire', *The Journal of Modern History*, LXXVIII/2 (June 2006), p. 377.
101 See his reminiscences in Ilya Zbarsky, *Lenin und andere Leichen. Ein Leben im Schatten des Mausoleums* (Munich 2000), pp. 184–90.
102 For archival footage and the destruction of the mausoleum, see the U.S. TV documentary 'A Better Tomorrow: The Georgi Dmitrov Mausoleum. Hope and Disappointment in Bulgaria', www.uctv.tv, accessed 30 October 2012; for

Dimitrov see 'Georgi Mikhailovich Dimitrov', www.britannica.com, accessed 30 October 2012.
103 Todorova, 'The Mausoleum', p. 387.
104 Radio Prague: 'Stalin and Gottwald: Together in Life and Death', www.radio.cz, accessed 1 December 2012.
105 Zbarsky, *Lenin und andere Leichen*, pp. 191–2.
106 Daniela Lazarova, 'Exhibition at Vitkov Memorial highlights the Klement Gottwald Personality Cult', www.radio.cz, accessed 1 December 2012.
107 'Albanian Civil Movement Protests Against Demolition of Enver Hoxha's Mausoleum', http://espressostalinist.wordpress.com, accessed 4 December 2012.

3 Fantasy and Reality: The Burial Places of Fascist Leaders

1 OSS Source Book 410, quoted by R.G.L. Waite, in 'Adolf Hitler's Guilt Feelings: A Problem in History and Psychology', *The Journal of Interdisciplinary History*, I/2 (Winter 1971), p. 17, n. 49. See also Paul Paxa, 'Capturing the Fascist Moment: Hitler's Visit to Italy in 1938 and the Radicalization of Fascist Italy', *Journal of Contemporary History*, XLII (April 2007), pp. 227–42).
2 Waite, 'Adolf Hitler's Guilt Feelings', p. 243; Karl Arndt, review of Alex Scobie, *Hitler's State Architecture: The Impact of Classical Antiquity*, in *Gnomon*, LXV/7 (1993), pp. 631–4.
3 See Thomas Friedrich, *Hitler's Berlin: Abused City*. (London and New Haven, CT, 2012); 'What might the Austrian town of Linz Have looked like if Hitler had won the War?' BBC History programme, bbc.co.uk, accessed 27 May 2013; 'Hitler's Hauptstädte: Nazibauten in München und Berlin', www.spiegel.de, accessed 27 May 2013.
4 James D. Plaut, 'Hitler's Capital', *Atlantic Monthly* (October 1946), www.theatlantic.com, accessed 27 May 2013.
5 See Hermann Giesler, *Ein anderer Hitler. Bericht seines Architekten: Erlebnisse, Gespräche, Reflexionen* (Leoni am Starnberger See, 1978).
6 See Erika und Helmuth Kern, 'Linz: die "Heimatstadt" Adolf Hitlers', www.deutschlandundeuropa.de; for the 2009 Exhibition in Linz, which featured plans and models, see www.linz09.at/sixcms/media.php/4974/2_The%20Exhibition.401606.pdf.
7 For English language coverage, see 'Headstone of Hitler's Parents' Grave removed', http://usatoday30, accessed 5 December 2012. .
8 Diane Yvonne Ghirardo, 'Italian Architects and Fascist Politics: An Evaluation of the Rationalist's Role in Regime Building', *Journal of the Society of Architectural Historians*, XXXIX/2 (May 1980), p. 144.
9 See 'Predappio Tricolore', www.mussolini.net, first accessed 6 June 2010.
10 Sean Anderson, 'The Light and the Line: Florestano Di Fausto and the Politics of '*Mediterraneità*', *California Italian Studies Journal*, I/1 (2010). Retrieved from www.escholarship.org, accessed 13 June 2010.
11 As described in the hagiography by Giorgio Pini, *The Official Life of Benito Mussolini*, trans. Luigi Vilari (London, 1939), p. 235.
12 The comments translate as: 'Proud to be Fascists', 'Yours faithfully in love with the idea. We shall never forget', 'In your honour and to you, everlasting Leader of Italy', 'Always Present'.
13 Paul Preston, *Franco* (London, 1993), p. 287.
14 Quoted by Preston, *Franco*, p. 290.
15 Quoted by Preston, *Franco*, p. 322.
16 Fernando Olmeda, *El Valle de Los Caídos. Una memoria de España* (Barcelona, 2009), p. 24 (my translation).
17 Olmeda, *El Valle de Los Caídos*, pp. 20–21 (my translation).
18 General José Millan Astray, *Franco, el caudillo* (Salamanca, 1939), pp. 11–12
19 He also shared Hitler's interest in art and took up painting, which became a lifelong hobby. See Preston, *Franco*, p. 352 and p. 630.
20 Olmeda, *El Valle de Los Caídos*, p. 52 (my translation).
21 Preston, *Franco*, p. 351 Preston is citing the decree dated 1 April 1940.
22 Olmeda, *El Valle de Los Caídos*, p. 37.
23 For a detailed history of the building process, see Daniel Sueiro, *El Valle de los Caídos. Idea, Proyecto y construcción* (Madrid, 1982).
24 This is unlike the basilica at Yamoussoukro, built for the Ivorian president and dictator Felix

Houphouët Boigny, which is taller than St Peter's. It is in fact the largest Catholic cathedral in the world. It also serves as final resting place for Houphouët Boigny, who raised it not least to his own glory.

25 Provision for further future entombments is afforded by chambers set behind the six chapels along the main nave.

26 Preston, *Franco*, p. 679.

27 To this day, Falangists take umbrage at the fact that a monument to the 'fallen' soldiers should accommodate the body of a person who died a civilian death, unlike their former leader José Antonio Primo de Rivera.

28 'Well then Mendez, when the day comes I'll be right here', quoted in Olmeda, *El Valle de Los Caídos*, p. 338.

29 Michael Richards, 'From War Culture to Civil Society: Francoism, Social Change and Memories of the Spanish Civil War', *History and Memory*, XIV/1–2, 'Special Issue: Images of a Contested Past' (Spring–Winter 2002), pp. 93–120; p. 106.

30 Richards, 'From War Culture to Civil Society', p. 107.

31 See Javier Caceres, 'Ruhestörung im Tal der Gefallenen', *Süddeutsche Zeitung* (30 November 2011), p. 13.

32 Ismael Saz, 'Was There Francoism in Spain?: Impertinent Reflections on the Historic Place of the Dictatorship', *Review (Fernand Braudel Center)*, XXVIII/3 (2005), p. 297.

4 New Nations, New Monuments: Mausolea for Fathers of the Nation

1 'When I administered my thirteenth consulate (2 BCE), the senate and Equestrian order and Roman people all called me father of the country, and voted that the same be inscribed in the vestibule of my temple, in the Julian senate-house, and in the forum of Augustus under the chariot which had been placed there for me by a decision of the senate. When I wrote this I was seventy-six years old.' See 'The Res Gestae of Augustus', http://penelope.uchicago.edu, accessed 20 July 2012.

2 Karl Galinsky, *Augustan Culture: An Interpretive Introduction* (Princeton, NJ, 1996), pp. 35–7.

3 Ovid, *Fasti, Book* II: *February 5: Nones*. Translation from www.poetryintranslation.com, accessed 20 July 2012.

4 He was called '*pater rbi*', the Father of the City of Rome, in recognition of the lavish investments in the new capital, centre of the new world. See Diane Favro, '"Pater urbis": Augustus as City Father of Rome', *Journal of the Society of Architectural Historians*, LI/1 (March 1992), pp. 61–84.

5 Article published on the occasion of Washington's 277th anniversary by Patrick Perry, 'Happy Birthday, President Washington', see www.saturdayeveningpost.com, accessed 23 July 2012. See also Barry Schwartz, *George Washington: The Making of an American Symbol* (New York and London, 1990).

6 Harris Memel-Fotê, 'Des ancêtres fondateurs aux Pères de la nation. Introduction à une anthropologie de la démocratie', *Cahiers d'Études Africaines*, XXXI /Cahier 123 (1991), pp. 263–85.

7 Peter Zarrow points out that Taiwan still calls itself the 'Republic of China', tracing its origin to Sun Yat-sen, while in official PRC historiography the 1911 revolution is described as only the beginning of the 'bourgeois phase' of a longer revolutionary struggle against feudalism and imperialism. See Zarrow, *China in War and Revolution 1895–1949* (London and New York, 2005), p. 30.

8 C. Voonping Yui, 'Some Experiences at the Siege of Nanking during the Revolution', *The Journal of Race Development*, IV/1 (July 1913), p. 90.

9 The name 'Yat-sen' was acquired later, when he attended school in Hong Kong.

10 James Gregor and Maria Hsia, 'Wang Yang-ming and the Ideology of Sun Yat-sen', *The Review of Politics*, XLII/3 (July 1980), p. 400.

11 Bernard Martin, *Strange Vigour: A Biography of Sun Yat-sen* (London, 1968), p. 225. According to a Reuters report, Sun had expressed the wish to be buried in a casket similar to Lenin's and for a glass-topped bronze coffin to be dispatched by rail from Moscow. See Malcom Rosholt, 'The Shoe-Box Letters from China', *The Wisconsin Magazine of History*, LXXIII/2 (Winter 1989–1990), p. 121. It was later alleged that this coffin was of poor quality and would not have been suitable to

preserve an embalmed corpse. On this point, see Jonathan Fenby, *Generalissimo: Chiang Kai-shek and The China He Lost* (New York, 2005), p. 74.

12 James Cantlie and C. Sheridan, *Sun Yat-sen and the Awakening of China* (London 1912), p. 154.

13 Delin Lai, 'Searching for a Modern Chinese Monument: The Design of the Sun Yat-sen Mausoleum in Nanjing', *Journal of the Society of Architectural Historians*, LXIV/1 (March 2005), p. 40.

14 Liping Wang quoted in Lai, 'Searching for a Modern Chinese Monument', p. 24.

15 Lai, 'Searching for a Modern Chinese Monument', p. 25.

16 The jury consisted of three Chinese (a civil engineer, a sculptor and a traditional Chinese painter) and, in the absence of so few Chinese architects in 1920s China, a German architect, Emil Busch (who worked for a company in Shanghai), 'who was chosen to give the jury international credibility', according to Delin Lai. See Lai, 'Searching for a Modern Chinese Monument', p. 29.

17 Guo Qinghua, 'Tomb Architecture of Dynastic China: Old and New Questions', *Architectural History*, XLVII (2004), p. 1.

18 Lü passed away in 1929, at the age of 35 years. He was taken as 'a fair sample of the energy, the brilliance and the personal sacrifices of the Nationalist Revolution of the 1920s'. From John Fitzgerald, *Awakening China: Politics, Culture, and Class in the Nationalist Revolution* (Stanford, CA, 1996), p. 1.

19 In the regions controlled by the KMT, his portrait hung in every office, school and barracks, in front of which a ritual had to be carried out. This involved bowing to Sun's likeness three times, reading aloud his 'Final Political Testament' and a three-minute silence. See Lai, 'Searching for a Modern Chinese Monument', pp. 40–41.

20 Rudolf Wagner recounts that those relics were 'later removed, hidden again and eventually burned on Chiang-Kai-shek's orders' because they were 'politically contaminated through their association with the traitorous Wang'. See Rudolf Wagner, 'Ritual, Architecture, Politics and Publicity during the Republic: Enshrining Sun Yat-sen', from a paper presented to the conference 'The Beaux-Arts, Paul Philippe Cret, and 20th-Century Architecture in China', 3–5 October 2003, University of Pennsylvania, Philadelphia, p. 413. Afterwards published in Jeffrey Cody, Nancy S. Steinhardt and Tony Atkin, eds, *Chinese Architecture and the Beaux-Arts* (2011).

21 In 2005 it was rated 'AAAAA' by the China National Tourism Authority.

22 This had been chiselled out by Red Guards during the Cultural Revolution and subsequently restored.

23 A skyscraper-sized statue of Sun's widow, Soong Ching-ling, is currently under construction in Zhengzhou, the capital of Henan province: 'Standing 24 m [around 78 ft] in height, what is soon to be the world's tallest statue of a female from the modern era shares its home with what is currently the tallest statue in the world, the 128 m [419 ft] Spring Temple Buddha. According to *China Daily*, the towering Soong Ching-ling is part of a 800 sq m complex under construction [. . . and] will include four six-storey buildings, housing cinemas, studios and meeting halls.' See 'Henan's Colossal Statue of Madame Sun Yat-Sen Exposes Scandal', 16 November 2011, www.architizer.com, accessed 20 December 2011.

24 Adolf Loos, 'Architektur' (1910), in *Über Architektur* (Vienna, 1995), p. 84.

25 The Turkish word means 'memorial tomb'.

26 The National Assembly then passed a law that restricted this surname to its sole use by Mustafa Kemal. See Andrew Mango, *Atatürk* (London, 1999), p. 498.

27 His surname derived from the place called 'İnönü', where he won two important battles in the War of Liberation.

28 Andrew Mango, *Atatürk,* p. 396.

29 Kim Shively, 'Religious Bodies and the Secular State: The Merve Kavakci Affair', *Journal of Middle East Women's Studies*, 1/3 (Fall 2005), p. 63.

30 Turkish archaeologists excavated these tombs in the 1940s and their contents are now displayed in the Museum of Anatolian Civilization.

31 Christopher Wilson, 'The Persistence of the Turkish Nation in the Mausoleum of Mustafa Kemal Atatürk', in *Nationalism in a Global Era,*

ed. Mitchell Young, Eric Zuelow and Andreas Storm (London, 2007), p. 97.
32 Ibid.
33 Sibel Bozdogan, Suha Özkan and Engin Yenal, *Sedad Elder: Architect in Turkey* (Istanbul, 1987), p. 68.
34 This contrasts with the detailed explanations supplied at Sun Yat-Sen's mausoleum at every stage of the visit.
35 See Nayanika Mookherjee 'The Aesthetics of Nations', *Journal of the Royal Anthropological Institute*, (NS) Special Issue (2011), p. 55.
36 They accommodate administrative offices, a research and archive library, a video screening room and exhibition spaces.
37 They consist of two panels of text, designed by calligrapher Emin Barim, excerpts from famous Atatürk speeches. The one on the right, addressed to the 'Youth of Turkey', has to be memorized by every Turkish pupil.
38 He was buried there in 1973 There used to also be the burials of 30 'martyrs' of the 1980 Civil War, but they have since been removed, though I could not find out when this happened.
39 Only in the subterranean galleries does a strict spatial sequence operate.
40 The columns are around two-and-a-half times the size of a man.
41 Shively, 'Religious Bodies', p. 63.
42 For these examples, see *Turkey's Engagement With Modernity: Conflict and Change in the Twentieth Century* ed. Celia Kerslake, Kerem Öktem and Philip Robins (Basingstoke, 2010), pp. 101–2.
43 For quotations from his speeches on the subject, see Stephen Philip Cohen, *The Idea of Pakistan* (Washington, DC, 2004), p. 41, n. 28.
44 Shahid Javed Burki, *Historical Dictionary of Pakistan* (Lanham MD, 2006).
45 The Urdu word means 'Land of the Pure'.
46 Cohen, *The Idea of Pakistan*, p. 45.
47 As told by Zahir-ud Din Khwaja, *Memoirs of an Architect* (Lahore, 1998), pp. 63–6.
48 There were and still are a range of different Islamic sects active in Pakistan, as well as Shia and Sunni factions. See Farzana Shaikh, *Making Sense of Pakistan* (London, 2009).
49 The foundation stone was ceremoniously laid on 31 July 1960.
50 For drawings (elevations and plans), see 'Competition for Ali Jinnah's Tomb: Winning Design by Raglan Squire and Partners', *Architects' Journal* (6 March 1958), pp. 346–7. See also, *Architect & Building News* (12 March 1958), pp. 340–41 Models are depicted in 'Mausoleé Qaide-Azam Mohammed Ali Jinnah, Karachi, Pakistan', *Architecture d'aujourd'hui*, 81 (1958), p. xxviii.
51 Zahir-ud Din Khwaja, *Memoirs of an Architect*, p. 65.
52 The architect especially referenced the tomb of Shah Rukn-i-Alam at Multan. In fact, the raised brick profile is closer to the much earlier mausoleum of Ismail Samani in Bukhara (I am grateful to Bruce Wannell for pointing this out).
53 Ahmed Humayun and Ali Jafri Karachi, 'Ethnic Tinderbox', *Small Wars Journal*, 2, http://small-warsjournal.com, 2 December 2010.
54 The official description insists that they derive from the curvature of the inclination of the walls. See Ahmad Hasan Dani and Hussain Afsar Akhtar, *The Quaid-i-Azam Mausoleum in Pictures* (Islamabad, 1976), p. 3.
55 There was no English notice here to explain to whom these tombs belonged.
56 'Mazar-e Quaid-Azam: Symbol of Hope for all Mankind', www.humsafar.info, accessed 26 June 2011.
57 Ahmad Hasan Dani and Husain Afsar Akhtar, *The Quaid-i-Azam Mausoleum.* See 'Victory Day Celebrated', http://redtimesbd.com/english, accessed 4 June 2011.
58 Available at http://redtimesbd.com/english_details.php?cat=4&id=752.
59 Marcus Franda, 'Ziaur Rahman and Bangladeshi Nationalism', *Economic and Political Weekly* XVI/10/12, Annual Number (March 1981), p. 379.
60 The one represented the interests of *jotedar*s and urban people and had greatest support in the western part, while the latter, known as the 'Krishak Praja Party' in Bengali, opposed absentee landlordism, was more rurally based and most popular in the erstwhile eastern province. On this point, Craig Baxter, *Bangladesh: From a Nation to a State* (Boulder, CO, 1997), p. 50.
61 He resigned again in 1943, after having formed another coalition ministry without the Muslim League's support in 1941.

62 One of the greatest disparities was in the army, where only a very small fraction of officers were Bengali, partially owing to the lack of family military traditions in Bengal.
63 Discrimination against Bengali Muslims was rife from the beginning. Sonia Preti, *Nationalism in Bangladesh: Genesis and Evolution* (Delhi, 2004), p. 17: 'In his preference for feudal aristocrats who were hardly aware of the plight of middle class Bengali-Muslims, Jinnah and his clique never allowed the deserving Bengali-Muslims to hold the highest decision-making position in the Muslim League.'
64 On the rigging of the election, see Craig Baxter, *Bangladesh*, p. 91.
65 Willem van Schendel comments that 'it [the constitution] stated that the Bangladeshi nation was the ultimate manifestation of the delta's Muslim-Bengali identity, which had been maturing during the British and Pakistan periods' and 'that the creation of Pakistan had enabled the emergence of Bangladesh'. See Willem van Schendel, *A History of Bangladesh* (Cambridge, 2009), p. 203.
66 According to Jeremy Seabrook, 'Their dynastic struggle makes them symbols as much of what their opponents loath as of what they positively represent. In any case, governments of both BNP and Awami League have been defined by corruption, rapacity, maladministration and neglect of the poor.' See Jeremy Seabrook, *Freedom Unfinished: Fundamentalism and Popular Resistance in Bangladesh Today* (London, 2001), p. 6.
67 It took 21 years from the initial commission by the government of Pakistan in 1961 to the inauguration in 1982. Louis Kahn died in 1974. See *Regionalism in Architecture: Proceedings of the Regional Seminar Sponsored by the Aga Khan Award for Architecture, Bangladesh University of Engineering and Technology and Institute of Architects, Bangladesh, held in Dhaka, Bangladesh, December 17–22, 1985* (Singapore, 1985).
68 Syed Serajul Islam, 'Bangladesh in 1986: Entering a New Phase', *Asian Survey*, XXVII/2, A Survey of Asia in 1986: Part 2 (February 1987), p. 166, note 7.
69 I have not been able to find any documentation of the original tomb. According to personal communication from Masud Bashat, the architect of the mausoleum, the sarcophagus was retained in their scheme.
70 According to the architect's notes, the openness of the plan 'reflects the life style of Late President Ziaur Rahman' (personal communication, email, 10 September 2011).
71 Masud Bashat, Architect's final text (personal communication, ibid.
72 A virtual museum is currently under construction See http://bangabandhu.net, accessed, 20 September 2011.

5 Not the Final Resting Place: Temporary Mausolea

1 An excerpt from the KMT official news organ, 'A Nation Mourns', *Vista*, 3 (1975), p. 19. Quoted in Frederic Wakeman Jr., 'Revolutionary Rites: The Remains of Chiang Kai-shek and Mao Tse Tung', *Representations*, 10 (Spring 1985), p. 164.
2 See Muray A. Rubeinstein, *Taiwan: A New History* (Armouth, New York and London, 1999) and Jonathan Manthorpe, *Forbidden Nation: A History of Taiwan* (New York, 2000).
3 See Peter Zarrow, *China in War and Revolution, 1895–1949* (London and New York, 2005), p. 343f.
4 Jonathan Fenby, *Generalissimo: Chiang Kai-shek and the China He Lost* (New York, 2005), p. 488.
5 See for instance, Congressional Research Service: 'Evolution of the "One China" policy', http://assets.opencrs.com, accessed 10 July 2011.
6 Quoted in Wakeman, 'Revolutionary Rites': p. 155.
7 Ibid., p. 156.
8 Older photographs show that the colours were added later. Even on the official brochure, the shutters are red.
9 Wakeman, 'Revolutionary Rites', p. 164.
10 Mahmoud Darwish, 'And We Have a Land', see www.othervoicespoetry.org, accessed 28 May 2013.
11 See Thomas Kiernan, *Yasir Arafat: The Man and the Myth* (London, 1976), pp. 16–29. For an account of the genealogy of his childhood and on the matter of his birth, see David Hulme, *Identity, Ideology, and the Future of Jerusalem* (London, 2006), p. 144.

12 Arafat always preferred to rely on oral accounts; he never wrote personal memoirs or autobiographical accounts, quite unlike, for instance, Kwame Nkrumah, Ho Chi Minh, or the other great myth-maker, Kim Il Sung.
13 His other sobriquet, 'Abu Ammar' (literally 'father of the builder'), dates from this period.
14 The number of settlers had grown from around 200,000 to nearly half a million. See Laleh Khalili, *Heroes and Martyrs of Palestine: The Poetics of National Commemoration* (Cambridge, 2007), p. xxi.
15 For his bodyguards' account of the siege, see Bassam Abu Sharif, *Arafat and the Dream of Palestine: An Insider's Account* (Basingstoke, 2009), pp. 237–43.
16 Many people, including his senior adviser and press officer, Abu Sharif, believed that he had been poisoned by Israeli agents. See Sharif, *Arafat*, pp 249–51. An alternative view, much circulated in the Israeli and U.S. media, was that Arafat had suffered from AIDS or alcoholism. In July 2012, the Palestinian Authority called for new examinations and the exhumation of Arafat's remains. See 'Call for Yasser Arafat death probe gains first international backer', www.telegraph.co.uk, 5 July 2012.
17 These included Jordan's King Abdullah II, Lebanese President Émile Lahoud and Syrian President Bashar al-Assad, UK Foreign Secretary Jack Straw and U.S. envoy Williams Burns.
18 Sarah Left, and agencies, 'Arafat begins final journey', www.guardian.co.uk, 11 November 2004. See also, 'Arafat's body begins final return', http://news.bbc.co.uk, 11 November 2004.
19 Israel also barred people from Gaza from travelling to Ramallah. Another symbolic funeral service was celebrated there instead. There were also travelling restrictions within the West Bank.
20 Martin Asser, 'Arafat's funeral held in Cairo', news.bbc.co.uk, 12 November 2004.
21 As reported in Khalili, *Heroes and Martyrs of Palestine*, p. 188.
22 Ibid., p. 187.
23 Tukan has Palestinian background. He was born in 1930 in Jerusalem and graduated from the American University in Beirut in 1960. He worked for the Jordanian Ministry of Public Works, then established a private practice in Beirut, before moving to Amman, where he was involved in designing a number of public works. He received the Aga Khan Award for Architecture in 2001 for his SOS children's village in Aqaba, which made good use of traditional building solutions for the hot and humid climate of the Persian Gulf. He also won the plaudits of architectural critics Charles Correa and Kenneth Frampton. See Charles Correa, Kenneth Frampton, David Robson, *Modernity and Community Architecture in the Islamic World* (London, 2001).
24 According to the architect's website, Queen Noor had also commissioned designs for a mausoleum destined for King Hussein, 'an open-air pavilion in Jordanian stone with elements from classical Islamic art and exquisite calligraphy'. See www.ccjo.com.
25 Rami G. Khouri, 'Arafat's mausoleum represents a fixed past and a possible future on the move', www.dailystar.com.lb, 25 June 2005.
26 See 'Yasser Arafat's tomb', http://newscoopramallah.wordpress.com, accessed 19 January 2011.
27 'Mausoleum of late Palestinian leader Yasser Arafat unveiled in Ramallah', www.haaretz.com, 10 November 2007.

6 Appropriated Traditions

1 The officially recognized religions were Islam, Hinduism, Buddhism, Catholicism and Protestantism.
2 He always stressed his humble origin as a son of the soil but given his unusual access to education and various inconsistencies in the accounts of his early life, it has been surmised that he was the illegitimate offspring of 'a well-placed villager', some say a wealthy Chinese, if not, as he himself publicly refuted, that of a minor member of the Yogyakarta nobility. See Robert E. Elson, *Suharto: A Political Biography* (Cambridge, 2008), pp. 3–5.
3 Sukarno died five years later of kidney failure (on 21 June 1970).
4 Elson, *Suharto*, p. 398.
5 David Bourchier, *Dynamics of Dissent in Indonesia: Sawita and the Phantom Coup* (Singapore, 2010), p. 112.

6 According to the authorized biography by Retnowati Abdulgani-Knapp, Ibu Tien was 'the daughter of a *wedana* and an employee of Mangkunegara', stressing that all employees of a *kraton* 'had to have royal blood.' See Retnowati Abdulgani-Knapp, *Soeharto: The Life and Legacy of Indonesia's Second President* (Singapore, 2007), p. 29.

7 See Benedict Anderson, 'Exit Suharto. Obituary for a Mediocre Tyrant', *New Left Review*, 50 (March–April 2008), p. 27.

8 Elson, *Suharto*, p. 194.

9 Stephan Fitzpatrick, 'Mystical powers sustain ailing Suharto', www.opensubscriber.com, 19 January 2008.

10 For details of his will, see the quoted passage in Pier Paolo de Giosa, 'Kudus and Blitar: A Tale of Two Javanese Iconic Cities', in *Cities Full of Symbols: A Theory of Urban Space and Culture*, ed. Peter J. M. Nas (Leiden, 2011), p. 204.

11 Retnowati Abdulgani-Knapp remarks that the Mangadeg Foundation, which built and continues to manage the site, also has the right to bury its members and their families. There are three levels and up to 339 available grave sites. Ibu Tien and her parents, with Suharto next to her, are on the highest level, Pak Suharto's six children on the second, while foundation members and their children can be accommodated on the third level. See Abdulgani-Knapp, *Soeharto*, p. 327.

12 Marshall Clark, 'Pipit Rochijat's Subversive Mythologies: The Suharto Era and Beyond', *Asian Folklore Studies*, LXV/1 (2006), p. 40.

13 Abidin Kusno, *Behind the Postcolonial: Architecture, Urban Space and Political Cultures in Indonesia* (London and New York, 2000).

14 For the importance of photographs of the dead in the context of Chinese forms of ancestor worship, which has spread to become a universal practice in mainly Muslim Java, see Karen Strassler, *Refracted Visions: Popular Photography and National Modernity in Java* (Durham and London, 2000), pp. 148–55.

15 According to a Javanese tourist website, a tunnel links the two sites that is only accessible on certain days. See www.javaisbeautiful.com, accessed 6 January 2011.

16 See Benedict Anderson, 'Exit Suharto', p. 27.

17 See www.jogjatrip.com, accessed 6 January 2011.

18 Quoted in Arif Zamhari, *Rituals of Islamic Spirituality: A Study of Majils Dhikr Groups in East Java* (Canberra, 2010), p. 200.

19 De Giosa, 'Kudus and Blitar', pp. 204–5.

20 Cf. George Quinn, 'Local Pilgrimage in Java and Madura: why is it booming?', IIAS Newsletter, 35 (November 2004), www.iias.nl, accessed 20 November 2011.

21 De Giosa, 'Kudus and Blitar'', p. 208.

22 See Dietrich Brandenburg, *Die Seldschuken: Baukunst des Islam in Persien und Turkmenistan* (Graz, 2005), p. 46, and Robert Hillenbrand, *Islamic Architecture: Form, Function and Meaning* (New York, 1994), pp. 294–306.

23 In Shia theology the Imamate passed from the Prophet Muhammad to Ali and then to designated successors. The twelfth Imam (born 868), Abul Qasim Muhammed, disappeared and thereafter declared that he had been hidden until God would permit him to be seen again. This is a doctrine known as 'occultation', whereby imams had to be designated, were sinless and infallible. See Moojan Momen, *An Introduction to Shi'i Islam* (New Haven, CT, and London, 1985), p. 23, pp. 153–60 and p. 163.

24 It was also the burial place of Ismail I (Shah Ismail). See Kishwar Rizvi, *The Safavid Dynastic Shrine: Architecture, Religion and Power in Early Modern Iran* (London, 2011), pp. 3–6.

25 Also know as '*liana*', originally the vaulted hall of a domestic building, they could form a deeply recessed and often elaborately decorated entrance niche in the facades of mosques and other monumental buildings.

26 Rizvi, *The Safavid Dynastic Shrine*, p. 3.

27 Kishwar Rizvi, 'Religious Icon and National Symbol: The Tomb of Ayatollah Khomeini in Iran', *Muqarnas*, XX (2003), p. 216.

28 The exact date is not substantiated owing to the unreliability of record keeping in rural Iran at the time. His official birthday happens to coincide with that of the much-revered Fatima Ma'suma, sister of Imam Ali Riza. See Colin Coughlin, *Khomeini's Ghost* (Basingstoke and Oxford, 2009), p. 32.

29 *Sayyids* have the right to wear a black turban as a mark of distinction.
30 He was said to have achieved the rank of an *ayatollah*, a claim not unanimously accepted.
31 He died probably from a heart attack, though many people believed that he was killed by SAVAK agents.
32 Colin Coughlin, *Khomeini's Ghost*, p. 162.
33 Vanessa Martin, *Creating an Islamic State: Khomeini and the Making of a New Iran* (London and New York, 2000), p. 203.
34 As reported in the *Washington Post*, 18 April 1980. Quoted in Coughlin, *Khomeini's Ghost*, pp. 183–4.
35 Ervand I. Abrahamian, *Khomeinism: Essays on the Islamic Republic* (London and New York, 1993), p. 27.
36 Coughlin, *Khomeini's Ghost*, p. 247.
37 Colin Coughlin quotes Iranian radio reports that stated that 10,000 people were treated for injuries sustained during the funeral ceremonies. The cemetery had been Khomeini's first stopping place after his return from exile. It was from here that he made his first public speech to a crowd of 250,000 supporters. See Coughlin, *Khomeini's Ghost*, p. 249.
38 This is according to the descriptions by Brigitte Hoffman, in Hoffmann, 'Das Mausoleum Khomeinis in Teheran. Überlegungen zur persisch-islamischen Gedächtnisarchitektur', *Die Welt des Islams*, N.S. XXXIX/ 1 (March 1999), pp. 1–30, and Kishwar Rizvi, 'Religious Icon and National Symbol: The Tomb of Ayatollah Khomeini in Iran', *Muqarnas*, XX (2003), pp. 209–24.
39 Brigitte Hoffman, remarks that that the 68 metres refers to the year of Khomeini's death in 1368, according to Islamic reckoning. See Hoffmann, 'Das Mausoleum Khomeinis in Teheran', p. 4, n. 8.
40 Rizvi, 'Religious Icon and National Symbol', p. 220.
41 The presence and demeanour of these women was for me the most impressive aspect of the mausoleum and in striking contrast to the atmosphere at Fatima Ma'suma's shrine in Qum, where the abundant male clergy is very evidently in control and women are confined to particular enclaves.
42 They offered editions of the Koran and religious tracts, headscarves, prayer beads, pictures of Khomeini and the shrines of Karbala and Najaf. There were no mementoes of the Khomeini mausoleum at all, however, and my requests for them were met with puzzlement. Once the whole project is finished, it will be interesting to see whether the Khomeini mausoleum will join the ranks of the major Shia holy sites and sell site specific merchandise.
43 For a brief summary of his life and legacy, see Anna Marveeva, 'After the Father', *The World Today*, LXIII/2 (February 2007), p. 20.
44 A Turkmenistan website reports that 'According to the state mass media, the mausoleum was erected as a gift to the Turkmen leader from Martin Bouygues, the president of the famous French Bouygues company that built the new mosque and a number of other large administrative and cultural buildings in Turkmenistan'. See 'Saparmurat Niyazov reburies ashes of parents, brothers at family mausoleum', www.turkmenistan.ru, 12 December 2004.

7 Political Mausolea in Africa

1 'The Tomb of Saal Zaghloul, http://cairobserver.com, 30 March 2012; see also Ali Labib Gabr, 'Neo Pharaonic Architecture in Cairo: A Western Legacy, in *Medina Premier Issue: Architecture, Interiors & Fine Art* (1998), pp. 44–72.
2 See 'Le Mausolée de Bourguiba à Monastir', http://tunisie.co, accessed 20 December 2011.
3 See Abdelaziz Barrouhi, 'Un mausolée construit sur mesure', www.jeuneafrique.com, accessed 27 June 2013.
4 See 'Funerailles solenelles pour Ahmed ben Bella, à Alger, www.rfi.fr, 13 April 2012.
5 See Hakim Adi and Marika Sherwood, *Pan-African History: Political Figures from Africa and the Diaspora Since 1787* (London 2003); Marika Sherwood, *Origins of Pan-Africanism: Henry Sylvester Williams, Africa, and the African Diaspora* (London 2010).
6 His exact birth date is not known but it around 1894, which means that he was in his late eighties when he died. See Jeremy Murray Brown, *Kenyatta*

7. Vincent B. Khapoya, 'The Politics of Succession in Africa: Kenya after Kenyatta', *Africa Today*, XXVI/3 (1979), p. 8.

8. For the history of Congo-Brazzaville, see John F. Clark, *The Failure of Democracy in the Republic of Congo* (Boulder, CO, 2008); on the mausoleum, see http://brazza.tv, and www.brazzavilleadiac.com, both accessed 21 December 2011.

9. I have only seen TV footage of this mausoleum on videos posted on the Web. It is not clear from these images, which show politicians depositing floral bouquets on the grave, whether there are normally guards on site but, given the ongoing relevance of Ngouabi to the present regime under Sassou Ngouesso, it is likely.

10. See 'Un mausolée pour Brazza', www.rfi.fr, 4 October 2006.

11. For Neto's life, see his biography in Russian by Anatoly M. Khazanov, *Agostinho Neto* (Moscow, 1986); for a review of Angolan history, see Patrick Chabal and Nuno Vidal, *Angola: The Weight of History* (London, 2007).

12. Ilya Zbarsky recalls that the preservation of Neto's 'ebony skin' had been 'a challenge'. See Ilya Zbarsky, *Lenin und andere Leichen. Mein Leben im Schatten des Mausoleums,* (Stuttgart, 2000), pp. 199–201.

13. Khazanov, *Agostinho Neto*, pp. 293–4 (my translation).

14. 'Memorial a Agostinho Neto inaugurado no dia do seu 90°', www.africatoday.co.ao.

15. Roger S. Gocking reports that over 65,000 soldiers were recruited; their main contribution was to serve overseas in other tropical war zones, such as Burma. See Roger S. Gocking, *The History of Ghana* (Westport, CT, 2005).

16. Kwame Nkrumah, *Revolutionary Path* (London, 1973), pp. 181–2.

17. Quoted by Basil Davidson, *Black Star: A View of the Life and Times of Kwame Nkrumah* (Plymouth, 1973), p. 200.

18. Roger S. Gocking, *The History of Ghana*, p. 138. For the possible involvement of the CIA in the coup under the CIA chief Howard Bane in Accra, see David Rooney, *Kwame Nkrumah: A Political Kingdom in the Third World* (London, 1988), pp. 252–4. See also Akwasi P. Osei, *Ghana: Recurrence and Change in a Post-Independence African State*, Society and Politics in Africa, vol. IV (New York, 1999), pp. 76–7.

19. See Gocking, *The History of Ghana*, p. 166.

20. Ibid., p. 169.

21. For an account of the funeral, see June Milne, *Kwame Nkrumah: A Biography* (London, 2000), pp. 262–7.

22. Berry Hess shows an image of a single room space, closed by a stone wall at the back, open to the front and shielded by glass-panelled walls on either side covered by a pitched timber roof. In the image there is a bust of Nkrumah against the wall and from the sarcophagus emerged a symbolic hand 'holding aloft the flame of liberty'. See Janet Berry Hess, *Art and Architecture in Postcolonial Africa* (Jefferson, NC, 2006), p. 86, image p. 87.

23. In 1985 he called for Nkrumah's vision to be kept alive and in the same year also inaugurated the W.E.B. Du Bois Memorial Centre for African Culture, which includes the mausoleum of the famous African-American pan-Africanist. See Hess, *Art and Architecture*, p. 86.

24. According to the official tour guide leaflet, 'the project [of the mausoleum] was said to be the dream of Lt-Gen. Kutu Acheampong [. . .] who unfortunately could not see the project incarnated.' See Isaac M. Quist, *Kwame Nkrumah. An Undying Flame. Tour Guide to Kwame Nkrumah Memorial Park, Accra, Ghana* (Tema, Ghana, 2002), p. 6.

25. On the election and the not uncontested outcome, see Paul Nugent, *Big Men, Small Boys, and Politics in Ghana: Power, Ideology, and the Burden of History, 1982–1994* (London, 1995), pp. 215–66. Nugent does not refer to the inauguration of the Nkrumah Memorial.

26. On the history Ghana from 1993 onwards, see Kwame Boafo-Arthur, ed*., Ghana: One Decade of the Liberal State* (London and New York, 2007).

27. In actual ceremonies hornblowers neither kneel nor stand in or near water. Here, however, this symbolizes both great reverence and the 'significance of water in Ghanaian belief', as the official leaflet explains. Also cf. Quist, *Kwame Nkrumah* p. 29. Owing to various plumbing problems, the

28. See Mike Summerton, 'Kwame Nkrumah Memorial Park', http://onsitereview.blogspot.com, accessed 9 August 2011.
29. The actual grave is in a sunken, normally inaccessible vault, underneath. His wife Fatima is buried in a smaller sarcophagus in the space between the pillars on the south side.
30. See 'Ghanians thrilled by re enactment of declaration of independence', www.ghanabusiness-news.com, 6 March 2011.
31. '*M'zee*' is the Swahili word for 'old man' or '*le vieux*' in French and is the common soubriquet for Kabila.
32. The USA was the first state to recognize Leopold's claim on Congo. Germany under Bismarck followed suit a year later in 1885. On 29 May of that year the Congo Free State (CFS) was officially established by royal decree. See Georges Nzongola-Ntalaja, *The Congo from Leopold to Kabila* (London and New York, 2002), p. 265.
33. Bogumil Jewsiewicki, 'Kinshasa: (auto)representation d'une société 'moderne' en (dé)construction, in *La Nouvelle Histoire du Congo : mélanges eurafricains offerts à Fran Bontinck*, C.I.C.I.M, ed. Pamphile Mabiala Mantuba-Ngoma (Tervuren and Paris, 2004), p. 254.
34. Belgian colonizers refused to educate black students at secondary and university level. By June 1960 the country had no more than ten university graduates. See Kasongo-Numbi Kashemukunda, *L'Afrique se recolonise: une relecture du demi-siècle de l'indépendance du Congo-Kinshasa* (Paris, 2008), p. 203.
35. For accounts of Lumumba's death, see Ludo De Witte, *The Assassination of Lumumba*, trans. Ann Wright and Renée Fenby (London and New York, 2002), and Jean Omasombo Tshonda, 'Lumumba, drame sans fin et deuil inachevé de la colonisation' *Cahiers d'études africaines*, XLIV/ 173/174, *Réparations, restitutions, réconciliations: Entre Afriques, Europe et Amériques* (2004), pp. 221–61.
36. His 'colonial' name at birth was 'Joseph-Désiré Mobutu', which once in power he changed to 'Mobutu Sese Seko Kuku Ngbendu Wa Za Banga'. According to Pamphile Mabiala Mantuba-Ngoma, the name means 'frightening sand/earth, ripe fruit, very hot pepper, fire on the other side of the river': [he] presents himself as a complex personality, enigmatically sand and earth at the same time, fearless, hot like green pepper and fire that burns at the other side of the river'. See Pamphile Mabiala Mantuba-Ngoma, 'Anthroponymie et histoire du Congo des origins à nos jours', in Pamphile Mabiala Mantuba-Ngoma, ed., *La Nouvelle Histoire du Congo : mélanges eurafricains offerts à Frans Bontinck*, C.I.C.I.M (Paris, 2004), p. 162.
37. Kinshasa was originally a part of the city, situated to the north of the original site of Port Stanley.
38. See Bogumil Jewsiewicki, 'Kinshasa: (auto)representation d'une société "moderne"', p. 256.
39. The date of birth is not clearly established, a biographical note given by Benoît Verhaegen says that he was born at Jadotville on 27 November 1939. See Benoît Verhaegen, *Rebellions au Congo*, vol. II (1969). In an interview, Laurent-Désiré Kabila himself claimed his date of birth was 27 November 1941. See Erik Kennes and Munkana N'Ge, *Essai Biographique sur Laurent Désiré Kabila. Cahiers africains,* 57–58–59 (2003), p. 13. Official Congolese sources use the 1941 date.
40. Guevara said of Kabila that he had the necessary qualities to be a great leader 'but not enough of them', quoted by Kennes and N'Ge, *Essai biographique* p. 336.
41. See Francis Kpatindé, 'Jeune Afrique L'Intelligent', 23–29 January 2001, www.jeuneafrique.com.
42. For a summary of circumstances, see Emmanuel M. A. Nashi, *Pourquoi ont-ils tué Laurent-Désiré Kabila?* (Paris, 2007). On p. 184 he quotes a passage from a speech by Kabila from 18 February 2001: 'What really irks these powers is our decision to rely on our own power and to refuse the order of those who still consider themselves our masters. Our diamonds, our gold, copper, cobalt belongs to us. We need to make use of them. We need to sell our riches ourselves, whereas before it was others who sold them and contributed nothing to the welfare of our people [. . .] This does not mean that

we do not want any help. But we do not want to be beggars forever because we have to wait for help and lose our independence.' (My translation.)

43 Kennes and N'Ge, *Essai biographique*, p. 331 (my translation).

44 Nashi, *Pourqoi ont-ils tué Laurent-Désiré Kabila?*, p. 181 (my translation).

45 His open coffin was carried through the streets of Kinshasa, with a white cloth covering the part of his face destroyed by the bullet wound. See Tim Butcher, 'War allies attend Kabila funeral', www.telegraph.co.uk, 24 January 2001.

46 I was not able to locate the original plans and drawings for the mausoleum. According to a colleague of Christophe Meko's at the Académie des Beaux-Arts at Kinshasa, several artists were involved.

47 For the history of the palace design by Marcel Lambrichs, which was only started in 1956, see Johan Lagae, 'Palais de la Nation, Kinshasa: architect Marcel Lambrichs', online at A+ BELGISCH TIJDSCHRIFT VOOR ARCHITECTUUR (2007), p. 106.

48 It is 65 metres high (213 feet) and weighs four tons. See excerpts from the official document published by the Fondation Mzee KDL and quoted by Laetitia Mbuyi, in 'Congo-Kinshasa : Revoici Mzee Laurent-*Désiré* Kabila sur toutes les levrès, http://fr.allafrica.com, 18 January 2010. I have no proof for my hunch that this was indeed made in North Korea other than the strong stylistic similarity between the monumental statues of Kim Il Sung and that of Kabila's, and the remark made by my guides in Pyongyang there the Mansudae Art Studios were always busy making such large-scale bronze for Africa and Latin America. In the absence of similar foundries in the Congo, it is likely that Kabila's statue was made in North Korea. Such public art is one of the few exports of that sanctions-ridden country.

49 See Laetitia Mbuyi, 'Congo-Kinshasa'.

50 These fists have some similarity with the forearms of Saddam Hussein's Victory Arch in Baghdad, for which he had his very own forearms cast, brandishing two crossing swords above a multi-lane highway. See Samir al-Khalil, *The Monument: Art, Vulgarity and Responsibility in Iraq* (London, 1991).

51 This had been removed when I visited the mausoleum, which was undergoing further maintenance. I do not know whether this flame, which recalls the torch on the national flag under Mobutu, will be replaced or not.

52 This star had been removed temporarily for restoration while I was in Kinshasa.

53 Kennes and N'Ge, *Essai biographique*, p. 336 (my translation).

54 Richard Dowden, 'Obituary: Dr Hastings Banda', www.independent.co.uk, 27 November 1997.

55 See www2timesdispatch.com, 6 June 2009, accessed 28 May 2013.

56 'Mausoleum for founding President Banda', www.sadocc.at, 16 May 2006.

57 Aubrey Sumbuleta, 'New tomb for Malawi's Banda', http://news.bbc.co.uk, 13 May 2005.

58 Geoffrey York, 'Nostalgia washes away sins of Malawi dictator', www2timesdispatch.com, 6 June 2009, accessed 28 May 2013.

59 For the timetable of the event, see 'Birth of a Nation: The Republic of South Sudan', http://www.gurtong.net, 15 December 2011. See also the official South Sudan website for details of events on 16 July 2011, www.goss.org, accessed 15 December 2011.

60 See 'Son of John Garang mourns and helps prepare grave in Juba', http://sudanwatch.blogspot.com, accessed 28 May 2013.

61 See John Littell, 'Infisal! Infisal! Infisal', *London Review of Books*, XXXIII/13 (June 2011), pp. 9–14. See www.lrb.co.uk, accessed 29 August 2011.

62 For classic ethnographic accounts, see E. E. Evans-Pritchard, *The Nuer* (London, 1940); Godfrey R. Lienhardt, *Divinity and Experience: The Religion of the Dinka* (Oxford, 1961), and more recently, Sharon Hutchinson, *Nuer Dilemmas: Coping with Money, War, and the State* (Berkeley, Los Angeles, London, 1996).

63 The Sudanese Defence Force (SDF) located in Torit, in the south, had been ordered to relocate to the north. It triggered the mutiny that resulted in most of the northern members of the SDF being killed. See Peter Lam Both, *South Sudan: Forgotten Tragedy* (Calgary, Alberta, 2003), p. 34.

64 For accounts of Garang's life, see the article Abdelaziz Barrouhi, 'John Garang, le dernier

guérillo', *Jeune Afrique*, www.jeuneafrique.com, 6 August 2003, and the obituary by Nicolas Michel, 'John Garang', *Jeune Afrique*, www.jeuneafrique.com, 17 January 2005. See also Zygmunt L. Ostrowski, *Le Soudan à l'aube de la paix: le combat de John Garang* (Paris, 2005).

65 Muammar Gaddafi likewise was hostile to Nimeiri and supplied arms and offered military training facilities to the SPLA.

66 For an autobiographical account of such 'lost boys', see Emmanuel Jal, *War Child: A Boy Soldier's Story* (London, 2010). For Jal's encounter with Garang, see pp. 152–5 of the work.

67 See John Young, 'Sudan: Liberation Movements, Regional Armies, Ethnic Militias and Peace', *Review of African Political Economy*, xxx/97, *The Horn of Conflict* (September 2003), pp. 542–4.

68 Ibid., p. 539.

69 Al-Bashir had after all invited Osama bin Laden and provided operational support for al-Qaeda in the 1990s.

70 The position had been created as part of the power sharing agreement.

71 For a South Sudanese article summarizing some of the conspiracy theories concerning this accident, see 'Who killed Garang: the conspiracy theories', http://bloggingjuba.blogspot.co.uk, accessed 28 May 2013.

72 For the account of his funeral, based on that of Garang's son, Chol Garang, see 'Son of John Garang mourns and helps', http://sudanwatch.blogspot.com.

Chronological List of Tombs and Mausolea

Lenin's mausoleum on Red Square in Moscow (built 1924–30)
Sun Yat-sen's mausoleum on Purple Mountain in Nanjing (built 1926–29)
Mussolini's crypt in the cemetery of Predappio (built 1928–30)
Anıtkabir: the Memorial Tomb of Mustafa Kemal Atatürk in Ankara (built 1941–53)
Mazar-i-Quaid-e-Azam, 'The Mausoleum of the Great Leader' Mohammed Ali Jinnah in Karachi (built 1960–71)
Mausoleum of Ho Chi Minh in Hanoi (built 1971–75)
Astana Giribangun, Suharto's mausoleum near Karangpandan, Java (built 1970–76)
Chiang Kai-shek's temporary mausoleum at Chihu, Taiwan (built 1975)
Mao Zedong Memorial Hall (*Mao Zhuxi Jinian Tang*) on Tiananmen Square, Beijing (1976–77)
Mausoleum of Ayatollah Ruhollah Musawi Khomeini in Tehran (under construction since 1989)
Mausoleum of Shaheed President Ziaur Rahman in Dhaka (1991)
Dr Kwame Nkrumah Memorial Park, Accra (1992)
Mausoleum of *M'zee* Laurent-Desiré Kabila in Kinshasa (2001–02)
Mausoleum of Dr John Garang de Mabior, Juba, South Sudan (2005)
Mausoleum of Yasser Arafat at the PLO *Muqata*, Ramallah, West Bank (2004–07)

Bibliographies

1 Enduring Signification: Mounds, Monuments and Mausolea

Boullée, Étienne-Louis, 'Architecture, Essay of Art', in *Boullée and Visionary Architecture*, ed. Helen Rosenau (London and New York, 1976), pp. 117–44

Colvin, Howard, *Architecture and the After-Life* (New Haven and London 1991)

Curl, James Stevens, *Death and Architecture: An Introduction to Funerary and Commemorative Buildings in the Western Tradition, with Some Considerations of their Settings* (Stroud, 1980) (revd edn 2002))

Davies, Penelope J. E., *Death and the Emperor: Roman Imperial Funerary Monuments from Augustus to Marcus Aurelius* (Cambridge, 2000)

Driskel, Michael Paul, *As Befits a Legend: Building a Tomb for Napoleon 1840–1861* (Kent, OH, and London, 1993)

Etlin, Richard A., *Symbolic Space: French Enlightenment Architecture and its Legacy* (Chicago and London 1994)

Fedak, Janos, 'Tombs and Commemorative Monuments', in Frederick E. Winter, *Studies in Hellenistic Architecture* (Toronto, Buffalo, London, 2006), pp. 71–95

Hodder, Ian, 'Spatiality and Meaning: The Example of Neolithic Houses and Tombs', in *Architecture and Order: Approaches to Social Space*, ed. Michael Parker Pearson and Colin Richards (London, 1994), pp. 84–101

Johnson, Mark J., *The Roman Imperial Mausoleum in Late Antiquity* (Cambridge, 2009)

Pettitt, Paul, *The Palaeolithic Origins of Human Burial* (London and New York, 2010)

Russell, Miles, *Monuments of the British Neolithic: The Roots of Architecture* (Stroud, 2002)

2 Safeguarding the Immortality of Revolutionary Leaders: Mausolea in Communist Countries

Barmé, Geremie R., *Shades of Mao: The Posthumous Cult of the Great Leader* (Armonk, New York, London, 1996)

Binns, Christopher, A. P., 'The Changing Face of Power: Revolution and Accommodation in the Development of the Soviet Ceremonial System: Part I', *Man*, NS, XIV/4 (1979), pp. 585–606

——, 'The Changing Face of Power: Revolution and Accommodation in the Development of the Soviet Ceremonial System': Part II', *Man*, NS, XV/1 (1980), pp.170–87

Becker, Jasper, *Rogue Regime: Kim Jong Il and the Looming Threat of North Korea* (Oxford and New York, 2005)

Boudarel, George and Nguyen Van Ky, *Hanoi: City of the Rising Dragon* (Lanham, 2002)

Bradley Martin K., *Under the Loving Care of the Fatherly Leader: North Korea and the Kim Dynasty* (New York, 2004)

Brandt, V. S. R, 'North Korea: Anthropological Speculation', *Korea and World Affairs*, VII/4 (1983), pp. 617–28

Brocheux, Pierre, *Ho Chi Minh: A Biography* (Cambridge, 2011)

Buzo, Adrian, *The Guerilla Dynasty: Politics and Leadership in North Korea* (London and New York, 1999)

——, *The Making of Modern Korea* (London and New York, 2002)

Cheater, A. P., 'Death Ritual as Political Trickster in the People's Republic of China', *The Australian Journal of Chinese Affairs*, XXVI (July 1991), pp. 77–97

Cohen, Stephen, 'Boshevism and Stalinism', in *Stalinism: Essays in Historical Interpretation*, ed. Robert C. Tucker (New York and London 1977), pp. 3–29

Cong, Dachang, *When Heroes Pass Away: The Invention of a Chinese Communist Pantheon* (Lanham, New York, Oxford, 1997)

Conquest, Robert, *Stalin: Breaker of Nations* (London, 1991)

Duiker, William, *Ho Chi Minh: A Life* (London, 2000)

French, Paul, *North Korea, the Paranoid Peninsula: A Modern History* (London and New York, 2005)

Hémery, Daniel, *Ho Chi Minh. De l'indochine au Vietnam* (Paris, 1990)

Hingley, Ronald, *Russia: A Concise History* (London, 2003)

Ho Tai, Hue-Tam, 'Monuments of Ambiguity: The State Commemoration of Ho Chi Minh', in *Essays into Vietnamese Pasts*, ed. K. W. Taylor and John K. Whitmore (Ithaca, NY, 1995)

Hoare, J. E., and Susan Pares, *North Korea in the 21st Century: An Interpretative Guide* (Folkstone, 2005)

Hunt, David, *Vietnam's Southern Revolution: From Peasant Insurrection to Total War* (Amhurst, 2008)

Jack, Andrew, *Inside Putin's Russia* (London, 2004)

Jamieson, Neil J., *Understanding Vietnam* (Berkeley and London, 1993)

Jeon, Jei Guk, 'The Politics of Mourning Ritual in North Korea (1994–97)', *World Affairs*, CLXII/3 (Winter 2000), pp. 126–36

Karl, Rebecca E., *Mao Zedong and China in the Twentieth-Century World* (Durham, NC, 2010)

Laing, Ellen, *The Winking Owl* (Berkeley, Los Angeles and London, 1988)

Ledderose, Lothar, 'Die Gedenkhalle für Mao Zedong', in *Kultur und Gedächtnis*, ed. Jan Assmann and Tonio Hölscher (Frankfurt, 1988), pp. 311–39

Li, Zhisui, *The Private Life of Chairman Mao: The Inside Story of the Man Who Made Modern China* (London, 1994)

Lintner, Bertil, *Great Leader, Dear Leader: Demystifying North Korea Under the Kim Clan* (Chiang Mai, 2005)

Logan, William S., *Hanoi: Biography of a City* (Sydney, 2000)

Malarney, Shaun, Kingsley, *Culture, Ritual and Revolution in Vietnam* (London and New York, 2002)

Merridale, Catherine, *Night of Stone: Death and Memory in Twentieth-Century Russia* (London and New York, 2000)

Meuser, Philipp, ed., *Architekturführer Pjöngjang*, 2 vols (Berlin, 2011)

Ngoc, Ba, *Memorial Site of Ho Chi Minh in Ha Noi* (Hanoi, 2006)

Portal, Jane, *Art Under Control in North Korea* (London, 2005)

Post, Ken, *Revolution, Socialism and Nationalism in Vietnam*, vol. I: *An Interrupted Revolution* (The Hague, 1999)

Ryang, Sonia, 'Biopolitics or the Logic of Sovereign Love – Love's Whereabouts in North Korea', in *North Korea: Toward a Better Understanding*, ed. Sonia Ryang (Boulder, CO, New York, Toronto, Plymouth, 2009), pp. 57–83

Sawka, Richard, ed. *Power and Politics in Putin's Russia* (London and New York, 2009)

Seiler, Sydney A., *Kim Il-song 1941–1948: the Creation of a Legend, the Building of a Regime*, (Lanham, MD, 1994)

Service, Robert, *Lenin: A Political Life*, vol. 1 (London, 1985)

Short, Philip, *Mao: A Life* (London, 1999)

Terrill, Ross, *Mao: A Biography* (Stanford, 1999)

Thomas, Mandy, 'Spatiality and Political Change in Urban Vietnam', in *Consuming Urban Culture in Contemporary Vietnam*, ed., Lisa B. W. Drummond and Mandy Thomas (London and New York, 2003), pp. 170–188

Tumarkin, Nina, *Lenin Lives! The Lenin Cult in the Soviet Union* (Cambridge, MA, 1983)

Vladimirov, Katya 'Dead Men Walking: Soviet Elite Cemeteries and Social Control', Department of History and Philosophy, Kennesaw State University, *The Forum on Public Policy* (2008); www.forumonpublicpolicy.com

Wagner, Rudolf G., 'Reading the Chairman Mao Memorial Hall in Peking: The Tribulations of the

Implied Pilgrim', in *Pilgrims and Sacred Sites in China*, ed. Susan Naquin and Chüng-fang Yü (Berkeley, CA, 1992), pp. 378–423
White, Stephen, ed., *Media, Culture and Society in Putin's Russia* (Basingstoke, 2008)
Wu, Hung, 'Tiananmen Square: A Political History of Monuments'*Representation*, xxv, Special Issue: 'Monumental Histories' (Summer 1991), pp. 84–88
——, *Remaking Beijing: Tiananmen Square and the Creation of a Political Space* (London, 2005)
Zbarsky, Ilya, *Lenin's Embalmers* trans. Samuel Hutchinson (London, 1998)

3 Fantasy and Reality: The Burial Places of Fascist Leaders

Blinkhorn, Martin, *Mussolini and Fascist Italy* (London and New York, 1984)
Brooker, Paul, 'The Fascist Examples', in *Twentieth-Century Dictatorships: The Ideological One-Party States* (New York, 1995), pp. 23–50
Olmeda, Fernando, *El Valle de Los Caídos. Una memoria de España* (Barcelona, 2009)
Preston, Paul, *Franco* (London, 1993)
Sancho, José Luis, *Guide Santa Cruz del valle de los Caídos* (Madrid, 2008)
Smith, Dennis Mack, *Mussolini* (London, 1981)
Sueiro, Daniel, *El Valle de los Caídos. Idea, Proyecto y construccíon* (Madrid, 1982)
——, *El Valle de los Caídos: los secretos de la cripta fraquista* (Barcelona, 1983)
Waite, R.G.L., 'Adolf Hitler's Guilt Feelings: A Problem in History and Psychology', *The Journal of Interdisciplinary History*, 1/2 (Winter 1971), pp. 229–49

4 New Nations, New Monuments: Mausolea for Fathers of the Nation

Ali, S. Mahmud, *Understanding Bangladesh* (London, 2009)
Arda, Orhan, Emin Onat, 'Mausoleum to Atatürk', *Mimarlik*, v/3 (1944)
——, 'Mausoleum of Kemal Atatürk, Ankara', *Arkitekt*, 280 (1955), pp. 51–61
Bandyopadhyay, P. K., *The Bangladesh Dichotomy and Politicisation of Culture* (New Delhi, 2004)
Baxter, Craig, *Historical Dictionary of Bangladesh*, 2nd edn (Lanham, MD, 2003)
——, *Bangladesh: From a Nation to a State* (Boulder, CO, 1997)
Burki, Shahid Javed, *Historical Dictionary of Pakistan*, 3rd edn (Lanham, MD, 2006)
Cohen, Stephen Philip, *The Idea of Pakistan* (Washington DC, 2004)
Dani, Ahmad Hasan, Husain Afsar Akhtar, *The Quaid-i-Azam Mausoleum in Pictures* (Islamabad, 1976)
Hakim, S. Abdul, *Begum Khaleda Zia of Bangladesh: A Political Biography* (New Delhi, 1992)
Khan, Shamsul I., *Political Culture, Political Parties and the Democratic Transition in Bangladesh* (Dhaka, 1996)
Kerslake, Celia, Kerem Öktem, Philip Robins, eds, *Turkey's Engagement with Modernity: Conflict and Change in the Twentieth Century* (Basingstoke, 2010)
Kinross, John P., *Atatürk: The Rebirth of a Nation,* (London, 1998)
Lai, Delin, 'Searching for a Modern Chinese Monument: The Design of the Sun Yat-sen Mausoleum in Nanjing', *Journal of the Society of Architectural Historians*, LXIV/1 (March 2005), pp. 22–55
Loschak, David, *Pakistan in Crisis* (London, 1971)
Mango, Andrew, *Atatürk* (London, 1999)
Martin, Bernard, *Strange Vigour: A Biography of Sun Yat-sen* (London, 1968)
Metz, William S., *The Political Career of Mohammad Ali Jinnah* (Karachi, 2010)
Özyürek, Esra, *Nostalgia for the Modernist State: Secularism of Everyday Politics in Turkey* (Durham, NC, 2006)
Riaz, Ali and Christine Fair, eds, *Political Islam and Governance in Bangladesh* (New York, 2010)
Schendel, Willem van, *A History of Bangladesh* (Cambridge, 2009)
Schiffren, Harold Z., *Sun Yat-sen and the Origins of the Chinese Revolution* (Berkeley, Los Angeles and London, 1970)
Seabrook, Jeremy, *Freedom Unfinished: Fundamentalism and Popular Resistance in Bangladesh Today* (London, 2001)
Shaikh, Farzana, *Making Sense of Pakistan* (London, 2009)
Wagner, Rudolf G., 'Ritual, Architecture, Politics and Publicity during the Republic: Enshrining Sun Yat-sen', a paper presented to the conference 'The Beaux-Arts, Paul Philippe Cret, and 20th

Century Architecture in China' (3–5 October 2003), University of Pennsylvania, Philadelphia, afterwards published in *Chinese Architecture and the Beaux-Arts*, ed. Jeffrey Cody, Nancy S. Steinhardt and Tony Atkin (Honolulu, Hawaii, 2011)

Wang, Liping, 'Creating a National Symbol: The Sun Yatsen Memorial in Nanjing', *Republican China*, XXI/2 (April 1996), pp. 23–63

Wells, Audrey, *The Political Thought of Sun Yat Sen* (Basingstoke, 2001)

Wilbur, C. Martin, *Sun Yat-sen, Frustrated Patriot* (New York, 1976)

Wilson, Christopher, 'The Persistence of the Turkish Nation in the Mausoleum of Mustafa Kemal Atatürk', in *Nationalism in a Global Era*, ed. Mitchell Young, Eric Zuelow and Andreas Storm (London, 2007), pp. 93–114

——, 'Representing National Identity and Memory in the Mausoleum of Mustafa Kemal Atatürk', *Society of Architectural Historians Journal*, LXVIII/2 (June 2009), pp. 224–253

Wolpert, Stanley, *Jinnah of Pakistan* (Delhi, 2005)

Upreti, Sonia, *Nationalism in Bangladesh: Genesis and Evolution* (New Delhi, 2004)

Vale, Lawrence J., *Architecture, Power and National Identity* (New Haven, 1992)

Yao, Qian Zhong shan ling, *Sun Yat-sen Mausoleum Beijing*, 1981)

Zarrow, Peter, *China in War and Revolution, 1895–1949* (London and New York, 2005)

Zürcher, Erik J., *Turkey: A Modern History* (London and New York, 1993)

5 Not the Final Resting Place: Temporary Mausolea

Copper, John F., *Taiwan: Nation-State or Province?* (2nd edn, Boulder, CO, 1996)

Eastman, Lloyd E., 'Nationalist China during the Nanking Decade, 1927–1937', in *The Nationalist Era in China 1929–1949*, ed. Lloyd, E. Eastman, Jerome Ch'en, Suzanne Pepper et al. (Cambridge, 1986), pp. 1–53

Fenby, Jonathan, *Generalissimo: Chiang Kai-shek and the China He Lost* (New York, 2005)

——, *The Penguin History of Modern China: The Fall and Rise of a Great Power, 1850—2008* (London, 2008)

Ghanem, As'ad, *Palestinian Politics After Arafat: A Failed National Movement* (Bloomington, 2010)

Grinberg, Lev Luis, *Politics and Violence in Israel/Palestine: Democracy Versus Military Rule* (London and New York, 2010)

Hulme, David, *Identity, Ideology and the Future of Jerusalem* (London, 2006)

Khalidi, Rashid, *Palestinian Identity: The Construction of Modern National Consciousness* (New York, 1997; repr 2010)

Khalili, Laleh, *Heroes and Martyrs of Palestine: The Poetics of National Commemoration*, (Cambridge, 2007)

Kiernan, Thomas, *Yasir Arafat: The Man and the Myth* (London, 1976)

Manthorpe, Jonathan, *Forbidden Nation: A History of Taiwan* (New York, 2000)

Rubin, Barry and Judith Colp Rubin, *Yasir Arafat: A Political Biography* (London, 2003)

Rubinstein, Murray A., ed, *Taiwan: A New History* (Arming, NY, 1999)

Tukan, Jafar, 'Beacon of Hope; Architects: Consolidated Consultants – Principal Architect: Jafar Tukan', *Architecture Plus*, 14 (2006), pp. 22–5

Walker, Tony and Andrew Gowers, *Arafat: The Biography* (London, 2003)

Wakeman, Frederic, 'Revolutionary Rites: The Remains of Chiang Kai-shek and Mao Tse Tung', *Representations*, 10 (Spring 1985), pp. 146–93

Zarrow, Peter, *China in War and Revolution, 1895–1949* (London and New York, 2005)

6 Appropriated Traditions

Abrahamian, Ervand I., *Khomeinism: Essays on the Islamic Republic* (London and New York, 1993)

Anderson, Benedict, *Language and Power: Exploring Political Cultures in Indonesia* (Ithaca, NY, 1990)

——, 'Exit Suharto. Obituary for a mediocre tyrant', *New Left Review*, 50, (March-April 2008), pp. 27–59

Brandenburg, Dietrich, *Die Seldschuken: Baukunst des Islam in Persien und Turkmenistan* (Graz, 2005)

Canby, Sheila R., ed, *Safavid Art and Architecture* (London, 2002)

Coughlin, Con, *Khomeini's Ghost* (Basingstoke and Oxford, 2009)

Elson, R. E., *Suharto: A Political Biography* (Cambridge 2001; paperback 2008)

Golombek, Lisa and Donald N. Wilber, *The Timurid Architecture of Iran and Turan* (New Jersey, 1988)

Hillenbrand, Robert, *Islamic Architecture: Form, Function and Meaning* (New York, 1994)

Hoffman, Brigitte, 'Das Mausoleum Khomeinis in Teheran. Überlegungen zu persisch-islamischen Gedächtnisarchitektur', *Die Welt des Islams*, XXXIX/1 (March 1999), pp.1–30

Khosronejad, Pedram, *The Art and Material Culture of Iranian Shi'ism: Iconography and Religious Devotion in Shi'i Islam* (London, 2010)

Kusno, Abidin, *Architecture, Urban Space and Political Cultures in Indonesia* (London and New York, 2000)

Legge, J. D., *Sukarno: A Political Biography* (3rd edn, Singapore, 2003)

McIntyre, Angus, *The Indonesian Presidency: The Shift from Personal Toward Constitutional Rule* (Lanham, MD, 2005)

Martin, Vanessa, *Creating an Islamic State: Khomeini and the Making of a New Iran* (London and New York, 2000)

Momen, Moojan, *An Introduction to Shi'i Islam* (New Haven and London, 1985)

Priyambudi, Sulistiyanto, *Reconciliation in Post-Suharto Indonesia* (London, 2009)

Rizvi, Kishwar, *The Safavid Dynastic Shrine: Architecture, Religion and Power in Early Modern Iran* (London, 2011)

——, 'Religious Icon and National Symbol: The Tomb of Ayatollah Khomeini in Iran', *Muqarnas*, XX (2003), pp. 209–24

Tjahjono, Gunawan, ed, *Indonesian Heritage: Architecture* (Singapore, 1998)

Tonna, Jo, 'The Poetics of Arab-Islamic Architecture', *Muqarnas*, VII (1990), pp. 182–97

Wright, Robin, *The Last Great Revolution: Turmoil and Transformation in Iran* (New York, 2000)

7 Political Mausolea in Africa

Babatope, Ebenezer, *The Ghana Revolution: From Nkrumah to Jerry Rawlings* (Enugu, Nigeria, 1982; 2002)

Bobb, F. Scott, *Historical Dictionary of the Democratic Republic of the Congo (Zaire)* (Lanham, MD, 1999)

Braeckman, Colette, *Les nouveaux prédateurs. Politique des puissances en afrique centrale* (Paris, 2003)

Bwatshia, Kambayi, *L'illusion tragique du pouvoir au Congo-Zaïre* (Paris, 2007)

Davidson, Basil, *Black Star: A View of the Life and Times of Kwame Nkrumah* (Plymouth, 1973)

De Boeck, Filip and Marie Françoise Plissart, *Kinshasa: Tales of the Invisible City* (Tervuren, 2004)

De Witte, Ludo, *The Assassination of Lumumba*, trans. Ann Wright and Renée Fenby (London and New York, 2002)

Fabian, Johannes, *Moments of Freedom: Anthropology and Popular Culture* (Charlottesville and London, 1998)

Gocking, Roger S., *The History of Ghana* (Westport, CT, 2005)

Hadjor, Kofu Buenor, *Nkrumah and Ghana: The Dilemma of Post-Colonial Power* (London and New York, 1988)

Hansen, Emmanuel, *Ghana Under Rawlings* (Oxford, 1991)

Hess, Janet Berry, 'Imagining Architecture: The Structure of Nationalism in Ghana', *Africa Today*, XLVII/2 (Spring 2000)

——, *Art and Architecture in Postcolonial Africa* (Jefferson, NC, 2006)

James, Cyril Lionel Robert, *Nkrumah and the Ghana Revolution* (London, 1977)

Jewsiewicki, Bogumil, 'Kinshasa: (auto)representation d'une société 'moderne' en (dé)construction, in *La Nouvelle Histoire du Congo: mélanges eurafricains offerts à Fran Bontinck*, C.I.C.I.M, ed. Pamphile Mabiala Mantuba-Ngoma (Tervuren and Paris, 2004), p. 252–65

Johnson, Douglas H., *The Root Causes of Sudan's Civil Wars* (Bloomington, IN, 2003)

Kabuya-Lumuna Sando, 'Laurent Désiré Kabila', *Review of African Political Economy*, XXIX, 93/94, State Failure in the Congo: Perceptions & Realities (Le Congo entre Crise et Régénération) (September-December 2002), pp. 616–19

Kasongo-Numbi Kashemukunda, L'Afrique se recolonise: une relecture du demi-siècle de l'indépendance du Congo-Kinshasa (Paris, 2008)

Khazanov, Anatoly Mikhailovich, *Agostinho Neto* (Moscow, 1986)

Kennes, Erik and Munkana N'Ge, *Essai Biographique sur Laurent Désiré Kabila. Cahiers africains,* 57-58-59 (2003)

Lam Booth, Peter, *South Sudan: Forgotten Tragedy* (Calgary, Alberta 2002)

Lwanda, John Lloyd, *Kamuzu Banda of Malawi: A Study*

in *Promise, Power and Paralysis: (Malawi Under Dr Banda) (1961 to 1993)* (Glasgow, 1993)

Malok, E., *The Southern Sudan: Struggle for Liberty* (Nairobi, 2009)

Malu-Malu, Jean Jacques, *Le Congo Kinshasa* (Paris, 2002)

Mantuba-Ngoma, Pamphile Mabiala, ed., *La nouvelle histoire du Congo: mélanges eurafricains offerts à Frans Bontinck* (Paris, 2004)

Martens, Ludo, *Kabila et la revolution congolaise: Panafricanisme ou néocolonialisme?* (Brussels, 2002)

Milne, June, *Kwame Nkrumah: A Biography* (London, 2000)

Mukendi, Germain, Bruno Kasonga, *Kabila, le retour du Congo* (Ottignies, 1999)

Nashi, Emmanuel M. A. *Pourqoui ont-ils tué Laurent-Désiré Kabila?* (Paris, 2007)

Ngolet, François, *Crisis in the Congo: The Rise and Fall of Laurent Kabila* (New York, 2010)

Nugent, Paul, *Big Men, Small Boys, and Politics in Ghana: Power, Ideology, and the Burden of History, 1982–1994* (London, 1995)

Nzongola-Ntalaja, Georges, *The Congo from Leopold to Kabila* (London and New York, 2002)

Osei, Akwasi P., *Ghana: Recurrence and Change in a Post-Independence African State*, Society and Politics in Africa, vol IV: *Society and Politics in Africa* (New York, 1999)

Power, Joey, *Political Culture and Nationalism in Malawi: Building Kwacha* (Rochester, NY, 2010)

Quist, Isaac M., *Kwame Nkrumah: An Undying Flame. Tour Guide to Kwame Nkrumah Memorial Park, Accra, Ghana* (Tema, Ghana, 2002)

Ramazani, Yvon, Omer Nsongo and Henri Mova Sakanyi, *De L-.D. Kabila à J. Kabila, la vérité des faits* (Paris, 2008)

Rooney, David, *Kwame Nkrumah: The Political Kingdom in the Third World* (London, 1988)

——, *Kwame Nkrumah: Vision and Tragedy* (Accra, 2007)

Shillington, Kevin, *Ghana and the Rawlings Factor* (London, 1992)

——, 'Kwame Nkrumah Memorial Park', *Ghana Review* (1995), pp. 135–8

Tshonda, Jean Omasombo, 'Lumumba, drame sans fin et deuil inachevé de la colonisation' *Cahiers d'études africaines*, XLIV/ 173–174, *Réparations, restitutions, réconciliations: Entre Afriques, Europe et Amériques* (2004), pp. 221–61

Willame, Jean-Claude, *L'odyssée Kabila. Trajectoire pour un Congo nouveau?* (Paris, 1999)

——, *Les 'faiseurs de paix' au Congo* (Brussels, 2007)

Young, John, Sudan: Liberation Movements, Regional Armies, Ethnic Militias & Peace', *Review of African Political Economy*, XXX/97, *The Horn of Conflict* (September 2003), pp. 542–4

——, 'John Garang's Legacy to the Peace Process, the SPLM/A and the South', *Review of African Political Economy*, XXIII/106, *Africa from SAP to PRSP: Plus ça change plus c'est la même chose* (December 2005), pp. 535–48

Acknowledgements

The original idea for this book came after an invitation by convenors Felicia Hughes-Freeland and Penelope Dransart to contribute to the panel 'Monumentalising the past, archaeologies of the future' for the 2009 Association of Social Anthropologists Conference in Bristol, where I spoke about Atatürk's tomb in Ankara. It was during discussions with colleagues after giving my paper that I began to think of preparing a more comprehensive account of such buildings and their context.

   I owe many thanks for practical assistance, local information, advice and hospitality to many people, notably Canan Barım Alioglu in Turkey, Francis Kirk in Spain, Susan Brewer in Italy, Ashkan Sadeghi in Iran, Maen Tafish in the West Bank, Henri Kalama Akulez in the Congo, Jok Thon in South Sudan, Joseph Kwabena in Ghana, Imadul Ikbal in Bangladesh, Xia Chan in China, Jang and Han in North Korea, Ying-Wen Chang, Chin-Chin Yu, Ching-Chiang Chang and Peter Ching in Taiwan and Nguyen Huy Duc in Vietnam.

   I am also grateful to Bruce Wannell, Petra Laidlaw, Felicia Hughes-Freeland and Alexander Kessler for their comments on draft chapters and to Sarah Bolton and Cyril Shing for their line drawings.

Illustration Acknowledgements

By kind permission of Masud Bashat: p. 180. Drawn by Sarah Bolton: pp. 14 (after image by Wessex Archaeology Ltd); 16 (after image by the University of Pennsylvania); 17, 19 and 21 (after Mark J. Johnson, *The Roman Imperial Mausoleum in Late Antiquity*, Cambridge University Press: Cambridge, 2009, figs. 7 and 8); 40 centre and bottom and 41 (after original photographs); 71, 72 (based on *China Pictorial*, issue 9, 1977); 99; 100 (after Hermann Giesler); 111 (after José Luis Sancho, Santa Cruz del Valle de los Caídos); 129; 133 (from photograph at Sun Yat-sen's mausoleum); 217. Photo and © Joan Gaffiney: p. 242. Photo Walter Karlik: p. 22. Photos Petra Laidlaw: pp. 102, 103. Photos Gwendolyn Leick: pp. 44, 45, 55, 59, 67, 82, 84, 85, 101, 109, 115, 116, 130, 132, 135, 136, 137, 144, 146, 147, 148, 149, 150, 153, 161, 162, 164, 165, 166, 167, 169, 178, 182, 183, 186, 192, 194, 196, 197, 198, 206, 207, 208, 209, 210, 211, 212, 219, 220, 221, 222, 233, 234, 235, 244, 245, 247 bottom, 252, 254, 255, 256, 257, 258, 259, 266, 267, 268, 269, 270, 274, 275, 276, 277. Photo Panoramio / Frederico Santa Martha: p. 247 top. Photo RIA Novosti, Moscow: p. 46. Photos Ashkan Sadeghi: pp. 236, 237. Drawn by Cyril Shing: pp. 26, 29, 95.

Colour section: Photo and © Richard Pare (Lenin's Tomb Chamber); Photo and © Boris Kester (Hastings Banda Mausoleum); other photos by Gwendolyn Leick.

Index

Aachen (Aix la Chapelle) 23
Abbas, Mahmoud 203, 205, 211, 212
Acheampong, Ignatious Kutu 251
Accra 248, 249, 251–3
Aeneas 19, 119, 120
African Union 273
Ahmadinejad, Mahmoud 237
Ahmed, Masud 172
Albania 97
Al-Bashir, Omar 279, 280
Alexander the Great 17, 20
Alfonso VIII 23
Alfonso XIII 105
Algeria 243
Algiers 243, 245
Ali Khan, Nawabzada Liaqat 158, 159, 168
Altar of Peace (*ara pacis*) 19
Amin, Idi 10
Amorites 15
Anatolia 140, 143, 148
Andrade, Ramon 112
Andropov, Yuri 46
Angola 246, 261, 263
Anıtkabir 138–55, 144, 145, 242
Ankara 8, 138–40, 143, 144, 146, 148, 151, 171, 185
Annam 51, 52
Arafat, Yasser 9, 88, 199–212, 272
architects 8, 25, 56, 58, 109, 110, 112, 143, 144, 146, 149, 159, 160, 179, 185, 187, 205

architecture parlante 8
Arda, Orhan 144
Arthur, Don 254, 255
Ashgabat 238
Astana Giribangun 217, 219, 222, 223
Atatürk, Mustafa Kemal 8, 138–55, 163, 171, 185, 187, 227, 242
Augustus 19–20, 21, 100, 119, 120, 121
Austria 7, 98, 99, 143
Awami League 171, 173, 175, 176, 177, 178, 180, 187
Awami Party 177
Ayub Khan, Muhammed 159, 160, 178

Ba Dinh Square, Hanoi 51, 56, 57, 58, 60
Babaoshan 65, 66
Bachelard, Gaston 7
Bangabandhu 171, 175, 185, 293
Bangladesh 9, 171–3, 175, 176, 177, 178, 181, 184, 186, 187
Bangladeshi National Party (BNP) 172, 173, 175, 176, 177, 179, 180
Bao Dai, Emperor 51, 52
Baroque 7, 26
barrows 13–14
Bashat, Masud 179, 180
Basilica Ulpia, Rome 20
Bataille, Georges 91
Bazargan, Mehdi 229
Behesht-e Zara 231, 232, 237

313

Beijing 61, 62–5, 68, 69, 75, 131, 134, 171, 189
Ben Bella, Ahmed 243
Bengal 160, 173–6, 181, 184, 187
Berlin 98, 99, 100, 108
Bhutto, Zulfikar Ali 175
Blitar 216, 217
Bokassa, Jean-Bédél 10, 88
Bolsheviks 34, 35, 43
Bonch-Bruevich, Vladimir 38
Borodin, Mikhail 125, 126
Borujerdi, Seyyid Hussein, Ayatollah 227, 228
Boullé, Etienne-Louis 16, 25
Bourbon dynasty 25, 27, 43
Bourguiba, Habib 242
Brazzà, Pierre Savorgnan di 245
Brazzaville 245, 246
Brezhnev, Leonid 46
Bronze Age 15–17
Bukharin, Nikolai 37
Bulgaria 54, 94–6
Burgos 23
burial 9, 12–14, 15, 19, 21, 23, 24, 28, 29, 31, 43, 46, 64, 65, 66, 96, 98, 100, 105, 112, 103, 126, 129, 132, 138, 139, 142, 143, 150, 160, 179, 197, 199, 202, 204, 212, 216, 217, 222, 231, 232, 251, 252, 267
    reburial 107, 108, 109, 117
Bush, George W. 202, 279
Byzantium 23, 102, 143

Cacoub, Olivier-Clément 241
Caesar, Julius 119
Cairo 79, 189, 200, 203, 210, 241
Campus Martius, Rome 19
Canton (Guangzhou) 49, 62, 122, 124, 125, 129
Carolingian empire 23
Castello degli Angeli 21
Castro, Fidel 94, 88
Çatalhöyük 13
Catalonia 106, 107
Catholicism 107, 117
cemeteries 25, 27, 65, 66, 83, 95, 96, 97, 101, 102, 110, 113, 117, 134, 217, 222, 231, 232, 235, 243
Charlemagne 23, 24
Chen Shui-Bian 192
Chen Yu 70, 125
Chiang Ching-kuo 192, 193

Chiang Kai-shek 9, 49, 63, 67, 121, 129, 130, 131, 132, 171, 186, 188–99, 287, 239
Chihu 188–99
China 9, 49, 50–53, 62–5, 67–9, 72–5, 77–82, 93, 121–32, 135, 158, 167, 171, 186, 188–91, 197–9, 255, 262, 193, 263
Chinese Communist Party (CCP) 62, 63, 64, 66, 75, 125, 129
Choibalsan, Khorloogiin 91–3
Christianity 21, 122
civil war
    Angola 246, 276
    China 131
    Congo 261
    Russia 35, 36
    Spain 107–11, 112
    Sudan 278
    West Pakistan 175
Clovis 23
Cochinchina 52
Cold War 52, 57, 189, 190, 191, 215, 227, 243, 240, 250, 261, 279
Comintern 49, 94, 125
commemoration 16, 37, 47, 110, 228
Communism 32, 43, 49, 85, 107, 116, 190, 191, 192, 215, 250
Congo 245, 260–69
Constantine 21
corpses 11, 31, 32, 188
    Arafat 203–4
    Atatürk 151–2
    Banda 271
    Chiang Kai-shek 188, 189, 191–2
    Dimitrov 95
    Ho Chi Minh 54–6, 58–9, 61
    Garang 273, 279
    Gottwald 96
    Kabila 264
    Kim Il-Sung 83, 88
    Kim Jong Il 76–7
    Lenin 32, 37, 38, 40–42, 58, 89
    Lincoln 28
    Lumumba 261
    Mao Zedong 66, 68, 70, 73–5
    Mussolini 100
    Neto 246, 248
    Nkrumah 251–3

Royal 23, 35
Suharto 216
Sun Yat-sen 126, 130–31
Zia 179
Counter-Reformation 8, 24
cremation 11, 20, 64, 65
crypts 26, 28, 29, 58, 102, 103, 104, 109, 100, 110, 111, 112, 151, 154, 163, 168
Cuelgamuros 110
cults
  funerary 16, 18, 20
  personality 21, 25, 35, 42, 57, 61, 66, 69, 80, 81, 90, 97, 98, 118, 121, 127, 129, 131, 138, 139, 141, 142, 179, 193, 198, 211, 228, 328, 240, 271, 272
Cultural Revolution 64, 70, 132, 171
Czechoslovakia 96–7

Dani, Ahmad Hasan 170
Darwish, Mahmoud 209
'Dear Leader' *see* Kim Jong Il
Deng Xiaoping 64, 66, 70
Dhaka 171–2, 174, 175, 179, 180, 184, 185, 267
Dien Bien Phu 52
Dimitrov, Georgi 93–6
Doi Moi 58
Du Bois, W.E.B. 243
Duban, Félix 26
Duvalier, Francois, 'Papa Doc' 10
Dzerzhinsky, Felix 37

Egli, Ernst 159
Egypt 16, 17, 19, 129, 200, 202, 203, 241, 242, 255, 276
El Escorial near Madrid 24, 108, 110, 114, 116
Eldem, Sedat Hakki 146
elite 16, 43, 48, 77, 123, 156, 159, 173, 249
  burials 15, 17, 19, 143
embalming 7, 32–3, 37, 38, 43, 54, 66, 75–7, 82, 83, 91, 92, 94, 96, 98, 126–7, 130, 131, 134, 152, 154, 189, 192, 199, 246, 251
enlightenment 9, 16, 24, 29, 37, 46
Erdogan, Recep Tayyib 155
Ershad, Hussain Muhammed 176–7, 179
Etruscans 19

Fahmy, Mustafa 241
Falange Española 106, 110

Fascism 102, 106
Fatah 201, 202, 211
Fausto, Florestano 102
fenmu 128
Ferdinand II 7, 8
flagpoles 206, 244, 254, 268, 273
flags 43, 45, 47, 102, 148, 180, 195, 236, 240, 245, 253, 268, 273
Forbidden City 64, 65, 67, 68, 73, 74
Franco, Francisco y Bahamonde 9, 104–18
Funeral Commission (or Committee) 38–9
funerals 12, 15, 16, 27, 36, 42, 54, 64, 65, 66, 76, 92, 96, 107, 112, 126, 127, 129, 158, 191, 203, 210, 216, 231, 245, 251, 263, 264, 271

Gaddafi, Muammar 88
Gandhi, Indira 94, 175
Gandhi, Mahatma 156, 254, 261
'Gang of Four' 64, 66
Garang, John de Mabior 272–81
Ghana 248–59
Giap, Vo Nguyen 52
Giesler, Hermann 99
'God-building' movement 37
Gorbachev, Mikhail 94
Gordion, Turkey 16
Gottwald, Klement 96–7
Graz, Austria 7, 24
Great Britain 25, 49, 140, 156, 174, 249, 270
'Great Leader' *see* Kim Il Sung
Greeks 18
Guangzhou 49 *see also* Canton
Guevara, Ernesto 'Che' 262

Habsburg dynasty and empire 7, 24
Hadrian, Emperor 20, 22
Halikarnassos, Turkey 17
'Hall of Honour', Anıtkabir, Turkey 149, 150, 151, 152
'Hall of Mourning', Moscow 39
'Hall of Tears', Pyongyang, North Korea 87, 89
Hamas 201, 202, 211
Han dynasty 69
Hanoi 50, 53, 55, 56, 60, 61, 188, 264
Haq, Fazlul 172, 174
Hellenism 17
Hémery, David 61

315

Heroon 19, 20
Herrera, Juan de 110
Hezbollah 154, 229
Hindu 173, 156, 158, 172, 174, 213, 224
Hitler, Adolf 43, 98–100, 101, 104, 106, 108, 227
  'Hitropolis' 99
Hittites 143, 147, 153, 185
Ho Chi Minh 33, 48–61, 62, 76, 84, 87, 105, 188
Holy Roman Empire 23
Honorius 21
'House of the Nation', Cairo 241
Hoxha, Enver 97, 289
Hua Guofeng 66, 68, 69
Hussein, Saddam 230, 231

ideology 14, 15, 48, 80, 81, 83, 86, 117, 124, 154, 176, 215, 226, 229, 249
'imagined community' 10
Imam 225, 226, 230, 231, 235, 236
immortality 16, 17, 28, 31–98
inauguration ceremonies 39, 111, 112, 178, 205, 248, 251, 271
India 155–60, 173, 174, 175, 176, 249, 255
Indian National Congress 156, 174
independence declaration 51, 56 60, 84, 91, 125, 158, 172, 175, 200, 214, 241, 244, 246, 250, 254, 257, 258, 261, 264, 270, 273, 281
Indochina 48–50
Indonesia 9, 213, 214, 215, 216, 218, 223, 224, 225
Inönü, Ismet 140, 141, 142, 144, 150
Iran 9, 213, 225–32, 237, 243
Isakovich, Garold Grigorievich 56, 60
Islam 156, 158–9, 169, 173, 176, 177, 186, 211, 219, 228, 233, 230, 231, 238, 278
'Islamism' 154, 155, 202, 279
Istanbul 141, 143, 155

Japan 50, 51, 52, 63, 78, 77, 79, 122, 123, 124, 130, 131, 174, 189, 192, 214
Java 213–25
Jensen, Hermann 143
Jericho 13
Jerusalem 21, 199, 200, 201, 203, 204, 205, 206, 209, 211, 212
Jiang Qing 64, 65, 66
Jinnah, Mohammad Ali 155–70, 226
Jinnah, Fatima 160, 168

Jordan 201, 205
Joseon dynasty 77
Juan Carlos, King 112, 118
Juba 272–5, 279
Juche 76, 80, 81, 82, 86, 90–91, 199

Kabila, Laurent-Désiré 260–72
Kabila, Joseph 260, 263, 268
Kahn, Louis 178, 179, 180, 181, 185
Karachi 155, 156, 157, 159, 159, 160–70, 181, 184, 185, 226
Kemal Mustafa *see* Atatürk
'Kemalism' 141
Kensal Green Cemetery, London 25
Kenya 243–5, 277, 278, 279, 281
Kenyatta, Jomo 243–5, 281, 297
Khaleda Zia, Begum 171, 172, 177, 179, 180, 184, 185
Khameini, Ali Hossseini Ayatollah 231, 237
Khartoum 276, 278, 279, 280
Khomeni, Ruholla Mustafavi, Ayatollah 213, 296, 225–31, 235, 237, 238
Khwaja, Zaha-ud Din 159, 292
Kiir, Salva Mayardit 273, 275, 280
Kim Il Sung 76–91, 199, 265
  'Kimilsungism' 82, 90
Kim Jong Il 76, 77, 81, 82, 83, 84, 90
Kim Jong Un 82
Kinshasa 260–72, 298–9
Koci, Bohuslav 128
Korea
  North 33, 76–91, 238, 260, 285, 288
  South 63, 78–81, 190
Korean War 63, 79–80, 83, 287
Kremlin, Moscow 31, 41, 43, 44, 46, 46
Krupskaya, Nadezhda 33, 35, 37
Krushchev, Nikita 43, 45
Kumsusan 33, 76, 77, 83, 87, 260
Kuomintang 50, 51, 62, 124, 125, 127, 123, 126, 129, 134

Laing, Ellen 74, 286, 287
'landscapes of eternity' 25
Latin America 24, 299
Lavinium 19
Ledoux, Claude-Nicolas 25
Lenin, Vladimir Illich 9, 32, 33–48, 49, 54, 56, 57, 59, 61, 62, 63, 77, 84, 89, 91, 92, 94, 96, 98, 105, 127, 146, 185, 246, 255

316

Leninism (also Marxism-Leninism) 47, 58, 78, 81, 90, 245
liberation war 240
    Bangladesh 171, 172
    Indonesia 214
    South Sudan 275–9
    Turkey 140, 142, 146, 151
    Vietnam 50–53
Lilongwe 269–72
Lincoln, Abraham 27–9, 284
Lincoln Memorial, Washington, DC 27–9
Lingmu 121, 128, 135
Linz, Austria 98–9, 100, 101
Liu, Shaoqi 70
London 123, 156, 175, 249
'Long March', the 63, 64, 70
Loos, Adolf 138, 291
Louis IX (St Louis) 23
Louis Philippe I 26
Lü Yanzi 128
Luanda 246–8
Lumumba, Patrice 260, 261, 262, 263, 264, 268, 281
Lunarchsky, Anatoly 37
Lycians 18

Madrid 107, 108, 112, 113,
Makam Bung Karno 223–5
Malawi 269–72, 299
Manchu dynasty 121, 122, 123, 124, 127
Manchuria 77, 78, 80, 131, 287
Mangadeg Cemetery, Java 217, 222
Mangkunegaran royal house 217
Mansudae Art Studio 84, 299
Mao Zedong 33, 61–76, 87, 131, 189, 190, 236, 250
Marochetti, Carlo (Charles) 26, 284
martyrs 83, 107, 116, 171, 172, 232, 238, 275
Marx, Karl 121, 123
Marxism 49, 107, 214, 227, 278, 279
Mashhad 226, 235
mass graves 24, 25, 31, 107, 109
Massamba-Débat, Alphonse 245
Mausolus 17–19
Maussoleion 17–19
Mayakovsky, Vladimir 36
Mead, Larkin G. 28
Megawati Sukarnoputri 224
Melnikov, Victor 40, 45, 89
Memel-Fotê, Harris 120–21

memorabilia 28, 59, 102, 104, 221
'Memorial Hall' 128
    Beijing 68–76, 97, 134, 236
    Dhaka 181
    Pyongyang *see* Kumsusan
    Taipei 131, 191, 198–9
'Memorial Park' (Accra) 253–9
Méndez, Diego 109, 111, 112
Mengistu, Haile Mariam 278, 279
Merchant, Yaya C. 160, 169, 185
Ming dynasty 67, 127, 185
Middle Ages 21–4, 144, 146
Mobuto, Sese Seko 10, 260
Moi, Daniel arap 243, 281
Mongolia 54, 91–3
Moscow 9, 31, 42, 46–50, 53, 54, 57, 66, 92, 94, 96, 107, 246, 254, 255
mounds 13, 14, 15, 17, 19, 143
mourning rites 11, 66 *see also* funerary rites
Mughal tombs 156
Muguruza, Otaño Pedro 109–10
Mujibbad 175
Muluzi, Elson Bakili 271
mummification 38
mummy 31, 96, 97
Munich 98, 99
Munthali, Knight 271–2
Muqata, Ramallah 199, 204
Muslim League 156, 157, 158, 160, 168, 173, 174
Mussolini, Benito 98, 100–104, 106
Mutharika, Bingu wa 271–2

Nabateans 18
Nader Shah 226
Nairobi 243–5, 279, 281
Najaf, Iraq 225, 228, 229
'Nakba' 200
Nanjing 66, 121–38, 185, 187, 189, 190, 198, 199
Napoleon I 9, 25–7, 28, 98, 134
National Front
    Bangladesh (JAGODAL) 176
    Spain 106
National Socialism (Nazism) 43, 100, 102, 143, 200
nationalism 117, 123, 155, 156, 175, 176, 177, 181, 187, 214, 249
Nazimuddin, Khawaja 172
necropolis 23, 31, 43, 44

Neo-Confucianism 77, 81
Neolithic burial sites 12–14
Neto, Agostinho 246–8, 282
Ngouabi, Marien 245, 246
N'Guesso, Sasson 245
Nguyen Ai Quoc (Ho Chi Minh) 48–50, 56
Nguyen Ngoc Chai 56
Nguyen Van Thieu 53
Nicolas II 43
Nivinsky, Ignaty Ignatievich 41, 45
Niyazov, Saparmurat ('Turkmenbashi') 238
Nkrumah, Kwameh 248–9, 260, 268, 277, 281

Oak Ridge Cemetery, Springfield, Illinois 27–30
October Revolution 31, 34
Olmeda, Fernand 107
Olšany Cemetery, Prague 96
Onat, Emin 144, 146
Orejas, Antonio 112
Osagyefo 254, 257, 258
Ottoman empire 139, 140, 200, 225

Padmore, George 243
Pakistan 9, 155–70, 171, 172, 174–5, 178, 185, 187
Palestine 140, 199, 200, 202, 203, 208, 228, 272
Pan-Africanism 243, 246, 248, 249
Pancasila 214
Pantheon 137
   National 24
   'Of the Fallen' 105, 108, 109, 118
   Paris 24
   'Proletarian' 96, 97
   Rome 21
Paris 23, 24, 31, 49, 53, 56, 98, 128, 134, 202, 203, 205, 210, 229, 264, 265
Pasargadae, Iran 225
pater patriae 119
Persian empire 17
personality cult *see* cult
Petacci, Clara 100
pharaohs 16, 105, 242
Philip II 24, 105, 108, 110
Phrygians 143
pilgrimage 21, 60, 75, 100, 104, 138, 192, 216, 224, 223, 225, 226, 237, 238, 281
pilgrims 23, 69, 75, 103, 121, 132, 146, 170, 213, 221, 223, 224, 225, 235, 236, 243

Politburo 32, 35, 36, 39, 53, 54, 65
Popular Front
   China 50
   Spain 106
Prague 24, 96, 97
Predappio, Emilia-Romagna, Italy 100–104
Preston, Paul 112, 289
Primo de Rivera, José Antonio 106, 107
Primo de Rivera, Miguel José 105, 112, 117
Purple Mountain, Nanjing, China 66, 121, 127, 132, 135, 138, 163
Putin, Vladimir 43, 47, 61
pyramids 16, 17, 25, 255

Qing dynasty 62, 77, 121, 122, 123, 127
Quaid-e Azam 155, 158, 160, 169
Qum, Iran 226, 227, 228, 229, 232, 235

Rabin, Yizhak 210
Rahman, Mujib(ur) 172, 175–6, 177, 178, 179, 184, 185, 186, 187
Rahman, Ziaur (Zia) 170–87
Ramallah 9, 205–12
Ravenna 22, 102
Rawlings, Jeremy 252–3
Red Army
   China 63, 64, 131, 190
   Russia 35, 92, 100
   South Sudan 278
   Spain 107
Red Square, Moscow 43–7
relics 21, 23, 31, 70, 88, 103, 105, 151, 193, 210, 272
revolution 27, 49, 63, 91, 230
   China 62–3, 75, 121, 122, 123, 124, 125
   France 24, 31
   Iran 213, 226, 229
   Korea 80, 82
   Russia 33–4, 36, 45, 48, 62, 121
   Vietnam 49, 51
Reza Shah Pahlavi 226
Reza Shah Pahlavi, Mohammed 227
Richards, Michael 112, 113, 290
'Righteous Fallen' 104, 105, 108, 112,
Risco de la Nava, Alto de Léon 108, 109, 110, 111, 116
Rizvi, Kishwar 226
Roberto, Holden 246
rock tombs 17, 18

INDEX

Roman empire 19
Rome 21, 22, 23, 98, 100, 119, 120, 121, 187
Ryang, Sonia 90

'Sacrificial Hall', Nanjing, China 128, 134, 135, 137
Sadat, Anwar al- 88
Sadr, Mohammed al- 230
Safavid empire 225, 226, 237
Saigon 51, 52, 53, 54,
St Peter's basilica, Vatican City 21, 111
St Petersburg, Russia 33, 43
Ste-Geneviève, Paris 24
saints 24, 31, 32, 170, 219, 223, 224, 225, 230, 238, 281
Salazar, António de Oliveira 117, 118, 246
Santa Cruz del Valle de los Caídos 104–18
sarcophagus 26, 27, 28, 33, 39, 40, 43, 45, 59, 88, 89, 73, 99, 102, 103, 136, 150, 152, 159, 167, 168, 181, 184, 189, 192, 195, 211, 221, 241, 242, 244, 245, 255, 282
Savimbi, Joseph 246
Second World War 47, 51, 79, 132, 142, 157, 240, 243, 249, 276
Seljuks 143, 146, 150, 225, 238
Seoul 77, 79
Shchusev, Alexey 39, 41
Sheikh Hasina Wajid 171, 172, 173, 177–9, 180, 181, 184
Sheikh Safi 225–6
Shiism 170, 225–6, 228, 230, 243
Sima de los Huesos, Spain 11
Sino-Japanese War 77, 189
Siti Hartinah 216
Sofia 93–5
Solo (Surakarta) 216, 218, 222
Soon Ching Ling 127, 291
Soon Tzu Wen 128
South Sudan 272–81
souvenirs 74, 134, 135, 137, 168, 211, 221
Spain 11, 24, 105–8, 110, 113, 114, 116, 117
Speer, Albert 99
Springfield, Illinois 27–9
Stalin, Joseph 35, 37, 38, 41–3, 46, 52, 64, 79, 92, 94, 96, 98, 125
statues 28, 29, 41, 43, 71, 70, 73, 76, 87, 89, 90, 93, 94, 116, 128, 134, 135, 137, 141, 186, 198, 199, 224, 236, 251, 254, 257, 258, 190, 195, 198, 240, 264, 265, 266, 268, 269, 272, 273, 274, 280

Stone Age 12–14
Sudan 273, 275–9
Suger, Abbot of St-Denis, Paris 23
Suharto, Kemuso Argamulja 213–39
Sühbaatar, Damdin 91
Suhrawardy, Hussain Shaheed 172, 174
Sukarno (Kusno Sosrodihardjo) 214–16, 218, 223–5, 238
Sumerians 16
'Sunism' 125
Sun Yat-sen 66, 67, 121–38, 158, 185, 189, 190, 191, 192, 198, 199
symbolic coffin 28, 148, 149, 150, 152, 272
symbolism 29, 43, 74, 75, 128, 133, 170, 265

Taipei 131, 171, 188, 190, 191, 193, 198
Taiwan 9, 63, 64, 69, 121, 131, 133, 188–99
Tatlin, Vladimir 39
Tehran 225, 226, 229, 231, 232, 236, 237
Tehrani, Mohammed 231
Theoderic, mausoleum of 22
tholos 19
Tiananmen Gate 63, 64, 67, 68, 70, 75, 76
Tiananmen 'Incident' 71
Tiananmen Square 64, 66–68, 70, 71, 74–6, 89
Tirana 97
Tito, Josip Broz 94
Todorov, Vladimir 32
Todorova, Maria 94, 95
Touré, Ahmed Sékou 251
tourists 44, 48, 74, 76, 86, 138, 195, 212, 213, 224
Trajan, Emperor 20
Trotsky, Leon 37, 41
Truman, Harry S. 52, 79
Tumarkin, Nina 42
Tunis 201, 242–3
Tunisia 23, 242
Turkmenbashi *see* Niyazov, Saparmurat
Turkmenistan 238

Ulan Bator 91–93, 95
United Front (China) 49, 125, 132, 174
USA 27–30, 32, 44, 52, 54, 79, 120, 123, 131, 200, 249, 269, 277, 281

Valley of the Fallen, Spain 104–18
vaults 28, 104, 112, 114, 134, 150, 151, 225, 232, 255

Vespasian 20
Vertov, Dziga 42, 44
Via Appia near Rome 25
Vienna 24, 99
Vietcong 53
Vietminh 50–52
Vietnam 48–61, 215, 251
Villanueva, Juan de 110
Visconti, Louis 26–7
Vitkov Hall, Prague 96
Vorobiev, Vladimir 38
Vuong Goc Ny 56

Xiaoling Tomb, Nanjing, China 132

Yang Zhao-cheng 198
Yeltsin, Boris 43, 94
Yhombi-Opanga, Joachim 245
Yogyakarta, Java 214
Yuan Shih-k'ai 123–4
Yunan 50, 63, 78

Zaghloul, Saad 241–2
Zapatero, José Luis Rodriguez 113, 116, 117
Zbarsky, Boris 94
Zbarsky, Ilya 96
Zhou Enlai 64, 66, 70, 132
Zhu De 64–6, 68, 70
Zhu Yuanzhang 127, 138
Ziaur Rahman, Bir Uttam *see* Rahman